W9-BMO-768

Bolt's
Christmas 04

Worth
Repeating

Worth Repeating: More Than 5,000 Classic and Contemporary Quotes

© 2003 by Bob Kelly

Published by Kregel Publications, a division of Kregel, Inc., P.O. Box 2607, Grand Rapids, MI 49501.

All rights reserved. No part of this book may be reproduced, stored in a retrieval system, or transmitted in any form or by any means—electronic, mechanical, photocopy, recording, or otherwise—without written permission of the publisher, except for brief quotations in printed reviews.

Library of Congress Cataloging-in-Publication Data
Worth repeating: more than 5000 classic and
contemporary quotes / compiled by Bob Kelly.
    p. cm.
Includes index.
   1. Quotations, English. 2. Religion—Quotations,
maxims, etc. I. Kelly, Bob.
PN6081.W64 2003
082—dc21
2003001781

ISBN 0-8254-2985-4

Printed in the United States of America

03 04 05 06 07 / 5 4 3 2 1

Worth Repeating

More Than 5,000
Classic and Contemporary
Quotes

Bob Kelly

Kregel
Academic & Professional

Preface

My interest in quotations was probably sparked when I was about 12 or 13 years old. My father was a newspaper editor, and my mom had been a schoolteacher before she married him. There were always lots of magazines in the house, and one of my favorites was *Reader's Digest*, especially its "Quotable Quotes" feature.

However, it wasn't until many years later that my interest turned into passion, or perhaps more accurately, obsession. In 1982, I became editor and publisher of a small local newspaper. When my layout person asked me to provide small items to help fill some open spaces, I immediately thought about quotations. My library included four or five of the popular quote volumes, but I quickly decided they weren't enough.

Before long, I owned 50 of them, and then 100. Whenever I traveled, I'd comb the used-book section of area bookstores, and I began uncovering many old and rare volumes. My collection grew to 200, then 300, and is now approaching the 400-volumes mark, and still growing. Many of these books were published more than a century ago. In all, my collection numbers about 1.5 million entries.

My collection is by no means limited to these published volumes. I record quotes from books and magazines I read and from sermons and speeches I hear, and friends often send me their favorites.

I've chosen the quotations in this book from the materials described above. In some instances, I failed to duly record the source and, in other cases, found the same quote attributed to different individuals. I've made every effort to give proper credit to the original author of each selection, where known. In the event I've failed to acknowledge the correct source of any of this material, I sincerely apologize and, if the inaccuracy is called to my attention, I'll see that the appropriate corrections are made in future editions.

As you read the following selections, may you be blessed, enriched, motivated, challenged, encouraged and, in some cases, amused. In the words of Henry Ward Beecher, "A book is a garden, an orchard, a storehouse, a party, a company by the way, a counsellor, a multitude of counsellors." May you find that this book fits that description.

A

ABILITY

Ability will never catch up with the demand for it.

—Malcolm S. Forbes

Abilities are like tax deductions—we use them or we lose them.

—Sam Jennings

We are sometimes born into wealth, but not ability. Ability must be acquired by earnest desire; it is not inherited.

—Paul P. Parker

Whatever we believe about ourselves and our ability comes true for us.

—Susan L. Taylor

Ability is a poor man's wealth.

—Matthew Wren

ABORTION

Abortion: The simple fact is that God certainly intended to create a human being and that this nascent human being has been deliberately deprived of his life. And that is nothing but murder.

—Dietrich Bonhoeffer

Abortion . . . interferes with God's plan—a plan He willed before He created the universe. Abortion is in violation of God-given life.

—Richard C. Halverson

When the sacredness of life before birth is attacked, we will stand up and proclaim that no one ever has the authority to destroy unborn life.

—Pope John Paul II

Abortion is advocated only by persons who have themselves been born.

—Ronald Reagan

Abortion is murder in the womb. . . . A child is a gift from God. If you do not want him, give him to me.

—Mother Teresa

I feel the greatest destroyer of peace today is abortion, because it is a direct killing of the innocent child.

—Mother Teresa

Please don't kill the child. I want the child. I am willing to accept any child who would be aborted and to give that child to a married couple who will love the child, and be loved by the child.

—Mother Teresa

To forbid birth is only quicker murder. . . . He is a man, who is to be a man; the fruit is always present in the seed.

—Tertullian

ABSENCE

Absence is to love what wind is to a fire; it puts out the little, it kindles the great.

—Roger de Bussy-Rabutin

Friends, though absent, are still present.

—Cicero

ABSURDITY

Every absurdity has a champion to defend it.

—Oliver Goldsmith

ACCOMPLISHMENT

There is nothing that God has judged good for us that He has not given us the means to accomplish, both in the natural and moral world.

—Edmund Burke

Knowledge may give weight, but accomplishments give luster, and many more people can see than weigh.

—Lord Chesterfield

Great thoughts converted to practice will become great accomplishments.

—William Hazlitt

The great accomplishments of the world have been achieved by men who had high ideals and who have received great visions. The path is not easy, the climbing is rugged and hard, but the glory at the end is worthwhile.

—Matthew Henson

I long to accomplish a great and noble task, but it is my chief duty to accomplish small tasks as if they were great and noble.

—Helen Keller

Some of the world's greatest feats were accomplished by people not smart enough to know they were impossible.

—Doug Larson

We judge ourselves by what we feel capable of doing; others judge us by what we have done.

—Henry Wadsworth Longfellow

Great things are not something accidental, but must certainly be willed.

—Vincent Van Gogh

Every accomplishment starts with the decision to try.

—Anonymous

ACHIEVEMENT

Think of yourself as on the threshold of unparalleled success. A whole clear, glorious life lies before you. Achieve! Achieve!

—Andrew Carnegie

The virtue of all achievement is victory over oneself. Those who know this victory can never know defeat.

—A. J. Cronin

Somewhere in your make-up there lies sleeping the seed of achievement, which, if aroused and put into action, would carry you to heights such as you may never have hoped to attain.

—Napoleon Hill

Keep a definite goal of achievement constantly in view. Realize that work well and worthily done makes life truly worth living.

—Grenville Kleiser

The roots of true achievement lie in the will to become the best that you can become.

—Harold Taylor

The key to achievement lies in being a *How* thinker, not an *If* thinker.

—Anonymous

ACQUAINTANCES

An acquaintance is a person whom we know well enough to borrow from, but not well enough to lend to.

—Ambrose Bierce

ACTION

What you want to do, you do. The rest is just talk.

—John Cleek

Not only strike while the iron is hot, but make it hot by striking.

—Oliver Cromwell

Action may not always bring happiness, but there is no happiness without action.

—Benjamin Disraeli

One that would have the fruit must climb the tree.

—Thomas Fuller

Why wait? Life is not a dress rehearsal. Quit practicing what you are going to do, and just do it.

—Marilyn Grey

I cannot do everything, but still I can do something, and because I cannot do everything, I will not refuse to do the something I can do.

—Edward Everett Hale

The vision must be followed by the venture. It is not enough to stare up the steps—we must step up the stairs.

—Vance Havner

You will never stub your toe standing still. The faster you go, the more chance there is of stubbing your toe, but the more chance you have of getting somewhere.

—Charles F. Kettering

Things may come to those who wait, but only the things left by those who hustle.

—Abraham Lincoln

To take action is always dangerous, but to sit and wait for the good things of life to fall into thy lap is the only calling where failures excel.

—Og Mandino

Do what you can, with what you have, where you are.

—Theodore Roosevelt

You can't just sit there and wait for people to give you that golden dream, you've got to get out there and make it happen for yourself.

—Diana Ross

Begin somewhere; you cannot build a reputation on what you intend to do.

—Liz Smith

It is the greatest of all mistakes to do nothing because you can only do little. Do what you can.

—Sydney Smith

The important thing is to start, to lay a plan and then follow it step-by-step, no matter how small or large each step by itself may seem.

—Robert Louis Stevenson

Do a little more each day than you think you possibly can.

—Lowell Thomas

Don't let what you can't do interfere with what you can do.

—John Wooden

Those who say, "It cannot be done," should get out of the way of those who are doing it.

—Anonymous

ACTIVITY
The individual activity of one man with backbone will do more than a thousand men with a mere wishbone.

—J. H. Boetcher

It is more important to know where you are going than to get there quickly. Do not mistake activity for achievement.

—Mabel Newcomer

ADAM AND EVE
The first time Adam had a chance, he laid the blame on women.

—Nancy Astor

Adam invented love at first sight, one of the greatest labor-saving machines the world ever saw.

—Josh Billings

Adam and Eve were the first bookkeepers. They invented the loose-leaf system.

—Eddie Cantor

Ever since the world began, it has been mostly wickedness that has made the headlines. How many people even know that Adam and Eve had a third son, who never got into trouble?

—Sydney J. Harris

Jesus was willing to sacrifice His life; Adam was willing to sacrifice his wife.

—Wes Harty

The woman was made of a rib out of the side of Adam; not out of his feet to be trampled upon by him, but out of his side to be equal with him, to be under his arm to be protected, and near his heart to be loved.

—Matthew Henry

The Devil did not tempt Adam and Eve to steal, to lie, to kill, to commit adultery; he tempted them to live independently of God.

—Bob Jones Sr.

Woman was made from Adam's side that she might walk beside him, not from his foot that he should step on her.

—Harold Lindsell

I've learned the same thing about my garden that Adam and Eve learned about theirs. It's best to follow instructions.

—Robert Orben

Adam was the driver of the bus of humanity. When he drove the bus over the cliff, we went down with him.

—Ray Pritchard

Conversation between Adam and Eve must have been difficult at times—they had nobody to talk about.

—Agnes Repplier

Ever since Eve gave Adam the apple, there has been a misunderstanding between the sexes about gifts.

—Nan Robertson

Adam and Eve had many advantages, but the principal one was that they escaped teething.

—Mark Twain

What a good thing Adam had. When he said a thing, he knew nobody had said it before.

—Mark Twain

If Adam and Eve were alive today, they would probably sue the snake.

—Bern Williams

Adam ate the apple and our teeth still ache.

—Hungarian Proverb

When Adam was lonely, God created for him not ten friends but one wife.

—The Samaritan

When Adam's son asked him why they didn't live in the Garden of Eden any more, he answered, "Your mother ate us out of house and home."

—Anonymous

Adam's comment to his wife, when he first saw her wearing a fig leaf, was "Eve, I'll wear the plants in this family."

—Anonymous

Whilst Adam slept, Eve from his side arose;
Strange his first sleep should be his last repose.

—Anonymous

Adam and Eve had an ideal marriage. He didn't have to hear about all the men she could have married, and she didn't have to listen to him tell how his mother used to cook.

—Anonymous

ADMIRATION

Admiration is our polite recognition of another man's resemblance to ourselves.

—Ambrose Bierce

To love is to admire with the heart; to admire is to love with the mind.

—Theophile Gautier

ADOLESCENCE
(See also Teenagers, Youth)

As I vaguely recalled from my own experience, adolescence was a time … when the very idea that anything interesting might have happened during your parents' lifetime was unthinkable.

—Russell Baker

Adolescence is perhaps nature's way of preparing parents to welcome the empty nest.

—Karen Savage and Patricia Adams

Snow and adolescence are the only problems that disappear if you ignore them long enough.

—Earl Wilson

ADVANCEMENT

There is no advancement to him who stands trembling because he cannot see the end from the beginning.

—E. J. Klemme

Slumber not in the tents of your fathers. The world is advancing. Advance with it.

—Guiseppe Mazzini

ADVERSITY

(See also Affliction, Burdens, Misfortune, Suffering, Trials, Troubles)

People and nations are forged in the fires of adversity.

—John Adams

If thou faint in the day of adversity, thy strength is small—too small to be worth talking about, for the day of adversity is its first real opportunity.

—Maltbie D. Babcock

Rightly conceived, time is the friend of all who are in any way in adversity, for its mazy road winds in and out of the shadows sooner or later into sunshine, and when one is at [time's] darkest point one can be certain that presently it will grow brighter.

—Arthur Bryant

If adversity hath killed his thousands, prosperity hath killed his ten thousands; therefore adversity is to be preferred. The one deceives, the other instructs; the one miserably happy, the other happily miserable; and therefore many philosophers have voluntarily sought adversity and so much commend it in their precepts.

—Robert Burton

Adversity, although painful to all and fatal to some, can be extremely rewarding to the survivors.

—Jack Flobeck

God takes hold when we break down. We go as far as we can and then God takes hold when we can't go any farther.

—A. P. Gouthey

Adversity toughens manhood, and the characteristic of the good or the great man is not that he has been exempted from the evils of life, but that he has surmounted them.

—Patrick Henry

Adversity has the effect of eliciting talents that in times of prosperity would have lain dormant.

—Horace

Adversity is the diamond dust Heaven polishes its jewels with.

—Robert Leighton

Stars may be seen from the bottom of a deep well, when they cannot be seen from the top of the mountain. So many things are learned in adversity that the prosperous man dreams not of.

—Charles H. Spurgeon

ADVERTISING

Advertising is the very essence of democracy. An election goes on every minute of the business day . . . where the customers state their preferences and determine which manufacturer and which product shall be the leader today, and which shall lead tomorrow.

—Bruce Barton

Doing business without advertising is like winking at a girl in the dark. You know what you are doing, but nobody else does.

—Steuart H. Britt

A good ad should be like a good sermon.

—Bernice Fitz-Gibbon

You have to do a little bragging on yourself, even to your relatives. Men just don't get anywhere without advertising.

—John Nance Garner

Advertising begins when the first crying child advertises his wants to his mother, and ends only with the epitaph on the headstone in the village cemetery.

—Edward S. Jordan

Advertising treats all products with the reverence and the seriousness due to sacraments.

—Thomas Merton

If you think advertising doesn't work, consider the millions of Americans who now think that yogurt tastes good.

—Joe L. Whitley

ADVICE

As time passes, we all get better at blazing a trail through the thicket of advice.

—Margot Bennett

When a man comes to me for advice, I find out what kind of advice he wants, and I give it to him.

—Josh Billings

Advice is like snow: the softer it falls, the longer it dwells upon, and the deeper it sinks into, the mind.

—Samuel Taylor Coleridge

When we ask for advice, we are usually looking for an accomplice.

—Marquis de la Grange

By the time a man asks you for advice, he has generally made up his mind what he wants to do, and is looking for confirmation rather than counseling.

—Sidney J. Harris

We all admire the wisdom of people who come to us for advice.

—Jack Herbert

The trouble with giving advice is that people want to repay you.

—Franklin P. Jones

Advice is what we ask for when we already know the answer but wish we didn't.

—Erica Jong

Ask advice of him who governs himself well.

—Leonardo da Vinci

"Be yourself!" is about the worst advice you can give to some people.

—Thomas L. Masson

I sometimes give myself admirable advice, but I am incapable of taking it.

—Mary Wortley Montagu

The people sensible enough to give good advice are usually sensible enough to give none.

—Eden Phillpotts

The true secret of giving advice is, after you have honestly given it, to be perfectly indifferent whether it is taken or not and never persist in trying to set people right.

—Hannah Whitall Smith

If you ask enough people, you can usually find someone who will advise you to do what you were going to do anyway.

—Weston Smith

The art of giving advice is to make the recipient believe he thought of it himself.

—Frank Tyger

The thing to do with good advice is to pass it on. It is never good to oneself.

—Oscar Wilde

AFFECTION

As the rolling stone gathers no moss, so the roving heart gathers no affections.

—Anna Jameson

Praise is well, compliment is well, but affection—that is the last and final and most precious reward that any man can win, whether by character or achievement.

—Mark Twain

AFFLICTION
(See also Adversity, Suffering, Trials, Troubles)

In the actual tribulations and circumstances of the moment, pain works for us an eternal hope. We have all had the experience that it is only in the days of affliction that our true interests are furthered.

—Oswald Chambers

The brightest crowns that are worn in heaven have been tried, and smelted, and polished, and glorified through the furnace of affliction.

—Edwin H. Chapin

The only way to meet affliction is to pass through it solemnly, slowly, with humility and faith, as the Israelites passed through the sea. Then its very waves of misery will divide, and become to us a wall, on the right side and on the left, until the gulf narrows before our eyes, and we land safe on the opposite shore.

—Dinah Maria Mulock Craik

Let us be patient! These severe afflictions
Not from the ground arise,
But oftentimes celestial benedictions
Assume this dark disguise.

—Henry Wadsworth Longfellow

Afflictions are but the shadow of God's wings.

—George MacDonald

We can stand affliction better than we can prosperity, for in prosperity we forget God.

—Dwight L. Moody

The Lord gets His best soldiers out of the highlands of affliction.

—Charles H. Spurgeon

As sure as God puts His children in the furnace of affliction, He will be with them in it.

—Charles H. Spurgeon

AGING

(See also Childhood, Middle Age, Old Age)

You don't grow old gradually, or on purpose, the way you go downtown on a subway. It's more like finding yourself standing in the last station, wondering how you got there.

—Robert Thomas Allen

It was charming of God! I never expected it! . . . That as beauty vanishes the eyes grow dimmer.

—Enid Bagnold

You know you're getting old when you stoop to tie your shoes and wonder what else you can do while you're down there.

—George Burns

Some people, no matter how old they get, never lose their beauty—they merely move it from their faces into their hearts.

—Martin Buxbaum

If you continue to work and to absorb the beauty in the world around you, you will find that age does not necessarily mean getting old.

—Pablo Casals

If wrinkles must be written upon our brows, let them not be written upon the heart. The spirit should not grow old.

—James A. Garfield

Most people say that as you get old, you have to give up things. I think you get old *because* you give up things.

—Theodore Francis Green

Either you have to face up to it and tell yourself you're not going to be eighteen all your life, or be prepared for a terrible shock when you see the wrinkles and white hair.

—Audrey Hepburn

If you survive long enough, you're revered—rather like an old building.

—Katharine Hepburn

You'll find as you grow older that you weren't born such a very great while ago after all. The time shortens up.

—William Dean Howells

Nobody grows old by merely living a number of years. People grow old only by deserting their ideals. Years wrinkle the face, but to give up enthusiasm wrinkles the soul.

—Watterson Lowe

I cannot conceive of getting old. I have a life that is never going to end.

—Dwight L. Moody

Age is a matter of mind. If you don't mind, it don't matter.

—Leroy "Satchel" Paige

Age should not have its face lifted but it should rather teach the world to admire wrinkles as the etchings of experience and the firm lines of character.

—Ralph Barton Perry

Growing old is like being increasingly penalized for a crime you haven't committed.

—Anthony Powell

You don't stop laughing because you grow old; you grow old because you stop laughing.

—Michael Pritchard

No one grows old by living—only by losing interest in living.

Marie Beynon Ray

You know you're getting old when you come across your childhood treasures in an antique shop.

—Dave Schultheis

The gradually declining years are among the sweetest in a man's life.

—Seneca

When men reach their sixties and retire, they go to pieces. Women just go right on cooking.

—Gail Sheehy

You've heard of the three ages of man: youth, middle age, and "you're looking wonderful."

—Francis J. Spellman

If you live long enough, the venerability factor creeps in; you get accused of things you never did, and praised for virtues you never had.

—I. F. Stone

I shall resolve never to resent growing old—so many folks are denied the privilege.

—Anonymous

It's easier to get older than it is to get wiser.

—Anonymous

AGNOSTICISM

The mistake of agnosticism, it seems to me, has been that it has said not merely, "I do not know," but "I will not consider."

—G. Lowes Dickinson

Agnosticism solves not, but merely shelves, the mysteries of life. When agnosticism has done its withering work in the mind of man, the mysteries remain as before.

—Vincent McNabb

Agnosticism is not an intellectual position, but a moral position, or better still, an intellectual defense for a life that is afraid of the light.

—Fulton J. Sheen

AGREEMENT

When you say that you agree to a thing in principle, you mean that you have not the slightest intention of carrying it out.
—Otto von Bismarck

Those who agree with us may not be right, but we admire their astuteness.
—Cullen Hightower

AIM

Aim at the sun, and you may not reach it; but your arrow will fly far higher than if aimed at an object on a level with yourself.
—J. Hawes

Next in importance to having good aim is to know when to pull the trigger.
—Elmer G. Leterman

An aim in life is the only fortune worth finding.
—Robert Louis Stevenson

AMBITION

Children, you must remember something. A man without ambition is dead. A man with ambition but no love is dead. A man with ambition and love for his blessings here on earth is ever so alive. Having been alive, it won't be hard in the end to lie down and rest.
—Pearl Bailey

A cemetery is a place where a lot of over-ambitious young men come to a dead stop.
—O. A. Battista

Great ambition is the passion of a great character. He who is endowed with it may perform very good or very bad actions; all depends upon the principles that direct him.
—Napoleon Bonaparte

Ah, but a man's reach should exceed his grasp—or what's a heaven for?
—Robert Browning

Ambition is in fact the avarice of power.
—Charles Caleb Colton

Ambition is like love, impatient both of delays and rivals.
—John Denham

Hitch your wagon to a star.
—Ralph Waldo Emerson

Whether life is rough or smooth, ambition we must have, or die at the hands of our own laziness.
—A. P. Gouthey

Most people would succeed in small things if they were not troubled by great ambition.
—Henry Wadsworth Longfellow

To do something, however small, to make others happier and better, is the highest ambition, the most elevating hope, that can inspire a human being.
—John Lubbock

Ambition is so powerful a passion in the human breast that however high we reach we are never satisfied.
—Niccolo Machiavelli

Ambition, old as mankind, the imme-
morial weakness of the strong.

—Vita Sackville-West

Fling away ambition; by that sin fell the
angels.

—William Shakespeare

Let your heart soar as high as it will.
Refuse to be average.

—A. W. Tozer

Keep away from people who try to
belittle your ambitions. Small people
always do that, but the really great make
you feel that you, too, can become great.

—Mark Twain

There is a loftier ambition than merely
to stand high in the world. It is to stoop
down and lift mankind a little higher.

—Henry Van Dyke

Ambition's a good thing if you've got it
headed in the right direction.

—Josh Wise

Ambition can be cultivated. But we
must not overlook the danger in over-
ambition. The successful man constantly watches lest his ambition may
ruin him. The desire to be champion
has caused the death of many a person
who let his ambition run wild.

—A. B. ZuTavern

AMERICA

A nation is made great not by its acres,
but by the men who cultivate them; not
by its great forests, but by the men who
use them. America was a great land
when Columbus discovered it. Americans have made it a great nation.

—Lyman Abbott

America is a place where Jewish
merchants sell Zen love beads to
agnostics for Christmas.

—John Burton Brimer

The historic glory of America lies in the
fact that it is the one nation that was
founded like a church. That is, it was
founded on a faith that was not merely
summed up after it had existed; it was
defined before it existed.

—Gilbert Keith Chesterton

Ours is the only country deliberately
founded on a good idea.

—John Gunther

Americanism means the virtues of
courage, honor, justice, truth, sincerity
and hardihood—the virtues that made
America. The things that will destroy
America are prosperity at any price,
peace at any price, safety first instead of
duty first, and the love of soft living and
the get-rich-quick theory of life.

—Theodore Roosevelt

The American people never carry an
umbrella. They prepare to walk in
eternal sunshine.

—Alfred E. Smith

America lives in the heart of every man everywhere who wishes to find a region where he will be free to work out his destiny as he chooses.

—Woodrow Wilson

AMUSEMENT

You can't live on amusement. It is the froth on water—an inch deep and then the mud.

—George MacDonald

ANCESTORS
(See also Heredity, Inheritance)

Misers aren't fun to live with, but they make wonderful ancestors.

—David Brenner

The man who boasts only of his ancestors confesses that he belongs to a family that is better dead than alive.

—J. Gilchrist Lawson

We pay for the mistakes of our ancestors. It seems only fair that they should leave us the money to pay with.

—Don Marquis

The man who has nothing to boast of but his illustrious ancestors is like a potato—the only good belonging to him is under ground.

—Thomas Overbury

ANGELS

We are all angels with only one wing; we can only fly while embracing one another.

—Luciano De Crescenzo

The empire of angels is as vast as God's creation.

—Billy Graham

The word *angel* simply means "messenger." If angels are messengers, then someone, somewhere must be sending a message.

—Dan Schaeffer

I do not how to explain it; I cannot tell how it is, but I believe angels have a great deal to do with the business of this world.

—Charles H. Spurgeon

ANGER
(See also Temper)

Speak when you are angry and you will make the best speech you will ever regret.

—Ambrose Bierce

An angry man opens his mouth and shuts his eyes.

—Marcus Porcius Cato

Whenever you are angry, be assured that it is not only a present evil, but that you have increased a habit.

—Epictetus

If a small thing has the power to make you angry, does that not indicate something about your size?

—Sydney J. Harris

He who blows his stack adds to the world's pollution.

—Will Henry

Anger is a wind that blows out the lamp
of the mind.

—Robert G. Ingersoll

Many a day has been saddened and
darkened by an angry word.

—John Lubbock

Mildness governs more than anger.

—Proverb

ANNIVERSARIES

A woman has reached real women's-lib
status when she is the one who forgets
the wedding anniversary.

—Harold Coffin

A wedding anniversary is the celebra-
tion of love, trust, partnership, tolerance, and tenacity. The order varies for
any given year.

—Paul Sweeney

A twentieth wedding anniversary is
difficult to celebrate. It's too soon to
brag and too late to complain.

—Anonymous

The most impressive example of tolerance
is a golden wedding anniversary.

—Anonymous

ANSWERS

A child can ask a thousand questions
that the wisest man cannot answer.

—Jacob Abbott

If you desire a wise answer, you must
ask a reasonable question.

—Johann von Goethe

ANXIETY
(See also Fear, Worry)

Anxiety in human life is what squeak-
ing and grinding are in machinery that
is not oiled. In life, trust is the oil.

—Henry Ward Beecher

If you trust in God and yourself, you can
surmount every obstacle. Do not yield to
restless anxiety. One must not always be
asking what may happen to one in life, but
one must advance, fearlessly and bravely.

—Otto von Bismarck

Anxiety is the rust of life, destroying its
brightness and weakening its power. A
childlike and abiding trust in Providence is the best preventive and remedy.

—Tryon Edwards

It is not God who loads us until we bend
or crack with an ulcer, nervous breakdown, heart attack, or stroke. These come
from our inner compulsions coupled
with the pressure of circumstances.

—Charles E. Hummel

What does your anxiety do? It does not
empty tomorrow, brother, of its sorrow;
but oh! It empties today of its strength.

—Ian Maclaren

The beginning of anxiety is the end of
faith; and the beginning of true faith is
the end of anxiety.

—George Mueller

The biggest big business in America is
not steel, automobiles, or television. It is
the manufacture, refinement, and
distribution of anxiety.

—Eric Sevareid

Are you in a hurry, flurried, distressed? Look up! See the Man in the glory! Let the face of Jesus shine upon you—the face of the Lord Jesus Christ. Is He worried, troubled, distressed? There is no wrinkle on His brow, no least shade of anxiety. Yet the affairs are His as much as yours.

—J. Hudson Taylor

APATHY

Science may have found a cure for most evils; but it has found no remedy for the worst of them all—the apathy of human beings.

—Helen Keller

Apathy is the glove into which evil slips its hand.

—Bodie Thoene

APPLAUSE

Of all music, that which most pleases the ear is applause. But it has no score. It ends and is carried off by the wind. Nothing remains.

—Enrique Solari

APPRECIATION

People want to be appreciated, not impressed. They want to be regarded as human beings, not as mere sounding boards for other people's egos. They want to be treated as an end in them- selves, not as a means toward the gratification of another's vanity.

—Sydney J. Harris

The deepest principle in human nature is the craving to be appreciated.

—William James

Be generous in giving credit to others. It's infinitely divisible.

—Darrel Le Barron

It's hard for a fellow to keep a chip on his shoulder if you allow him to take a bow.

—Billy Rose

ARGUMENT

There is no good in arguing with the inevitable. The only argument available with an east wind is to put on your overcoat.

—James Russell Lowell

Argument is the worst sort of conversation.

—Jonathan Swift

In a heated argument we are apt to lose sight of the truth.

—Publilius Syrus

There's nothing so annoying as arguing with a person who knows what he's talking about.

—Anonymous

ART

Art is a collaboration between God and the artist, and the less the artist does the better.

—André Gide

Art is like a border of flowers along the course of civilization.
— Lincoln Steffens

ASPIRATIONS
(See also Dreams)

Far away there in the sunshine are my highest aspirations. I may not reach them, but I can look up and see their beauty, believe in them, and try to follow where they lead.
— Louisa May Alcott

Whatever your present environment may be, you will fall, remain, or rise with your thoughts, your vision, your ideal. You will become as small as your controlling desire, as great as your dominant aspiration.
— James Lane Allen

Our aspirations are our possibilities.
— Robert Browning

ATHEISM
(See also God—Denial of)

An atheist is a man without any invisible means of support.
— John Buchan

The three great apostles of practical atheism that make converts without persecuting, and retain them without preaching, are health, wealth, and power.
— Charles Caleb Colton

The Devil divides the world between atheism and superstition.
— George Herbert

Sometimes when I'm faced with an unbeliever, an atheist, I am tempted to invite him to the greatest gourmet dinner that one could ever serve, and when we finished eating that magnificent dinner, to ask him if he believes there's a cook.
— Ronald Reagan

The worst moment for the atheist is when he is really thankful, and has nobody to thank.
— Dante Gabriel Rossetti

The religion of the atheist has a God-shaped blank at its heart.
— H. G. Wells

Atheism is the death of hope, the suicide of the soul.
— Anonymous

Why is the atheist's main target always Jesus of Nazareth, and never Buddha, Confucius, or Mohammed? Why is the aspiring athlete's target always the true champion and never the also-rans?
— Anonymous

ATONEMENT

When we think of the atonement we are apt to think only of what man gains. We must remember what it cost God and what it costs Him now when men refuse His love.
— Frank Fitt

I must die or get somebody to die for me. If the Bible doesn't teach that, it doesn't teach anything. And that is where the atonement of Jesus Christ comes in.

—Dwight L. Moody

The Lord alone must be exalted in the work of atonement, and not a single mark of man's chisel or hammer will be endured. There is an inherent blasphemy in seeking to add to what Christ Jesus in His dying moments declared to be finished, or to improve that in which the Lord Jehovah finds perfect satisfaction.

—Charles H. Spurgeon

ATTITUDE

The worth of a man is revealed in his attitude to ordinary things when he is not before the footlights.

—Oswald Chambers

Attitude is the mind's paintbrush. It can color a situation gloomy or gray, or cheerful.... In fact, attitudes are more important than facts.

—Mary C. Crowley

A chip on the shoulder is too heavy a piece of baggage to carry through life.

—John Hancock

Ability is what you're capable of doing. Motivation determines what you do. Attitude determines how well you do it.

—Lou Holtz

The greatest discovery is that a human being can alter his life by altering his attitudes of mind.

—William James

Your attitude about who you are and what you have is a very little thing that makes a very big difference.

—Theodore Roosevelt

There is one thing over which each person has absolute, inherent control, and that is his mental attitude.

—W. Clement Stone

If I keep a green bough in my heart, the singing bird will come.

—Chinese Proverb

AUTUMN

Autumn: a gypsy with jewels in her hair.

—Isla Paschal Richardson

Listen! The wind is rising, and the air is
    wild with leaves.
We have had our summer evenings;
    now for October eves.

—Humbert Wolfe

AVERAGE
(See also Statistics)

The average woman of thirty-five isn't.

—Franklin P. Jones

Not doing more than the average is what keeps the average down.

—William Winans

B

BABIES

(See also Birth, Childhood, Children)

Baby: an alimentary canal with a loud voice at one end and no sense of responsibility at the other.

—Elizabeth I. Adamson

Babies are bits of stardust blown from the hand of God. Lucky the woman who knows the pangs of birth, for she has held a star.

—Larry Barratto

When the first baby laughed for the first time, the laugh broke into a thousand pieces and they all went skipping about, and that was the beginning of fairies.

—James M. Barrie

The first handshake in life is the greatest of all: the clasp of an infant fist around a parent's finger.

—Mark Beltaire

Training a baby by the book is a good idea, only you need a different book for each baby.

—Dan Bennett

There are two things in this life for which we are never fully prepared: twins.

—Josh Billings

Except that right side up is best, there is not much to learn about holding a baby. There are 152 distinctly different ways—and all are right! At least all will do.

—Heywood Broun

I have never understood the fear of some parents about babies getting mixed up in the hospital. What difference does it make as long as you get a good one?

—Heywood Broun

A baby is born with a need to be loved—and never outgrows it.

—Frank A. Clark

Babies are unreasonable; they expect far too much of existence. Each new generation that comes takes one look at the world, thinks wildly, "Is this all they've done to it?" and bursts into tears.

—Clarence Day

Here we have a baby. It is composed of a bald head and a pair of lungs.

—Eugene Field

Babies are such a nice way to start people.

—Don Herold

A child is helpless in inverse ratio to his age. He is at the zenith of his powers while he is an infant in arms. What on earth is more powerful than a very young baby?

—Aline Kilmer

Baby: a tight little bundle of wailing and flannel.

—Frederick Locker-Lampson

She who gives a baby birth,
Brings Savior Christ again to earth.

—John Masefield

Babies are always more trouble than you thought—and more wonderful.

—Charles Osgood

A baby is God's opinion that life should go on.... Never will a time come when the most marvelous recent invention is as marvelous as a newborn baby.

—Carl Sandburg

It sometimes happens, even in the best of families, that a baby is born. This is not necessarily a cause for alarm. The important thing is to keep your wits about you and borrow some money.

—Elinor Goulding Smith

A babe in the house is a wellspring of pleasure, a messenger of peace and love, a resting place for innocence on earth, a link between angels and men.

—Martin F. Tupper

If you want a baby, have a new one. Don't baby the old one.

—Jessamyn West

Most non-negotiable demand you'll ever hear: the baby calling for his three A.M. feeding.

—Anonymous

There's a new baby food on the market. It's half orange juice and half garlic. It not only makes the baby healthier, but also easier to find in the dark.

—Anonymous

A physician says babies don't need that traditional slap on the rear end when they're born. But at least it gives them an immediate idea of what life is going to be like.

—Anonymous

BACHELOR

A bachelor never gets over the idea that he is a thing of beauty and a boy forever.

—Helen Rowland

BACKSLIDING

Backsliding starts in such a subtle way that most of us are not aware of it, and many of us may be backslidden and may not realize it.

—Theodore H. Epp

With deep repentance and sincere faith, find your way back from your backsliding. It is your duty, for you have turned away from Him whom you have professed to serve.

—Charles H. Spurgeon

BALANCE

Work, love, and play are the great balance-wheels of man's being.

—Orison Swett Marden

In the relentless busyness of modern life, we have lost the rhythm between action and rest.

—Wayne Muller

Keep your eyes on the stars, and your
feet on the ground.

—Theodore Roosevelt

The balanced man is he whose thoughts
soar on the wings of vision—but whose
feet remain on the rocks of reality.

—J. A. Rosenkranz

BAPTISM

The babe, with a cry brief and dismal,
Fell into the water baptismal;
E're they'd gathered its plight,
It had sunk out of sight,
For the depth of the font was abysmal.

—Edward Gorey

The promises of God are never spoken
to the individual alone, but to all at one
time. Baptism, on the contrary, is
something that God does to the
individual.

—O. Hallesby

Baptism points back to the work of God,
and forward to the life of faith.

—J. A. Motyer

BEAUTY

Beauty is an all-pervading presence.... It
waves in the branches of the trees and in
the green blades of grass.... The
mountains, the clouds, the heavens, the
stars, the rising and the setting sun, all
overflow with beauty.... The greatest
truths are wronged if not linked with
beauty, and they win their way most
surely and deeply into the soul when
arrayed in this their natural and fit attire.

—William Ellery Channing

Never lose an opportunity of seeing
anything that is beautiful; for beauty
is God's handwriting—a wayside
sacrament.

—Ralph Waldo Emerson

Though we travel the world over to find
the beautiful, we must carry it with us
or find it not.

—Ralph Waldo Emerson

As a beauty I'm not a great star,
There are others more handsome by far,
    But my face I don't mind it
    Because I'm behind it—
'Tis the folks in the front that I jar.

—Anthony Euwer

I don't think of all the misery, but of all
the beauty that still remains.

—Anne Frank

The best and most beautiful things in
the world cannot be seen or even
touched. They must be felt with the
heart.

—Helen Keller

In every man's heart, there is a secret
nerve that answers to the vibrations of
beauty.

—Christopher Morley

God's definition of beauty is a lot
different than the world's. God says that
beauty is found in a gentle, quiet, and
obedient spirit.

—Heather Whitestone

Beautiful hands are they that do deeds
that are noble, good, and true; beautiful

feet are they that go swiftly to lighten another's woe.

—Anonymous

The average girl would rather have beauty than brains because she knows the average man can see better than he can think.

—Anonymous

BEHAVIOR

Behavior is a mirror in which everyone shows his true image.

—Johann von Goethe

There are two things to do about the gospel—believe it and behave it.

—Susannah Wesley

BELIEF

A belief is not true because it is useful.

—Henri Frédéric Amiel

He does not believe that does not live according to his belief.

—Thomas Fuller

Believe. No pessimist ever discovered the secrets of the stars, or sailed to an uncharted land, or opened a new heaven to the human spirit.

—Helen Keller

The man who believes he can do it is probably right, and so is the man who believes he can't.

—Laurence J. Peter

Live your beliefs and you can turn the world around.

—Henry David Thoreau

BIBLE

So great is my veneration for the Bible that the earlier my children begin to read it, the more confident my hope that they will prove useful citizens, and respectful members of society.

—John Quincy Adams

The reason people are down on the Bible is that they are not up on the Bible.

—William Ward Ayer

Few events tend more powerfully to impress the mind as to the overwhelming power of the evidence attending true Christianity, than the fact that many who have sat down to read the sacred volume with the view of opposing it have been compelled, by the force of conviction, cordially to embrace its truths.

—Thomas T. Biddulph

The Bible is a window in this prison-world through which we may look into eternity.

—Timothy Dwight

The Bible is endorsed by the ages. Our civilization is built upon its words. In no other book is there such a collection of inspired wisdom.

—Dwight D. Eisenhower

Hold fast to the Bible as the anchor of your liberty; write its precepts in your hearts and practice them in your lives.

—Ulysses S. Grant

To the influence of the Bible we are indebted for the progress made in civilization, and to this we must look as our guide in the future.

—Ulysses S. Grant

It is impossible to enslave mentally or socially a Bible reading people. The principles of the Bible are the groundwork of human freedom.

—Horace Greeley

The Bible is the rock on which our republic rests.

—Andrew Jackson

Unless we form the habit of going to the Bible in bright moments as well as in trouble, we cannot fully respond to its consolations, because we lack equilibrium between light and darkness.

—Helen Keller

The Bible is a book in comparison with which all others are of minor importance, and . . . has never failed to give me light and strength.

—Robert E. Lee

The book to read is not the one that thinks for you, but the one that makes you think. No book in the world equals the Bible for that.

—James McCosh

In all literature, there is nothing that compares with the Bible.

—John Milton

I find more marks of authenticity in the Bible than in any profane history whatever.

—Isaac Newton

Inside the Bible's pages lie all the answers to all the problems man has ever known. . . . The Bible can touch our hearts, order our minds, and refresh our souls.

—Ronald Reagan

Throughout the centuries, men of many faiths and diverse origins have found in the sacred Book [the Bible], words of wisdom, counsel, and inspiration. It is a foundation of strength, and now, as always, an aid in attaining the highest aspirations of the human soul.

—Franklin Delano Roosevelt

If a man is not familiar with the Bible, he has suffered a loss that he had better make all possible haste to correct.

—Theodore Roosevelt

Nobody ever outgrows Scripture; the book widens and deepens with our years.

—Charles H. Spurgeon

The sacred page is not meant to be the end, but only the means toward the end, which is knowing God Himself.

—A. W. Tozer

Most people are bothered by those passages in Scripture that they cannot understand; but as for me, I always noticed that the passages in Scripture that trouble me most are those that I do understand.

—Mark Twain

I believe no one can read the history of our country without realizing that the Good Book and the spirit of the Savior have from the beginning been our guiding geniuses. . . . I like to believe that we are living today in the spirit of the Christian religion. I also like to believe that as long as we do, no great harm can come to our country.

—Earl Warren

A man has deprived himself of the best there is in the world who has deprived himself of the Bible.

—Woodrow Wilson

BIGOTRY
(See also Intolerance, Prejudice)

Bigotry does not consist in a man being convinced he is right; that is not bigotry, but sanity. Bigotry consists in a man being convinced that another man must be wrong.

—Gilbert Keith Chesterton

Bigotry tries to keep truth safe in its hands—with a grip that kills it.

—Rabindranath Tagore

BIRTH
(See also Babies, Children)

Birth is the sudden opening of a window through which you look out upon a stupendous prospect. For what has happened? A miracle! You have exchanged nothing for the possibility of everything.

—William M. Dixon

Of all the joys that lighten suffering earth, what joy is welcomed like a new-born child?

—Caroline Norton

Giving birth is like trying to push a piano through a transom.

—Alice Roosevelt Longworth

Making a decision to have a child—it's wondrous. It is to decide forever to have your heart go walking around outside your body.

—Elizabeth Stone

The three most beautiful sights—a potato garden in bloom, a ship in sail, and a woman after the birth of her child.

—Irish Proverb

BIRTHDAYS

Birthdays are mentioned only twice in the Bible. On the first one, Pharaoh's birthday, he had his chief baker beheaded. On King Herod's birthday, he had John the Baptist beheaded.

—Bernice T. Cory

Do you number your birthdays with thankfulness?

—Horace

Birthdays are good for you. Statistics show that the people who have the most live the longest.

—Larry Lorenzoni

Birthdays are feathers in the broad wing of time.

—Jean Paul Richter

BLAME

If something goes wrong, it is more

important to talk about who is going to fix it than who is to blame.

—Francis J. Gable

The search for someone to blame is always successful.

—Robert Half

BLESSINGS

Come what may, I have been blessed.

—Lord Byron

The tendency to seldom think of what we have but always of what we lack is the greatest tragedy on earth. Count your blessings—not your troubles!

—Dale Carnegie

Reflect upon your present blessings, of which every man has many—not on your past misfortunes, of which all men have some.

—Charles Dickens

Blessings are not valued till they are gone.

—Thomas Fuller

My God! How little do my countrymen know what precious blessings they are in possession of, and which no other people on earth enjoy.

—Thomas Jefferson

When God blesses you, He always has more than you in mind.

—Ron Jutze

Remember the wonderful blessings that come to you each day from the hands of a generous God, and forget the irrita-

tions that would detract from your happiness.

—William Arthur Ward

BLINDNESS

My old eyes grow dimmer; the specialist says the light will fade altogether. So I gird myself for darkness, quote James 1:2–4, shout "Hallelujah," and go on.

—Samuel L. Brengle

In the country of the blind, the one-eyed man is king.

—Desiderious Erasmus

Better be blind than to see ill.

—George Herbert

Folk oft times are most blind in their own cause.

—John Heywood

To be blind is bad, but worse it is to have eyes and not to see.

—Helen Keller

There is none so blind as they that will not see.

—Jonathan Swift

The eyes are blind when the mind is elsewhere.

—Publilius Syrus

BLOOD

There are many things more horrible than bloodshed, and slavery is one of them.

—Padraic Pearse

The blood of the martyrs is the seed of the church.

—Tertullian

BODY

The body is a thing of shreds and patches, borrowed unequally from good and bad ancestors and a misfit from the start.

—Ralph Waldo Emerson

The human body was designed to walk, run or stop; it wasn't designed for coasting.

—Cullen Hightower

Our body has this defect that, the more it is provided care and comforts, the more needs and desires it finds.

—Saint Teresa of Avila

BOLDNESS

Whatever you can do, or dream you can,
    begin it.
Boldness has genius, power, and magic
    in it.

—Johann von Goethe

Put a grain of boldness in everything you do.

—Baltasar Gracian

BOOKS

(See also Library, Reading)

A book is a friend; a good book is a good friend. It will talk to you when you want it to talk, and it will keep still when you want it to keep still—and there are not many who know enough to do that.

—Lyman Abbott

Books are the legacies that a great genius leaves to mankind, which are delivered down from generation to generation, as presents to the posterity of those who are yet unborn.

—Joseph Addison

Books are ships that pass through the vast seas of time.

—Francis Bacon

A book is a garden, an orchard, a storehouse, a party, a company by the way, a counselor, a multitude of counselors.

—Henry Ward Beecher

Among the many inventions of man, the book, without a doubt, is the most astounding.... Only the book is an extension of our imagination and memory.

—Jorge Luis Borges

All that mankind has done, thought, gained, or been, it is lying as in magic preservation in the pages of books. They are the choicest possessions of men.

—Thomas Carlyle

We should make the same use of a book that the bee does of a flower; she steals sweets from it, but does not injure it.

—Charles Caleb Colton

My books are my tools, and the greater their variety and perfection, the greater the help to my literary work.

—Tryon Edwards

I make it a rule not to clutter my mind with simple information that I can find in a book in five minutes.

—Albert Einstein

Without the love of books the richest man is poor, but endowed with this treasure, the poorest man is rich.

—Leon Gutterman

What refuge is there for the victim who is oppressed with the knowledge that there are a thousand new books he ought to read, while life is only long enough for him to attempt to read a hundred?

—Oliver Wendell Holmes

A house without books is like a home without windows.

—Horace Mann

When I am attacked by gloomy thoughts, nothing helps me so much as running to my books. They quickly absorb me and banish the clouds from my mind.

—Michel de Montaigne

Books are readily available, and what companions they are. A good book is the same today as yesterday. It is never displeased when we put it down; it is always inspiring when we pick it up. It never fails us in times of adversity.

—Fulton J. Sheen

Books are lighthouses erected in the great sea of time.

—E. P. Whipple

A book, tight shut, is but a block of paper.

—Chinese Proverb

BOREDOM

It is not the fast tempo of modern life that kills but the boredom, a lack of strong interest, and a failure to grow that destroy.

—Harold Dodds

Is not life a hundred times too short for us to bore ourselves?

—Friedrich Nietzsche

The most bored people in life are not the underprivileged but the overprivileged.

—Fulton J. Sheen

BORN AGAIN
(See also Regeneration, Salvation)

Being born from above is a perennial, perpetual, and eternal beginning, a freshness all the time in thinking and in talking and in living, the continual surprise of the life of God.

—Oswald Chambers

BOYS
(See also Sons)

I don't want to go to school and learn solemn things. No one is going to catch me, lady, and make me a man. I want always to be a little boy and to have fun.

—James M. Barrie

A father of five boys will hardly agree that there is safety in numbers.

—O. A. Battista

A boy is a magical creature—you can lock him out of your workshop, but you can't lock him out of your heart.

—Allan Beck

A boy is a piece of existence quite separate from all things else and deserves separate chapters in the natural history of man.

—Henry Ward Beecher

I'm convinced that every boy, in his heart, would rather steal second base than an automobile.

—Tom Clark

Boys do not grow up gradually. They move forward in spurts like the hands of clocks in railway stations.

—Cyril Connolly

Never be surprised when you shake a cherry tree if a boy drops out of it; never be disturbed when you think yourself in complete solitude if you discover a boy peering out at you from a fence corner.

—David Grayson

When I grow up I want to be a little boy.

—Joseph Heller

A boy becomes an adult three years before his parents think he does, and about two years after he thinks he does.

—Lewis B. Hershey

A boy is a man in a cocoon—you do not know what it is going to become—his life is big with many possibilities.

—Elbert Hubbard

Be patient with the boys—you are dealing with soul-stuff. Destiny awaits just around the corner.

—Elbert Hubbard

Kaplan's Law of the Instrument: Give a small boy a hammer and he will find that everything he encounters needs pounding.

—Abraham Kaplan

You save an old man and you save a unit; but save a boy, and you save a multiplication table.

—Rodney "Gipsy" Smith

One of the best things in the world is to be a boy; it requires no experience, but needs some practice to be a good one.

—Charles Dudley Warner

The sweetest roamer is a boy's young heart.

—G. E. Woodberry

A boy is a stick of dynamite, a bundle of energy and potential power, waiting to be ignited. Guard him zealously from careless sparks that would dissipate his energies. . . . Guide him carefully to a place where his vigor and strength will be used to build a better world.

—Anonymous

A good man dies when a boy goes wrong.

—Anonymous

A boy is a noise with some dirt on it.
—Anonymous

Home, to the small boy, is merely a filling station.
—Anonymous

BRAINS
(See also Mind)

Brains aren't everything, but they are important.
—William Feather

The brain is a mass of cranial nerve tissue, most of it in mint condition.
—Robert Half

I use not only all the brains I have, but all I can borrow.
—Woodrow Wilson

BRAVERY
(See also Courage)

Bravery is the capacity to perform properly even when scared half to death.
—General Omar Bradley

True bravery is shown by performing without witnesses what one might be capable of doing before all the world.
—François de La Rochefoucauld

Where there is one brave man, in the thickest of the fight, there is the post of honor.
—Henry David Thoreau

BROTHERHOOD

Our doctrine of equality and liberty and humanity comes from our belief in the brotherhood of man through the fatherhood of God.
—Calvin Coolidge

If you really believe in the brotherhood of man, and you want to come into its fold, you've got to let everyone else in too.
—Oscar Hammerstein

Brotherhood doesn't come in a package. It is not a commodity to be taken down from the shelf with one hand—it is an accomplishment of soul-searching prayer and perseverance.
—Oveta Culp Hobby

The answer to the question, "Am I my brother's keeper?" must always be "No! I am my brother's brother."
—Paul Klapper

You may call for peace as loudly as you wish, but where there is no brother-hood, there can in the end be no peace.
—Max Lerner

BUDGET

A budget tells us what we can't afford, but it doesn't keep us from buying it.
—William Feather

BUILD

Many men build as cathedrals were built, the part nearest the ground finished, but that part that soars toward heaven, the turrets and the spires, forever incomplete.
—Henry Ward Beecher

Too low they build who build beneath the stars.

—Edward Young

BURDENS
(See also Trials, Worry)

When we come to the Lord with our burden, He just lifts up His child, burden and all, and bears him all the way home.

—Charles A. Fox

No one ever sank under the burden of the day. It is when tomorrow's burden is added to the burden of today that the weight is more than a man can bear. Never load yourself so.

—George MacDonald

BUREAUCRACY

Bureaucracy is a giant mechanism operated by pygmies.

—Honoré de Balzac

I hate being a bureaucrat and will resign as soon as I know the proper procedure.

—Hector Breeze

Government machinery has been described as a marvelous labor saving device that enables ten men to do the work of one.

—John Maynard Keynes

Giving a bureaucrat a new rule is like handing a pyromaniac a lighted match in a haymow.

—Ronald Reagan

BUSINESS

Some regard private enterprise as if it were a predatory tiger to be shot. Others look upon it as a cow that they can milk. Only a handful see it for what it really is—the strong horse that pulls the whole cart.

—Winston Churchill

All business proceeds on beliefs, or judgments of probabilities, and not on certainties.

—Charles Eliot

Agriculture, manufacturers, commerce, and navigation, the four pillars of our prosperity, are most thriving when left most to free enterprise.

—Thomas Jefferson

Every business organization should have a vice president in charge of constant renewal.

—Dwayne Orton

Business is what, if you don't have any, you go out of.

—Earl Wilson

Business is like riding a bicycle—either you keep moving or you fall down.

—Anonymous

BUSYNESS

It is so easy to confuse our daily busyness with our daily business. Many of us earn our living in business, but waste much of the rest of our time on busyness that profits us little.

—David Dunn

Busyness

In the relentless busyness of modern
life, we have lost the rhythm between
action and rest.

—Wayne Muller

It is not enough to be busy; so are the
ants. The question is, What are we busy
about?

—Henry David Thoreau

C

CALLING

We can't do what God has called us to do without involving others.

—Darrel Le Barron

You cannot choose your calling. Your calling chooses you. You have been blessed with special skills that are yours alone. Use them, whatever they may be, and forget about wearing another's hat.

—Og Mandino

If a man has any brains at all, let him hold on to his calling, and, in the grand sweep of things, his turn will come at last.

—William McCune

God doesn't call people who are qualified. He calls people who are willing, and then He qualifies them.

—Richard Parker

CALVARY

There is something in Calvary that passes our understanding, and the words about the precious blood should never be read or sung except on the knees of our spirit.

—Amy Carmichael

CANDOR

Candor is a compliment; it implies equality. It's how true friends talk.

—Peggy Noonan

Frankness consists in always telling the truth, but not always all the truth.

—Mme. Anne Louise de Staël

CARE

Nobody cares how much you know— until they know how much you care.

—John Cassis

CAREERS

Think not of yourself as the architect of your career but as the sculptor. Expect to have to do a lot of hard hammering and chiseling and scraping and polishing.

—B. C. Forbes

Careers, like rockets, don't always take off on schedule. The key is to keep working on the engines.

—Gary Sinise

CENSORSHIP

The argument that pornography cannot be censored without destroying our civil liberties is fundamentally wrong. We have censored pornography since the nation was established, and there is no evidence of an adverse effect on our civil liberties.

—Winton M. Blount

Pontius Pilate was the first great censor, and Jesus Christ the first great victim of censorship.

—Ben Lindsey

CHALLENGE

Our prayers are answered not when we are given what we ask, but when we are challenged to be what we can be.

—Morris Adler

Think so big that you can't do it alone, so big you can't do it this year, this decade or even in your lifetime. Have a dream worth dreaming, a challenge so big that even credit isn't necessary.

—Bobb Biehl

Always take a job that is too big for you.

—Harry Emerson Fosdick

God's road is all uphill, but do not tire: rejoice that we may still keep climbing higher.

—Arthur Guiterman

Life's greatest challenge is not being a man's man, but God's man.

—Charlie "T" Jones

The way to face a challenge is to be convinced that the challenge can be met.

—C. Randall Powell

CHANCE

There is no such thing as chance or accident; the words merely signify our ignorance of some real and immediate cause.

—Adam Clarke

Those who trust to chance must abide by the results of chance. They have no legitimate complaint against anyone but themselves.

—Calvin Coolidge

When we count on chance in lieu of law and labor, we weaken our healthy attitudes toward work, our fellow men, and our God.

—Ralph W. Sockman

CHANGE

When you're through changing, you're through.

—Bruce Barton

To exist is to change, to change is to mature, to mature is to go on creating oneself endlessly.

—Henri Bergson

Change of fashions is the tax that industry imposes on the vanity of the rich.

—Sebastien R. N. Chamfort

I thought I could change the world. It took me a hundred years to figure out I can't change the world. I can only change Bessie. And honey, that ain't easy either.

—Bessie Delaney

Christians are supposed not merely to endure change, nor even to profit by it, but to cause it.

—Harry Emerson Fosdick

Little men with little minds and little imagination jog through life in little ruts, smugly resisting all changes that would jar their little worlds.

—Marie Fraser

All change is not growth; as all movement is not forward.

—Ellen Glasgow

We must always change, renew, rejuvenate ourselves; otherwise we harden.

—Johann von Goethe

Blessed is the man who has discovered that there is nothing permanent in life but change.

—A. P. Gouthey

I wanted to change the world. But I have found that the only thing one can be sure of changing is one's self.

—Aldous Huxley

There is a certain relief in change, even though it be from bad to worse; as I have found in traveling in a stagecoach, it is often a comfort to shift one's position and be bruised in a new place.

—Washington Irving

If one is going to change things, one has to make a fuss and catch the eye of the world.

—Elizabeth Janeway

Such is the state of life that none are happy but by the anticipation of change. The change itself is nothing; when we have made it, the next wish is to change again.

—Samuel Johnson

If you are wedded to today's trends, you'll be widowed by the weekend.

—E. Stanley Jones

We live in a moment of history where change is so speeded up that we begin to see the present only when it is already disappearing.

—R. D. Laing

If you want truly to understand something, try to change it.

—Kurt Lewin

Not everything that is faced may be changed, but nothing can be changed until it is faced.

—James B. Lytton

It's the most unhappy people who most fear change.

—Mignon McLaughlin

None of us knows what the next change is going to be, what unexpected opportunity is just around the corner, waiting a few months or a few years to change all the tenor of our lives.

—Kathleen Norris

Change is always powerful. Let your hook be always cast. In the pool where you least expect it, will be a fish.

—Ovid

Just because everything is different doesn't mean anything has changed.

—Irene Peter

Welcome change as a friend; try to visualize new possibilities and the blessings it is bound to bring you. . . . Never stop learning and never stop growing; that is the key to a rich and fascinating life.

—Alexander de Seversky

Those who cannot change their minds cannot change anything.

—George Bernard Shaw

When people shake their heads because we are living in a restless age, ask them how they would like to live in a stationary one and do without change.

—George Bernard Shaw

It is the nature of a man as he grows older . . . to protest against change, particularly change for the better.

—John Steinbeck

Change is always hard for the man who is in a rut. For he has scaled down his living to that which he can handle comfortably and welcomes no change—or challenge—that would lift him.

—C. Neil Strait

The great world spins forever down the ringing grooves of change.

—Alfred Lord Tennyson

You can't change circumstances and you can't change other people, but God can change you.

—Evelyn A. Thiessen

Everybody thinks of changing humanity and nobody thinks of changing himself.

—Leo Tolstoy

The art of progress is to preserve order amid change, and to preserve change amid order.

—Alfred North Whitehead

There is no growth without challenge, and there is no challenge without change.

—Warren Wiersbe

If you want to make enemies, try to change something. You know why it is: to do things today exactly the way you did them yesterday saves thinking.

—Woodrow Wilson

Change yourself, and your fortune will change too.

—Portuguese Proverb

It might be just as offensive to be around a man who never changed his mind as one who never changed his clothes.

—Anonymous

Remember that change and change for the better are often two different things.

—Anonymous

CHARACTER
(See also Reputation)

Let us not say, every man is the architect of his own fortune; but let us say, every man is the architect of his own character.

—G. D. Boardman

Of all the properties that belong to honorable men, not one is so highly prized as that of character.

—Henry Clay

There is no substitute for character. You can buy brains, but you cannot buy character.

—Robert A. Cook

Character needs no epitaph. You can bury a man, but character will bear the hearse back from the graveyard.

—Benjamin R. De Jong

Character is not made in a crisis—it is only exhibited.

—Robert Freeman

You cannot dream yourself into a character; you must hammer and forge yourself one.

—James A. Froude

Talents are best nurtured in solitude; character is best formed in the stormy billows of the world.

—Johann von Goethe

Character is like every other structure; its weaknesses show up when it is tested. No man knows of what stuff he is made until prosperity and ease try him.

—A. P. Gouthey

Fame is a vapor, popularity an accident, riches take wing. Only one thing endures—character.

—Horace Greeley

Success is the product of character. The development of your character is in your own hands, and poverty plus honest ambition is the best environment for character-building.

—Charlie "T" Jones

Character cannot be developed in ease and quiet. Only through experience of trial and suffering can the soul be strengthened, ambition inspired, and success achieved.

—Helen Keller

Nearly all men can stand adversity, but if you want to test a man's character give him power.

—Abraham Lincoln

The measure of a man's real character is what he would do if he knew he never would be found out.

—Thomas B. Macaulay

Character is what God and the angels know of us; reputation is what men and women think of us.

—Horace Mann

You can easily judge the character of a man by how he treats those who can do nothing for him.

—James D. Miles

Character is what you are in the dark.

—Dwight L. Moody

A man never discloses his own character so clearly as when he describes another's.

—Jean Paul Richter

I believe in the sacredness of a promise, that a man's word should be as good as his bond, that character—not wealth or power or position—is of supreme worth.

—John D. Rockefeller Jr.

It is with trifles, and when he is off guard, that a man best reveals his character.

—Arthur Schopenhauer

Character is a strange blending of flinty strength and pliable warmth.

—Robert Shaffer

To be worth anything, character must be capable of standing firm upon its feet in the world of daily work, temptation and trial; and able to bear the wear and tear of actual life. Cloistered virtues do not count for much.

—Samuel Smiles

Character is something each one of us must build for himself, out of the laws of God and nature, the examples of others, and—most of all—out of the trials and errors of daily life. Character is the total of thousands of small daily strivings to live up to the best that is in us.

—Alfred G. Trudeau

A man's strength of character may be measured by his ability to control his temper, instead of letting his temper control him.

—J. Sherman Wallace

Character, not circumstances, makes the man.

—Booker T. Washington

Of genius there is no dearth; but character is a rare article.

—Richard Willstatter

The principle of isometrics is that you can build muscle by pushing firmly against an unyielding object. You can build character the same way.

—Anonymous

Character is like the foundation of a house—it is below the surface.

—Anonymous

The most beautiful side of character, hidden in prosperity, is oftenest revealed in the night time of affliction.

—Anonymous

CHARITY

Charity is a virtue of the heart, and not of the hands.

—Joseph Addison

Real charity doesn't care if it's tax-deductible or not.

—Dan Bennett

The highest exercise of charity is charity toward the uncharitable.

—Joseph S. Buckminster

Charity is a principle of prevailing love to God and goodwill to men, which effectually inclines one endued with it to glorify God, and to do good to others.

—Alexander Cruden

If you haven't any charity in your heart, you have the worst kind of heart trouble.

—Bob Hope

Charity is injurious unless it helps the recipient to become independent of it.

—John D. Rockefeller Jr.

Charity sees the need, not the cause.

—German Proverb

CHEERFULNESS

Cheerfulness keeps up a kind of daylight in the mind, and fills it with a steady and perpetual serenity.

—Joseph Addison

Wondrous is the strength of cheerfulness, and its power of endurance—the cheerful man will do more in the same time, will do it better, will persevere in it longer than the sad or sullen.

—Thomas Carlyle

I feel an earnest and humble desire, and shall till I die, to increase the stock of harmless cheerfulness.

—Charles Dickens

Cheerfulness costs nothing; yet is beyond price. It is an asset for both business and body. The big men of today, the leaders of tomorrow, are those who can blend cheerfulness with their brains.

—B. C. Forbes

Cheerfulness is among the most laudable virtues. It gains you the good will and friendship of others. It blesses those who practice it and those upon whom it is bestowed.

—B. C. Forbes

Cheerfulness is the sunny ray of life.

—Baron Humboldt

Let us be of good cheer, remembering that the misfortunes hardest to bear are those that never come.

—James Russell Lowell

The most certain sign of wisdom is a continual cheerfulness. Her state is like that of things in the regions above the moon, always clear and serene.

—Michel de Montaigne

Cheerfulness is the heaven under which everything but poison thrives.

—Jean Paul Richter

Laughing cheerfulness throws the light of day on all the paths of life.

—Jean Paul Richter

Cheerfulness, like spring, opens all the blossoms of the inward man.

—Jean Paul Richter

Cheerfulness means a contented spirit, a pure heart, a kind and loving disposition; it means humility and charity, a generous appreciation of others, and a modest opinion of self.

—William Makepeace Thackeray

Assume a cheerfulness you do not feel and shortly you will feel the cheerfulness you assumed.

—Chinese Proverb

Cheerful people, the doctors say, resist disease better than the glum ones. In other words, the surly bird catches the germ.

—Anonymous

Cheerfulness is the window-cleaner of the mind.

—Anonymous

CHILDHOOD
(See also Children)

There is in most men's minds a secret instinct of reverence and affection towards the days of their childhood. They cannot help sighing with regret and tenderness when they think of it.

—Saint Ailred of Rievaulx

Backward, turn backward, O Time, in
   your flight,
Make me a child again just for tonight!

—Elizabeth Chase Akers

Blessed be childhood, which brings down something of heaven into the midst of our rough earthliness.

—Henri Frédéric Amiel

Childhood and genius have the same master-organ in common—inquisitiveness.

—Edward G. Bulwer-Lytton

Childhood, the bud of life, unfolding forms the youth, full-blown, becomes a man.

—Ella E. Dodson

For me, the greatest tragedy of life is that childhood is such a short part of our lives.

—Henry Dormann

There is always one moment in childhood when the door opens and lets the future in.

—Graham Greene

Childhood is the world of miracle and wonder: as if creation rose, bathed in light, out of the darkness, utterly new and fresh and astonishing.

—Eugene Ionesco

The primary need of children is not better laws or public programs. It is better childhoods.

—Jack Kemp

Childhood: the kingdom where nobody dies.

—Edna St. Vincent Millay

Childhood is frequently a solemn business for those inside it.

—George F. Will

CHILDREN
(See also Babies, Boys, Childhood, Girls)

A child is a beam of sunlight from the Infinite and Eternal, with possibilities of virtue and vice—but as yet unstained.

—Lyman Abbott

In every child who is born, under no matter what circumstances and of no matter what parents, the potentiality of

the human race is born again.
—James Agee

Ideals and principles continue from generation to generation only when they are built into the hearts of children as they grow up.
—George S. Benson

No one who has ever brought up a child can doubt for a moment that love is literally the life-giving fluid of human existence.
—Smiley Blanton

Words of praise, indeed, are almost as necessary to warm a child into congenial life as acts of kindness and affection. Judicious praise is to children what sun is to flowers.
—Christian Bovée

Never fear spoiling children by making them too happy. Happiness is the atmosphere in which all good affections grow.
—Ann Eliza Bray

There are only two lasting bequests we can hope to give our children. One of these is roots, the other wings.
—Hodding Carter

A child is a seed. You water it. You care for it the best you can. And then it grows all by itself into a beautiful flower.
—Suzanne Chazin

The work will wait while you show the child the rainbow, but the rainbow won't wait while you do the work.
—Patricia Clafford

There's nothing that can help you understand your beliefs more than trying to explain them to an inquisitive child.
—Frank A. Clark

The purest affection the heart can hold is the honest love of a nine-year-old.
—Holman F. Day

I love these little people; and it is not a slight thing when they, who are so fresh from God, love us.
—Charles Dickens

Love your children with all your hearts, love them enough to discipline them before it is too late. . . . Praise them for important things, even if you have to stretch them a bit. Praise them a lot. They live on it like bread and butter and they need it more than bread and butter.
—Lavina Christensen Fugal

Children—the fruit of the seeds of all your finest hopes.
—Gloria Gaither

Children are like wet cement. Whatever falls on them makes an impression.
—Haim Ginott

When we are confused by the world, we can gain a renewed feeling of security from seeing the light in the eyes of a happy, trusting child.
—Harry Hepner

What feeling is so nice as a child's hand in yours?—so small, so soft and warm, like a kitten huddling in the shelter of your clasp.
—Marjorie Holmes

One laugh of a child will make the holiest day more sacred still.
—Robert G. Ingersoll

A child is the root of the heart.
—Carolina Maria de Jesus

Children are the true connoisseurs. What's precious to them has no price— only value.
—Bel Kaufman

Children are not things to be molded, but are people to be unfolded.
—Jess Lair

A child is a person who can't understand why someone would give away a perfectly good kitten.
—Doug Larson

A torn jacket is soon mended, but hard words bruise the heart of a child.
—Henry Wadsworth Longfellow

Children: God's apostles, day by day sent forth to preach of love, and hope, and peace.
—James Russell Lowell

Children know the grace of God better than most of us. They see the world the way the morning brings it back to them, new and born and fresh and wonderful.
—Archibald MacLeish

Children seldom misquote you. They more often repeat word for word what you shouldn't have said.
—Mae Maloo

The hearts of small children are delicate organs. A cruel beginning in this world can twist them into curious shapes.
—Carson McCullers

A child's eyes! Those clear wells of undefiled thought! What on earth can be more beautiful? Full of hope, love, and curiosity, they meet your own. In prayer, how earnest! In joy, how sparkling! In sympathy, how tender!
—Caroline Norton

When you are dealing with a child, keep all your wits about you, and sit on the floor.
—Austin O'Malley

All children wear the sign, "I want to be important NOW." Many of our juvenile delinquency problems arise because nobody reads the sign.
—Dan Pursuit

A child is not a vase to be filled, but a fire to be lit.
—François Rabelais

The smallest children are nearest to God, as the smallest planets are nearest the sun.
—Jean Paul Richter

If you want your child to walk the righteous path, do not merely point the way—lead the way.
—J. A. Rosenkranz

Once you've loved a child, you love all children. You give your love away to one, and you find that by the giving you have made yourself an inexhaustible treasury.

—Margaret Lee Runbeck

Kids are always the only future the human race has.

—William Saroyan

Blessed is the man who does not insist upon talking about his children when I want to talk about mine.

—Roy L. Smith

We are apt to forget that children watch examples better than they listen to preaching.

—Roy L. Smith

Children are the keys of paradise.

—Richard H. Stoddard

There are no seven wonders of the world in the eyes of a child. There are seven million.

—Walt Streightiff

Where children are not, heaven is not.

—Algernon G. Swinburne

Every child comes with the message that God is not yet discouraged of man.

—Rabindranath Tagore

Having a young child explain something exciting he has seen is the finest example of communication you will ever see or hear.

—Bob Talbert

Know what it is to be a child? . . . It is to believe in love, to believe in loveliness, to believe in belief; it is to be so little

that the elves can reach to whisper in your ear; it is to turn pumpkins into coaches, and mice into horses, lowness into loftiness, and nothing into everything, for each child has its fairy godmother in its own soul.

—Francis Thompson

It is true that a child is always hungry all over; but he is also curious all over, and his curiosity is excited about as early as his hunger.

—Charles Dudley Warner

Children are the living messages we send to a time we will not see.

—John W. Whitehead

Every child born into the world is a new thought of God, an ever-fresh and radiant possibility.

—Kate Douglas Wiggin

It's a little frustrating sometimes when you listen to your children saying their prayers. It costs thousands and thousands of dollars to raise them and you get mentioned ahead of the goldfish but after the gerbil.

—Pat Williams and Ken Hussar

A child is like an axe; even if it hurts you, you still carry it on your shoulder.

—African Proverb

A child's life is like a piece of paper on which every passerby leaves a mark.
—Chinese Proverb

A truly rich man is one whose children run into his arms when his hands are empty.
—Anonymous

A child is an island of curiosity surrounded by a sea of question marks.
—Anonymous

There's nothing thirstier than a child who has just gone to bed.
—Anonymous

Fifty years from now, it will not matter what kind of car you drove, what kind of house you lived in, how much you had in your bank account, nor what your clothes looked like. But the world will be a little better place because you were important in the life of a child.
—Anonymous

Our children are the only possessions we can take to heaven.
—Anonymous

Almost every child would learn to write sooner if allowed to do his homework in wet cement.
—Anonymous

CHOICE

All of us are in process all the time. We all choose to grow or retreat. It is a choice we make daily.
—Robert Docter

Between two evils, choose neither; between two goods, choose both.
—Tryon Edwards

The freedom to choose can be very stimulating for us—indeed, without it, life would be dull and uninteresting. The right to choose, or free will if you like, is a precious gift, and we can easily lose it by letting ourselves get so hidebound by habit that we forget the art of choosing wisely.
—Francis Gay

Every time you make a choice, you are turning the central part of you, the part that chooses, into something a little different from what it was before.
—C. S. Lewis

One's philosophy is not best expressed in words. It is expressed in the choices one makes. The process never ends, until we die. And the choices we make are ultimately our responsibility.
—Eleanor Roosevelt

Objective observers in a society that virtually worships freedom of choice must see the irony of forbidding a form of expression [prayer] so basic to people of every culture.
—Forrest Turpen

There is now set before us life and good, death and evil.... But if our hearts shall turn away so that we will not obey, but shall be seduced and worship other gods ... we shall surely perish.
—John Winthrop

The longer I live, the more I begin to grasp that our choice in life is never between pain and no pain. It is rather a choice between enduring it and using it. And God, in His great patience and love, gently paves the way for its use.

—Anonymous

CHRIST

The older I grow in years, the more my wonder and my joy increases when I see the power of these words of Jesus—"I have called you friends"—to move the human heart. The one word "friend" breaks down each barrier of reserve, and we have boldness in His presence. Our hearts go out in love to meet His love.

—Charles F. Andrews

The religion of Jesus is the religion of a little child. There is no affectation about a disciple of Jesus, he is as a little child, amazingly simple but unfathomably deep. Many of us are not childlike enough, we are childish.

—Oswald Chambers

Jesus was God, spelling Himself out in language humanity could understand.

—S. D. Gordon

In the restless sea of human passions, Christ stands steadfast and calm, ready to welcome all who will turn to Him and accept the blessings of safety and peace.

—Billy Graham

Take Jesus Christ seriously. Enter into the most delightful and fulfilling life that anyone could imagine.

—Richard C. Halverson

Of all the systems of morality, ancient or modern, that have come under my observation, none appear to me so pure as that of Jesus.

—Thomas Jefferson

Had the doctrines of Jesus been preached always as pure as they came from his lips, the whole civilized world would now have been Christian.

—Thomas Jefferson

The Son of God became a man to enable men to become the sons of God.

—C. S. Lewis

Not in the emergencies, not in the great crises, but in everything, we must cultivate the habit of dependence on Christ. Habitually recognize that He has undertaken the business of your life in all its departments.

—J. Gregory Mantle

Jesus is not only that [the vine]: He is soil and sunshine, air and showers, and ten thousand times more than we have ever dreamed, wished for, or needed.

—J. Hudson Taylor

You'll never realize Jesus is all you need until Jesus is all you've got.

—Mother Teresa

Without the Way, there is no going; without the Truth, there is no knowing; without the Life, there is no living.

—Thomas à Kempis

Jesus Christ does not want to be our helper; He wants to be our life. He does not want us to work for Him. He wants us to let Him do His work through us, using us as we use a pencil to write with—better still, using us as one of the fingers on His hand.

—Charles G. Trumbull

All that is best in the civilization of today is the fruit of Christ's appearance among men.

—Daniel Webster

If our greatest need had been information, God would have sent us an educator. If our greatest need had been technology, God would have sent us a scientist. If our greatest need had been money, God would have sent us an economist. If our greatest need had been pleasure, God would have sent us an entertainer. But our greatest need was forgiveness, so God sent us a Savior.

—Anonymous

The crucifixion of Jesus is *sufficient* for all, but is *efficient* only for those who accept His gift.

—Anonymous

Titles of Jesus Christ

To the architect, He is the chief cornerstone. (1 Peter 2:6)

To the bride, He is the bridegroom. (Matt. 25:1)

To the carpenter, He is the door. (John 10:9)

To the engineer, He is the new and living way. (Heb. 10:20)

To the farmer, He is the Lord of the harvest. (Matt. 9:38)

To the horticulturist, He is the true vine. (John 15:1)

To the jurist, He is the righteous judge. (2 Tim. 4:8)

To the philanthropist, He is the unspeakable gift. (2 Cor. 9:15)

To the philosopher, He is the wisdom of God. (1 Cor. 1:24)

To the preacher, He is the Word of God. (Rev. 19:13)

To the soldier, He is the captain of his salvation. (Heb. 2:10)

To the statesman, He is the desire of the nations. (Hag. 2:7)

To the sinner, He is the Lamb of God. (John 1:29)

—Henrietta C. Mears

CHRISTIANITY

There is no longer any room in the world for a merely external form of Christianity, based upon custom. The world is entering upon a period of catastrophe and crisis when we are being forced to take sides, and in which a higher and more intense spiritual life will be demanded of Christians.

—Alexander Berdyaev

I saw about a peck of counterfeit dollars once. Did I go to the window and throw away all my good dollars? No! Yet you reject Christianity because there are hypocrites, or counterfeit Christians.

—William E. Biederwolf

There is between Christianity and all other religions whatsoever, the distance of infinity.

—Napoleon Bonaparte

Christianity is not a theory or speculation, but a life; not a philosophy of life, but a living presence.

—Samuel Taylor Coleridge

Christianity has a cross at its heart! Crossless Christianity is a contradiction!

—Richard C. Halverson

Christian faith is a grand cathedral, with divinely pictured windows. Standing without, you can see no glory, nor can imagine any, but standing within, every ray of light reveals a harmony of unspeakable splendors.

—Nathaniel Hawthorne

When I became a Christian, Jesus Christ came to live in my heart in the person of His Holy Spirit. Real Christianity is really Christ-in-you-ity.

—John Hunter

I believe in Christianity as I believe the sun has risen, not only because I see it, but because by it I see everything else.

—C. S. Lewis

Vulnerability is believability and Christianity is believable when it is lived out by vulnerable Christians.

—Elisa Morgan

Christianity is the religion of *done,* all done by God. Every other religion is one of *doing,* seeking to attain God from man's end.

—Malcolm Smith

Christianity must mean everything to us before it can mean anything to others.

—Donald Soper

There never has been a period of history in which the Common Law did not recognize Christianity as laying at its foundation.

—Joseph Story

Stop playing around with Christianity. Go all out at any cost so that when you get to the end of the road you will have that deep and abiding assurance from the Lord of "well done." There is not one thing in this life that is worth contending for except to preach the gospel in all its purity.

—Morris M. Townsend

CHRISTIANS

The Christian should be an alleluia from head to foot.

—Saint Augustine

Often the most useful Christians are those who serve their Master in little things. He never despises the day of small things, or else He would not hide His oaks in tiny acorns, or the wealth of a wheat field in bags of little seeds.

—Theodore Ledyard Cuyler

It cannot be emphasized too strongly or too often that this great nation was founded, not by religionists, but by Christians, not on religions, but on the gospel of Jesus Christ! For this very reason peoples of other faiths have been afforded asylum, prosperity, and freedom of worship here.

—Patrick Henry

Christians ought to rise together in defense of spiritual and moral values against the pressure of materialism and moral permissiveness.

—Pope John Paul II

For a Christian, life is not divided into the secular and the sacred. To him all ground is sacred ground, every bush a burning bush, and every place a temple of worship.

—Bob Jones Sr.

It is impossible for a man to be a Christian without having Christ; and if he has Christ he has at the same time all that is in Christ.

—Martin Luther

A true Christian's enthusiasm for the Lord Jesus Christ should be so exuberant that it would be far more likely to set others on fire than to be extinguished by worldly influences. Have a Christianity that is contagious.

—Henrietta C. Mears

Christians are useless if they are fruitless.

—Henrietta C. Mears

If our faith is not relevant to our daily life in the world and in the parish, then it is no use; and if we cannot be Christians in our work, in the neighborhood, in our political decisions, then we had better stop being Christians. A piety

reserved for Sundays is no message for this age.

—Douglas Rhymes

Next to the wicked lives of men, nothing is so great a disparagement and weakening to religion as the divisions of Christians.

—John Tillotson

CHRISTLIKENESS

The expression of Christian character is not good doing, but God-likeness. If the Spirit of God has transformed you within, you will exhibit divine characteristics in your life, not good human characteristics.

—Oswald Chambers

Brothers, you are Christ to the world. Christ has no hands but your hands to touch and bless and heal, no feet but your feet to lead men in the path of truth, no arms but your arms to gather the scattered, no tongue but your tongues to cheer a suffering mankind, no heart but your heart to love, to pity, to care.

—Saint Francis of Assisi

In the footsteps of my Savior
I would walk each day,
Following ever where they'd lead me,
Close to Him to stay.

—B. K.

Do little things as though they were great, because of the majesty of Jesus Christ who does them in us, and who lives our life; and do the greatest things as though they were little and easy, because of His omnipotence.

—Blaise Pascal

CHRISTMAS

Christmas is a Son away from home.

—Norma Alloway

There has been only one Christmas (the rest are anniversaries), and it is not over yet.

—W. J. Cameron

The place that the shepherds found was not an academy or an abstract republic; it was not a place of myths allegorized or dissected or explained away. It was a place of dreams come true.

—Gilbert Keith Chesterton

It is good to be children sometimes, and never better than at Christmas, when its mighty Founder was a child Himself.

—Charles Dickens

I will honor Christmas in my heart, and try to keep it all the year.

—Charles Dickens

It is Christmas in the heart that puts Christmas in the air.

—W. T. Ellis

There is love at Christmas because Christmas was born of love. Let us, each one, keep alive this spirit of love and glorify God.

—Josepha Emms

God grant you the light of Christmas, which is faith; the warmth of Christmas,

which is love; the radiance of Christmas, which is purity; the righteousness of Christmas, which is justice; the belief in Christmas, which is truth; the all of Christmas, which is Christ.

—Wilda English

Some businessmen are saying that this could be the greatest Christmas ever. I always thought the first one was.

—Art Fettig

Christmas is based on an exchange of gifts: the gift of God to man—His Son; and the gift of man to God when ... we first give ourselves to God.

—Vance Havner

And thus was kept the first Christmas, the Christmas in the year one, with carols by the choir of heaven, and God's own Son, the Savior of the world, coming as a Christmas gift for all mankind.

—George Hodges

In the hustle and bustle, amidst the trappings and the wrappings, it's good to pause and reflect on the reason for the Christmas season. As we rush to buy our gifts, let's remember what happened on that first Christmas morn. The trappings were a stable in Bethlehem, and the wrappings were swaddling clothes that became the royal garments of the infant King. The gift—Jesus Christ, the Son of God, made flesh.

—B. K.

Let this Christmas season be a renewing of the mind of Christ in our thinking, and a cleansing of our lives by

His pure presence. Let His joy come to our weary world through us.

—Gerald Kennedy

I wish we could put some of the Christmas spirit in jars and open a jar of it every month.

—Harlan Miller

Christmas waves a magic wand over this world, and behold, everything is softer and more beautiful. If only for one short day, ill will is set aside, and the effect on our lives is miraculous.

—Norman Vincent Peale

Nothing during the year is so impressively convincing as the vision Christmas brings of what this world would be if love became the daily practice of human beings.

—Norman Vincent Peale

He who has not Christmas in his heart will never find it under a tree.

—Roy L. Smith

The first Christmas is a miraculous story of the eternal God's becoming of no reputation and then humbling Himself to accept a cruel death on a cross. Sure there were angel choirs. Kings came from far away to worship Him. But the true Christmas story is about smallness, humility, and servanthood.... Let us consider becoming unknown and squeezing into small places in the lives of those around us who have great need to know this babe from Bethlehem, Jesus Christ.

—Bob Snyder

Holiday and holy day, Christmas is more than a Yule log, holly, or tree. It is more than natural good cheer and the giving of gifts. Christmas is even more than the feast of the home and of children, the feast of love and friendship. It is more than all of these together. Christmas is Christ, the Christ of justice and charity, of freedom and peace.

—Francis J. Spellman

Christmas is when God came down the stairs of heaven with a Baby in His arms.

—R. Eugene Sterner

The coming of Christ by way of a Bethlehem manger seems strange and stunning. But when we take Him out of the manger and invite Him into our hearts, then the meaning unfolds and the strangeness vanishes.

—C. Neil Strait

May the spirit of Christmas ignite in the hearts of patriotic Americans a determination to redouble efforts at recapturing control of our national destiny, so that our children and their children may know, as we have known, the joy of true freedom and the infinite glory that shines from the humble manger of the newborn Christ.

—James Thornton

I do hope your Christmas has had a little touch of Eternity in among the rush and pitter patter and all. It always seems such a mixing of this world and the next—but that after all is the idea.

—Evelyn Underhill

Light of the world so clear and bright,
Enter our homes this Christmas night;
Re-light our souls so tenderly,
That we may grow to be like Thee.

—Anonymous

Christmas is a gift from God that a man
cannot keep unless he gives it to
someone else.

—Anonymous

Under most Christmas trees on
December 25 there will be many gifts.
On Calvary's tree there was only one gift
but it included all others—God's gift of
his only begotten Son.

—Anonymous

CHURCH

Only the church stood squarely across
the path of Hitler's campaign for
suppressing the truth. I never had any
special interest in the church before, but
now I feel a great affection and admiration for it because the church alone has
had the courage and persistence to
stand for intellectual and moral
freedom. I am forced to confess that
what I once despised I now praise
unreservedly.

—Albert Einstein

The only way any church can get a
blessing is to lay aside all difference, all
criticism, all coldness and party feeling,
and come to the Lord as one.

—Dwight L. Moody

What is the church? . . . The best way to
kill a church is to squeeze it into a
building. For without contact with
people in need and publicly witnessing
faith and trust in Jesus, a church will
quietly die.

—Bob Snyder

The church is not a dormitory for
sleepers, it is an institution for workers;
it is not a rest camp, it is a front-line
trench.

—Billy Sunday

In too many churches today, head tables
have replaced towels and wash basins as
symbols of leadership among God's
people.

—C. Gene Wilkes

CHURCH MEMBERS

Too many church members are starched
and ironed, but not washed.

—Vance Havner

Church members are either pillars or
caterpillars. The pillars hold up the
church; the caterpillars just crawl in and
out.

—Wendell Phillips

The problem is not that the churches are
filled with empty pews, but that the
pews are filled with empty people.

—Charlie Shedd

Every Christian's place is in a local
church . . . sharing in its worship, its
fellowship, and its witness.

—John R. W. Stott

CIRCUMSTANCES

Circumstances do not make or break you—they simply reveal your real self.
—Robert D. Foster

Circumstances never made the man do right who didn't do right in spite of them.
—Coulson Kernahan

Circumstances are things round about; we are *in* them, not *under* them.
—Walter Savage Landor

People are always blaming circumstances for what they are. I don't believe in circumstances. The people who get on in this world are the people who get up and look for the circumstances they want, and if they can't find them, make them.
—George Bernard Shaw

CIVILIZATION

The true civilization is where every man gives to every other every right that he claims for himself.
—Robert G. Ingersoll

You can't say civilizations don't advance ...in every war they kill you in a new way.
—Will Rogers

There is no solid basis for civilization but in the Word of God.
—Daniel Webster

Unless our civilization is redeemed spiritually, it cannot endure materially.
—Woodrow Wilson

COMFORT

Comfort comes as a guest, lingers to become a host, and stays to enslave us.
—Lee S. Bickmore

Oh, the comfort, the inexpressible comfort, of feeling safe with a person, having neither to weigh thoughts nor measure words, but pouring them all right out, just as they are, chaff and grain together, certain that a faithful hand will take and sift them, keep what is worth keeping, and with the breath of kindness blow the rest away.
—Rex Cole

God does not comfort us to make us comfortable, but to make us comforters.
—J. H. Jowett

Words of comfort, skillfully administered, are the oldest therapy known to man.
—Louis Nizer

Creature comforts are like the soft morning dews, which, while they water the branches of the tree, leave the roots dry.
—William Secker

COMMITMENT
(See also Consecration)

To the wrongs that need resistance,
To the right that needs assistance,

To the future in the distance,
Give yourselves.

—Carrie Lane Chapman Catt

It is not a question of being willing to go straight through, but of going straight through—not a question of saying, "Lord, I will do it," but of doing it. There must be the reckless committal of everything to Him with no regard for the consequences.

—Oswald Chambers

If you have people who will only come [to Africa] if they know there is a good road, I don't want them. I want men and women who are willing to come if there is no road at all.

—David Livingstone

Nothing earthly will make me give up my work in despair.

—David Livingstone

The moment one definitely commits oneself, then Providence moves too. All sorts of things occur to help one that would never otherwise have occurred. A whole stream of events issues from the decision, raising in one's favor all manner of unforeseen incidents and meetings and material assistance that no man could have dreamed would have come his way.

—W. H. Murray

If we could but show the world that being committed to Christ is no tame humdrum, sheltered monotony, but the most thrilling, exciting adventure the human spirit could ever know.

—James S. Stewart

We are committed to feed Christ who is hungry, committed to clothe Christ who is naked, committed to take in Christ who has no home—and to do all this with a smile on our faces and bursting with joy.

—Mother Teresa

COMMITTEES
(See also Conferences, Meetings)

If Moses had been a committee the Israelites would still be in Egypt.

—J. B. Hughes

A committee is an arrangement, enabling one to share the blame with others.

—Franklin P. Jones

If you want to kill any idea in the world today, get a committee working on it.

—Charles F. Kettering

A committee is an animal with four back legs.

—John Le Carré

A committee is a cul-de-sac down which ideas are lured, then quietly strangled.

—John A. Lincoln

A committee should consist of three men, two of whom are absent.

—Herbert Beerbohm Tree

For God so loved the world that He didn't send a committee.

—Anonymous

The ideal committee consists of two, four, or six people who haven't time, and one person who likes to do things his own way.

—Anonymous

COMMON SENSE

Nothing is more fairly distributed than common sense: no one thinks he needs more of it than he already has.

—René Descartes

Common sense is, of all kinds, the most uncommon.

—Tryon Edwards

Common sense is genius dressed in its working clothes.

—Ralph Waldo Emerson

Nothing astonishes men so much as common sense and plain dealing.

—Ralph Waldo Emerson

Common sense is compelled to make its way without the enthusiasm of anyone.

—Edgar Watson Howe

It is a thousand times better to have common sense without education than to have education without common sense.

—Robert G. Ingersoll

Common sense suits itself to the ways of the world. Wisdom tries to conform to the ways of heaven.

—Joseph Joubert

Common sense is instinct. Enough of it is genius.

—George Bernard Shaw

Common sense is the knack of seeing things as they are, and doing things as they ought to be done.

—Harriet Beecher Stowe

COMMUNICATION

We should have all our communications with men as in the presence of God, and with God as in the presence of men.

—Charles Caleb Colton

The constant use of long, involved words proves two things: 1) that you're learned; 2) that you're ignorant of how best to communicate with people.

—Will Conway

What a man really says when he says that someone else can be persuaded by force, is that he himself is incapable of more rational means of communication.

—Norman Cousins

Strides in communication now permit us to talk with people around the globe, but cannot bridge the ever-widening gaps within our own families.

—Gloria France

We can communicate an idea around the world in seven seconds, but it sometimes takes years for an idea to get through one-fourth inch of human skull.

—Charles F. Kettering

The purpose of all higher education is to make men aware of what was and what is, to incite them to probe into what may be. It seeks to teach them to understand, to evaluate, to communicate.

—Otto Kleppner

Communication is something so simple and difficult that we can never put it in simple words.

—T. S. Matthews

The marvels—of film, radio, and television—are marvels of one-way communication, which is not communication at all.

—Milton Mayer

There is no pleasure to me without communication; there is not so much as a sprightly thought comes into my mind but I grieve that I have no one to tell it to.

—Michel de Montaigne

Good communication is as stimulating as black coffee, and just as hard to sleep after.

—Anne Morrow

The more we elaborate our means of communication, the less we communicate.

—J. B. Priestley

Extremists think "communication" means agreeing with them.

—Leo Rosten

Precision of communication is important, more important than ever, in our era of hair-trigger balances, when a false or misunderstood word may create as much disaster as a sudden thoughtless act.

—James Thurber

Half the world's problems are caused by poor communications. The other half are caused by good communications.

—Anonymous

The greatest problem in communication is the illusion that it has been achieved.

—Anonymous

COMPASSION

Compassion will cure more sins than condemnation.

—Henry Ward Beecher

The dew of compassion is a tear.

—Lord Byron

Even if you can't prevent another's sorrow, caring will lessen it.

—Frank A. Clark

He best can pity who has felt the woe.

—John Gay

To ease another's heartache is to forget one's own.

—Abraham Lincoln

Pity weeps and runs away;
Compassion comes to help and stay.
—Janet Curtis O'Leary

Compassion is almost never practical.
—Kathleen Parker

What value has compassion that does
not take its object in its arms?
—Antoine de Saint-Exupéry

There never was any heart truly great
and gracious that was not also tender
and compassionate.
—Robert South

COMPETITION

Without the spur of competition we'd
loaf out our life.
—Arnold H. Glasow

The carpenter or plumber or painter,
the butcher or baker or candlestick
maker who would naturally prosper is
he who does the same work better than
his competitors.
—H. M. Kallen

Don't knock your competitors. . . . A
little competition is a good thing and
severe competition is a blessing. Thank
God for competition.
—Jacob Kindleberger

Our competitors are often our greatest
benefactors. He that wrestles with us
strengthens our muscles and sharpens
our skills.
—Alfred A. Montapert

COMPLAINT
(See also Grumbling)

Constant complaint is the poorest sort
of pay for all the comforts we enjoy.
—Benjamin Franklin

Complaining minds send a wagon to
bring their troubles home in.
—Charles H. Spurgeon

COMPLIMENTS

Some fellows pay a compliment like
they expect a receipt.
—Frank McKinney Hubbard

I have been complimented many times
and they always embarrass me; I always
feel that they have not said enough.
—Mark Twain

COMPROMISE

Compromise is but the sacrifice of one
right or good in the hope of attaining
another—too often ending in the loss
of both.
—Tryon Edwards

A compromise is the art of dividing a
cake in such a way that everyone
believes that he has gotten the biggest
piece.
—Ludwig Erhard

Compromise is simply changing the
question to fit the answer.
—Merrit Malloy

CONCEIT

Conceit is the most incurable disease that is known to the human soul.
—Henry Ward Beecher

There are many kinds of conceit, but the chief one is to let people know what a very ancient and gifted family one descends from.
—Benvenuto Cellini

The greatest curse in spiritual life is conceit. If we ever have had a glimpse of what we are like in the sight of God, we shall never say, "Oh, I am so unworthy," because we shall know we are, beyond the possibility of stating it.
—Oswald Chambers

He who falls in love with himself will have no rivals.
—Benjamin Franklin

Conceit is characteristic of the man with easy targets.
—Richard C. Halverson

CONDUCT

Confront improper conduct, not by retaliation, but by example.
—John Foster

Every man is valued in this world as he shows by his conduct that he wishes to be valued.
—Jean de La Bruyère

The virtue of man ought to be measured, not by his extraordinary exertions, but by his everyday conduct.
—Blaise Pascal

The world is made better by every man improving his own conduct.
—William Allen White

CONFERENCES
(See also Committees, Meetings)

A conference is a gathering of important people who, singly, can do nothing, but together can decide that nothing can be done.
—Fred Allen

A conference is just an admission that you want somebody to join you in your troubles.
—Will Rogers

Perhaps hell is nothing more than an enormous conference of those who, with little or nothing to say, take an eternity to say it.
—Dudley C. Stone

CONFESSION

The confession of evil works is the beginning of good works.
—Saint Augustine

We only confess our little faults to persuade people that we have no big ones.
—François de La Rochefoucauld

A man should never be ashamed to own he has been wrong, which is but saying in other words that he is wiser today than he was yesterday.
—Alexander Pope

CONFIDENCE

He who has lost confidence can lose nothing more.

—Boiste

God expects of us the one thing that glorifies Him—and that is to remain absolutely confident in Him, remembering what He has said beforehand, and sure that His purposes will be fulfilled.

—Oswald Chambers

Confidence is that feeling by which the mind embarks in great and honorable courses with a sure hope and trust in itself.

—Cicero

"I can do all things through Christ which strengtheneth me." The man who believes this has calm quiet confidence, but, because his confidence is based upon God's power and not his own power, there is never the slightest speck of egotism.

—Clinton Davidson

The mutual confidence on which all else depends can be maintained only by an open mind and a brave reliance upon free discussion.

—Learned Hand

Skill and confidence are an unconquered army.

—George Herbert

The confidence that we have in ourselves gives birth to much of that which we have in others.

—François de La Rochefoucauld

Confidence always gives pleasure to the man in whom it is placed.

—François de La Rochefoucauld

Why should there not be a patient confidence in the ultimate justice of the people? Is there any better or equal hope in the world?

—Abraham Lincoln

Confidence . . . thrives only on honesty, on honor, on the sacredness of obligations, on faithful protection, and on unselfish performance. Without them, it cannot live.

—Franklin Delano Roosevelt

Lack of confidence is not the result of difficulty; the difficulty comes from lack of confidence.

—Seneca

No man has a right to expect others to display confidence in him if he has no confidence in himself.

—Roy L. Smith

Society is built upon trust and trust upon confidence in one another's integrity.

—Robert South

Confidence! Confidence! Confidence! That is your capital.

—John Wanamaker

Be courteous to all, but intimate with few, and let those few be well tried before you give them your confidence.

—George Washington

Confidence is a thing not to be produced by compulsion. Men cannot be forced into trust.

—Daniel Webster

Confidence never comes from having all the answers; it comes from being open to all the questions.

—Anonymous

CONQUEST

They conquer who believe they can.

—John Dryden

Make me a captive, Lord,
And then I shall be free.
Force me to render up my sword,
And I shall conqueror be.

—George Matheson

CONSCIENCE

Conscience: a small, still voice that makes minority reports.

—Franklin P. Adams

It is an accepted law of ethics that punishment in the court of conscience, unlike that in courts of law, lessens with each repeated and unrebuked offense.

—Joseph S. Auerbach

The world has achieved brilliance without conscience. Ours is a world of nuclear giants and ethical infants. We have grasped the mystery of the atom and rejected the Sermon on the Mount.

—Omar N. Bradley

Conscience is thoroughly well-bred and soon leaves off talking to those who do not wish to hear it.

—Samuel Butler

If your conscience won't stop you, pray for cold feet.

—Elmer G. Leterman

Conscience is the most sacred of all property.

—James Madison

In the courtroom of our conscience, we call only witnesses for the defense.

—François Mauriac

Conscience is the inner voice that warns us that someone may be looking.

—H. L. Mencken

Conscience is a mother-in-law whose visit never ends.

—H. L. Mencken

Conscience is the voice of the soul; the passions are the voice of the body.

—Jean Jacques Rousseau

Conscience is God's presence in man.

—Emanuel Swedenborg

The conscience is a thousand witnesses.

—Richard Tavener

He that loses his conscience has nothing left that is worth keeping.

—Izaak Walton

Labor to keep alive in your breast that little spark of celestial fire, called conscience.

—George Washington

Conscience is the small clear voice deep down inside of you, where the acoustics are very bad.

—Anonymous

Conscience warns us as a friend before it punishes us as a judge.

—Anonymous

CONSECRATION
(See also Commitment)

There can be no compulsion in consecration.

—J. Sidlow Baxter

He is no fool who gives what he cannot keep to gain what he cannot lose.

—Jim Elliot

Consecration is not synonymous with activity. Consecration concerns our relationship to Jesus Christ as a Person.

—Eric S. Fife

The purpose of my life is to make me what the Almighty wants me to be. Then I shall not measure things by their capacity to delight and please my tastes, ambitions, desires, and senses . . . but only by their power to mold me in His likeness.

—Robert D. Foster

No friend or anything else shall ever come first in my life. I have resolved that the Lord Jesus Christ shall have all of me. I care not what the future holds. I have determined to follow Him at any cost.

—Billy Graham

God will give us opportunities to try our consecration, whether it be a true one or not. No man can be wholly the Lord's unless he is wholly consecrated to the Lord; and no man can know whether he is wholly consecrated except by tribulation.

—Madame Jean Guyon

Lord, send me anywhere, only go with me; lay any burden on me, only sustain me; sever every tie but the tie that binds me to Thy service and to Thy heart.

—David Livingstone

CONSEQUENCES

Sooner or later, everyone sits down to a banquet of consequences.

—Robert Louis Stevenson

CONSISTENCY

A foolish consistency is the hobgoblin of little minds.

—Ralph Waldo Emerson

Consistency is contrary to nature, contrary to life. The only consistent people are the dead.

—Aldous Huxley

CONSTITUTION, THE U.S.

Our Constitution was made only for a moral and religious people.

—John Adams

The Constitution is not neutral. It was designed to take the government off the backs of people.

—William O. Douglas

The Constitution is not an instrument for the government to restrain the people, it is an instrument for the people to restrain the government—lest it come to dominate our lives and interests.

—Patrick Henry

[An] act of the Congress of the United States . . . that assumes powers . . . not delegated by the Constitution, is not law, but is altogether void and of no force.

—Thomas Jefferson

Hold on, my friends, to the Constitution and to the republic for which it stands. Miracles do not cluster, and what has happened once in six thousand years may not happen again. Hold on to the Constitution, for if the American Constitution should fail, there will be anarchy throughout the world.

—Daniel Webster

CONTEMPT

To exercise contempt is to invite contempt. Any person who looks with contempt upon another sets in motion an evil force that rarely ever stops.

—Charles Ashcraft

Whatever you hold in contempt is your jailer.

—Brendan Francis

CONTENTMENT
(See also Satisfaction)

Contentment is more satisfying than exhilaration; and contentment means simply the sum of small and quiet pleasures.

—Henry Ward Beecher

True contentment is the power of getting out of any situation all that there is in it.

—Gilbert Keith Chesterton

A contented spirit is the sweetness of existence.

—Charles Dickens

Contentment comes not so much from great wealth as from few wants.

—Epictetus

Fortify yourself with contentment, for this is an impregnable fortress.

—Epictetus

I am always content with what happens; for I know that what God chooses is better than what I choose.

—Epictetus

Content makes poor men rich; discontent makes rich men poor.

—Benjamin Franklin

Contentment consisteth not in adding more fuel, but in taking away some fire.

—Thomas Fuller

When we cannot find contentment in ourselves, it is useless to seek it elsewhere.

—François de La Rochefoucauld

Contentment will make a cottage look
as fair as a palace.

—William Secker

Contentment is the best food to
preserve a sound man, and the best
medicine to restore a sick man.

—William Secker

Contentment is natural wealth; luxury is
artificial poverty.

—Socrates

Contentment is the best of all riches—
and it's not taxed!

—Anonymous

CONTRADICTION

Trust only those who have the courage
to contradict you with respect, and who
value your character more than your
favor.

—François de la Fenelon

Contradiction is the salt that keeps
truth from corruption.

—John Lancaster Spalding

CONVERSATION

The art of conversation consists as
much in listening politely as in talking
agreeably.

—George Atwell

A good conversationalist is not one who
remembers what was said, but says
what someone wants to remember.

—John Mason Brown

Conversation is an art in which a man
has all mankind for competitors.

—Ralph Waldo Emerson

Conversation is the handmaid of
learning. It would be impossible to put
too high a price on all we stand to lose
by suffering its decay.

—A. Whitney Griswold

The reason why so few people are
agreeable in conversation is that each is
thinking more on what he is intending
to say than on what others are saying,
and that we never listen when we are
desirous to speak.

—François de La Rochefoucauld

CONVERSION

Conversion is the end of the Christian
life—but it's the front end!

—J. B. Gambrell

There isn't any doubt about it, the
human soul cannot go on forever in sin
without some desire to free itself. . . .
Conversion simply means turning
around.

—Vincent McNabb

CONVICTIONS

Conviction is worthless till it convert
itself into conduct.

—Thomas Carlyle

Give me the benefit of your convictions,
if you have any; but keep your doubts to
yourself, for I have enough of my own.

—Johann von Goethe

Have convictions, but be sure your convictions are convictions, not prejudices.

—Bob Jones Sr.

When principles that run against your deepest convictions begin to win the day, then battle is your calling, and peace has become sin; you must, at the price of dearest peace, lay your convictions bare before friend and enemy, with all the fire of your faith.

—Abraham Kuyper

Every man is encompassed by a cloud of comforting convictions, which move with him like flies on a summer day.

—Bertrand Russell

COOPERATION

We are born for cooperation, as are the feet, the hands, the eyelids, and the upper and lower jaws.

—Marcus Aurelius Antoninus

The world must learn to work together, or finally it will not work at all.

—Dwight D. Eisenhower

COURAGE

It is a lovely thing to live with courage and die, leaving an everlasting flame.

—Alexander the Great

Whether you be man or woman, you will never do anything in this world without courage. It is the greatest quality of the mind next to honor.

—James Lane Allen

Courage: The lovely virtue—the rib of Himself that God sent down to His children.

—James M. Barrie

Courage is the first of human qualities, because it is the quality that guarantees all others.

—Winston Churchill

Physical courage, which despises all danger, will make a man brave in one way; and moral courage, which despises all opinion, will make a man brave in another.

—Charles Caleb Colton

It takes courage to live—courage and strength and hope and humor. And courage and strength and hope and humor have to be bought and paid for with pain and work and prayers and tears.

—Jerome P. Fleishman

Courage is very important. Like a muscle, it is strengthened by use.

—Ruth Gordon

One man with courage makes a majority.

—Andrew Jackson

Courage is not simply one of the virtues but the form of every virtue at the testing point, which means at the point of highest reality.

—C. S. Lewis

It takes as much courage to have tried and failed as it does to have tried and succeeded.

—Anne Morrow Lindbergh

Courage can't see around corners, but goes around them anyway.

—Mignon McLaughlin

Happy is he who dares courageously to defend what he loves.

—Ovid

Courage is not the absence of fear, but rather the judgment that something else is more important than fear.

—Ambrose Redmoon

Courage is doing what you're afraid to do. There can be no courage unless you're scared.

—Eddie Rickenbacker

Courage is resistance to fear, mastery of fear—not absence of fear.

—Mark Twain

Courage is the standing army of the soul, which keeps it from conquest, pillage, and slavery.

—Henry Van Dyke

Hope awakens courage. He who can implant courage in the human soul is the best physician.

—Karl Von Knebel

It isn't life that matters, but the courage you bring to it.

—Hugh Walpole

All courage comes from daring to begin.

—Eugene Ware

Courage is what it takes to stand up and speak; courage is also what it takes to sit down and listen.

—Anonymous

COURTESY

Life is not so short but that there is always time for courtesy.

—Ralph Waldo Emerson

Courtesy is a science of the highest importance, which ought to be on the curriculum of every Christian.

—Anonymous

Courtesy opens every gate and doesn't cost a cent.

—Anonymous

COWARDICE

To know what is right and not to do it is the worst cowardice.

—Confucius

Fear has its use but cowardice has none.

—Mohandas K. Gandhi

It is the coward who fawns on those above him. It is the coward who is insolent whenever he dares be so.

—Junius

To sin by silence when they should protest makes cowards out of men.

—Abraham Lincoln

The world has no room for cowards. We must all be ready somehow to toil, to suffer, to die. And yours is not the less noble because no drum beats before

you when you go out into your daily
battlefields, and no crowds shout about
your coming when you return from
your daily victory or defeat.

—Robert Louis Stevenson

CREATION
(See also Evolution)

All things bright and beautiful,
All creatures great and small,
All things wise and wonderful,
The Lord God made them all.

—Cecil Frances Alexander

God created the world out of nothing.
As long as you are not yet nothing, God
cannot make something out of you.

—Martin Luther

CREATIVITY
(See also Imagination)

Creativity is bound to stir up contro-
versy because its ultimate impact
always is to change the status quo.

—O. A. Battista

Without appearing to work as hard, the
highly creative person appears to learn
as much as, if not more than, the one
with a high IQ. My guess is that these
highly creative people are learning and
thinking when they appear to be
playing around.

—Emma Birkmaier

One must not lose desires. They are
mighty stimulants to creativeness, to
love, and to long life.

—Alexander A. Bogomoletz

There is a correlation between the
creative and the screwball. So we must
suffer the screwball gladly.

—Kingman Brewster

A hunch is creativity trying to tell you
something.

—Frank Capra

No matter how old you get, if you can
keep the desire to be creative, you're
keeping the man-child alive.

—John Cassavetes

I believe all of us subconsciously want
to be creative. This is a very human trait
and probably what makes the difference
between us and the animals. The
trouble is that for most of us imagination has been suppressed to the point
where we have stopped using it. We
need to stop and daydream once in a
while. We need to let our imaginations
roam and give them a chance to breathe.
It's never really too late for anyone to
start thinking more creatively.

—J. P. Dubois

To raise new questions, new possibilities, to regard old problems from a new
angle requires creative imagination and
marks real advances in science.

—Albert Einstein

Creative thinking may mean simply the
realization that there's no particular
virtue in doing things the way they've
always been done.

—Rudolf Flesch

Creativity

Creative minds have always been known to survive any kind of bad training.

—Anna Freud

No man can be absolutely true to himself ... without becoming original, for there is in every creature a fountain of life that, if not choked back by stones and other dead rubbish, will create a fresh atmosphere and bring to life fresh beauty.

—Margaret Fuller

Creativity requires the freedom to consider "unthinkable" alternatives, to doubt the worth of cherished practices.

—John W. Gardner

The value of the creative faculty derives from the fact that that faculty is the primary mark of man. To deprive man of its exercise is to reduce him to subhumanity.

—Eric Gill

Discontent is at the root of the creative process ... the most gifted members of the human species are at their creative best when they cannot have their way, and they must compensate for what they miss by realizing and cultivating their capacities and talents.

—Eric Hoffer

Take an object. Do something to it. Do something else to it.

—Jasper Johns

You don't reach in and duplicate yesterday; you create tomorrow.

—Charles Kaman

Creative activity could be described as a type of learning process where teacher and pupil are located in the same individual.

—Arthur Koestler

You cannot order people to be creative. People are creative only when they are doing the things they want to do.

—Herman Krannert

When patterns are broken, new worlds can emerge.

—Tuli Kupferberg

A first-rate soup is more creative than a second-rate painting.

—Abraham Maslow

The great creative individual ... is capable of more wisdom and virtue than collective man ever can be.

—John Stuart Mill

Making the simple complicated is commonplace; making the complicated simple, awesomely simple, that's creativity.

—Charles Mingus

It is better to create than to be learned; creating is the very essence of life.

—Reinhold Niebuhr

Nobody is a creative thinker unless continually he has a thorn in his flesh, that is, unless he is disturbed by something. The thick-skinned people do no creative thinking; to them everything is understood; they have no problems; nothing baffles them.

—F. S. C. Northrop

Creativity is so delicate a flower that praise tends to make it bloom, while discouragement often nips it in the bud. Any of us will put out more and better ideas if our efforts are truly appreciated.
—Alexander F. Osborn

In the average person, judgment grows automatically with years, while creativity dwindles unless consciously kept up.
—Alexander F. Osborn

True creativeness is finding new possibilities in old situations.
—J. G. Saxe

The intellect must surely harden as fast as the arteries. Creativity depends on action. Trust no thought arrived at sitting down.
—George Sheehan

One of the most pressing problems of our country today is the urgent need for new creative talent. It is not enough that we train more engineers, scientists, or mathematicians; what is demanded is more creative individuals.
—Alexander Whitson

Since there is nothing new under the sun, creativity means simply putting old things together in a fresh way.
—Sherwood E. Wirt

Teamwork may be good for morale, but when new ideas are needed, it's best to let people work on their own. . . . Researchers believe that when people work in groups, their creativity is inhibited by fear of criticism and real or perceived pressures to conform.
—Anonymous

CRISIS
Crises refine life. In them you discover who you are.
—Allan K. Chalmers

The strong man meets his crisis with the most practical tools at hand. They may not be the best tools but they are available, which is all-important. He would rather use them, such as they are, than do nothing.
—Raymond Clapper

There cannot be a crisis next week. My schedule is already full.
—Henry Kissinger

We must learn to live with crisis in an age that calls for cool heads and accurate appraisals.
—Percey C. Spender

In every crisis there is a message. Crises are nature's way of forcing change— breaking down old structures, shaking loose negative habits so that something new and better can take their place.
—Susan L. Taylor

CRITICISM
(See also Critics)
The most beneficial criticism in the world is self-criticism.
—O. A. Battista

A man's character is determined not by the criticism he gives but by the criticism he forgives.

—O. A. Battista

Criticism is easy; achievement is more difficult.

—Winston Churchill

Criticism, like rain, should be gentle enough to nourish a man's growth without destroying his roots.

—Frank A. Clark

Worse than the sin you criticize is the sin of criticism.

—Benjamin R. De Jong

How much easier to be critical than to be correct.

—Benjamin Disraeli

Any fool can criticize, and many of them do.

—C. Garbett

I hate being asked to criticize what I cannot praise.

—Gerard Manley Hopkins

Criticism is a study by which men grow important and formidable at very small expense.

—Samuel Johnson

He has a right to criticize, who has a heart to help.

—Abraham Lincoln

Criticism is asserted superiority.

—Henry Manning

People ask you for criticism, but they only want praise.

—W. Somerset Maugham

Keep your judgment of other people to yourself. Do not criticize.

—Alfred A. Montapert

Criticism often takes from the tree, caterpillars and blossoms together.

—Jean Paul Richter

I have yet to find a man, however exalted his station, who did not do better work and put forth greater effort under a spirit of approval than under a spirit of criticism.

—Charles M. Schwab

He who is critical is the one most deserving of criticism.

—Philippine Proverb

Before you criticize someone, you should walk a mile in his shoes. That way, when you criticize him, you're a mile away and you have his shoes.

—Anonymous

Don't criticize your wife's judgment. See whom she married.

—Anonymous

CRITICS
(See also Criticism)

To be a good critic demands more brains and judgment than most men possess.

—Josh Billings

Love your critics and hate your flatterers.
—Jonah Gerondi

A critic is a man created to praise greater men than himself, but he is never able to find them.
—Richard Le Gallienne

Pay no attention to what critics say. There has never been set up a statue in honor of a critic.
—Jan Sibelius

Critics search for ages for the wrong word, which, to give them credit, they eventually find.
—Peter Ustinov

CROSS, THE

That there was no room in the inn was symbolic of what was to happen to Jesus. The only place there was room for Him was on the cross.
—William Barclay

The Cross is the ladder to heaven.
—Thomas Drake

The cross God now sends you he has considered with His all-knowing eyes, understood with His divine mind, tested with His wise justice, warmed with loving arms, and weighed with His own hands to see that it not be one inch too large and not one ounce too heavy for you.
—Saint Francis de Sales

The Cross is God's connection between time and eternity. He planned it from before the foundation of the world, and it is intended for the whole world.
—Richard C. Halverson

The cross is a symbol of God's heartbreak over a world that is gone astray.
—Sam Jones

There is a great difference between realizing, "On that cross He was crucified *for* me," and "On that cross I am crucified *with* Him." The one aspect brings us deliverance from *sin's condemnation,* the other from *sin's power.*
—J. Gregory Mantle

The Cross is the blazing fire at which the flame of our love is kindled, and we have to get near enough for its sparks to fall on us.
—John R. W. Stott

If you rightly bear your cross, it will bear you.
—Thomas à Kempis

The cross is "I" crossed out.
—Anonymous

CURIOSITY
(See also Discovery, Exploration)

Be curious always! For knowledge will not acquire you; you must acquire it.
—Sudie Back

Too much curiosity lost Paradise.
—Aphra Behn

A sense of curiosity is nature's original school of education.
—Smiley Blanton

Curiosity

The first and simplest emotion that we discover in the human mind is curiosity.

—Edmund Burke

The curiosity of an honorable mind willingly rests where the love of truth does not urge it further onward and the love of its neighbor bids it stop.

—Samuel Taylor Coleridge

Curiosity is free-wheeling intelligence. . . . It endows the people who have it with a generosity in argument and a serenity in their own mode of life that spring from the cheerful willingness to let life take the forms it will.

—Alistair Cooke

The important thing is not to stop questioning. Curiosity has its own reason for existing. One cannot help but be in awe when he contemplates the mysteries of eternity, of life, of the marvelous structure of reality. It is enough if one tries merely to comprehend a little of this mystery every day. Never lose a hold on curiosity.

—Albert Einstein

Curiosity is lying in wait for every secret.

—Ralph Waldo Emerson

Curiosity is little more than another name for hope.

—A. W. and J. C. Hare

There are different kinds of curiosity, one of interest, which causes us to learn that which would be useful to us, and the other of pride, which springs from a desire to know that of which others are ignorant.

—François de La Rochefoucauld

Curiosity in children is but an appetite for knowledge.

—John Locke

There are two sorts of curiosity—the momentary and the permanent. The momentary is concerned with the odd appearance on the surface of things. The permanent is attracted by the amazing and consecutive life that flows on beneath the surface of things.

—Robert S. Lynd

A curious person who asks questions may be a fool for five minutes; he who never asks questions remains a fool forever.

—Vern McLellan

The cure for boredom is curiosity. There is no cure for curiosity.

—Ellen Parr

A person who is too nice an observer of the business of the crowd, like one who is too curious in observing the labor of bees, will often be stung for his curiosity.

—Alexander Pope

Curiosity is an instinct of infinite scope: on the one hand it leads to listening behind closed doors; on the other, it leads to the discovery of America.

—José Maria Queiros

Life was meant to be lived, and curiosity must be kept alive. One must never, for whatever reason, turn his back on life.

—Eleanor Roosevelt

I think, at a child's birth, if a mother could ask a fairy godmother to endow it with the most useful gift, that gift would be curiosity.

—Eleanor Roosevelt

Curiosity will conquer fear even more than bravery will; indeed it has led many people into dangers that mere physical courage would shudder away from, for hunger and love and curiosity are the great impelling forces of life.

—James Stephens

Life can be one dreary day after another or a Baghdad of fascinating things to keep learning. Get more out of every phase of your life—stay incurably curious.

—L. Perry Wilbur

You know what a woman's curiosity is. Almost as great as a man's!

—Oscar Wilde

CYNICS

A cynic is not merely one who reads bitter lessons from the past; he is one who is prematurely disappointed in the future.

—Sydney J. Harris

Cynics build no bridges; they make no discoveries; no gaps are spanned by them. Cynics may pride themselves in being realistic in their approach, but progress and the onward march of Christian civilization demand an inspiration and motivation that cynicism never affords.

—Paul L. McKay

A cynic is a man who, when he smells flowers, looks around for a coffin.

—H. L. Mencken

Cynics and critics wake us up. Kindness often covers up the truth and allows us to sleep on in our ignorance.

—Wilfred A. Peterson

A cynic is a man who knows the price of everything and the value of nothing.

—Oscar Wilde

DANGER

A danger foreseen is half avoided.

—Thomas Fuller

Wherever there is danger, there lurks opportunity; whenever there is opportunity, there lurks danger. The two are inseparable.

—Earl Nightingale

He is most free from danger, who, even when safe, is on his guard.

—Publilius Syrus

DARING

Dare and the world always yields; or if it beats you sometimes, dare it again and it will succumb.

—William Makepeace Thackeray

A sheltered life can be a daring life as well. For all serious daring starts from within.

—Eudora Welty

DARKNESS

When it is dark enough, men see the stars.

—Ralph Waldo Emerson

It is in the encircling gloom that we come to realize the importance of being led by the kindly light of the Eternal One.

—Hyman J. Schachtel

DAUGHTERS

Any astronomer can predict with absolute accuracy just where every star in the heavens will be at half-past eleven tonight. He can make no such prediction about his young daughter.

—James Truslow Adams

No father has really tasted the thrill of fatherhood until his six-year-old daughter starts waiting on him hand-and-foot.

—O. A. Battista

This is the third of four daughters [to get engaged]. Every time it happens, I'm obsessed with the feeling that I'm giving a million-dollar Stradivarius to a gorilla.

—Jim Bishop

A daughter is mystery and enchantment and magic and fantasy all rolled up in a small, strange package.

—Dan Valentine

The whisper of a pretty daughter can be heard above the roar of a mighty storm.

—Hungarian Proverb

A man who has only sons and who has never fathered a daughter has lost a little bit of heaven on earth.

—Irish Proverb

He who has daughters is always a shepherd.

—Spanish Proverb

Raise your daughter to know the Lord
and she will have a built-in chaperone.

—Anonymous

DAWN
(See also Morning, Sunrise)

Every dawn signs a new contract with
existence.

—Henri Frédéric Amiel

Where others see but the dawn coming
over the hill, I see the soul of God
shouting for joy.

—William Blake

It is always darkest just before the day
dawneth.

—Thomas Fuller

Your attitude toward life in general is
reflected in your response to the dawn
of a new day.

—J. N. Gehman

Oft when the white, still dawn
Lifted the skies and pushed the hills
    apart,
I have felt it like a glory in my heart.

—Edwin Markham

Each day's dawn is like a recurrence of
the first act of the Creation—as if again
a decree had gone forth: "Let there be
light." And as the earth whirls on its
orbit, there sweeps westward a band of
brightness, fringed by the half-light of
daybreak. The sun's rays, themselves all
energy, bring new energy to every living
thing.

—Thomas Moore

Dawn-wind in tree-tops is a thrilling
murmur and stir: it gives the feeling
that something is going to happen; that
feeling of half-blissful, half-terrified
expectancy that is the summit of life.

—Christopher Morley

Just listen to the whispers in the quiet of
    the dawn,
A thousand little muffled sounds along
    the winds are borne.
The gentle rustling of a tree, the
    trembling leaves that sigh,
The reed that bends and quivers when
    the breeze goes laughing by.

—Patience Strong

Now the frosty stars are gone;
I have watched them one by one,
Fading on the shores of Dawn.

—Bayard Taylor

For the mind disturbed, the still beauty
of dawn is nature's finest balm.

—Edwin Way Teale

Only that day dawns to which we are
awake. There is more day to dawn. The
sun is but a morning star.

—Henry David Thoreau

You have never seen God, my friend?
Then you've never watched the dawn
silently, swiftly, swallow up the night.
You've never seen the splendor and
beauty in the heavens as the sun bursts
forth upon yon horizon. . . . Rise at early
morn and be still. You, too, can see God
all around you.

—Norma Turner

Day's sweetest moments are at dawn.
—Ella Wheeler Wilcox

Greet the dawn with enthusiasm and
you may expect satisfaction by sunset.
—Anonymous

DEATH
(See also Death—Children, Grave)
It's not that I'm afraid to die. I just don't
want to be there when it happens.
—Woody Allen

I think of death as a glad awakening
from this troubled sleep, which we call
life, as an emancipation from a world,
which, beautiful though it be, is still a
land of captivity.
—Lyman Abbott

Death is not the enemy; living in
constant fear of it is.
—Norman Cousins

This world is the land of the dying; the
next is the land of the living.
—Tryon Edwards

In the night of death hope sees a star
and glistening love can hear the rustle
of a wing.
—Robert G. Ingersoll

Death and the sun are two things a man
cannot outstare.
—François de La Rochefoucauld

We see but dimly through the mists and
vapors
Amid these early damps,

What seem to us like sad funeral tapers,
May be Heaven's distant lamps.
—Henry Wadsworth Longfellow

Death is a very dull, dreary affair, and
my advice to you is to have nothing to
do with it.
—W. Somerset Maugham

If you ever happen to see in the obituary
column that Henrietta Mears has died,
don't you believe it! This old body may
die, but I'll be glad of that. . . . I'll have a
new body. And what will I do when I get
to heaven? Well, I am going to ask the
Lord to show me around. I'll want to get
in a rocket ship to inspect all the
galaxies He has made. And maybe He
will give me a planet of my own, so that
I can start building something. Oh, it's
going to be so wonderful!
—Henrietta C. Mears

Death is the golden key that opens the
palace of eternity.
—John Milton

He that lives to live forever never fears
dying.
—William Penn

Death gives us sleep, eternal youth, and
immortality.
—Jean Paul Richter

Let us so endeavor to live that when we
come to die even the undertaker will be
sorry.
—Mark Twain

Some people are so afraid to die that they never begin to live.

—Henry Van Dyke

Think not of death as the extinguishing of life, but rather the snuffing out of a candle because dawn has come.

—Anonymous

DEATH—CHILDREN

Every mother who has lost an infant has gained a child of immortal youth.

—George William Curtis

We weep over the graves of infants and the little ones taken from us by death; but an early grave may be the shortest way to heaven.

—Tryon Edwards

They who have lost an infant are never, as it were, without an infant child. Their other children grow up to manhood and womanhood, and suffer all the changes of mortality; but this one is rendered an immortal child, for death has arrested it with his kindly harshness, and blessed it into an eternal image of youth and innocence.

—Leigh Hunt

To me, my son didn't die—he's more alive than ever. Each of us has to keep a rendezvous with death . . . but I believe that life is the childhood of immortality.

—Daniel A. Poling

DEBT

Debt is the secret foe of thrift. . . . The debt habit is the twin brother of poverty.

—Theodore T. Munger

Some debts are fun when you are acquiring them, but none are fun when you set about retiring them.

—Ogden Nash

A man in debt is caught in a net.

—John Ray

DECISIONS

When decisions have to be made, don't look back and wonder what I would have done. Look up, and the light will come to do what our Lord and Master would have you do.

—Amy Carmichael

We make so few genuine decisions in life. Most of the choices we make are affected by outside forces and demands. But when it comes to the most important decision in life—our decision about God—He seeks only a genuine one. . . . God refuses to violate our personhood and our power to choose.

—Gayle Erwin

I have to be wrong a certain number of times in order to be right a certain number of times. However, in order to be either, I must first make a decision.

—Frank N. Giampietro

Decision is a sharp knife that cuts clean and straight; indecision, a dull one that hacks and tears and leaves ragged edges around it.

—Gordon Graham

When we let somebody else decide what our reaction shall be, we are no longer free persons, whether we decide to agree or disagree.

—Sydney J. Harris

Make your decision, make it yours, and live and die by it.

—Charlie "T" Jones

When we make our decisions, we must use the brains God has given us. But we must also use our hearts, which He also gave us.

—Fulton Oursler

When a decision has to be made, make it. There is no totally right time for anything.

—George S. Patton

DEEDS

Small deeds done are better than great deeds planned.

—Peter Marshall

Our deeds are like stones cast in the pool of time; they themselves may disappear, but their ripples extend to eternity.

—Anonymous

DEFEAT

Defeat is a school in which truth always grows stronger.

—Henry Ward Beecher

When we start talking of defeat, too often the Devil has the victory already.

—Jess Kaufman

Believe you are defeated, believe it long enough, and it is likely to become a fact.

—Norman Vincent Peale

What is defeat? Nothing but education, nothing but the first step to something better.

—Wendell Phillips

Some defeats are only installments to victory.

—Jacob A. Riis

On earth we have nothing to do with success or results, but only with being true to God and for God. Defeat in doing the right is nevertheless victory.

—Frederick W. Robertson

DEMOCRACY
(See also Voting)
Democracy is the worst form of government—except all others.

—Winston Churchill

The moment our democracy ceases to respect God, it will cease to respect your value as an individual. The moment it ceases to respect your value as an individual, it ceases to be democracy.

—Thomas J. Curran

Two cheers for democracy: one because it admits variety and two because it permits criticism.

—E. M. Forster

Democracy is based upon the conviction that there are extraordinary possibilities in ordinary people.

—Harry Emerson Fosdick

Democracy without morality is impossible.

—Jack Kemp

Democracy and religion stand or fall together. Where democracy has been destroyed, religion has been doomed. Where religion has been trampled down, democracy has ceased to exist.

—Herbert H. Lehman

Under democracy, one party always devotes its chief efforts to trying to prove that the other is unfit to rule—and both commonly succeed and are right.

—H. L. Mencken

Man's capacity for justice makes democracy possible, but man's inclination to injustice makes democracy necessary.

—Reinhold Niebuhr

Too many people expect wonders from democracy when the most wonderful thing of all is just having it.

—Walter Winchell

DEPENDABILITY

The greatest ability is dependability.

—Bob Jones Sr.

You may depend on the Lord, but can He depend on you?

—Croft M. Pentz

DESIRE

We should aim rather at leveling down our desires than leveling up our means.

—Aristotle

Freedom is not procured by a full enjoyment of what is desired, but by controlling the desire.

—Epictetus

'Tis easier to suppress that first desire than to satisfy all that follows it.

—Benjamin Franklin

If your desires be endless, your cares and fears will be also.

—Thomas Fuller

Lord, grant that I may always desire more than I can accomplish.

—Michelangelo

We live in our desires rather than in our achievements.

—George Moore

There are two tragedies in life. One is not to get your heart's desire. The other is to get it.

—George Bernard Shaw

We desire nothing so much as what we ought not to have.

—Publilius Syrus

DESPAIR

Don't despair. Even the sun has a sinking spell every night, but rises again in the morning.

—Miguel de Cervantes

Don't despair. Only the mediocre person is always at his best.

—W. Somerset Maugham

Life begins on the other side of despair.

—Jean Paul Sartre

It is impossible for that man to despair who remembers that his Helper is omnipotent.

—Jeremy Taylor

DESPERATION

The mass of men lead lives of quiet desperation. What is called resignation is confirmed desperation.

—Henry David Thoreau

DESTINY

Destiny is not a matter of chance, it is a matter of choice; it is not a thing to be waited for, it is a thing to be achieved.

—William Jennings Bryan

It is a mistake to look too far ahead. Only one link of the chain of destiny can be handled at a time.

—Winston Churchill

Men heap together the mistakes of their lives, and create a monster they call destiny.

—John Oliver Hobbes

DETERMINATION
(See also Perseverance, Persistence)

We shall not fail or falter; we shall not weaken or tire.... Give us the tools and we will finish the job.

—Winston Churchill

The difference between the impossible and the possible lies in a person's determination.

—Tommy Lasorda

Act with determination not to be turned aside by thoughts of the past or fears of the future.

—Robert E. Lee

I determined never to stop until I had come to the end and achieved my purpose.

—David Livingstone

Let us not be content to wait and see what will happen, but give us the determination to make the right thing happen.

—Peter Marshall

If people knew how hard I had to work to gain my mastery, it wouldn't seem wonderful at all.

—Michelangelo

When faced with a mountain, I will not quit! I will keep on striving until I climb over, find a pass through, tunnel underneath—or simply stay and turn the mountain into a gold mine, with God's help!

—Robert Schuller Sr.

DEVIL

Our Adversary majors in three things: noise, hurry, and crowds. If he can keep us engaged in "muchness" and "manyness," he will rest satisfied.

—Richard J. Foster

That there is a devil is a thing doubted by none but such as are under the influences of the Devil.

—Cotton Mather

When you drive the Devil out of the human heart, the stream of life will be sweet, happy, and peaceful.

—Charles Clifford Peale

He who has no mind to trade with the Devil should be so wise as to keep away from his shop.

—Robert South

The Devil never tempted a man whom he found judiciously employed.

—Charles H. Spurgeon

DEVOTIONS
(See also Quiet Time)

Every morning I spend fifteen minutes filling my mind full of God; and so there's no room for worry thoughts.

—Howard Chandler Christy

Put your morning devotions into your personal grooming. You would not go out to work with a dirty face. Why start the day with the face of your soul unwashed?

—Robert A. Cook

DIET
(See also Eating)

It would be far easier to lose weight permanently if replacement parts weren't so handy in the refrigerator.

—Hugh Allen

What you eat standing up doesn't count.

—Beth Barnes

The toughest part of dieting isn't watching what you eat—it's watching what your friends eat.

—Wilfred Beaver

Probably nothing in the world arouses more false hopes than the first four hours on a diet.

—Dan Bennett

You can lead a person to cottage cheese, but you can't make him shrink.

—Hilde Bruch

A diet is what helps a person gain weight more slowly.

—Bill Copeland

An optimist is a person who starts a new diet on Thanksgiving Day.

—Irv Kupcinet

If you wish to grow thinner, diminish your dinner.

—H. S. Leigh

So far on my thirty-day diet, I lost eighteen days.

—Terry McEntire

Self-delusion is pulling in your stomach when you step on the scales.

—Paul Sweeney

Stomachs shouldn't be waist baskets.

—P. K. Thomajan

A balanced diet is a cookie in each hand.

—Anonymous

DIFFERENCES

If men would consider not so much wherein they differ, as wherein they agree, there would be far less of uncharitableness and angry feeling in the world.

—Joseph Addison

Honest differences of views and honest debate are not disunity. They are the vital process of policy-making among free men.

—Herbert Hoover

DIFFICULTY

Difficulties are God's errands; and when we are sent upon them, we should esteem it a proof of God's confidence.

—Henry Ward Beecher

Difficulty is a miracle in its first stage.

—William D. Brown

Difficulties mastered are opportunities won.

—Winston Churchill

Difficult times have helped me to understand better than before how infinitely rich and beautiful life is in every way and that so many things that one goes worrying about are of no importance whatsoever.

—Isak Dinesen

Make chariot wheels out of your difficulties and ride to success.

—Bob Jones Sr.

The person who has not struggled with difficulty after difficulty cannot know the joy of genuine success. Face the problems and fight your way over them. There is more satisfaction in putting forth effort than in gloating over easily won profits. The rungs in the ladder of success are composed of difficulties.

—Vern McLellan

Undertake something that is difficult; it will do you good. Unless you try to do something beyond what you have already mastered, you will never grow.

—Ronald E. Osborn

The individual who knows the score about life sees difficulties as opportunities.

—Noman Vincent Peale

Many men owe the grandeur of their lives to their tremendous difficulties.

—Charles H. Spurgeon

Have the courage to face a difficulty, lest it kick you harder than you bargain for.

—King Stanislaus I

Real difficulties can be overcome; it is only the imaginary ones that are unconquerable.

—Theodore N. Vail

It is a good rule to face difficulties at the time they arise and not allow them to increase unacknowledged.

—Edward W. Ziegler

DIGNITY

The ultimate end of all revolutionary social change is to establish the sanctity of human life, the dignity of man, the right of every human being to liberty and well-being.

—Emma Goldman

Human rights rest on human dignity. The dignity of man is an ideal worth fighting for and worth dying for.

—Robert Maynard

No race can prosper until it learns that there is as much dignity in tilling a field as in writing a poem.

—Booker T. Washington

DILIGENCE

Diligence is the mother of good fortune.

—Miguel de Cervantes

The expectations of life depend upon diligence; the mechanic that would perfect his work must first sharpen his tools.

—Confucius

What we hope ever to do with ease, we must first learn to do with diligence.

—Samuel Johnson

DIRECTION

If you board the wrong train, it is no use running along the corridor in the other direction.

—Dietrich Bonhoeffer

Society has erected the gallows at the end of the lane instead of guideposts and direction boards at the beginning.

—Edward G. Bulwer-Lytton

I find the great thing in this world is not so much where we stand, as in what direction we are moving: To reach the port of heaven, we must sail sometimes with the wind and sometimes against it—but we must sail, and not drift, nor lie at anchor.

—Oliver Wendell Holmes

DISAGREEMENT

The people to fear are not those who disagree with you, but those who disagree with you and are too cowardly to let you know.

—Napoleon Bonaparte

He who has learned to disagree without being disagreeable has discovered the most valuable secret of a diplomat.

—Robert Estabrook

DISAPPOINTMENT

There is no room for the word *disappointment* in the happy life of entire trust in Jesus and satisfaction with His perfect and glorious will.

—Frances Ridley Havergal

Disappointment is often the salt of life.

—Theodore W. Parker

Disappointment to a noble soul is what cold water is to burning metal; it strengthens, tempers, intensifies, but never destroys it.

—Eliza Tabor

DISCERNMENT

Discernment is God's call to intercession, never to fault finding.

—Oswald Chambers

Give us grace and strength to forbear
and to persevere. . . . Give us courage
and . . . the quiet mind, spare to us our
friends, soften to us our enemies.

—Robert Louis Stevenson

God grant me the serenity to delegate
tasks when necessary, the courage to say
no, and the wisdom to know when to go
home.

—Anonymous

DISCIPLESHIP

Discipleship is not a second step in
Christianity, as if one first becomes a
believer in Jesus and then (if he
chooses) a disciple, but from the
beginning, discipleship is involved in
what it means to be a Christian.

—James Montgomery Boice

Salvation is free . . . but discipleship will
cost you your life.

—Dietrich Bonhoeffer

If the heart is devoted to the mirage of
the world, to the creature instead of the
Creator, the disciple is lost. . . . However
urgently Jesus may call us, His call fails
to find access to our hearts. Our hearts
are closed, because they have already
been given to another.

—Dietrich Bonhoeffer

Whenever our Lord talked about
discipleship, He always prefaced it with
an "IF," never with an emphatic assertion—"You must." Discipleship carries
an option with it.

—Oswald Chambers

The people God is using mightily today
are those who have chosen the road of
discipleship, which is the route to
fruitfulness.

—Francis M. Cosgrove Jr.

He [Christ] looks today as He ever
looks, not for crowds drifting aimlessly
in His track, but for the individual man
or woman whose undying allegiance
will spring from their having recognized that He wants those who are
prepared to follow Him through the
path of self-renunciation, which He trod
before them.

—H. A. Evan Hopkins

The Savior is not looking for men and
women who will give their spare
evenings to Him or their weekends or
their years of retirement. Rather He
seeks those who will give Him first
place in their lives.

—William MacDonald

DISCIPLINE
(See also Self-control, Self-discipline)
Some people regard discipline as a
chore. For me, it is a kind of order that
sets me free to fly.

—Julie Andrews

No one ever reached any eminence, and no one having reached it ever maintained it, without discipline.
—William Barclay

There is no man that lives who does not need to be drilled, disciplined, and developed into something higher and better and nobler than he is by nature.
—Henry Ward Beecher

Your disciplines today will govern you tomorrow.
—Thomas Blandi

As soon as we renounced the precepts of the gospel, we renounced all interior discipline. The new generation is not even aware that such a discipline ever existed.
—Alexis Carrel

It is one thing to praise discipline and another to submit to it.
—Miguel de Cervantes

No horse ever gets anywhere until he is harnessed. No steam or gas ever drives anything until it is confined. No Niagara is ever turned into light and power until it is tunneled. No life ever grows great until it is focused, dedicated, disciplined.
—Benjamin R. De Jong

Discipline is inevitable; if it does not come from within a man, it will be imposed from without.
—David Grayson

To live a disciplined life, and to accept the result of that discipline as the will of God—that is the mark of a man.
—Tom Landry

Character is, by its very nature, the product of . . . discipline.
—Austin Phelps

Discipline is the refining fire by which talent becomes ability.
—Roy L. Smith

Discipline is like broccoli. We may not care for it ourselves, but feel sure it would be good for everybody else.
—Bill Vaughan

DISCOVERY
(See also Curiosity, Exploration)

Greater even than the greatest discovery is to keep the way open to future discovery.
—John Jacob Abel

They are ill discoverers that think there is no land, when they can see nothing but sea.
—Francis Bacon

"Theirs not to make reply, theirs not to reason why" may be a good enough motto for men who are on their way to be shot, but from such men expect no empires to be built, no inventions made, no great discoveries brought to life.
—Bruce Barton

Don't keep forever on the public road. Leave the beaten path occasionally and dive into the woods. You will be certain to find something that you have never seen before. One discovery will lead to another, and before you know it you will have something worth thinking about to occupy your mind. All really big discoveries are the results of thoughts.

—Alexander Graham Bell

Great discoveries and improvements invariably involve the cooperation of many minds. I may be given credit for having blazed the trail but when I look at the subsequent developments I feel the credit is due to others rather than to myself.

—Alexander Graham Bell

We get closer to God as we get more intimately and understandingly acquainted with the things He has created. I know of nothing more inspiring than that of making discoveries for one's self.

—George Washington Carver

Men of strong minds and who think for themselves should not be discouraged on finding occasionally that some of their best ideas have been anticipated by former writers; they will neither anathematize others nor despair themselves. They will rather go on discovering things before discovered, until they are rewarded with a land hitherto unknown, an empire indisputably their own, both by right of conquest and of discovery.

—Charles Caleb Colton

The intellect has little to do on the road to discovery. There comes a leap in consciousness, call it intuition or what you will, and the solution comes to you and you don't know how or why. All great discoveries are made this way.

—Albert Einstein

Man cannot discover new oceans unless he has courage to lose sight of the shore.

—André Gide

All human discoveries seem to be made only for the purpose of confirming more and more strongly the truths contained in the Holy Scriptures.

—John Herschel

When all the mountains in the world have been scaled, when the poles hold no more secrets, when the last acre of the last continent has been traversed, when, in short, everything on our planet is known and catalogued, the way will still be open for discovery. The world will never be conquered so long as the zest for conquest, for adventure, is in men's hearts.

—Maurice Herzog

The progress of the world depends upon the men who walk in the fresh furrows and through the rustling corn; upon those whose faces are radiant with the glare of furnace fires; upon the delvers in mines, and the workers in shops; upon those who give to the winter air the ringing music of the axe; upon those who battle with the boisterous billows of the sea; upon the inventors and discoverers; upon the brave thinkers.

—Robert Ingersoll

A man of genius makes no mistakes. His errors are volitional and are the portals of discovery.

—James Joyce

Where there is an open mind, there will always be a frontier.

—Charles F. Kettering

It is a profound mistake to think that everything has been discovered; as well think the horizon the boundary of the world.

—Antoine Lemièrre

The secret of all those who make discoveries is that they regard nothing as impossible.

—Justus Liebig

The real voyage of discovery comes not in seeking new landscapes but in having new eyes.

—Marcel Proust

Discovery consists of seeing what everybody has seen and thinking what nobody has thought.

—Albert Szent-Györgyi

It is at night that the astronomers discover new worlds. It is often in the night of failure that men discover the light of a new hope.

—Anonymous

DISHONESTY
(See also Lies)

Don't place too much confidence in the man who boasts of being as honest as the day is long. Wait until you meet him at night.

—Robert C. Edwards

Brooks become crooked from taking the path of least resistance. So do people.

—Harold E. Kohn

False words are not only evil in themselves, but they infect the soul with evil.

—Socrates

DISOBEDIENCE

When a person's faith seems to collapse without warning, one can be sure it has been the result of inner conflicts—the termites of disobedience.

—Quinton J. Everest

DOUBT

If a man will begin in certainties he shall end in doubts; but if he will be content to begin in doubts he shall end in certainties.

—Francis Bacon

Doubt is the vestibule through which all must pass before they can enter the temple of wisdom.

—Charles Caleb Colton

A person who doubts himself is like a man who would enlist in the ranks of his enemies and bear arms against himself. He makes his failure certain by himself being the first person to be convinced of it.

—Alexandre Dumas

Those who doubt most, and yet strive to overcome their doubts, turn out to be some of Christ's strongest disciples.

—Selwyn Hughes

The only limit to our realization of tomorrow will be our doubts of today.

—Franklin Delano Roosevelt

Our doubts are traitors, and make us lose the good we oft might win by fearing to attempt.

—William Shakespeare

DREAMS

(See also Aspirations)

The greatest achievement was at first and for a time a dream.... Dreams are the seedlings of realities.

—James Lane Allen

The mightiest works have been accomplished by men who have kept their ability to dream great dreams.

—W. R. Bowie

Life is for dreaming dreams, but few have the courage or will to realize them.

—Crenner Bradley

To dream anything that you want to
  dream,
That is the beauty of the human mind.

—Bernard Edmonds

You are only one step away from God's doing a fresh thing in your life. Choose to dream His dream.

—David Edwards

Always dream and shoot higher than you know you can do. Don't bother just to be better than your contemporaries or predecessors. Try to be better than yourself.

—William Faulkner

To accomplish great things, we must not only act, but also dream, not only plan, but also believe.

—Anatole France

I am a dreamer. I am, indeed, a practical dreamer. My dreams are not airy nothings. I want to convert my dreams into realities, as far as possible.

—Mohandas K. Gandhi

Behind every advance of the human race is a germ of creation, growing in the mind of some lone individual—an individual whose dreams waken him in the night while others lie contentedly asleep.

—Crawford H. Greenewalt

Man, with God's help and personal dedication, is capable of anything he can dream.

—Conrad Hilton

There is nothing like a dream to create the future.

—Victor Hugo

Dreamers are the architects of great-ness. Their brains have wrought all human miracles.... Your homes are set upon a land a dreamer found. The pictures on its walls are visions from a dreamer's soul.... They are the chosen few—the blazers of the way—who

never wear doubt's bandage on their
eyes.

—Herbert Kaufman

Nothing ever built arose to touch the
skies unless some man dreamed that it
should, some man believed that it could,
and some man willed that it must.

—Charles F. Kettering

The greatest thing about man is his
ability to transcend himself, his
ancestry, and his environment and to
become what he dreams of being.

—Tully C. Knoles

All men dream but not equally. Those
who dream by night in the dusty
recesses of their minds wake in the day
to find that it was vanity; but the
dreamers of the day are dangerous men,
for they may act their dreams with open
eyes to make it possible.

—T. E. Lawrence

It may be that those who do most,
dream most.

—Stephen Leacock

Dreams are extremely important. You
can't do it unless you imagine it.

—George Lucas

Do you believe in dreams? Don't
oversleep if you want your dreams to
come true! Don't let dreams become
nightmares.

—Henrietta C. Mears

A man's gotta dream; it comes with the
territory.

—Arthur Miller

Dreaming is just another name for
thinking, planning, devising—another
way of saying that a man exercises his
soul. A steadfast soul, holding steadily
to a dream ideal, plus a sturdy will
determined to succeed in any venture,
can make any dream come true.

—B. N. Mills

A man is no greater than his dream, his
ideal, his hope, and his plan. Man
dreams the dream—and fulfilling it, it's
the dream that makes the man.

—Alfred A. Montapert

Let me dream as of old by the river.
And be loved for the dream alway;
For a dreamer lives forever,
And a toiler dies in a day.

—John Boyle O'Reilly

I don't allow anyone to put a limit on my
dreaming, and I dream big. Always.

—Gordon Parks

Stay young by hanging on to your
dreams. A philosopher writes, "There is
not much to do but bury a man when
the last of his dreams is dead."

—Wilfred A. Peterson

They who dream by day are cognizant
of many things that escape those who
dream only by night.

—Edgar Allen Poe

The best way to make your dreams
come true is to wake up.

—J. M. Power

Dreams grow holy put in action.

—Adelaide Ann Procter

I simply dream dreams and see visions, and then I paint around those dreams and visions.

—Raphael

Your hopes, dreams, and aspirations are legitimate. They are trying to take you airborne, above the storms, above the clouds—if you will only let them.

—Diane Roger

Nothing happens unless first a dream.

—Carl Sandburg

An artist is a dreamer, consenting to dream of the actual world.

—George Santayana

Some men see things as they are and say "Why?" I dream things that never were and say "Why not?"

—George Bernard Shaw

If one advances confidently in the direction of his dreams, and endeavors to live the life that he has imagined, he will meet with a success unexpected in common hours.

—Henry David Thoreau

Dreams are the touchstones of our characters.

—Henry David Thoreau

If you have built castles in the air, your work need not be lost; that is where they should be. Now put foundations under them.

—Henry David Thoreau

Dreams are renewable. No matter what our age or condition, there are still untapped possibilities within us waiting to be born.

—Dale Turner

When we dare to dream, many marvels can be accomplished. The trouble is, most people never start dreaming their impossible dream.

—Glenn Van Ekeren

We grow great by dreams. All big men are dreamers. They see things in the soft haze of a spring day or in the red fire of a long winter's evening. Some of us let these great dreams die, but others nourish and protect them, nurse them through bad days till they bring them to the sunshine and light, which come always to those who sincerely hope that their dreams will come true.

—Woodrow Wilson

Dreams never hurt anybody if he keeps working right behind the dream to make as much of it come real as he can.

—F. W. Woolworth

I've dreamed many dreams that never
    came true,
I've seen them vanish at dawn;
But I've realized enough of my dreams,
    thank God,
To make me want to dream on.

—Anonymous

If your dreams turn to dust—vacuum.

—Anonymous

Without dreams, there is no reason to work. Without work, there is no reason to dream.

—Anonymous

Have a dream that gets you up early and excited and keeps you going all day.

—Anonymous

A man's stature is measured by his dreams, by the love he is able to show, by the values he respects, by the happiness he is able to share, by the truths he is able to express, by the help he is able to give, by the life he leads, and by the destiny of which he dreams.

—Anonymous

DRINKING

Many guys and girls drink to prop up their sagging courage—to help them do what they really want to do, and what they know is the wrong thing to do. Alcohol could be called a false set of guts.

—Bill Glass

Even though a number of people have tried, no one has yet found a way to drink for a living.

—Jean Kerr

DUTY

Do your duty, and leave the rest to God.

—Richard Cecil

Once we become rightly related to God, duty will never be a disagreeable thing of which we have to say with a sigh, "Oh, well, I must do my duty." Duty is the daughter of God.

—Oswald Chambers

Duty is not collective, it is personal. Let every individual make known his determination to support law and order. That duty is supreme.

—Calvin Coolidge

Do your duty in all things. You cannot do more. You should never wish to do less.

—Robert E. Lee

To do one's duty sounds a rather cold and cheerless business, but somehow in the end it does give one a queer sense of satisfaction.

—W. Somerset Maugham

Duty does not have to be dull. Love can make it beautiful and fill it with life.

—Thomas Merton

A duty dodged is like a debt unpaid; it is only deferred, and we must come back and settle the account at last.

—Joseph Fort Newton

The path of duty is the way to glory.

—Alfred Lord Tennyson

Duty is a very personal thing. It is what comes from knowing the need to take action and not just a need to urge others to do something.

—Mother Teresa

Make it a point to do something every day that you don't want to do. This is the golden rule for acquiring the habit of doing your duty without pain.

—Mark Twain

One trouble with the world is that so many people who stand up vigorously for their rights fall down miserably on their duties.

—Anonymous

ℰ

EASE

A life of ease is a difficult pursuit.
—William Cowper

The indulgence of ease is fatal to excellence.
—Anonymous

EASTER

(See also Resurrection)

The great Easter truth is not that we are to live newly after death—that is not the great thing—but that we are to be new here and now by the power of the Resurrection.
—Phillips Brooks

The message of Easter cannot be written in the past tense. It is a message for today and the days to come. It is God's message that must re-echo through your lives.
—Frank D. Getty

If Easter says anything to us today, it says this: You can put truth in a grave, but it won't stay there. You can nail it to a cross, wrap it up in winding sheets, and shut it up in a tomb, but it will rise!
—Clarence W. Hall

The story of Easter is the story of God's wonderful window of divine surprise.
—Carl Knudsen

The great day does not merely arrive, like a date on a calendar; it explodes!
—John W. Lynch

Easter morning is not merely a declaration that we are immortal, but a declaration that we are the immortal children of God.
—George Matheson

Angels, roll the rock away;
Death, yield up thy mighty prey;
See, He rises from the tomb,
Glowing with immortal bloom.
Al-le-lu-ia! Al-le-lu-ia!
Christ the Lord is risen today!
—Thomas Scott

Easter is the New Year's Day of the soul.
—A. B. Simpson

Today one grave is open, and from it has risen a sun that will never be obscured, that will never set, a sun that creates new life. This new sun is the crucified one, the Son of God.
—Jean Marie Vianney

Easter is the truth that turns a church from a museum into a ministry.
—Warren Wiersbe

EATING
(See also Diet)

When it comes to eating, you can sometimes help yourself more by helping yourself less.

—Richard Armour

Square meals often make round people.

—E. Joseph Cossman

If I were reincarnated, I'd want to come back as a buzzard. He can eat anything.

—William Faulkner

A good dinner is not to be despised. It paves the way for all the virtues.

—Louise Imogen Guiney

People sometimes praise a restaurant by saying it makes them feel at home....I don't want to feel at home in a restaurant. I want to feel that I'm having a night out.

—Alvin Kerr

My husband thinks that health food is anything he eats before the expiration date.

—Rita Rudner

If there were no such thing as eating, we should have to invent it to save man from despairing.

—Wilhelm Stekhel

After a good dinner, one can forgive anybody, even one's own relatives.

—Oscar Wilde

ECONOMY

He who will not economize will have to agonize.

—Confucius

I favor the policy of economy, not because I wish to save money, but because I wish to save people.

—Calvin Coolidge

Economy is half the battle of life; it is not so hard to earn money as to spend it well.

—Charles H. Spurgeon

EDUCATION
(See also Learning, School, Teachers, Teaching, University)

The primary purpose of education is not to teach you to earn your bread, but to make every mouthful sweeter.

—James Angell

The test and use of man's education is that he finds pleasure in the exercise of his mind.

—Jacques Barzun

All education should be directed toward the development of character. Sound character cannot be achieved if spiritual development is neglected. I do not like to think of turning out physical and mental giants who are spiritual pygmies.

—Walter G. Coffey

Abraham Lincoln had difficulty getting an education, but what do you expect from a guy who didn't play football, basketball, or baseball?

—Lloyd Cory

How is it that little children are so intelligent and men so stupid? It must be education that does it.

    —Alexandre Dumas

The great end of education is to discipline rather than to furnish the mind, to train it to the use of its own powers rather than fill it with the accumulation of others.

    —Tryon Edwards

Education's purpose is to replace an empty mind with an open one.

    —Malcolm S. Forbes

The main part of intellectual education is not the acquisition of facts but learning how to make facts live.

    —Oliver Wendell Holmes

Education is not to reform students or amuse them or to make them expert technicians. It is to unsettle their minds, widen their horizons, inflame their intellect, teach them to think straight, if possible.

    —Robert M. Hutchins

Education is our only political safety. Outside of this ark all is deluge.

    —Horace Mann

The aim of education should be to convert the mind into a living fountain, and not a reservoir. That which is filled by merely pumping in will be emptied by pumping out.

    —John M. Mason

To educate a man in mind and not in morals is to educate a menace to society.

    —Theodore Roosevelt

The only foundation for a useful education in a republic is to be laid in religion. Without this there can be no virtue, and without virtue there can be no liberty, and liberty is the object and life of all republican governments.

    —Benjamin Rush

The entire object of true education is to make people not merely do the right thing, but enjoy the right things; not merely industrious, but to love industry; not merely learned, but to love knowledge; not merely pure, but to love purity; not merely just, but to hunger and thirst after justice.

    —John Ruskin

Our lives revolved around education. Under no circumstances were we to miss a day of school. . . . No excuses would be accepted and all illnesses would presume to be feigned. Indeed, my grandfather announced that if we died, he would take us to school for three consecutive days to make sure that we were not faking.

    —Clarence Thomas

Education was the road to freedom and independence. It was the promise of possibilities beyond the cramped oppressive worlds of segregation and ignorance. It was the way to a better life and a bigger world.

    —Clarence Thomas

Education occurs both in and outside the classroom. There are certain bumps and bruises that befall us all during life. The manner in which we deal with them will have a lot to say about how we deal with future difficulties and what kind of people we become. Education most certainly gives us the means by which to earn a living, but it also provides the means to learn how to live.

—Clarence Thomas

Education is not the filling of a pail, but the lighting of a fire.

—William Butler Yeats

An educational system isn't worth a great deal if it teaches young people how to make a living but doesn't teach them how to make a life.

—Anonymous

Education without God is like a ship without a compass.

—Anonymous

EFFORT

In all human affairs there are efforts, and there are results, and the strength of the effort is the measure of the result.

—James Lane Allen

There is no comparison between that which is lost by not succeeding and that which is lost by not trying.

—Francis Bacon

How much easier our work would be if we put forth as much effort in trying to improve the quality of it as most of us

do in trying to find excuses for not properly attending to it.

—George W. Ballenger

Satisfaction lies in the effort, not in the attainment. Full effort is full victory.

—Mohandas K. Gandhi

It is hard to fail, but it is worse never to have tried to succeed. In this life we get nothing save by effort.

—Theodore Roosevelt

EGO
(See also Self)

An egotist is a conceited dolt who thinks he knows as much as you do.

—Hal Crane

You have an ego—a consciousness of being an individual. But that doesn't mean that you are to worship yourself, to think constantly of yourself, and to live entirely for self.

—Billy Graham

An egotist is not a man who thinks too much of himself; he is a man who thinks too little of other people.

—Joseph Fort Newton

When a man is wrapped up in himself, he makes a pretty small package.

—John Ruskin

No man has learned the meaning of life until he has surrendered his ego to the service of his fellow men.

—Beran Wolfe

ELOQUENCE

(See also Speech)

Eloquence is logic on fire.

—Lyman Beecher

Eloquence is the power to translate a truth into language perfectly intelligible to the person to whom you speak.

—Ralph Waldo Emerson

True eloquence consists in saying all that should be said, and that only.

—François de La Rochefoucauld

Eloquence is the art of saying things in such a way that those to whom we speak may listen to them with pleasure.

—Blaise Pascal

EMOTIONS

People are moved and motivated by emotions. Living is a constant process of trying to satisfy emotional needs and wants.

—Robert Conklin

This is the greatest paradox: the emotions cannot be trusted, yet it is they that tell us the greatest truths.

—Don Herold

All emotions are pure that gather you and lift you up; that emotion is impure that seizes only one side of your being and so distorts you.

—Rainer Maria Rilke

EMPATHY

Empathy—your pain in my heart.

—Jess Lair

One of the most poignant of all human experiences is empathy—the ability to feel what others feel when suffering pain or loss.

—Louis Jolyon West

ENCOURAGEMENT

We should seize every opportunity to give encouragement. Encouragement is oxygen to the soul. The days are always dark enough. There is no need for us to emphasize the fact by spreading further gloom.

—George Matthew Adams

One of the highest of human duties is the duty of encouragement. . . . It is easy to laugh at men's ideals; it is easy to pour cold water on their enthusiasm; it is easy to discourage others. The world is full of discouragers. We have a Christian duty to encourage one another. Many a time a word of praise or thanks or appreciation or cheer has kept a man on his feet. Blessed is the man who speaks such a word.

—William Barclay

If you want to change people without giving offense or arousing resentment, use encouragement.

—Dale Carnegie

Encouragement is perhaps one of the greatest gifts friends can ever give. An encouraging friend is a lifeline to steady a floundering heart, to bring sunshine to a cloudy day, and to deliver a blessing just looking for a place to land.

—Susan Duke

Correction does much, but encouragement does more. Encouragement after censure is as the sun after a shower.

—Johann von Goethe

Those who are lifting the world upward and onward are those who encourage more than criticize.

—Elizabeth Harrison

There is nothing better than the encouragement of a good friend.

—Katharine Butler Hathaway

Two solemn farewells we find our Lord Jesus giving to his church, and his parting word at both of them is very encouraging; one was here [in Matthew 28], when he closed up his personal converse with them, and then his parting word was, "Lo, I am with you always; I leave you, and yet still I am with you." (The other was in Revelation 22:20, when He says, "Yes, I am coming again soon.")

—Matthew Henry

A smile of encouragement at the right moment may act like sunlight on a closed up flower; it may be the turning point for a struggling life.

—Alfred A. Montapert

Encouragement is food for the heart, and every heart is a hungry heart.

—Pat Morley

People have a way of becoming what you encourage them to be—not what you nag them to be.

—Scudder N. Parker

I have never seen a man who could do real work except under the stimulus of encouragement and enthusiasm and the approval of the people for whom he is working.

—Charles M. Schwab

If others do not encourage us, let us encourage ourselves in the Lord. How much He encouraged others! On the stormy lake, and in the upper room. He spoke words of cheer to the paralytic, and to the stricken woman He administered words of comfort.

—A. Soutter

A pat on the back is only a few vertebrae removed from a kick in the pants, but is miles ahead in results.

—Ella Wheeler Wilcox

ENDURANCE

Endurance is patience concentrated.

—Thomas Carlyle

Endurance is the crowning quality
And patience all the passion of great hearts.

—James Russell Lowell

When a man has quietly made up his mind that there is nothing he cannot endure, his fears leave him.

—Grove Patterson

Endurance is nobler than strength, and patience than beauty.

—John Ruskin

ENEMIES

Pay attention to your enemies, for they are the first to discover your mistakes.

—Antisthenes

Everyone needs a warm personal enemy or two to keep him free from rust in the movable parts of his mind.

—Gene Fowler

Our real enemies are the people who make us feel so good that we are slowly, but inexorably, pulled down into the quicksand of smugness and self-satisfaction.

—Sydney J. Harris

Could we read the secret history of our enemies, we should find in each man's life sorrow and suffering enough to disarm all hostility.

—Henry Wadsworth Longfellow

If you must talk about your troubles, don't bore your friends with them—tell them to your enemies, who will be delighted to hear about them.

—Olin Miller

ENERGY

The difference between one man and another is not mere ability—it is energy.

—Thomas Arnold

Energy, like the biblical grain of the mustard-seed, will remove mountains.

—Hosea Ballou

The world belongs to the energetic.

—Ralph Waldo Emerson

The real difference between men is energy. A strong will, a settled purpose, an invincible determination, can accomplish almost anything; and in this lies the distinction between great men and little men.

—Thomas Fuller

Energy will do anything that can be done in the world, and no talents, no circumstances, no opportunities will make a two-legged animal a man without it.

—Johann von Goethe

ENJOYMENT

It is a beautiful and blessed world we live in, and while life lasts, to lose the enjoyment of it is a sin.

—A. W. Chambers

Some people are making such preparation for rainy days that they aren't enjoying today's sunshine.

—William Feather

I sincerely believe we are given life to enjoy and make it more enjoyable for others. . . . The best way to do this is to get in the middle of it.

—Henry L. Harrell

True enjoyment comes from activity of the mind and exercise of the body; the two are ever united.

—Karl Wilhelm von Humboldt

Enjoy the little you have while the fool is hunting for more.

—Spanish Proverb

ENTHUSIASM

The worst bankrupt in the world is the man who has lost his enthusiasm. Let a man lose everything else in the world but his enthusiasm, and he will come through again to success.

—H. W. Arnold

The greatest achievements of man have always depended upon a marriage between intense enthusiasm and creative genius.

—O. A. Battista

Every man is enthusiastic at times. One man has enthusiasm for thirty minutes—another man has it for thirty days, but it is the man who has it for thirty years who makes a success in life.

—Edward B. Butler

Enthusiasm, backed up by horse sense and persistence, is the quality that most frequently makes for success.

—Dale Carnegie

Enthusiasm is the mother of effort, and without it nothing great was ever accomplished.

—Ralph Waldo Emerson

Every great and commanding moment in the annals of the world is the triumph of some enthusiasm.

—Ralph Waldo Emerson

The enthusiastic, to those who are not, are always something of a trial.

—Alban Goodier

Enthusiasm finds the opportunities, and energy makes the most of them.

—Henry S. Haskins

It requires so infinitely much tact to handle enthusiasm.

—Jens Peter Jacobsen

There are incompetent enthusiasts, and they are a mighty dangerous lot.

—G. C. Lichtenberg

The world belongs to the enthusiast who keeps cool.

—William McFee

What the world really needs is more young people who will carry to their jobs the same enthusiasm for getting ahead that they display in traffic.

—Vern McLellan

A true Christian's enthusiasm for the Lord Jesus Christ should be so exuberant that it would be far more likely to set others on fire than to be extinguished by worldly influences.

—Henrietta C. Mears

Enthusiasm is the electricity of life. How do you get it? You act enthusiastic until you make it a habit. Enthusiasm is natural; it is being alive, taking the initiative, seeing the importance of what you do, giving it dignity, and making what you do important to yourself and to others.

—Gordon Parks

Like simplicity and candor, and other much-commended qualities, enthusiasm is charming until we meet it face to face, and cannot escape from its charm.

— Agnes Repplier

A man will succeed at anything about which he is really enthusiastic.

— Charles M. Schwab

Enthusiasm is the best protection in any situation. Wholeheartedness is contagious. Give yourself, if you wish to get others.

— David Seabury

The sense of this word among the Greeks affords the noblest definition of it: enthusiasm signifies God in us.

— Mme. Anne Louise de Staël

You don't ever want to sleep when you're enthusiastic. If you can't wait to get up until tomorrow to get back to work on something, then you won't sleep much anyway.

— Jim Trebig

Years wrinkle the skin, but to give up enthusiasm wrinkles the soul.

— Samuel Ullman

Enthusiasm is that temper of the mind in which the imagination has got the better of the judgment.

— William Warburton

Duty without enthusiasm becomes laborious; duty with enthusiasm becomes glorious.

— Artemus Ward

Without enthusiasm, there is no progress in the world.

— Woodrow Wilson

The man without enthusiasm is trying to move the machinery of his life with lukewarm water. Only one thing will happen; he will stall. Remember, enthusiasm is electricity in the battery.

— A. B. ZuTavern

ENVY

If there is any sin more deadly than envy, it is being pleased at being envied.

— Richard Armour

Envy is the art of counting the other fellow's blessings instead of your own.

— Harold Coffin

Envy ought to have no place allowed it in the heart of man; for the goods of this present world are so low and vile that they are beneath it, and those of the future world are so vast and exalted that they are above it.

— Charles Caleb Colton

Too many Christians envy the sinners their pleasure and the saints their joy, because they do not have either.

— Martin Luther

Men always hate most what they envy most.

— H. L. Mencken

If we did but know how little some enjoy of the great things that they possess, there would not be much envy in the world.

— Edward Young

Envy provides the mud that failure throws at success.

—Anonymous

EQUALITY

We are all born equal—equally helpless and equally indebted to others for whatever our survival turns out to be worth.

—Cullen Hightower

For the reason that we are equal before God, we are made equal before the law of this land. And when you have said that, you have summed up and tied with a bowknot the complete American doctrine of equality.

—Clarence E. Manion

ERROR

Error is the discipline through which we advance.

—William Ellery Channing

It is human to err; and the only final and deadly error, among all our errors, is denying that we have ever erred.

—Gilbert Keith Chesterton

The most fruitful lesson is the conquest of one's own error. Whoever refuses to admit error may be a great scholar, but he is not a great learner. Whoever is ashamed of error will struggle against recognizing and admitting it, which means that he struggles against his greatest inward gain.

—Johann von Goethe

ETERNAL LIFE

We may let go all things that we cannot carry into eternal life.

—Anna Robertson Brown

In the eternal life there is no greed. One hears of neither *mine* nor *thine*. All things are for all.

—Anna Robertson Brown

The real meaning of eternal life is a life that can face anything without wavering. If we take this view, life becomes one great romance, a glorious opportunity for seeing marvelous things all the time.

—Oswald Chambers

Unless you know that you have eternal life, everything you have ever done for Christ has been a sin—because your *motive* was wrong. If you don't know you *have* eternal life, everything you are doing is an effort to *get* eternal life, and thus your motive is gain and greed.

—D. James Kennedy

ETERNITY

One hour of eternity, one moment with the Lord, will make us utterly forget a lifetime of desolations.

—Horatio Bonar

He who has no vision of eternity has no hold on time.

—Thomas Carlyle

We are citizens of eternity.

—Fyodor Dostoyevsky

Eternity is not something that begins after you are dead. It is going on all the time. We are in it now.

—Charlotte P. Gilman

Eternity has no gray hairs! The flowers fade, the heart withers, man grows old and dies, the world lies down in the sepulchre of ages, but time writes no wrinkles on the brow of eternity.

—Reginald Heber

In the presence of eternity, the mountains are as transient as the clouds.

—Robert G. Ingersoll

God hath given to man a short time here upon earth, and yet upon this short time eternity depends.

—Jeremy Taylor

ETHICS
(See also Conscience, Integrity)

The real problem is in the hearts and minds of men. It is not a problem of physics but of ethics. It is easier to denature plutonium than to denature the evil from the spirit of man.

—Albert Einstein

A man without ethics is a wild beast loosed upon this world.

—Manly P. Hall

The justification of majority rule in politics is not to be found in its ethical superiority.

—Walter Lippman

There are no pastel shades in the Christian ethic.

—Arnold H. Lowe

A man is ethical only when life, as such, is sacred to him, that of plants and animals as well as that of his fellowman, and when he devotes himself helpfully to all life that is in need of help.

—Albert Schweitzer

The truth is, hardly any of us have ethical energy enough for more than one really inflexible point of honor.

—George Bernard Shaw

Ethical behavior is concerned above all with human values, not with legalisms.

—A. M. Sullivan

If we were half as concerned about our own ethics as we are about the other fellow's, there would be no serious problem.

—A. M. Sullivan

Ethics is the science of human duty.

—David Swing

In civilized life, law floats in a sea of ethics.

—Earl Warren

EVANGELISM
(See also Soul Winning, Witnessing)

Evangelism is not salesmanship! It is not urging people, pressing them, coercing them, overwhelming them, or subduing them. Evangelism is telling a message. Evangelism is reporting good news.

—Richard C. Halverson

Evangelism is the spontaneous overflow of a glad and free heart in Jesus Christ.

—Robert Boyd Munger

Evangelism is just one beggar telling another beggar where to find bread.

—D. T. Niles

Christians and non-Christians have something in common. We're both uptight about evangelism.

—Rebecca Manley Pippert

A charge to keep I have,
A God to glorify;
A never dying soul to save,
And fit it for the sky.

—Charles Wesley

EVIL

All that is necessary for the triumph of evil is that good men do nothing.

—Edmund Burke

Evils in the journey of life are like the hills that alarm travelers on the road. Both appear great at a distance, but when we approach them we find they are far less insurmountable than we had conceived.

—Charles Caleb Colton

Once we assuage our conscience by calling something a "necessary evil," it begins to look more and more necessary and less and less evil.

—Sydney J. Harris

A good end cannot sanctify evil means, nor must we ever do evil that good may come of it.

—William Penn

No man is justified in doing evil on the grounds of expediency.

—Theodore Roosevelt

For every thousand hacking at the leaves of evil, there is one striking at the root.

—Henry David Thoreau

Allow no thought of evil to intrude within the sacred sanctum of your mind.

—Anonymous

EVOLUTION
(See also Creation)

There is no more reason to believe that man descended from some inferior animal than there is to believe that a stately mansion has descended from a small cottage.

—William Jennings Bryan

The evolutionists seem to know everything about the missing link except the fact that it is missing.

—Gilbert Keith Chesterton

The probability of life originating from accident is comparable to the Un-abridged Dictionary resulting from an explosion in a printing factory.

—Edwin Conklin

What can be more foolish than to think that all this rare fabric of heaven and earth could come by chance, when all the skill or art is not able to make an oyster!

—Jeremy Taylor

To believe in evolution is to believe that the frog really does turn into a prince.

—Anonymous

EXAGGERATION

Exaggeration is a blood relation to falsehood and nearly as blamable.

—Hosea Ballou

We exaggerate misfortune and happiness alike. We are never so wretched or as happy as we say we are.

—Honoré de Balzac

An exaggeration is a truth that has lost its temper.

—Kahlil Gibran

EXAMPLE
(See also Influence)

Be such a man, and live such a life, that if every man were such as you, and every life such as yours, this earth would be God's paradise.

—Phillips Brooks

Example is the school of mankind and they will learn at no other.

—Edmund Burke

The world needs examples, not exhorters.

—Ella E. Dodson

You can preach a better sermon with your life than with your lips.

—Oliver Goldsmith

We're all role models, either positively or negatively, no matter what station in life we occupy. It's one of the things we attain simply by being human beings in a community of other human beings.

—Bill Norwood

One man cannot do it all, but one man with a lifetime can be enough of an example to have someone follow in his footsteps.

—Bob Pierce

Example is not the main thing in influencing others. It is the only thing.

—Albert Schweitzer

People may doubt what you say, but they will always believe what you do.

—Anonymous

EXCELLENCE

Excellence is an art won by training and habituation. We do not act rightly because we have virtue or excellence, but rather we have those because we have acted rightly. We are what we repeatedly do. Excellence, then, is not an act but a habit.

—Aristotle

I am thankful that God does not accept the limitations we put on our lives. Mediocrity is never His will for us. He calls us to excellence and challenges us to be more than we thought.

—Max Browning

The rareness of excellence should not be made into an excuse for the failure to recognize it.

—John Ciardi

EXCUSES

Ninety-nine percent of the failures come from people who have the habit of making excuses.

—George Washington Carver

He that is good at making excuses is seldom good at anything else.

—Benjamin Franklin

Whoever wants to be a judge of human nature should study people's excuses.

—John Peter Hebel

An excuse is the skin of a reason stuffed with lies.

—D. James Kennedy

We have forty million reasons for failure, but not a single excuse.

—Rudyard Kipling

Never give nor take an excuse.

—Florence Nightingale

Excuses are the nails used to build a house of failure.

—Don Wilder and Bill Rechin

EXERCISE
(See also Fitness)

If it weren't for the fact that the TV set and the refrigerator are so far apart, some of us wouldn't get any exercise at all.

—Joey Adams

I get my exercise acting as a pallbearer to my friends who exercise.

—Chauncey Depew

The only exercise some people get is jumping to conclusions, running down their friends, sidestepping responsibility, and pushing their luck.

—Arnold H. Glasow

A reason to smile: Every seven minutes of every day, someone in an aerobics class somewhere pulls a hamstring.

—Allan Roth

If God had wanted me to touch my toes, He would have put them on my knees.

—Anonymous

EXPECTANCY

Attempt great things for God; expect great things from God.

—William Carey

Always be in a state of expectancy, and see that you leave room for God to come in as He likes.

—Oswald Chambers

When we are rightly related to God, life is full of spontaneous, joyful uncertainty and expectancy.

—Oswald Chambers

EXPERIENCE

All experience is an arch to build upon.

—Henry Brooks Adams

Experience is very valuable. It keeps a man who makes the same mistake twice from admitting it the third time.

—Brook Benton

A person with an experience is never at a loss with a person with an argument.

—Ralph Byron

My own experience has taught me this: if you wait for the perfect moment when all is safe and assured it may never arrive. Mountains will not be climbed, races won, or lasting happiness achieved.

—Maurice Chevalier

To most men experience is like the stern lights of a ship, which illuminate only the track it has passed.

—Samuel Taylor Coleridge

Experience is not what happens to a man. It is what a man does with what happens to him.

—Aldous Huxley

I don't want men of experience working for me. The experienced man is always telling me why something can't be done. The fellow who has not had any experience is so dumb he doesn't know a thing can't be done—and he goes ahead and does it.

—Charles F. Kettering

Experience is the worst teacher; it gives the test before presenting the lesson.

—Vernon Law

One thorn of experience is worth a whole wilderness of warning.

—James Russell Lowell

Experience teaches you to recognize a mistake when you've made it again.

—Vin Scully

We should be careful to get out of an experience only the wisdom that is in it—and stop there, lest we be like the cat that sits down on a hot stove-lid. She will never sit down on a hot stove-lid again—and that is well; but also she will never sit down on a cold one anymore.

—Mark Twain

Experience is the name everyone gives to his mistakes.

—Oscar Wilde

We learn from experience. A man never wakes up his second baby just to see it smile.

—Grace Williams

Experience is the one thing you have plenty of when you're too old to get the job.

—Anonymous

EXPLORATION
(See also Discovery)

Do not go where the path may lead, go instead where there is no path and leave a trail.

—Ralph Waldo Emerson

Two roads diverged in a wood, and I took the one less traveled by, and that has made all the difference.

—Robert Frost

I will not follow where the path may lead, but I will go where there is no path, and I will leave a trail.

—Muriel Strode

EYES

An eye can threaten like a loaded and
leveled gun, or it can insult like hissing
or kicking; or, in its altered mood, by
beams of kindness, it can make the
heart dance for joy.

—Ralph Waldo Emerson

Eyes that look are common. Eyes that
see are rare.

—J. Oswald Sanders

FACTS

Facts are stubborn things; and whatever may be our wishes, our inclinations, or the dictates of our passions, they cannot alter the state of facts and evidence.
—John Adams

Facts do not cease to exist because they are ignored.
—Aldous Huxley

Comments are free, but facts are sacred.
—Charles P. Scott

FAILURE

(See also Success)

We mount to heaven mostly on the ruins of our cherished schemes, finding our failures were successes.
—Amos Bronson Alcott

Failure is an event, never a person.
—William D. Brown

Let the past sleep, but let it sleep on the bosom of Christ, and go out into the irresistible future with Him. . . . Never let the sense of failure corrupt your new actions.
—Oswald Chambers

Beware of succumbing to failure as inevitable; make it the stepping-stone to success.
—Oswald Chambers

The real legacy of my life was my biggest failure—that I was an ex-convict. My greatest humiliation—being sent to prison—was the beginning of God's greatest use of my life; He chose the one experience in which I could not glory for His glory.
—Charles Colson

The most beautiful mosaic is but pieces of broken glass. With divine aid, the scattered fragments of our lives are joined to make success.
—Ella E. Dodson

Most of us know that the joy of anticipated success can turn to ashes in the day of failure. Yet success is only possible if the potential for failure exists.
—Ted W. Engstrom

Failure: Often that early morning hour of darkness that precedes the dawning of the day of success.
—Leigh Mitchell Hodges

Failure is often God's own tool for carving some of the finest outlines in the character of His children; and, even in this life, bitter and crushing failures have often in them the germs of new and quite unimagined happiness.
—Thomas Hodgkin

There is no failure except in no longer trying. There is no defeat except from within, no really insurmountable barrier save our own inherent weakness of purpose.

—Frank McKinney Hubbard

The saddest of all failures is that of a soul, with its capabilities and possibilities, failing of life everlasting, and entering on that night of death upon which no morning ever dawns.

—Herrick Johnson

My great concern is not whether you have failed, but whether you are content with your failure.

—Abraham Lincoln

My conviction is that failure of some kind is common to us all. And since God had people like us in mind when Christ died, God's grace is adequate to make the best of any situation. Successful people are those who apply God's remedy for failure.

—Erwin W. Lutzer

Remind thyself, in the darkest moments, that every failure is only a step toward success.

—Og Mandino

There are always reasons for giving up. There is no such thing as failure except to those who accept and believe in failure.

—Orison Swett Marden

It is better to fail in a cause that will ultimately succeed than to succeed in a cause that will ultimately fail.

—Peter Marshall

God lets us fail in a secondary thing that we may succeed in a primary thing.

—Henrietta C. Mears

Failure was a part of God's training curriculum for the disciples over one hundred times in the Gospels. It wasn't until Peter had failed terribly that he was given his greatest responsibility.

—Roland Niednagel

If at first you don't succeed, try, try again. Don't think of it as failure. Think of it as timed-release success.

—Robert Orben

If you visualize a failure, you tend to create the conditions that produce failure. Visualize—believe—and thank God in advance.

—Norman Vincent Peale

He who hopes to avoid all failure and misfortune is trying to live in a fairyland; the wise man readily accepts failures as a part of life and builds a philosophy to meet them and make the most of them.

—Wilfred A. Peterson

Nothing succeeds like failure. We learn far more about ourselves in our failures than in our successes. Failure is the greatest teacher of all. Failure dramatizes where we are yet incomplete, and points the way to wholeness. So failure may be the future signaling to us.

—Robert A. Raines

Far better it is to dare mighty things, to win glorious triumphs, even though checkered by failure, than to take rank with those poor spirits who neither enjoy much nor suffer much, because they live in the gray twilight that knows neither victory nor defeat.

—Theodore Roosevelt

The successful man lengthens his stride when he discovers the signpost has deceived him; the failure looks for a place to sit down.

—John Ruskin

There is no such thing as failure inside the will of God. There is no such thing as real success outside the will of God.

—Robert C. Savage

Failure: Never anything but an invitation to have recourse to God.

—Antonin Sertillanges

I cannot give you the formula for success, but I can give you the formula for failure, which is—try to please everybody.

—Herbert Bayard Swope

Failure should be our teacher, not our undertaker. Failure is delay, not defeat. It is a temporary detour, not a dead-end street.

—William Arthur Ward

Failure is far more honorable than fossilization!

—Chick Yuill

Failure isn't so bad when it comes out of an honest attempt to bring Christ to the people and the people to Christ. And success when it comes—as it surely will—is even more glorious.

—Chick Yuill

Failure is a far better teacher than success, but she hardly ever finds any apples on her desk.

—Anonymous

If we fill our hours with regrets over the failures of yesterday, and with worries over the problems of tomorrow, we have no today in which to be thankful.

—Anonymous

FAITH

When you decide God's way shall be your way, immediately you begin to walk. You stop worrying about whether you will fail or not; you just launch, out of faith.

—Charles Allen

Faith is to believe what we do not see; and the reward of this faith is to see what we believe.

—Saint Augustine

Faith is not only a commitment to the promises of Christ; faith is also a commitment to the demands of Christ.

—William Barclay

Faith is not an opinion, but a certitude. "The substance of things hoped for," says the apostle—not the phantasies of empty conjecture.

—Saint Bernard of Clairvaux

Don't get the idea that if you can only muster up faith, you will be effective in prayer. Faith is not some mysterious commodity to be sought after. You do not need more faith; you need to learn how to appropriate the faith you already have.

—John Bisagno

Strong, serene, unquenchable faith in the loving kindness of God will enable us to look fearlessly toward the end of the temporal existence and the beginning of the eternal, and will make it possible for us to live our lives effectively, grandly!

—Anna Robertson Brown

I believe in grace, because I have seen it; in peace, because I have felt it; in forgiveness, because I have needed it.

—George W. Bush

Faith cannot be intellectually defined; faith is the inborn capacity to see God behind everything, the wonder that keeps you an eternal child.

—Oswald Chambers

We have an idea that God is leading us to a certain goal, a desired haven; He is not.... What men call the process, God calls the end. If you can stay in the midst of turmoil unperplexed and calm because you see Jesus, that is God's purpose in your life.... God's purpose for you is that you depend on Him and His power NOW; that you see Him walking on the waves—no shore in sight, no success, just the absolute

certainty that it is all right because you see Him.

—Oswald Chambers

Faith never knows where it is being led, but it loves and knows the One who is leading.

—Oswald Chambers

Jesus says, "He that believeth in me, out of him shall flow rivers of living water." If we begin to examine the outflow, we lose touch with the Source. We have to pay attention to the Source, and God will look after the outflow.

—Oswald Chambers

Faith is not trying to believe something regardless of the evidence: faith is daring to do something regardless of the consequences.

—Sherwood Eddy

The secret of strong and healthy faith is constant cultivation of the presence of God in Christ in the life. Center your attention—your affection on Him— faith comes along without any difficulty. Think of God—not faith!

—Richard C. Halverson

Christian faith is a grand cathedral, with divinely pictured windows. Standing without, you can see no glory, nor can imagine any, but standing within every ray of light reveals a harmony of unspeakable splendors.

—Nathaniel Hawthorne

When I cannot enjoy the faith of assurance, I live by the faith of adherence.

—Matthew Henry

Active faith gives thanks for a promise, even though it is not yet performed, knowing that God's contracts are as good as cash.

—Matthew Henry

Faith is the bird that feels the light and sings to greet the dawn while it is still dark.

—James S. Hewett

It is, I think, pertinent to recall that the achievement of the Christians of the first century was due to the fact that their faith was so exceptional as triumphantly to outbalance their numerical insignificance.

—Stanley High

Many of God's people, like the nation of Israel, waste forty years out in the desert of life because they do not believe God. Far too many Christians have "grass-hopper vision."

—Tim LaHaye

The principal part of faith is patience.

—George MacDonald

Faith does not wonder why. God has not done anything that needs to be explained.

—Pamela Rosewell

Faith is believing in things when common sense tells you not to.

—George Seaton

Faith goes up the stairs that love has made and looks out the window that hope has opened.

—Charles H. Spurgeon

It's not dying for faith that's so hard, it's living up to it.

—William Makepeace Thackeray

Faith is seeing the invisible, but not the nonexistent.

—A. W. Tozer

Faith is not belief without proof, but trust without reservations.

—Elton Trueblood

Faith is knowing there is an ocean because you have seen a brook.

—William Arthur Ward

Faith is the bucket of power lowered by the rope of prayer into the well of God's abundance. What we bring up depends upon what we let down. We have every encouragement to use a big bucket.

—Virginia Whitman

Feed your faith, and your doubts will starve to death.

—Anonymous

FAITHFULNESS

Our prayer will be most like the prayer of Christ if we do not ask God to show us what is going to be, or to make any particular thing happen, but only pray that we may be faithful in whatever happens.

—Father Andrew

No power outside, from the Devil downward, can take us out of God's hand; so long as we remain faithful, we are as eternally secure as God Himself.

—Oswald Chambers

We have to be so faithful to God that through us may come the awakening of those who have not yet realized that they are redeemed.

—Oswald Chambers

Watch where Jesus went. The one dominant note in His life was to do His Father's will. His was not the way of wisdom or of success, but the way of faithfulness.

—Oswald Chambers

Whether our work is a success or a failure has nothing to do with us. Our call is not to successful service, but to faithfulness.

—Oswald Chambers

It is, however, only by fidelity in little things that a true and constant love of God can be distinguished from a passing fervor of spirit.

—François de la Fenelon

Nothing in life can take the place of faithfulness and dependability. It is one of the greatest virtues. Brilliance, genius, competence—all are subservient to the quality of faithfulness.

—Wallace Fridy

Only the person who has faith in himself is able to be faithful to others.

—Erich Fromm

Not the maker of plans and promises, but rather he who offers faithful service in small matters is most welcome to one who would achieve what is good and lasting.

—Johann von Goethe

It is far harder to live for Christ moment by moment than it is to die once for Him; and if we wait for great occasions in which to display our fidelity, we shall find that our life has slipped away, and with it the opportunities that each hour has brought of proving our love to the Lord, by being faithful in that which is least.

—J. Gregory Mantle

Do little things as though they were great, because of the majesty of Jesus Christ who does them in us, and who lives our life; and do the greatest things as though they were little and easy, because of His omnipotence.

—Blaise Pascal

God does not ask how many talents one has; he asks for faithfulness.

—Croft M. Pentz

When faithfulness is most difficult, it is most rewarding.

—Croft M. Pentz

It is better to be faithful than famous.

—Theodore Roosevelt

When faithfulness is most difficult, it is most necessary.

—Anonymous

God has no larger field for the man who is not faithfully doing his work where he is.

—Anonymous

It is not success that God rewards but faithfulness in doing His will.

—Anonymous

FAME

The more inward a man's greatness, in proportion to the external show of it, the more substantial, and therefore lasting, his fame.

—John Ayscough

The anticipation of fame always is so much sweeter than actually tasting it.

—O. A. Battista

People who have the most contempt for fame are those who have long ago resigned themselves to mediocrity.

—O. A. Battista

Fame always brings loneliness. Success is as ice cold and lonely as the North Pole.

—Vicki Baum

Fame—a few words upon a tombstone, and the truth of those not to be depended on.

—Christian Bovée

Fame is a fickle food upon a shifting plate.

—Emily Dickinson

Fame is proof that people are gullible.

—Ralph Waldo Emerson

All fame is dangerous: good bringeth envy; bad, shame.

—Thomas Fuller

Fame! What a vain word, and what a vain recompense! Since I have known the simple life of the Pacific, I think only of withdrawing myself far from men, and in consequence far from fame.

—Paul Gauguin

A man comes to be famous because he has the matter of fame within him. To seek for, to hunt after fame, is a vain endeavor.

—Johann von Goethe

Fame is a vapor, popularity an accident, riches take wings, those who cheer today will curse tomorrow, only one thing endures—character.

—Horace Greeley

People seldom become famous for what they say until after they are famous for what they've done.

—Cullen Hightower

Fame usually comes to those who are thinking about something else.

—Oliver Wendell Holmes Jr.

Men have a solicitude about fame; and the greater share they have of it, the more afraid they are of losing it.

—Samuel Johnson

There is no business in this world so troublesome as the pursuit of fame; life is over before you have hardly begun your work.

—Jean de La Bruyère

The fame of great men ought always to be estimated by the means used to acquire it.

—François de La Rochefoucauld

It is an indiscreet and troublesome ambition that cares so much about fame; about what the world says of us; to be always looking in the faces of others for approval; to be always anxious about the effect of what we do or say; to be always shouting to hear the echoes of our own voices.

—Henry Wadsworth Longfellow

If fame is only to come after death, I am in no hurry for it.

—Martial

Fame is an illusive thing—here today, gone tomorrow. The fickle, shallow mob raises its heroes to the pinnacle of approval today and hurls them into oblivion tomorrow at the slightest whim; cheers today, hisses tomorrow; utter forgetfulness in a few months.

—Henry Miller

The charm of fame is so great that we like every object to which it is attached.

—Blaise Pascal

Fame is something that must be won; honor is something that must not be lost.

—Arthur Schopenhauer

Let us satisfy our own consciences, and trouble not ourselves by looking for fame. If we deserve it, we shall attain it; if we deserve it not, we cannot force it.

—Seneca

He who would acquire fame must not show himself afraid of censure. The dread of censure is the death of genius.

—William Simms

What is fame?—The advantage of being known by people of whom you yourself know nothing, and for whom you care as little.

—King Stanislaus I

No true and permanent fame can be founded except in labors that promote the happiness of mankind.

—Charles Sumner

I feel about fame as the fellow did who found himself in heaven. He didn't ask himself whether he deserved it. He just kept quiet and stayed.

—Walt Whitman

FAMILY
(See also Home)

In the all-important world of family relations, three other words are almost as powerful as the famous "I love you." They are, "Maybe you're right."

—Oren Arnold

Other things may change us, but we start and end with family.

—Anthony Brandt

Family faces are magic mirrors. Looking at people who belong to us, we see the past, present, and future. We make discoveries about ourselves.

—Gail Lumet Buckley

Where does the family start? It starts with a young man falling in love with a girl—no superior alternative has been found.

—Winston Churchill

Children in a family are like flowers in a bouquet: there's always one determined to face in the opposite direction from the way the arranger desires.

—Marcelene Cox

The family fireside is the best of schools.

—Arnold H. Glasow

The car trip can draw the family together, as it was in the days before television, when parents and children actually talked to each other.

—Andrew H. Malcolm

We fear the government may be powerful enough to destroy our families; we know that it is not powerful enough to replace them.

—Ronald Reagan

A happy family is but an earlier heaven.

—Chinese Proverb

FANATICISM

A fanatic is one who can't change his mind and won't change the subject.

—Winston Churchill

Fanaticism is the false fire of an overheated mind.

—William Cowper

A fanatic is a man who does what he thinks the Lord would do if only He knew the facts of the case.

—Finley Peter Dunne

Fanaticism consists in redoubling your efforts when you have forgotten your aim.

—George Santayana

FANTASY

Nothing, ultimately, costs more than the upkeep on castles in the air. Reality, no matter how taxing, is never as expensive (physically or financially) as fantasy.

—Sydney J. Harris

FATE

Whatever limits us we call Fate.

—Ralph Waldo Emerson

I do not believe in that word *fate*. It is the refuge of every self-confessed failure.

—Andrew Soutar

FATHERS

A father is a man who expects his son to be as good a man as he meant to be.

—Frank A. Clark

Fathers should never underestimate the priceless return they receive—both in this life and in the life to come—on time they invest in their children.

—Chris Halverson

One father is more than a hundred schoolmasters.

—George Herbert

The most important thing a father can do for his children is to love their mother.

—Theodore M. Hesburgh

My father didn't tell me how to live; he lived, and let me watch him do it.

—Clarence Budington Kelland

A good father is a little bit of a mother.

—Lee Salk

It doesn't matter who my father was; it matters who I *remember* he was.

—Anne Sexton

A child is not likely to find a father in God unless he finds something of God in his father.

—Austin L. Sorenson

When I was a boy of fourteen, my father was so ignorant I could hardly stand to have the old man around. But when I got to be twenty-one, I was astonished at how much he had learned in seven years.

—Mark Twain

Any father who thinks he's all-important should remind himself that this country honors fathers only one day a year while pickles get a whole week.

—Anonymous

By the time a man realizes that maybe his father was right, he usually has a son who thinks he's wrong.

—Anonymous

He can climb the highest mountain or swim the biggest ocean. He can fly the fastest plane and fight the strongest tiger. My father can do anything! But most of the time he just carries out the garbage.

—Anonymous (eight-year-old)

A father is one whose daughter marries a man who is vastly her inferior mentally but then gives birth to unbelievably brilliant grandchildren.

—Anonymous

FAULT-FINDING

Keep a fair-sized cemetery in your back yard, in which to bury the faults of your friends.

—Henry Ward Beecher

Everybody loves to find fault; it gives a feeling of superiority.

—William Feather

Don't find fault. Find a remedy.

—Henry Ford

There is no reward for finding fault.

—Arnold H. Glasow

Rare is the person who can weigh the faults of others without putting his thumb on the scales.

—Byron J. Langenfield

Don't be a fault-finding grouch; when you feel like finding fault with some-body or something, stop for a moment and think; there is apt to be something wrong within yourself.

—J. J. Reynolds

Some would find fault with the morning sky, if they ever got up early enough. The fault-finder will find faults even in paradise.

—Henry David Thoreau

Soiling another will never make one's self clean.

—Alfred Lord Tennyson

Nothing is easier than fault-finding; no talent, no self-denial, no brain, no character are required to set up in the grumbling business.

—Robert West

FEAR

(See also Anxiety, Courage, Worry)

If you are frightened and look for failure and poverty, you will get them, no matter how hard you try to succeed. Lack of faith in yourself, in what life will do for you, cuts you off from the good things of the world. Expect victory and you make victory.

—Preston Bradley

No passion so effectually robs the mind of all its powers of acting and reasoning as fear.

—Edmund Burke

Nothing in life is to be feared. It is only to be understood.

—Marie Curie

If a man harbors any sort of fear, it percolates through all his thinking, damages his personality, makes him landlord to a ghost.

—Lloyd Douglas

Do the thing you fear and the death of fear is certain.

—Ralph Waldo Emerson

All men are frightened. The more intelligent they are, the more they are frightened. The courageous man is the man who forces himself, in spite of his fear, to carry on.

—George S. Patton

We can easily forgive a child who is afraid of the dark; the real tragedy of life is when men are afraid of the light.

—Plato

You gain strength, courage, and confidence by every experience in which you really stop to look fear in the face.

—Eleanor Roosevelt

Thinking will not overcome fear, but action will.

—W. Clement Stone

Fear is the mother of foresight.

—J. Hudson Taylor

It is only the fear of God that can deliver us from the fear of man.

—John Witherspoon

Fear is the darkroom where negatives are developed.

—Anonymous

FEELINGS

Never apologize for showing feelings. Remember that when you do, you apologize for the truth.

—Benjamin Disraeli

Feelings are everywhere—be gentle.

—J. Masai

Between the life of feeling and the life of faith the Christian has to choose every day ...feeling seeks and aims at itself; faith honors God and shall be honored by Him.

—Andrew Murray

FELLOWSHIP

Fellowship is fundamental to mission! Commitment to Christ, commitment to each other in Christ, is prerequisite to authentic Christian witness.

—Richard C. Halverson

FINANCES
(See also Budget, Income, Money, Wealth)

If you make six figures and can't make ends meet, maybe your ends are a little too far apart.

—Ron Barnes

Financial sense is knowing that certain men will promise to do certain things, and fail.

—Edgar Watson Howe

FIRE
(See also Passion)

Men ablaze are invincible.... The stronghold of Satan is proof against everything but fire.

—Samuel Chadwick

In an age that is given over to cynicism, coldness, and doubt, and in which the fire and warmth of God is conspicuous for its absence in the world, my heart cry is, Let the fire fall.... Oh God, let the fire of your love fall on us.

—Billy Graham

Let us joyfully stand in the midst of the fiery furnace, knowing that we shall lose nothing in the fire but our bonds, and that ever in the midst thereof will be One who is the Son of God.

—J. Gregory Mantle

The supreme need of the church is the same in [this] century as it was in the first: it is men on fire for Christ.

—James S. Stewart

If the world is cold, make it your business to build fires.

—Horace Traubel

FITNESS

I have the body of a man half my age. Unfortunately, he's in terrible shape.

—George Foreman

Your body is the baggage you must carry through life. The more excess baggage, the shorter the trip.

—Arnold H. Glasow

It is impossible to attain proper physical condition without being sound both mentally and morally.

—John Wooden

FLATTERY

Beware the flatterer: he feeds you with an empty spoon.

—Cosimo DeGregorio

Flattery is the art of telling another person exactly what he thinks of himself.

—Paul H. Gilbert

Flattery is like perfume. The idea is to smell it, not swallow it.

—William Ralph Inge

Flattery is counterfeit money that, but for vanity, would have no circulation.

—François de La Rochefoucauld

Avoid flatterers, for they are thieves in disguise.

—William Penn

FLOWERS

Flowers are our greatest silent friends.

—J. G. Brown

The flower that follows the sun does so even on cloudy days.

—Robert Leighton

There is material enough in a single flower for the ornament of a score of cathedrals.

—John Ruskin

Flowers are the poetry of earth, as the stars are the poetry of heaven.

—Anonymous

FLYING

I feel about airplanes the way I feel about diets. It seems to me they are wonderful things for other people to go on.

—Jean Kerr

He who would learn to fly must first learn to walk and run and climb and dance; one cannot fly into flying.

—Friedrich Nietzsche

And when my combat's over and my flying days are done,
I will store my ship forever in the airdrome of the sun.
Then I'll meet the referee, Great God, my Flying Boss,
Whose Wingspread fills the heavens from Polaris to the Cross.

—Robert L. Scott Jr.

The mother eagle teaches her little ones to fly by making their nest so uncomfortable that they are forced to leave it and commit themselves to the unknown world of air outside. And just so does our God to us. He stirs up our comfortable nests, and pushes us over the edge of them, and we are forced to use our wings to save ourselves from fatal falling.

—Hannah Whitall Smith

You *can* fly—but the cocoon has got to go.

—Anonymous

The most dangerous part of any flight is the trip to the airport.

—Anonymous

Flying isn't dangerous. Crashing is what's dangerous.

—Anonymous

FOLLOWERS

Following Christ has nothing to do with success as the world sees it. It has to do with love.

—Madeleine L'Engle

If you haven't learned to follow, you can't lead.

—Henrietta C. Mears

Being a follower of Jesus is to be marked by His love and to share an attitude of humility and joy that cannot be explained by life's circumstances.

—Bob Snyder

FOOD
(See also Diet)

I'm allergic to food. Every time I eat, it breaks out in fat.

—Jennifer Greene Duncan

The first thing I remember liking that liked me back was food.

—Rhoda Morgenstern

FOOLISHNESS

There is a foolish corner in the brain of the wisest man.

—Aristotle

The fellow who's always declaring he's no fool usually has his suspicions.

—Wilson Mizner

The ultimate result of shielding men from the effects of folly is to fill the world with fools.

—Herbert Spencer

A fool can no more see his own folly than he can see his ears.

—William Makepeace Thackeray

FORBEARANCE

The kindest and the happiest pair
Will find occasion to forbear;
And something, every day they live,
To pity and perhaps forgive.

—William Cowper

Forbearance should be cultivated till your heart yields a fine crop of it. Pray for a short memory as to all unkindness.

—Charles H. Spurgeon

FORGIVENESS
(See also Forbearance, Grudges)

Forgiveness is the key to action and freedom.

—Hannah Arendt

Each night, before retiring, forgive whomever offended you.

—Asher

Without forgiveness life is governed by . . . an endless cycle of resentment and retaliation.

—Roberto Assagioli

If you are suffering from a bad man's injustice, forgive him lest there be two bad men.

—Saint Augustine

They who forgive most shall be most forgiven.

—Philip J. Bailey

We have a free, full, final, forever forgiveness in the atoning work of Christ.

—J. Sidlow Baxter

If we are to love others as we love ourselves, then we must learn to love the little self, who so often needs to be forgiven for doing the things we do not want to do and saying the things we do not want to say.

—Rebecca Beard

Forgiveness ought to be like a cancelled note, torn in two and burned up, so that it can never be shown against the man.

—Henry Ward Beecher

I can forgive, but I cannot forget, is only another way of saying, I cannot forgive.

—Henry Ward Beecher

I don't live a righteous life, but a forgiven life. My Rock is the rock of forgiveness.

—John Benton

There is no revenge so complete as forgiveness.

—Josh Billings

Forgiveness does not change the past, but it does enlarge the future.

—Paul Boese

It's easier to get forgiven than to get permission.

—Ralph Bus

Little, vicious minds abound with anger and revenge, and are incapable of feeling the pleasure of forgiving their enemies.

—Lord Chesterfield

To err is human,
To forgive takes restraint;
To forget you forgave
Is the mark of a saint.

—Suzanne Douglass

Forgiveness is better than revenge; for forgiveness is the sign of a gentle nature, but revenge the sign of a savage nature.

—Epictetus

The worst of men are those who will not forgive.

—Thomas Fuller

The weak can never forgive. Forgiveness is the attribute of the strong.

—Mohandas K. Gandhi

Forgiveness is radical! Forgiveness dissolves alienation, brings reconciliation, restoration, and renewal. Forgiveness is the most radical force in history. Jesus is the most radical person in history.

—Richard C. Halverson

Forgiveness is the answer to the child's dream of a miracle by which what is broken is made whole again, what is soiled is again made clean.

—Dag Hammarskjöld

He that cannot forgive others, breaks the bridge over which he himself must pass if he would ever reach heaven; for every one has need to be forgiven.

—George Herbert

Our unwillingness to forgive when we've been deeply hurt breeds self-pity and bitterness. If you will learn and experience God's love and forgiveness through Jesus, you will have no problem in forgiving anyone for anything.
—Charlie "T" Jones

He who has not forgiven an enemy has not yet tasted one of the most sublime enjoyments of life.
—Johann K. Lavater

Everyone says forgiveness is a lovely idea, until they have something to forgive.
—C. S. Lewis

Forgiveness saves the expense of anger, the cost of hatred, the waste of spirits.
—Hannah More

When a deep injury is done us, we never recover until we forgive.
—Alan Paton

We win by tenderness; we conquer by forgiveness.
—Frederick W. Robertson

If we really want to love, we must learn how to forgive.
—Mother Teresa

Forgiveness is the fragrance the violet sheds on the heel that has crushed it.
—Mark Twain

Friendship flourishes at the fountain of forgiveness.
—William Arthur Ward

It is very easy to forgive others their mistakes; it takes more grit and gumption to forgive them for having witnessed your own.
—Jessamyn West

Sign on a company bulletin board in Grand Rapids, Michigan: To err is human, to forgive is not company policy.
—Anonymous

Forgiveness is a funny thing. It warms the heart and cools the sting.
—Anonymous

Forgiveness from others is charity; from God, grace; from oneself, wisdom.
—Anonymous

We are most like beasts when we kill.
We are most like men when we judge.
We are most like God when we forgive.
—Anonymous

FORTUNE

Not only is fortune herself blind, but she generally blinds those on whom she bestows her favors.
—Cicero

He is a good man whom fortune makes better.
—Thomas Fuller

Industry is fortune's right hand and frugality her left.
—John Ray

This is the posture of fortune's slaves: one foot in the gravy, one foot in the grave.
—James Thurber

Fortune knocks at every man's door once in a life, but in a good many cases the man is in a neighboring saloon and does not hear her.

—Mark Twain

FREE WILL

Free will is God's gift of a do-it-yourself kit.

—Larry Eisenberg

Free will, though it makes evil possible, is also the only thing that makes possible any love or goodness or joy worth having.

—C. S. Lewis

FREEDOM

(See also Liberty)

Posterity—you will never know how much it has cost my generation to preserve your freedom. I hope you will make good use of it.

—John Quincy Adams

The spirit of man grows in freedom; it withers in chains.

—Bernard M. Baruch

The cause of freedom is the cause of God.

—William Lisle Bowles

Freedom—no word was ever spoken that has held out greater hope, de-manded greater sacrifice, needed more to be nurtured, blessed more the giver . . . or came closer to being God's will on earth.

—General Omar N. Bradley

In their cry for freedom, it may truly be said, the voice of the people is the voice of God.

—Grover Cleveland

There is always one man to state the case for freedom. That's all we need, one.

—Clarence Darrow

Freedom and duty always go hand in hand and if the free do not accept the duty of social responsibility, they will not long remain free.

—John Foster Dulles

Man is really free only in God, the source of his freedom.

—Sherwood Eddy

Everything that is really great and inspiring is created by the individual who can labor in freedom.

—Albert Einstein

Only our individual faith in freedom can keep us free.

—Dwight D. Eisenhower

The winning of freedom is not to be compared to the winning of a game—with the victory recorded forever in history. Freedom has its life in the hearts, the actions, the spirit of men and so it must be daily earned and refreshed—else like a flower cut from its life-giving roots, it will wither and die.

—Dwight D. Eisenhower

Only a virtuous people are capable of freedom. As nations become corrupt and vicious, they have more need of masters.

—Benjamin Franklin

Freedom is not worth having if it does not connote freedom to err.

—Mohandas K. Gandhi

If freedom is right and tyranny is wrong, why should those who believe in freedom treat it as if it were a roll of bologna to be bartered a slice at a time?

—Jesse Helms

Aye, call it holy ground,
The soil where first they trod!
They left unstained what there they
     found—
Freedom to worship God.

—Felicia D. Hemans

The basic test of freedom is perhaps less in what we are free to do than in what we are free not to do.

—Eric Hoffer

A splendid storehouse of integrity and freedom has been bequeathed to us by our forefathers. In this day of confusion, of peril to liberty, our duty is to see that this storehouse is not robbed of its contents.

—Herbert Hoover

Those who deny freedom to others deserve it not for themselves, and, under a just God, cannot long retain it.

—Abraham Lincoln

No man is entitled to the blessings of freedom unless he be vigilant in its preservation.

—Douglas MacArthur

Freedom fails when a people decide that it is their right to take and not to give.

—Stanley F. Maxwell

None can love freedom heartily, but good men; the rest love not freedom, but license.

—John Milton

The final contribution of religious faith to the whole problem of freedom is the freedom to confess our sins—the freedom to admit that we all stand under the ultimate judgment of God.

—Ursula W. Niebuhr

Those who expect to reap the blessings of freedom must, like men, undergo the fatigue of supporting it.

—Thomas Paine

Heaven knows how to put a proper price upon its goods; and it would be strange indeed if so celestial an article as freedom should not be highly rated.

—Thomas Paine

Necessity is the plea for every infringement of human freedom. It is the argument of tyrants; it is the creed of slaves.

—William Pitt

Under God we are determined that wheresoever, whensoever, or howsoever we shall be called to make our exit, we will die free men.

—Josiah Quincy

Freedom is indivisible, there is no *s* on the end of it. You can erode freedom, diminish it, but you cannot divide it and choose to keep "some freedoms" while giving up others.

—Ronald Reagan

We find freedom when we find God; we lose it when we lose Him.

—Paul E. Scherer

Man seeks freedom as the magnet seeks the pole or water its level, and society can have no peace until every member is really free.

—Josiah Warren

For those who fought for it, freedom has a flavor the protected will never know.

—Anonymous

FREEDOM OF THE PRESS
(See also Journalism, Media, News, Newspapers)

A free press can of course be good or bad, but, most certainly, without freedom it will never be anything but bad.

—Albert Camus

I, like every soldier in America, will die for the freedom of the press, even for the freedom of newspapers that call me everything that is a good deal less than being a gentleman.

—Dwight D. Eisenhower

Then hail to the press! Chosen guardian of freedom! Strong swordarm of justice! Bright sunbeam of truth.

—Horace Greeley

Absolute freedom of the press to discuss public questions is a foundation stone of American liberty.

—Herbert Hoover

Our liberty depends on freedom of the press, and that cannot be limited without being lost.

—Thomas Jefferson

The freedom of the press works in such a way that there is not much freedom from it.

—Grace Kelly

Freedom of the press is the staff of life for any vital democracy.

—Wendell Phillips

FRIENDSHIP

Let your friends come into your life; let them see you as you are, and not find you trying to be somebody else.

—Emma Whitcomb Babcock

I value the friend who for me finds time on his calendar, but I cherish the friend who for me does not consult his calendar.

—Robert Brault

It takes a great soul to be a true friend. One must forgive much, forget much, forbear much.

—Anna Robertson Brown

When once the relationship of being the friends of Jesus is understood, we shall be called upon to exhibit to everyone we meet the love He has shown us.

—Oswald Chambers

Let us learn to anoint our friends while they are yet among the living. Post-mortem kindness does not cheer the burdened heart; flowers on the coffin cast no fragrance backward over the weary way.

—George W. Childs

Treat your friends as you do your pictures, and place them in their best light.

—Jennie Jerome Churchill

My friends are my estate. Forgive me then the avarice to hoard them!

—Emily Dickinson

Friendship consists in forgetting what one gives, and remembering what one receives.

—Alexandre Dumas

God evidently does not intend us all to be rich, or powerful, or great, but He does intend us all to be friends.

—Ralph Waldo Emerson

We force no doors in friendship, but like the Christ in Revelation, we stand reverently at the door without, to knock.

—Ralph Waldo Emerson

A true friend never gets in your way unless you happen to be going down.

—Arnold H. Glasow

A loyal friend laughs at your jokes when they're not so good, and sympathizes with your problems when they're not so bad.

—Arnold H. Glasow

Imitating Christ is opening the door to friendship.

—Billy Graham

Blessed are they who have the gift of making friends, for it is one of God's best gifts. It involves many things, but above all, the power of going out of one's self, and appreciating whatever is noble and loving in another.

—Thomas Hughes

A friend is—a push when you've stopped; a word when you're lonely; a guide when you're searching; a smile when you're sad; a song when you're glad.

—Charlie "T" Jones

True and lasting friendships cannot be founded except on the foundation of a true and abiding friendship with God.

—D. James Kennedy

Friendliness is contagious. The trouble is, many of us wait to catch it from someone else, when we might be better giving them a chance to catch it from us.

—Donald A. Laird

True friends don't spend time gazing into each other's eyes. They may show great tenderness toward each other, but they face in the same direction—toward common projects, interests, goals—above all, toward a common Lord.

—C. S. Lewis

A friend hears the song of the heart and sings it when memory fails.

—Martin Luther

Real friends are those who, when you've made a fool of yourself, don't feel that you've done a permanent job.

—Erwin T. Randall

Friendship is one of the sweetest joys in life. Many might have failed beneath the bitterness of their trial had they not found a friend.

—Charles H. Spurgeon

Good friends are like shock absorbers. They help you take the lumps and bumps on the road of life.

—Frank Tyger

A faithful friend is an image of God.

—French Proverb

A friend is one who takes you to lunch even if you are not tax-deductible.

—Anonymous

Friends are God's way of taking care of us.

—Anonymous

A friend is a person who thinks you're a good egg even though you're slightly cracked.

—Anonymous

A friend will joyfully sing with you when you are on the mountain top, and silently walk beside you in the valley.

—Anonymous

FRUIT OF THE SPIRIT

The fruit of the Spirit is the harvest, marking growth and maturity. It produces ethical character. It is the true measure of holiness of life and practice in the believer. Every believer is expected to bear fruit.

—Milton S. Agnew

Paul will not call these virtues "works." He reserves that term for deeds done in obedience to the Law or acts prompted by the flesh. These virtues are "fruit," the results put forth by the indwelling energy of the Spirit.

—John A. Allan

Love is the key. Joy is love, singing; peace is love, resting; long-suffering is love, enduring; kindness is love's touch; goodness is love's character; faithfulness is love's habit; gentleness is love's self-forgetfulness; self-control is love, holding the reins.

—Donald Grey Barnhouse

Inevitably, the first word in the list is love, and Paul might well have contented himself with that word alone. Many of those that follow are special manifestations of love: long-suffering, kindness, goodness, faithfulness, meekness, and the others are not far removed—joy, peace, self-control. All are the consequence of the self-forgetfulness that looks away from itself to God.

—C. K. Barrett

Fruit, though a collective noun, is singular. The life that has been unified, with Christ at the center, produces a harvest of love, which has many expressions.

—Andrew W. Blackwood Jr.

They are all one, they are all of the heart, they are all of an abounding soul. There is hardly ever just one grape, for grapes grow in clusters. Not just one of them ripens, they all ripen. So the produce of the spirit is a cluster. It is many and the many are one.

—W. A. Criswell

The Spirit produces one fruit, not nine fruits. The fruit, however, has nine facets or qualities. If a believer is walking in the Spirit, he will possess all nine of these qualities. The source of the fruit is the Spirit who produces it in and through the believer.

—Robert G. Gromacki

The fruit of the Spirit is not the work of the believer. It is the work of Christ in his soul . . . that is being done in him and through him by the Lord Himself. It may be noted that the apple grows on the apple tree; the orchard owner does not have to do it. The Lord gives the increase: that fruit grows by the power of God.

—Manford George Gutzke

It is a cluster of fruit inseparable, not separate fruits—the total picture of Godly character.

—Gladys Hunt

What Paul calls fruit is the sole product of the Spirit-possessed life. It is the fruit of the Spirit; that is, it is His fruit and not that of the believer. All that the Christian can do is to bear the fruit; he cannot originate it.

—Herbert Lockyear

The term *love,* which heads the list of the Spirit's fruit, should not be regarded merely as one of the cluster; it is rather the stem from which all the rest hangs. Love stands at the head of the list, but it is the heart of the whole.

—H. D. McDonald

The fruit of the Spirit begins with love . . . love is the first thing, the first in that precious cluster of fruit. Someone has said that all other eight can be put in terms of love. Joy is love, exulting; peace is love in repose; long-suffering is love on trial; gentleness is love in society; goodness is love in action; faith is love on the battlefield; meekness is love at school; and temperance is love in training. So it is love all the way—love at the top, love at the bottom, and all the way along down this list of graces.

—Dwight L. Moody

How does the branch bear fruit? Not by incessant effort for sunshine and air, not by vain struggles. . . . It simply abides in the vine, in silent and undisturbed union, and blossoms, and fruit appear as of spontaneous growth. How then shall a Christian bear fruit? By efforts and struggles to obtain that which is freely given? . . . No: there must be a full concentration of the thoughts and affections on Christ, a complete surrender of the whole being to Him, a constant looking to Him for grace.

—Harriet Beecher Stowe

FRUITFULNESS

The man who concentrates on the root system of his life is going to bear fruit upward, but if he concentrates on the eye-appealing foliage he may end up a rootless failure.

—Robert D. Foster

FRUSTRATION

Frustration is when the same snow that covers the ski slopes makes the road to them impassable.

—James Holt McGavran

Frustration is commonly the difference between what you would like to be and what you are willing to sacrifice to become what you would like to be.

—Anonymous

FUN

Fun is like life insurance; the older you get, the more it costs.

—Frank McKinney Hubbard

What is funny about us is precisely that we take ourselves too seriously.

—Reinhold Niebuhr

One of the best things people can have up their sleeves is a funny bone.

—Richard L. Weaver II

FUTURE

The best thing about the future is that it comes only one day at a time.

—Dean Acheson

The best of prophets of the future is the past.

—Lord Byron

I never think of the future. It comes soon enough.

—Albert Einstein

The future that we study and plan for begins today.

—Chester O. Fischer

The future is the past, coming in through another gate.

—Arnold H. Glasow

What the future holds for us depends on what we hold for the future. Hard-working todays make high-winning tomorrows.

—William E. Holler

The future has several names. For the weak, it is the impossible. For the fainthearted, it is the unknown. For the thoughtful and valiant, it is the ideal.

—Victor Hugo

My interest is in the future because I am going to spend the rest of my life there.

—Charles F. Kettering

Passed years seem safe ones, vanquished ones, while the future lies in a cloud, formidable from a distance. The cloud clears as you enter it. I have learned this, but like everyone, I learned it late.

—Beryl Markham

The future belongs to those who believe in the beauty of their dreams.

—Eleanor Roosevelt

As for the future, your task is not to foresee but to enable.

—Antoine de Saint-Exupéry

The future is called "perhaps," which is the only possible thing to call the future. And the important thing is not to allow that to scare you.

—Tennessee Williams

Most of us spend a lot of time dreaming of the future, never realizing a little arrives each day.

—Anonymous

There is a past that is gone forever, but there is a future that is still our own.

—Anonymous

G

GENEALOGY
(See also Ancestry, Heredity)

Genealogy: A perverse preoccupation of those who seek to demonstrate that their forebears were better people than they are.

—Sydney J. Harris

GENERATIONS

Older generations are living proof that younger generations can survive their lunacy.

—Cullen Hightower

It is fortunate that each generation does not comprehend its own ignorance. We are thus enabled to call our ancestors barbarous.

—Charles Dudley Warner

Every generation has one big impulse in its heart—to exceed all generations of the past in all the things that make life worth living.

—William Allen White

GENEROSITY
(See also Gifts/Giving, Stewardship)

Generosity is giving more than you can.

—Kahlil Gibran

The truly generous is the truly wise;
And he who loves not others, lives unblest.

—John Home

The generous, who is always just, and the just who is always generous, may, unannounced, approach the throne of heaven.

—Johann K. Lavater

He who gives what he would as readily throw away gives without generosity, for the essence of generosity is in self-sacrifice.

—Henry J. Taylor

GENIUS

Doing easily what others find difficult is talent; doing what is impossible for talent is genius.

—Henri Frédéric Amiel

Genius, that power which dazzles human eyes,
Is oft but perseverance in disguise.

—Henry W. Austin

Genius, in one respect, is like gold—numbers of persons are constantly writing about both who have neither.

—Charles Caleb Colton

Fortune has rarely condescended to be the companion of genius.

—Benjamin Disraeli

To believe your own thought, to believe that what is true for you in your own heart is true for all men—that is genius. . . . A man should learn to detect and

watch that gleam of light that flashes
across his mind from within.
—Ralph Waldo Emerson

Genius is the ability to put into effect
what is on your mind.
—F. Scott Fitzgerald

The world is always ready to receive
talent with open arms. Very often it
does not know what to do with genius.
—Oliver Wendell Holmes

Genius means little more than the
faculty of perceiving in an unhabitual
way.
—William James

Genius is the ability to see things
invisible, to manipulate things intan-
gible, to paint things that have no
features.
—Joseph Joubert

The principal mark of genius is not
perfection but originality, the opening
of new frontiers.
—Arthur Koestler

Everyone is a genius at least once a year;
a real genius has his original ideas
closer together.
—G. C. Lichtenberg

Sometimes men come by the name of
genius in the same way that certain
insects come by the name of centi-
pede—not because they have a
hundred feet, but because most people
can't count above fourteen.
—G. C. Lichtenberg

Towering genius disdains a beaten path.
It seeks regions hitherto unexplored.
—Abraham Lincoln

Good sense travels on the well-worn
paths; genius never. And that is why the
crowd, not altogether without reason, is
so ready to treat great men as lunatics.
—Cesare Lombroso

Every man of genius is considerably
helped by being dead.
—Robert S. Lynd

Genius is eternal patience.
—Michelangelo

The genius so-called is only that one
who discerns the pattern of things
within the confusion of details a little
sooner than the average man.
—Ben Shahn

Some of the world's greatest geniuses
were self-educated men and women
who visualized success for themselves,
who saw themselves overcoming all
handicaps, who gained the heights, first
through achieving a thorough knowledge of their inner resources and how
and when to draw upon them.
—Harold Sherman

When a true genius appears in the
world, you may know him by this
sign—that the dunces are all in a
confederacy against him.
—Jonathan Swift

I'm all in favor of the democratic principle that one idiot is as good as one genius, but I draw the line when someone takes the next step and concludes that two idiots are better than one genius.

—Leo Szilard

Everybody is born with genius, but most people only keep it a few minutes.

—Edgard Varese

GENTLENESS

The gentleness of Christ is the comeliest ornament that a Christian can wear.

—William D. Arnot

Gentleness corrects whatever is offensive in our manners.

—Robert Blair

God does not come in and patch up our good works. He puts in the spirit that was characteristic of Jesus; it is His patience, His love, and His tenderness and gentleness that are exhibited through us.

—Oswald Chambers

How sweet it is when the strong are also gentle!

—Libbie Fudim

Gentleness! more powerful than Hercules.

—Ninon de L'Enclos

Gentle words fall lightly, but they have great weight.

—Croft M. Pentz

Be gentle in old age; peevishness is worse in second childhood than in first.

—George D. Prentice

Gentleness is a divine trait: nothing is so strong as gentleness; nothing is so gentle as real strength.

—Ralph W. Sockman

The gentle mind by gentle deeds is known.

—Edmund Spenser

Gentleness, when it weds with manhood, makes a man.

—Alfred Lord Tennyson

GIFTS/GIVING
(See also Generosity, God's Provision, Stewardship)

Blessed are those who can give without remembering and take without forgetting.

—Elizabeth Bibesco

It is an anomaly of modern life that many find giving to be a burden. Such persons have omitted a preliminary giving. If one first gives himself to the Lord, all other giving is easy.

—John S. Bonnell

A man there was and they called him mad; the more he gave, the more he had.

—John Bunyan

Some people give time, some money, some their skills and connections, some literally give their life's blood . . . but everyone has something to give.

—Barbara Bush

You can give without loving, but you cannot love without giving.

—Amy Carmichael

Giving is the thermometer of our love.

—Benjamin R. De Jong

God sees the heart, not the hand—the giver, not the gift.

—Benjamin R. De Jong

The only true gift is a portion of yourself.

—Ralph Waldo Emerson

In the sphere of material things, giving means being rich. Not he who has much is rich, but he who gives much.

—Erich Fromm

It's better to give than to lend, and it costs about the same.

—Philip Gibbs

You give but little when you give of your possessions. It is when you give of yourself that you truly give.

—Kahlil Gibran

Complete possession is proved only by giving. All you are unable to give possesses you.

—André Gide

There is no happiness in having and getting, but only in giving. Half the world is on the wrong scent in the pursuit of happiness.

—Frank Wakely Gunsaulus

Man is much like a hole: the more you take away from him the bigger he gets. Greatness is always in terms of giving, not getting.

—Richard C. Halverson

We hear a great deal about the Lord loving cheerful givers; we wonder where He finds them.

—Edgar Watson Howe

If you ever give something to get something, you're not giving, in the true sense of the word. You're trading!

—Charlie "T" Jones

The manner of giving shows the character of the giver more than the gift itself.

—Johann K. Lavater

Give what you may have; to some it may be better than you dare think.

—Henry Wadsworth Longfellow

When it comes to giving, some people stop at nothing.

—Vern McLellan

What you are is God's gift to you. What you make of yourself is your gift to God.

—Vern McLellan

You give to get. The surest way to get is to give—and one's getting will be gauged by one's giving. So said Christ. So testifies experience.

—Alfred A. Montapert

Rich gifts wax poor when givers prove unkind.

—William Shakespeare

God loveth a cheerful giver who does not talk too much about it nor expect too much credit for it.

—Roy L. Smith

If there be any truer measure of a man than by what he does, it must be by what he gives.

—Robert South

Feel for others—in your pocket.

—Charles H. Spurgeon

The less I spent on myself and the more I gave to others, the fuller of happiness and blessing did my soul become.

—Hudson Taylor

The excellence of a gift lies in its appropriateness rather than in its value.

—Charles Dudley Warner

A real gift is one we make through our own personal sacrifice.

—A. B. ZuTavern

Many look with one eye at what they give and with seven at what they receive.

—German Proverb

Who gives to me teaches me to give.

—Dutch Saying

As you give, so shall you receive. Contribute more and you will receive more. If you want a stronger rebound, throw the ball harder.

—Anonymous

Plenty of people are willing to give God credit, yet few are willing to give Him cash.

—Anonymous

The Sea of Galilee receives but does not keep the River Jordan. For every drop that flows into it, another drop flows out. The giving and receiving go on, equal in measure. The other sea is shrewder, hoarding income jealously. It will not be tempted into any generous impulse. Every drop it gets, it keeps. The Sea of Galilee gives and lives. This other sea gives nothing. It is named—the Dead!

—Anonymous

GIRLS

A girl is Innocence playing in the mud, Beauty standing on its head, and Motherhood dragging a doll by the foot.

—Allan Beck

Little girls are the nicest things that happen to people.

—Allan Beck

What do little girls talk about?
What is their mystic theme?
Those still too young for puppy love,
Yet old enough to dream.

—William Herschell

You cannot hammer a girl into anything. She grows as a flower does.

—John Ruskin

No symphony orchestra ever played music like a two-year-old girl laughing with a puppy.

—Bern Williams

GLORY

(See also God's Glory)

The promise of glory is the promise, almost incredible, and only possible by the work of Christ, that some of us, that any of us who really chooses . . . shall find approval, shall please God.

—C. S. Lewis

Of all the affections that attend human life, the love of glory is the most ardent.

—Richard Steele

The desire of glory clings even to the best men longer than any other passion.

—Tacitus

GOALS

If you stare into the mirror each morning, having no meaningful goals for the day, not even expecting to accomplish anything except routine things, you have a failure image!

—William H. Cook

First say to yourself what you would be; and then do what you have to do.

—Epictetus

Write out your goal. What are the obstacles? What are the rewards? Is it worth it? Are you willing to pay the price? If so, visualize the rewards and get excited about it. Keep reselling yourself! Go forward!

—Maxwell Maltz

Aim for a star, and keep your sights high! With a heart full of faith within, your feet on the ground and your eyes in the sky.

—Helen Lowrie Marshall

The human scene is crowded with the people who have gone as far as they're going simply because their goals aren't high enough.

—Paul J. Meyer

You have a rudder-like control on your life, and you get that control largely by the goals you set with deep desire.

—Earl Nightingale

You must have long-range goals to keep from being frustrated by short-term failures.

—Charles N. Noble

If you don't know where you're going, you will probably end up somewhere else.

—Laurence J. Peter

There are those who will frown upon those who set ambitious goals, and yet without goals there can be no achievement, and with no achievement life will be as it has been.

—Jim Rohn

The man with average mentality, but with control, a definite goal and a clear conception of how it can be gained and, above all, with the power of application and labor, wins in the end.

—William Howard Taft

Being easygoing when you have a goal
to reach seldom makes the going easier.
—Frank Tyger

GOD

Man's extremity is God's opportunity.
—Miguel de Cervantes

You are only one step away from God
doing a fresh thing in your life. Choose
to dream His dream.
—David Edwards

God enters by a private door into every
individual.
—Ralph Waldo Emerson

The history of the world suggests that
without love of God there is little
likelihood of a love for man that does
not become corrupt.
—François de la Fenelon

God is not some cosmic bellboy for
whom we can press a button to get
things done.
—Harry Emerson Fosdick

The longer I live, the more convincing
proofs I see of the truth—that God
governs in the affairs of men....We
have been assured, sir, in the sacred
writings, that "except the Lord build the
house, they labour in vain that build it."
—Benjamin Franklin

God will not look you over for medals,
degrees, or diplomas, but for scars.
—Elbert Hubbard

This great round world, on which we
live, is very old, so old that no one
knows when it was made. But long
before there was any earth, or sun, or
stars, God was living, for God never
began to be. He always was.
—Jesse Lyman Hurlbut

God is the same person yesterday, today,
and forever; but in the drama of the
ages, He plays many parts.
—Bob Jones Sr.

My great concern is not whether God is
on our side; my great concern is to be
on God's side.
—Abraham Lincoln

How often we look upon God as our last
and feeblest resource! We go to Him
because we have nowhere else to go.
And then we learn that the storms of
life have driven us, not upon the rocks,
but into the desired havens.
—George MacDonald

We cannot afford to let God's requirements become our options, any more
than we can afford to make our options
God's requirements.
—David McKenna

The living God is my partner.
—George Mueller

There is a God-shaped vacuum in every
man that can only be filled by God.
—Blaise Pascal

The time has come to turn to God and
reassert our trust in Him.
—Ronald Reagan

How calmly may we commit ourselves to the hands of Him who bears up the world.

—Jean Paul Richter

God always gives us strength enough, and sense enough, for everything that He wants us to do.

—John Ruskin

If our confidence in God had to depend upon our confidence in any human person, we would be on shifting sand.

—Francis Schaeffer

God is too wise to be mistaken. God is too wise to be unkind. When you can't trace His hand, that's when you must learn to trust His heart.

—Charles H. Spurgeon

What peace it brings to the Christian's heart to realize that our heavenly Father never differs from Himself. In coming to Him at any time, we need not wonder whether we shall find Him in a receptive mood. He is always receptive to misery and need, as well as to love and faith. He does not keep office hours nor set aside periods when He will see no one.

—A. W. Tozer

We get our moral bearings by looking at God. We must begin with God. We are right when, and only when, we stand in a right position relative to God, and we are wrong so far and so long as we stand in any other position.

—A. W. Tozer

None but God can satisfy the longings of the immortal soul; as the heart was made for Him; only He can fill it.

—Richard C. Trench

God has made thee to love Him, and not to understand Him.

—Voltaire

It is impossible to account for the creation of the universe without the agency of a Supreme Being. And it is impossible to govern the universe without the aid of a Supreme Being.

—George Washington

Good morning. This is God, I will be handling all your problems today. I will not require your help.

—Anonymous

GOD—DENIAL OF

They who deny a God destroy man's nobility; for certainly man is of kin to the beasts by his body; and, if he be not of kin to God by his spirit, he is a base and ignoble creature.

—Francis Bacon

If men not only cease to believe in God, but allow the very idea of God to vanish from their consciousness, they will become nothing more than a set of fantastically clever monkeys, and their ultimate fate will be too horrible to contemplate.

—Karl Rahner

GODLESSNESS

Godlessness! Whether you call it by its right name or another, it is at the root of the disintegration of any people or nation. Godlessness is not atheism! Godlessness is to live without regard for God, His will, His plan!

—Richard C. Halverson

GOD'S FAITHFULNESS

It's time to review God's faithfulness and offer Him your consecration, without reservations. As you take your eyes off your problems and look at His promises, you will possess your inheritance.

—Stanley Banks

God takes hold when we break down. We go as far as we can and then God takes hold when we can't go any farther.

—A. P. Gouthey

I have held many things in my hand and lost them all, but whatever I have placed in God's hands, that I always possess.

—Martin Luther

If God gave His own Son for us, how could He ever bring Himself to desert us in small things?

—Martin Luther

Each of us may be sure that, if God sends us over rocky paths, He will provide us with sturdy shoes. He will never send us on any journey without equipping us well.

—Alexander Maclaren

God will not be absent when His people are on trial; He will stand in court as their advocate, to plead on their behalf.

—Charles H. Spurgeon

All of God's greats have been weak men who did great exploits for God because they reckoned on His being faithful.

—J. Hudson Taylor

Cast all your care on God! That anchor holds.

—Alfred Lord Tennyson

When we look back at the faithfulness of God, we praise Him. When we look forward to God's faithfulness, we trust Him.

—Ken Watters

GOD'S GLORY

The higher the mountains, the more understandable is the glory of Him who made them and who holds them in His hand.

—Francis Schaeffer

GOD'S JUSTICE

And can the liberties of a nation be thought secure when we have removed their only firm basis, a conviction in the minds of the people that these liberties are the gift of God? That they are not to be violated but with His wrath? Indeed I tremble for my country when I reflect that God is just; that His justice cannot sleep forever.

—Thomas Jefferson

Man is unjust, but God is just; and finally justice triumphs.

—Henry Wadsworth Longfellow

GOD'S KINGDOM

The kingdom of God is a kingdom of love; and love is never a stagnant pool.

—Henry W. DuBose

Wherever a believer is, there is the kingdom—there is the witness to Christ—there is the influence of Christ. The kingdom of God is hidden in business, industry, the professions, education, government, labor, private clubs—in millions of homes.

—Richard C. Halverson

Wherever God rules over the human heart as King, there is the kingdom of God established.

—Paul W. Harrison

If you want to work for the kingdom of God, and to bring it, and to enter it, there is just one condition to be accepted. You must enter it as children, or not at all.

—John Ruskin

The blessed ones who possess the kingdom are they who have repudiated every external thing and have rooted from their hearts all sense of possessing.

—A. W. Tozer

GOD'S LEADING

Let God be sovereign in your affairs. Crown Him Dictator—then He shall direct your paths.

—Robert D. Foster

He who walks with God will tell you plainly, God does not ordinarily shout to make Himself heard. As Elijah discovered, God tends to whisper in the garden.

—Gordon MacDonald

The stops of a good man, as well as his steps, are ordered by the Lord.

—George Mueller

I am like a little pencil in God's hand. He does the writing. The pencil has nothing to do with it.

—Mother Teresa

Don't try to hold God's hand; let Him hold yours. Let Him do the holding, and you the trusting.

—Hammer William Webb-Peploe

GOD'S LOVE

God loves each of us as if there were only one of us.

—Saint Augustine

God's love for me is inexhaustible, and His love for me is the basis of my love for others. We have to love where we cannot respect and where we must not respect, and this can only be done on the basis of God's love for us.

—Oswald Chambers

He prayeth best who loveth best
All things both great and small;
For the dear God who loveth us,
He made and loveth all.

—Samuel Taylor Coleridge

Paul's description of love in 1 Corinthians 13 ... is a portrait for which Christ Himself has sat.

—C. H. Dodd

To believe in God's love is to believe that He's passionately interested in each of us personally and continually.

—Louis Evely

The love of God is broader than the measure of man's mind.

—Frederick W. Faber

Be persuaded, timid soul, that He has loved you too much to cease loving you.

—François de la Fenelon

God proved His love on the cross. When Christ hung, and bled, and died, it was God saying to the world, "I love you."

—Billy Graham

The love of God, with arms extended on a cross, bars the way to hell. But if that love is ignored, rejected, and finally refused, there comes a time when love can only weep while man pushes past into the self-chosen alienation that Christ went to the cross to avert.

—Michael Green

Love, it has been said, flows downward. The love of parents for their children has always been far more powerful than that of children for their parents; and who among the sons of men ever loved God with a thousandth part of the love 'that God has manifested to us?

—August W. Hare

Divine love is a sacred flower, which in its early bud is happiness, and in its full bloom is heaven.

—Thomas K. Hervey

The heart of him who truly loves is a paradise on earth; he has God in himself, for God is love.

—Hugo de Lamennais

Divine love is perfect peace and joy, it is a freedom from all disquiet, it is all content and happiness.

—William Law

Love is an image of God, and not a lifeless image, but the living essence of the divine nature that beams full of all goodness.

—Martin Luther

You take up the subject of love in the Bible! You will get so full of it that all you have to do is to open your lips, and a flood of the love of God flows out.

—Dwight L. Moody

Do you know the love of God, and does it make you from morning to night sing the song of the ransomed ones?

—Andrew Murray

There is tremendous relief in knowing that His love to me is utterly realistic, based at every point on prior knowledge of the worst about me, so that no discovery now can disillusion Him about me.

—J. I. Packer

Can a plant wander away even from the power of the sun? How then can man fall out of the love of God?
—Friedrich Ruckert

Love was bestowed on the world by God, in order to train the soul for God.
—Friedrich Ruckert

Love is the greatest thing that God can give us, and it is the greatest we can give God.
—Jeremy Taylor

God's love for us is not a love that always exempts us from trials, but rather, a love that sees us through trials.
—Anonymous

GOD'S PEACE
(See also Peace, Peace of Mind)

The heart of man is restless until it finds its rest in Thee.
—Saint Augustine

Peace, perfect peace, in this dark world of sin?
The blood of Jesus whispers peace within.
—Edward Henry Bickersteth

Whenever you obey God, His seal is always that of peace, the witness of an unfathomable peace, which is not natural, but the peace of Jesus. Whenever peace does not come, tarry till it does or find out the reason why it does not.
—Oswald Chambers

God cannot give us a happiness and peace apart from Himself, because it is not there. There is no such thing.
—C. S. Lewis

A great many people are trying to make peace, but that has already been done. God has not left it for us to do; all we have to do is enter into it.
—Dwight L. Moody

Peace with God brings the peace of God. It is a peace that settles our nerves, fills our minds, floods our spirits and, in the midst of the uproar around us, gives us the assurance that everything is all right.
—Bob Mumford

GOD'S PLAN

If God is really preparing us all to become that which is the very highest and best thing possible, there ought never to be a discouraged or uncheerful being in the world.
—Horace Bushnell

Not until each loom is silent
And the shuttles cease to fly,
Will God unroll the pattern
And explain the reason why
The dark threads are as needful
In the Weaver's skilful hand
As the threads of gold and silver
For the pattern that He planned.
—Anonymous

GOD'S PROMISES

God never made a promise that was too good to be true.

—Dwight L. Moody

He that builds his nest on a divine promise shall find that it abides and remains until he shall fly away to the land where promises are lost in fulfillments.

—Charles H. Spurgeon

Tarry at the promise till God meets you there. He always returns by way of His promises.

—Anonymous

GOD'S PROVISION

Abundance isn't God's provision for me to live in luxury, but his provision for me to help others live.

—Randy Alcorn

God is always trying to give good things to us, but our hands are too full to receive them.

—Saint Augustine

God's gifts put man's best dreams to shame.

—Elizabeth Barrett Browning

What a serene and quiet life might you lead if you would leave providing to the God of providence.

—Charles H. Spurgeon

GOD'S SUFFICIENCY

He who has God and everything has nothing more than he who has God alone.

—C. S. Lewis

I believe God is made sad at the sight of so many of us trying to work things out for ourselves. He longs to help us, but we won't let Him; we won't ask Him.

—Peter Marshall

When you have nothing left but God . . . you become aware that God is enough.

—A. Maude Royden

When you have nothing but God, see all in God; when you have everything, see God in everything. Under all conditions, stay thy heart only on the Lord.

—Charles H. Spurgeon

No man has ever tested the resources of God until he tries what is humanly impossible.

—Anonymous

GOD'S TIMING

God is never too late, nor too early, but just on time.

—R. T. Kendall

God often visits us, but most of the time we are not at home.

—Joseph Roux

GOD'S TRUTH

A man can never be the same after hearing God's truth spoken in the power of God's Holy Spirit; he will either obey and go forward, or ignore and die a little.

—Richard C. Halverson

GOD'S WILL

Opposition or obstacles do not necessarily mean that a certain course of action is not God's will for us.

—John Benton

If we honestly sought nothing save His will, we should always be in a state of perfect peace.

—Hyacinthe Besson

Never let someone else determine God's will for your life. No one else can understand God's unique call on your life as clearly as you.

—Bob Briner and Ray Pritchard

True union with God is to do His will without ceasing, in spite of all our natural disinclination.

—François de la Fenelon

What we usually pray to God is not that His will be done, but that He approve ours.

—Helga Bergold Gross

Why should God reveal any more of His will to us if we are not following that part of His will that is already revealed in His Word?

—Richard C. Halverson

God's will is revealed in the Word of God and He will never reveal anything to us that He hasn't first revealed in His Word.

—Wes Harty

I find that doing the will of God leaves me with no time for disputing about His plans.

—George MacDonald

Because the will of God is the glory of heaven, the doing of it is the blessedness of heaven. As the will is done, the kingdom of heaven comes into the heart.

—Andrew Murray

A God who filled the prayer-orders of people whose wills were not His own would be no God at all. He would be a heavenly vending machine.

—Malcolm Nygren

If the will of God is our will, and if He always has His way, then we always have our way also.

—Hannah Whitall Smith

The will of God has far more to do with my spiritual condition than with my geographical location.

—Paul B. Smith

The real problem of Christian life is not how to discover the will of God. The real problem is to want to do it. It is the issue of motivation.

—Ray C. Stedman

The whole duty of man is summed up in obedience to God's will.

—George Washington

The will of God will be done; but, oh, the unspeakable loss for us if we have missed our opportunity of doing it.

—Brooke Foss Westcott

147

God for His service needeth not proud
work of human skill;
They please Him best who labor most in
peace to do His will.

—William Wordsworth

To know God's will is life's greatest
treasure; to do God's will is life's greatest
pleasure.

—Anonymous

GOLDEN RULE

The Golden Rule is of no use to you
whatever unless you realize that it is
your move.

—Frank Crane

Commit the Golden Rule to memory—
now commit it to life.

—Edwin Markham

GOLF

(See also Sports)

One of the advantages bowling has over
golf is that you seldom lose a bowling
ball.

—Don Carter

Some of us worship in churches, some
in synagogues, some on golf courses.

—Adlai Stevenson

The only way . . . of really finding out a
man's true character is to play golf with
him. In no other walk of life does the
cloven hoof so quickly display itself.

—P. G. Wodehouse

Sunday is the day when we bow our
heads. Some of us are praying, and
some of us are putting.

—Anonymous

GOOD AND EVIL

Good and evil both increase at com-
pound interest. That is why the little
decisions you and I make every day are
of such infinite importance.

—C. S. Lewis

The sorrow of knowing that there is evil
in the world is far out-balanced by the
joy of discovering that there is good in
the worst.

—Austin Fox Riggs

GOOD NATURE

An inexhaustible good nature is one of
the most precious gifts of heaven,
spreading itself like oil over the troubled
sea of thought.

—Washington Irving

It is so easy to be good-natured that I
wonder why anybody takes the trouble
to be anything else.

—Douglas Jerrold

The world is good-natured to people
who are good-natured.

—William Makepeace Thackeray

GOOD SAMARITAN

No one would remember the Good
Samaritan if he'd only had good
intentions; he had money, too.

—Margaret Thatcher

The Good Samaritan has lived in
memory for centuries without a name.

—Katie F. Wiebe

GOOD WORKS

A Christian should always remember
that the value of his good works is not
based on their number and excellence,
but on the love of God that prompts him
to do those things.

—San Juan De la Cruz

Not only must a good work be something
that is commanded by God in His Word
and come from a purified heart, but it
must also be done to the right end.

—D. James Kennedy

People talk about being saved by faith
plus good works. This is not true. Good
works are the necessary consequence of
our salvation. They are not necessary to
be saved; they are the necessary result
of our salvation and the evidence that
we truly have faith.

—Martin Luther

One might better try to sail the Atlantic
in a paper boat than to get to heaven on
good works.

—Charles H. Spurgeon

GOODNESS

Waste no more time arguing what a
good man should be; be one.

—Marcus Aurelius

The goodness of the heart is shown in
deeds of peacefulness and kindness.

—Philip J. Bailey

Goodness is achieved, not in a vacuum
but in the company of other men,
attended by love.

—Saul Bellow

No man or woman of the humblest sort
can really be strong, gentle, pure, and
good without the world being better for
it, without somebody being helped and
comforted by the very existence of that
goodness.

—Phillips Brooks

The work an unknown good man has
done is like a vein of water flowing
hidden underground, secretly making
the ground green.

—Thomas Carlyle

Beware every time you notice yourself
doing a good thing because you ruin it
by the notice.

—Oswald Chambers

Goodness consists not in the outward
things we do, but in the inward thing we
are.

—Edwin H. Chapin

Little progress can be made by merely
attempting to repress what is evil; our
great hope lies in developing what is
good.

—Calvin Coolidge

The smallest good deed is better than
the grandest good intention.

—Duguet

He who loves goodness harbors angels,
reveres reverence, and lives with God.

—Ralph Waldo Emerson

Men of true wisdom and goodness are contented to take persons and things as they are, without complaining of their imperfections or attempting to amend them.

—Henry Fielding

Goodness is uneventful. It does not flash, it glows.

—David Grayson

Goodness is something so simple: Always live for others, never to seek one's own advantage.

—Dag Hammarskjöld

If you can see good in everybody, almost everyone will see some good in you.

—Henry F. Henrichs

No man is good but as he wishes the good of others.

—Samuel Johnson

Nothing is rarer than real goodness; those even who think they possess it are generally only good-natured and weak.

—François de La Rochefoucauld

An act of goodness, the least act of true goodness, is indeed the best proof of the existence of God.

—Jacques Maritain

Goodness is beauty in its best estate.

—Christopher Marlowe

Be not only good; be good for something.

—Henrietta C. Mears

To make the improving of our own character our central aim is hardly the highest kind of goodness. True goodness forgets itself and goes out to do the right thing for no other reason than that it is right.

—Lesslie Newbigin

Goodness is a special kind of truth and beauty. It is truth and beauty in human behavior.

—Croft M. Pentz

Goodness and love mold the form into their own image, and cause the joy and beauty of love to shine forth from every part of the face. When this form of love is seen, it appears ineffably beautiful, and affects with delight the inmost life of the soul.

—Emanuel Swedenborg

Goodness is the only investment that never fails.

—Henry David Thoreau

The value of our good is not measured by what it costs us but by the amount of good it does the one concerned.

—Anonymous

When you are good to others you are always best to yourself.

—Anonymous

GOODWILL

Goodwill is the mightiest practical force in the universe.

—Charles E. Dole

None of us can buy goodwill; we must earn it.

—William Feather

Henceforth in me instill, O God, a sweet goodwill to all mankind.

—Theodore Tilton

GOSPEL

Men may not read the gospel in sheep-skin, or the gospel in morocco, or the gospel in cloth covers, but they can't get away from the gospel in shoe leather.

—Donald Grey Barnhouse

The gospel is not a challenge, it is an offer.

—Joe Blinco

The gospel is not something we go to church to hear; it is something we go from church to tell.

—Vance Havner

It cannot be emphasized too strongly or too often that this great nation was founded, not by religionists, but by Christians, not on religions, but on the gospel of Jesus Christ! For this very reason peoples of other faiths have been afforded asylum, prosperity, and freedom of worship here.

—Patrick Henry

God writes the gospel not in the Bible alone, but on trees, and flowers, and clouds, and stars.

—Martin Luther

The gospel is a declaration, not a debate.

—James S. Stewart

GOSSIP

Gossip is a sort of smoke that comes from the dirty tobacco pipes of those who use it; it proves nothing but the bad taste of the smoker.

—George Eliot

This has to do with gossip. That juicy news you know about. Hold it. Swallow it. Don't allow it to pass through your lips. In many cases, silence is golden.

—Robert D. Foster

Nothing ever happens in a small town, but what you hear makes up for it.

—Virginia Safford

Fire and sword are but slow engines of destruction in comparison with the gossiper.

—Sir Richard Steele

Whoever gossips to you will gossip about you.

—Spanish Proverb

GOVERNMENT
(See also Taxes)

The worst thing in this world, next to anarchy, is government.

—Henry Ward Beecher

In the long-run every government is the exact symbol of its people, with their wisdom and unwisdom; we have to say, like people, like government.

—Thomas Carlyle

The budget should be balanced. The treasury should be refilled. Public debt should be reduced. The arrogance of officials should be tempered and controlled, and assistance to foreign lands should be curtailed, lest we become bankrupt. The people should be forced to work and not depend on the government for subsistence.

—Cicero

Government is a trust, and the officers of the government are trustees; and both the trust and the trustees are created for the benefit of the people.

—Henry Clay

Governments are not formed to achieve, but to protect.

—James Fenimore Cooper

The less government we have the better—the fewer laws and the less confided power. The antidote to this abuse of formal government is the influence of private character, the growth of the individual.

—Ralph Waldo Emerson

If men and women of capacity refuse to take part in politics and government, they condemn themselves, as well as the people, to the punishment of living under bad government.

—Sam J. Ervin

Everybody wants to eat at the government's table, but nobody wants to do the dishes.

—Werner Finck

The government solution to a problem is usually as bad as the problem.

—Milton Friedman

Providence has given to our people the choice of their rulers, and it is the duty as well as the privilege and interest of our Christian nation to select and prefer Christians for their rulers.

—John Jay

A government big enough to supply all your needs is big enough to take all you have.

—Thomas Jefferson

A wise and frugal government ... shall not take from the mouth of labor the bread it has earned.

—Thomas Jefferson

When a government entity talks about "matching funds," it usually means that for every dollar it plans to take out of your left pocket, it will take another one out of your right pocket.

—B. K.

Every public official should be recycled occasionally.

—John V. Lindsay

Government breaks your legs and then gives you a pair of crutches.

—Rob Moody

You know someone once likened government to a baby. It is an alimentary canal with an appetite at one end and no sense of responsibility at the other.

—Ronald Reagan

A government is the only known vessel that leaks from the top.

—James Reston

I believe that the law was made for man and not man for the law, that government is the servant of the people, not their master.

—John D. Rockefeller Jr.

If you make any money, the government shoves you in the creek once a year with it in your pockets, and all that don't get wet you can keep.

—Will Rogers

It is impossible to govern the world without God. He must be worse than an infidel who lacks faith, and more than wicked who has not gratitude enough to acknowledge his obligation.

—George Washington

Actually, there is only one first question of government, and it is "How should we live?" or (this is the same question) "What kind of people do we want our citizens to be?"

—George F. Will

GRACE

Grace creates liberated laughter. The grace of God in Jesus Christ is beautiful, and it radiates joy and awakens humor.

—Karl Barth

Grace freely justifies me and sets me free from slavery to sin.

—Saint Bernard of Clairvaux

Cheap grace is the deadly enemy of our church. . . . Cheap grace is the preaching of forgiveness without requiring repentance, baptism without church discipline, communion without confession, absolution without personal confession.

—Dietrich Bonhoeffer

Your worst days are never so bad that you are beyond the reach of God's grace. And your best days are never so good that you are beyond the need of God's grace.

—Jerry Bridges

Thank God, He does not measure grace out in teaspoons.

—Amy Carmichael

The surest sign that God has done a work of grace in my heart is that I love Jesus Christ best, not weakly and faintly, not intellectually, but passionately, personally, and devotedly, overwhelming every other love of my life.

—Oswald Chambers

The grace of our Lord Jesus Christ is the overflowing of God's nature in entire and absolute forgiveness through His own sacrifice.

—Oswald Chambers

Purity in God's children is not the outcome of obedience to His law, but the result of the supernatural work of His grace.

—Oswald Chambers

Grace is unconquerable love ... waits not for merit to call it forth, but flows out to the most guilty, is the sinner's only hope.

—William Ellery Channing

No one is safe by his own strength, but he is safe by the grace and mercy of God.

—Saint Cyprian

By "riches of grace" the apostle means all the spiritual resources that are at the disposal of Christians through the redeeming work of Christ and the gracious presence of his Holy Spirit.

—Henry W. DuBose

As grace is first from God, so it is continually from Him, as much as light is all day long from the sun, as well as at first dawn or at sun-rising.

—Jonathan Edwards

Grace is but glory begun, and glory is but grace perfected.

—Jonathan Edwards

Our heavenly Father, so far from ever overlooking us, is only waiting to find our hearts open, to pour into them the torrents of His grace.

—François de la Fenelon

Grace is not sought nor bought nor wrought. It is a free gift of almighty God to needy mankind.

—Billy Graham

The doctrines of grace humble a man without degrading him, and exalt a man without inflating him.

—Charles Hodge

The love that gives, that loves the unlovely and the unlovable, is given a special name in the New Testament—grace.

—Oswald C. J. Hoffmann

Sin had no sooner come into the world than God came in grace seeking the sinner, and so from the first question, "Adam, where art thou?" on to the incarnation, God has been speaking to man.

—Harry A. Ironside

Grace binds you with far stronger cords than the cords of duty or obligation can bind you. Grace is free, but when once you take it you are bound forever to the Giver, and bound to catch the spirit of the Giver.

—E. Stanley Jones

The word *grace* is unquestionably the most significant single word in the Bible.

—Ilion T. Jones

Grace is sufficient to enable us to be accounted entirely and completely righteous in God's sight.

—Martin Luther

Christ is no Moses, no exactor, no giver of laws, but a giver of grace, a Savior; He is infinite mercy and goodness, freely and bountifully given to us.

—Martin Luther

Grace is God's unmerited, free spontaneous love for sinful man, revealed and made effective in Jesus Christ.

—C. L. Mitton

Don't let Satan make you think you are so good that you don't need the grace of God. We are a bad lot, all of us, with nothing to pay.

—Dwight L. Moody

Remember the great need you have of the grace and assistance of God. You should never lose sight of Him—not for a moment.

—Andrew Murray

Man is born broken. He lives by mending. And the grace of God is glue.

—Eugene O'Neill

As the grace of God changes a man's heart, this is the great evidence of the change: that he begins to grow in love, to lay aside self-seeking, and to live for others.

—Francis Paget

We have a power implanted in us that would lift us up above all hindrances, carry us over all temptations—the almighty power of the grace of God.

—Edward B. Pusey

Millions of hells of sinners cannot come near to exhaust infinite grace.

—Samuel Rutherford

Grace is the one word for all that God is for us in the form of Jesus Christ.

—Lewis B. Smedes

There is nothing but God's grace. We walk upon it; we breathe it; we live and die by it; it makes the nails and axles of the universe.

—Robert Louis Stevenson

Grace is love that cares and stoops and rescues.

—John R. W. Stott

They travel lightly whom God's grace carries.

—Thomas à Kempis

God will always be Himself, and grace is an attribute of His holy being. He can no more hide His grace than the sun can hide its brightness.

—A. W. Tozer

It is by His grace that God imputes merit where none previously existed and declares no debt to be where one has been before.

—A. W. Tozer

Grace is God himself, his loving energy at work within his church and within our souls.

—Evelyn Underhill

G-R-A-C-E: God's **R**iches **a**t **C**hrist's **E**xpense

—Anonymous

Grace: unmerited favor to one deserving positive disfavor.

—Anonymous

GRANDCHILDREN/ GRANDPARENTS

Grandbabies are better than babies. You can tote them around the church, collecting compliments, whereas it would be unseemly if you were merely the father.

—Oren Arnold

Grandchildren don't make a man feel old; it's the knowledge that he's married to a grandmother.

—G. Norman Collie

Nobody can do for little children what grandparents do. Grandparents sort of sprinkle stardust over the lives of little children.

—Alex Haley

Few things are more delightful than grandchildren fighting over your lap.

—Doug Larson

There's nothing like having grandchildren to restore your faith in heredity.

—Doug Larson

The simplest toy, which even the youngest child can operate, is called a grandparent.

—Sam Levenson

I don't know who my grandfather was. I am much more concerned to know what his grandson will be.

—Abraham Lincoln

A grandmother is a person with too much wisdom to let that stop her from making a fool of herself over her grandchildren.

—Phil Moss

Our children are here to stay, but our babies and toddlers and preschoolers are gone as fast as they can grow up—and we have only a short moment with each. When you see a grandfather take a baby in his arms, you see that the moment hasn't always been long enough.

—St. Clair Adams Sullivan

My grandfather was cut down in the prime of his life. My grandmother used to say, "If he had been cut down fifteen minutes earlier, he could have been resuscitated."

—Mark Twain

Never have children, only grandchildren.

—Gore Vidal

Grandchildren are God's way of compensating us for growing old.

—Mary H. Waldrip

Perfect love does not come till the first grandchild.

—Welsh Proverb

One thing you can say for small children—they don't go around showing off pictures of their grandparents.

—Anonymous

A grandmother is a mother who has a second chance.

—Anonymous

When I die, I want to die like my grandmother who died peacefully in her sleep—not screaming like all the passengers in her car.

—Anonymous

GRATITUDE
(See also Thankfulness)

A true Christian is a man who never for a moment forgets what God has done for him in Christ, and whose whole comportment and whole activity have their root in the sentiment of gratitude.

—John Baillie

If gratitude is due from children to their earthly parents, how much more is the gratitude of the great family of men due to our Father in heaven?

—Hosea Ballou

In ordinary life we hardly realize that we receive a great deal more than we give, and that it is only with gratitude that life becomes rich. It is very easy to overestimate the importance of our own achievements in comparison with what we owe others.

—Dietrich Bonhoeffer

Gratitude is not only the greatest of virtues, but the parent of all the others.

—Cicero

Gratitude is something of which none of us can give too much.

—A. J. Cronin

Gratitude is riches. Complaining is poverty. Instead of complaining about what's wrong, be grateful for what's right.

—Zachary Fisher

Gratitude is born in hearts that take time to count up past mercies.

—Charles E. Jefferson

So much has been given to me, I have no time to ponder over that which has been denied.

—Helen Keller

Gratitude is the memory of the heart.

—J. B. Massieu

Gratitude is not a virtue that comes easy to the human race.

—W. Somerset Maugham

To be grateful is to recognize the love of God in everything He has given us— and He has given us everything. Every breath we draw is a gift of His love.

—Thomas Merton

How happy a person is depends on the depth of his gratitude.

—John Miller

Gratitude is a duty that ought to be paid, but that none have a right to expect.

—Jean Jacques Rousseau

An interesting phenomenon in children is that gratitude or thankfulness comes relatively late in their young lives. They almost have to be taught it; if not, they grow up thinking that the world owes them a living.

—Fulton J. Sheen

He who forgets the language of gratitude can never be on speaking terms with happiness.

—C. Neil Strait

Gratitude is the homage of the heart, rendered to God for his goodness.

—Nathaniel Parker Willis

Gratitude is a way of life, a temper of being, an index to spiritual health.

—Sherwood E. Wirt

A really thankful heart will extract motive for gratitude from everything, making the most even of scanty blessings.

—Anonymous

GRAVE

(See also Death)

The tomb is not a blind alley; it is a thoroughfare. It closes on the twilight, it opens on the dawn.

—Victor Hugo

The grave itself is but a covered bridge leading from light to light through a brief darkness.

—Henry Wadsworth Longfellow

GREATNESS

Greatness lies not in being strong, but in the right use of strength.

—Henry Ward Beecher

Great things are done when men and mountains meet.

—William Blake

Great men are meteors designed to burn so that the earth may be lighted.

—Napoleon Bonaparte

All your youth you want to have your greatness taken for granted; when you find it taken for granted, you are unnerved.

—Elizabeth Bowen

No man has come to true greatness who has not felt in some degree that his life belongs to his race, and that what God gives him He gives him for mankind.

—Phillips Brooks

Greatness lies, not in being strong, but in the right use of strength. . . . He is the greatest whose strength carries up the most hearts by the attraction of his own.

—William Cullen Bryant

No sadder proof can be given by a man of his own littleness than disbelief in great men.

—Thomas Carlyle

All greatness is unconscious, or it is little and naught.

—Thomas Carlyle

There is a great man who makes every man feel small. But the really great man is the man who makes every man feel great.

—Gilbert Keith Chesterton

The price of greatness is responsibility.

—Winston Churchill

Great men are they who see that the spiritual is stronger than any material force, that thoughts rule the world.

—Ralph Waldo Emerson

No man ever became great doing as he pleased. Little men do as they please— little nobodies. Great men submit themselves to the laws governing the realm of their greatness.

—Richard C. Halverson

The greatest truths are the simplest, and so are the greatest men.

—A. W. and J. C. Hare

No man is truly great who is great only in his lifetime. The test of greatness is the page of history.

—William Hazlitt

He who comes up to his own idea of greatness must always have had a very low standard of it in his mind.

—William Hazlitt

He is great who feeds other minds. He is great who inspires others to think for themselves.

—Elbert Hubbard

A retentive memory is a good thing, but the ability to forget is the true token of greatness.

—Elbert Hubbard

Shed no tears over your lack of early advantages. No really great man ever had any advantages that he himself did not create.

—Elbert Hubbard

Great minds have purposes, others have wishes. Little minds are tamed and subdued by misfortune; but great minds rise above them.

—Washington Irving

No man was ever great by imitation.

—Samuel Johnson

Lives of great men all remind us
We can make our lives sublime,
And, departing, leave behind us
Footprints on the sands of time.

—Henry Wadsworth Longfellow

The heights by great men reached and
    kept
Were not attained by sudden flight,
But they, while their companions slept,
Were toiling upward in the night.

—Henry Wadsworth Longfellow

If any man seeks for greatness, let him forget greatness and ask for truth, and he will find both.

—Horace Mann

The final measure of greatness is whether you and I, by our individual lives, have increased the freedom of man, enhanced his dignity, and brought him nearer to the nobility of the divine image in which he was created.

—Herbert V. Prochnow

Do not despise the bottom rungs in the ascent to greatness.

—Publilius Syrus

A solemn regard to spiritual and eternal things is an indispensable element of all true greatness.

—Daniel Webster

The truest greatness lies in being kind.

—Ella Wheeler Wilcox

GRIEF
(See also Sorrow, Tears)

I hope it helps to remember that we are never closer to God than when we grieve. Faith is tested in suffering. And faith is often born in suffering, for that is when we seek the hope we most need. That is when we awaken to the greatest hope there is, that is when we look beyond our lives to the hour when God will wipe away every tear, and death will be swallowed up in victory.

—George W. Bush

Those who have known grief seldom seem sad.

—Benjamin Disraeli

Grief knits two hearts in closer bonds than happiness ever can; and common sufferings are far stronger links than common joys.

—Alphonse de Lamartine

Waiting is worse than knowing. Grief rends the heart cleanly, that it may begin to heal. Waiting shreds the spirit.

—Morgan Llywelyn

GROWTH

If the shoe fits, you're not allowing for growth.

—Robert N. Coons

You cannot force the growth of human life and civilization, any more than you can force slow-growing trees. That is the economy of God, that all good growth is slow growth.

—William J. Gaynor

Everybody wants to be somebody; nobody wants to grow.

—Johann von Goethe

That which grows slowly endures.

—Josiah G. Holland

Mere change is not growth. Growth is the synthesis of change and continuity, and where there is no continuity there is no growth.

—C. S. Lewis

Growth is the only evidence of life.

—John Henry Newman

GRUDGES

Don't carry a grudge. While you're carrying a grudge, the other guy's out dancing.

—Buddy Hackett

Grudges get heavier the longer they are carried.

—P. K. Thomajan

The heaviest load any man carries on his back is a pack of grudges.

—Anonymous

GRUMBLING
(See also Complaint)

You can overcome anything if you don't bellyache.

—Bernard M. Baruch

Some people are always grumbling; if they had been born in the Garden of Eden, they would have found much to complain of.

—John Lubbock

Do not grumble or criticize; it takes neither heart nor brains to do that.

—Dwight L. Moody

Why be difficult, when with a little more effort you could be impossible?

—Anonymous

GUESTS
(See also Hospitality)

A guest should be permitted to graze, as it were, in the pastures of his host's kindness, left even to his own devices, like a rational being, and handsomely neglected.

—Louise Imogen Guiney

If you want to become the perfect guest, then try to make your host feel at home.

—W. A. Nance

GUIDANCE

We need to learn to set our course by the stars and not by the light of every passing ship.

—Omar N. Bradley

If you are not guided by God, you will be guided by someone or something else.

—Eric Liddell

Man gives advice; God gives guidance.

—Leonard Ravenhill

GUILT

Guilt is never a rational thing; it distorts all the faculties of the human mind, it perverts them, it leaves a man no longer in the free use of his reason, it puts him into confusion.

—Edmund Burke

H

HABITS

Habit, if not resisted, soon becomes necessity.

—Saint Augustine

It is easy to assume a habit; but when you try to cast it off, it will take skin and all.

—Josh Billings

The trouble with people who have broken a habit is that they usually have the pieces mounted and framed.

—Ivern Boyett

We must form the habit of love until it is the practice of our lives.

—Oswald Chambers

A habit is something you can do without thinking—which is why most of us have so many of them.

—Frank A. Clark

We first make our habits, and then our habits make us.

—John Dryden

Habit is either the best of servants or the worst of masters.

—Nathaniel Emmons

Each year, one vicious habit rooted out, In time might make the worst man
  good throughout.

—Benjamin Franklin

We are ruled by our habits. When habits are young they are like lion cubs, soft, fluffy, funny, frolicsome little animals. They grow day by day. Eventually they rule you. Choose ye this day the habit ye would have to rule over you.

—Elbert Hubbard

Ever' once in a while some feller without a single bad habit gets caught.

—Frank McKinney Hubbard

The chains of habit are too weak to be felt until they are too strong to be broken.

—Samuel Johnson

Everybody should have a few bad habits so he'll have something he can give up if his health fails.

—Franklin P. Jones

The beginning of a habit is like an invisible thread, but every time we repeat the act we strengthen the strand, add to it another filament, until it becomes a great cable and binds us irrevocably.

—Orison Swett Marden

The unfortunate thing about this world is that good habits are so much easier to give up than bad ones.

—W. Somerset Maugham

It is just as easy to form a good habit as it is a bad one. And it is just as hard to

break a good habit as a bad one. So get
the good ones and keep them.

—William McKinley

I never knew a man to overcome a bad
habit gradually.

—John R. Mott

Habit is habit, and not to be flung out of
the window by any man, but coaxed
downstairs a step at a time.

—Mark Twain

Nothing so needs reforming as other
people's habits.

—Mark Twain

A habit is a shirt made of iron.

—Czech Proverb

HANDICAPS

Every single one of us is handi-
capped—physically, mentally, socially,
and spiritually—to some degree; and
although we seldom think about it, the
person without faith has a far greater
handicap than the person without feet.

—Frank K. Ellis

Man has a handicap that is difficult to
overcome. We have the capacity to see
the faults, sins, and mistakes of others,
but we cannot see them in ourselves.

—Cort R. Flint

The one resolution, which was in my
mind long before it took the form of a
resolution, is the key-note of my life. It
is this: always to regard as mere
impertinences of fate the handicaps
that were placed upon my life almost at
the beginning. I resolved that they
should not crush or dwarf my soul, but
rather be made to blossom, like Aaron's
rod, with flowers.

—Helen Keller

I thank God for my handicaps, for,
through them, I have found myself, my
work, and my God.

—Helen Keller

HANDS

God has given us two hands—one to
receive with and the other to give with.

—Billy Graham

Take a look at those two open hands of
yours. They are tools with which to
serve, make friends, and reach out for
the best of life. Open hands open the
way to achievement. Put them to work
today.

—Wilfred A. Peterson

God has no other hands than ours.

—Dorothee Sölle

HAPPINESS

The grand essentials of happiness in
this life are something to do, someone
to love, and something to hope for.

—Joseph Addison

Happiness is nothing but the conquest
of God through love.

—Henri Frédéric Amiel

Happiness often sneaks in through a
door you didn't know you left open.

—John Barrymore

163

Happiness

If you ever find happiness by hunting for it, you will find it as the old woman did her spectacles, safe on her own nose all the time.

—Josh Billings

It is only possible to live happily-ever-after on a day-to-day basis.

—Margaret Bonano

If you are not happy today, you will never be happy! Strive to be patient, unselfish, purposeful, strong, and eager, and work mightily! If you do these things with a grateful heart, you will be happy—at least as happy as it is given man to be on earth.

—Anna Robertson Brown

The happiest people are rarely the richest, or the most beautiful, or even the most talented.... Their eyes are turned outward; they are aware, compassionate. They have the capacity to love.

—Jane Canfield

Happiness is no easy matter; 'tis very easy to find it within ourselves, and impossible to find it anywhere else.

—Sebastien R. N. Chamfort

Seek happiness for its own sake, and you will not find it; seek for duty, and happiness will follow as the shadow comes with the sunshine.

—Tryon Edwards

Happiness consists in activity; it is a running stream, and not a stagnant pool.

—John Mason Good

Happiness, I have discovered, is nearly always a rebound from hard work.

—David Grayson

Happiness is a butterfly, which when pursued is always just beyond your grasp, but which, if you will sit down quietly, will light upon you.

—Nathaniel Hawthorne

It's pretty hard to tell what does bring happiness; poverty and wealth have both failed.

—Frank McKinney Hubbard

Happiness is reflective, like the light of heaven.

—Washington Irving

It is an illusion to think that more comfort means more happiness. Happiness comes from the capacity to feel deeply, to enjoy simply, to think freely, to be needed.

—Storm Jameson

Many persons have a wrong idea about what constitutes true happiness. It is not attained through self-gratification, but through fidelity to a worthy purpose.

—Helen Keller

Happiness is neither within us nor without us; it is the union of ourselves with God.

—Blaise Pascal

Success is not the key to happiness. Happiness is the key to success. If you love what you are doing, you will be successful.

—Albert Schweitzer

Happiness consists in being happy with what we have got and with what we haven't got.

—Charles H. Spurgeon

Cherish all your happy moments; they make a fine cushion for old age.

—Booth Tarkington

Happiness walks on busy feet.

—Kitte Turmell

If we'd only stop trying to be happy, we could have a pretty good time.

—Edith Wharton

Now that I know Christ, I'm happier when I'm sad than I was before when I was glad.

—John C. Wheeler

Talk happiness. The world is sad enough without your woes.

—Ella Wheeler Wilcox

If you want happiness for an hour, take a nap. If you want happiness for a day, go fishing. If you want happiness for a year, inherit a fortune. If you want happiness for a lifetime, help somebody.

—Chinese Proverb

True happiness comes from the knowledge that we are of some use in this world.

—Anonymous

Happiness has no reason. It is not to be found in the facts of our lives, but in the color of the light by which we look at the facts.

—Anonymous

Happiness is in the heart, not in the circumstances.

—Anonymous

HARMONY

Minimize friction and create harmony. You can get friction for nothing, but harmony costs courage and self-control.

—Elbert Hubbard

Beauty is harmony.

—Juan Montalvo

If only the whole world could feel the power of harmony.

—Wolfgang Amadeus Mozart

It is indeed from the experience of beauty and happiness, from the occasional harmony between our nature and our environment, that we draw our conception of the divine life.

—George Santayana

Observe good faith and justice toward all nations. Cultivate peace and harmony with all.

—George Washington

HATRED

Hate is an acid that corrodes its container.

—Tonya Baker

Remember, to hate, to be violent, is demeaning. It means you're afraid of the other side of the coin—to love and be loved.

—James Baldwin

There isn't even enough time for love, so what does that leave for hate?

—Bill Copeland

Hatred is a snare in which the hater himself is caught.

—Ella E. Dodson

Hatred is a low and degrading emotion and is so poisonous that no man is strong enough to use it safely. The hatred we think we are directing against some person or thing has a devilish way of turning back upon us.

—Thomas Dreier

Hating people is like burning down your own house to get rid of a rat.

—Harry Emerson Fosdick

I never hated a man enough to give him his diamonds back.

—Zsa Zsa Gabor

A rattlesnake, if cornered, will become so angry it will bite itself. That is exactly what the harboring of hate and resentment against others is—a biting of oneself. We think that we are harming others in holding these spites and hates, but the deeper harm is to ourselves.

—E. Stanley Jones

Love must be learned and learned again and again; there is no end to it. Hate needs no instruction, but waits only to be provoked.

—Katherine Anne Porter

Long ago . . . I resolved that I would permit no man, no matter what his color might be, to narrow and degrade my soul by making me hate him.

—Booker T. Washington

Any one person can hate, but it takes two to get along.

—Anonymous

HEALTH
(See also Diet, Fitness)

Don't tell your friends about your indigestion; "How are you!" is a greeting, not a question.

—Arthur Guiterman

A healthy body makes for a healthy mind and a healthy soul.

—Robert J. McCracken

Modern concepts of health have lost their connection to God. They look at health as normal anatomical, physiological, and mental function. God would remind us that our intended spiritual state—holiness—forms the supreme description of health.

—Bob Snyder

Be careful of reading health books. You might die of a misprint.

—Mark Twain

Look to your health, and if you have it praise God, and value it next to a good conscience; for health is the second blessing that we mortals are capable of—a blessing that money cannot buy.

—Izaak Walton

Health is a trust from God.

—Anonymous

HEART

It is the heart that makes a man rich. He is rich according to what he is, not according to what he has.

—Henry Ward Beecher

Only the heart knows how to find what is precious.

—Fyodor Dostoyevsky

The best and most beautiful things in the world cannot be seen or even touched. They must be felt with the heart.

—Helen Keller

In making our decisions, we must use the brains that God has given us. But we must also use our hearts, which He also gave us.

—Fulton Oursler

Carve your name on hearts and not on marble.

—Charles H. Spurgeon

To wear your heart on your sleeve isn't a very good plan; you should wear it inside, where it functions best.

—Margaret Thatcher

Let your heart soar as high as it will. Refuse to be average.

—A. W. Tozer

God will accept a broken heart, but He must have all the pieces.

—Anonymous

HEAVEN

The kingdom of heaven is not for the well-meaning; it is for the desperate.

—James Denney

A man may go to heaven with half the pains it cost him to purchase hell.

—Henry Fielding

He will never get to heaven who desires to go there alone.

—Thomas Fuller

We talk about heaven being so far away. It is within speaking distance of those who belong there.

—Dwight L. Moody

If ever I reach heaven, I expect to find three wonders there: first, to meet some I had not thought to see there; second, to miss some I had expected to see there; and third, the greatest wonder of all, to find myself there.

—John F. Newton

Our destination is home with our Father in heaven. It is so easy on this journey to lose sight of our destination and to focus on the detours of this life instead. This life is only the trip to get home.

—Bob Snyder

Heaven may be defined as the place that men avoid.

—Henry David Thoreau

We ought to be no less persuaded that the propitious smiles of heaven can never be expected on a nation that disregards the eternal rules of order and right that heaven itself has ordained.

—George Washington

HELL

A man has to squeeze past the cross to get into hell.

—Richard C. Halverson

The safest road to hell is the gradual one—the gentle slope, soft underfoot, without sudden turnings, without milestones, without signposts.

—C. S. Lewis

Let me remind you that God does not send anyone to hell. He permits the soul a choice . . . and if a human being has chosen to gratify the lusts of the flesh rather than the longings of the spirit . . . that soul may be left with that choice.

—Peter Marshall

The proof of how real Jesus knew hell to be is that He came to earth to save us from it.

—Peter Marshall

HELP

It is one of the most beautiful compensations of this life that no man can sincerely try to help another without helping himself.

—Ralph Waldo Emerson

All the other pleasures of life seem to wear out, but the pleasure of helping others in distress never does.

—Julius Rosenwald

HEREDITY
(See also Ancestors, Inheritance)

Heredity: the traits that a disobedient child gets from the other parent.

—Luther Burbank

Heredity is an omnibus in which all our ancestors ride, and every now and then one of them puts his head out and embarrasses us.

—Oliver Wendell Holmes

Insanity is hereditary; you can get it from your children.

—Sam Levenson

Parents of bright children are always great believers in heredity.

—Pat Williams and Ken Hussar

Nearly every man is a firm believer in heredity until his son makes a fool of himself.

—Anonymous

Parenting is hereditary. If your parents didn't have any children, you're not likely to have any either.

—Anonymous

HERESY

The real heretic is not the atheist or agnostic (who are often decent people) but those who murmur "it doesn't matter what you believe, as long as it makes you feel good." This turns religion into a subjective matter, like taste in furnishings, and robs theology of its claim to ultimate truth.

—Sydney J. Harris

The most damnable and pernicious heresy that has ever plagued the mind of man is that somehow he can make himself good enough to deserve to live forever with an all-holy God.

—Martin Luther

HEROISM

The hero is one who kindles a great light in the world, who sets up blazing torches in the dark streets of life for men to see by.

—Felix Adler

Heroism is the dazzling and glorious concentration of courage.

—Henri Frédéric Amiel

True heroism is remarkably sober, very undramatic. It is not the urge to surpass all others at whatever cost, but the urge to serve others at whatever cost.

—Arthur Ashe

The hero is known for achievements, the celebrity for well-knownness. The hero reveals the possibilities of human nature. The celebrity reveals the possibilities of the press and media. Celebrities are people who make news, but heroes are people who make history. Time makes heroes but dissolves celebrities.

—Daniel J. Boorstin

Being positive is part of being a hero—maybe the hardest part, because if you are a hero you're smart enough to know all the reasons why you should be discouraged.

—Michael Dorris

No way has been found for making heroism easy, even for the scholar. Labor, iron labor, is for him. The world was created as an audience for him; the atoms of which it is made are opportunities.

—Ralph Waldo Emerson

It is the surmounting of difficulties that makes heroes.

—Louis Kossuth

It doesn't take a hero to order men into battle. It takes a hero to be one of those men who go into battle.

—H. Norman Schwarzkopf

We can't all be heroes because someone has to sit on the curb and clap as they go by.

—Mark Twain

A hero is one who hangs on one minute longer.

—Anonymous

HESITATION

On the Plains of Hesitation bleach the bones of countless millions who, at the Dawn of Victory, sat down to wait, and waiting—died!

—George W. Cecil

He who hesitates is sometimes saved.

—James Thurber

HISTORY

The history of free men is never really written by chance but by choice—their choice.

—Dwight D. Eisenhower

What experience and history teach is this—that people and governments never have learned anything from history, or acted on principles deduced from it.

—Georg Wilhelm Friedrich Hegel

History is to the nation . . . as memory is to the individual. An individual deprived of memory becomes disoriented and lost, not knowing where he has been or where he is going, so a nation denied a conception of its past will be disabled in dealing with its present and future.

—Arthur M. Schlesinger

History is His story.

—Abram Veradie

HOLINESS

There is no detour to holiness. Jesus came to the Resurrection through the Cross, not around it.

—Leighton Ford

To know Christ is the way to grow in holiness. Ask yourself, in the moment of perplexity or temptation, what would He do if He were here? Nothing else will so surely lead us into the way of holy living.

—George Hodges

Holiness is not the way to Christ, but Christ is the way to holiness.

—Henrietta C. Mears

It is a great deal better to live a holy life than to talk about it.

—Dwight L. Moody

Holiness is not a luxury for the few; it is not just for some people. It is meant for you and for me and for all of us. It is a simple duty, because if we learn to love, we learn to be holy.

—Mother Teresa

The essential part of Christian holiness lies in giving your heart wholly to God.

—John Wesley

HOLY SPIRIT

O Holy Spirit, descend plentifully into my heart. Enlighten the dark corners of this neglected dwelling and scatter there Thy cheerful beams.

—Saint Augustine

When the Spirit prays through us, He trims our praying down to the will of God. . . . The Holy Spirit is both teacher and lesson. We pray, not by the truth He reveals to us, but we pray by the actual presence of the Holy Spirit. He kindles the desire in hearts by His own flame.

—E. M. Bounds

Oh, the rapture mingled with reverential, holy fear—for it is a rapturous, yet divinely fearful thing—to be indwelt by the Holy Ghost, to be a temple of the living God!

—Samuel L. Brengle

God gives you the privilege and the indescribable honor of presenting your bodies to the Holy Spirit, to be His dwelling place on earth. If you have been washed in the blood of the Lamb, then yours is a holy body, washed whiter than snow, and will be accepted by the Spirit when you give it.

—James M. Gray

He who has the Holy Spirit in his heart and the Scripture in his hands has all he needs.

—Alexander Maclaren

One quickly gains a sense from the Bible that wherever the Holy Spirit is found in the lives of people, strange and wonderful things are likely to happen at any moment.

—Gordon McDonald

God commands us to be filled with the Spirit; and if we aren't filled, it's because we're living beneath our privileges.

—Dwight L. Moody

If the church is to rise to its fullest stature in God ... it must rely, not upon its numbers or skills, but upon the power of the Holy Spirit.

—A. J. Moore

I have learned to place myself before God every day as a vessel to be filled with His Holy Spirit.

—Andrew Murray

Being filled with the Spirit is an inside job. If you insist on an outer experience, then you make emotions the king.

—Jack R. Taylor

Know where your strength comes from. It is only the Holy Spirit who can make a message good and fruitful.

—Corrie ten Boom

Though every believer has the Holy Spirit, the Holy Spirit does not have every believer.

—A. W. Tozer

HOME

Where is home? Home is where the heart can laugh without shyness. Home is where the heart's tears can dry at their own pace.

—Vernon G. Baker

A happy home is one in which each spouse grants the possibility that the other may be right, though neither believes it.

—Don Fraser

The most important thing a man can know is that, as he approaches his own door, someone on the other side is listening for the sound of his footsteps.

—Clark Gable

In the homes of America are born the children of America, and from them go out into American life American men and women. They go out with the stamp of these homes upon them, and only as these homes are what they should be, will they be what they should be.

—Josiah G. Holland

Where we love is home—home that our feet may leave, but not our hearts.

—Oliver Wendell Holmes

The first home was made when a woman, cradling in her loving arms a baby, crooned a lullaby.

—Elbert Hubbard

Home is a place you grow up wanting to leave, and grow old wanting to get back to.

—John Ed Pearce

This is the true nature of home—it is the place of peace, the shelter, not only from injury, but from all terror, doubt, and division.

—John Ruskin

Every house where love abides
And friendship is a guest,
Is surely home, and home, sweet home;
For there the heart can rest.

—Henry Van Dyke

The factory that produces the most important product is the home.

—Carol Williams

HONESTY

How desperately difficult it is to be honest with one's self. It is much easier to be honest with other people.

—Edward F. Benson

Make yourself an honest man, and then you may be sure that there is one less rascal in the world.

—Thomas Carlyle

There is no twilight zone of honesty—a thing is right or wrong—it's black or white.

—John F. Dodge

Honesty is the first chapter in the book of wisdom.

—Thomas Jefferson

Honesty isn't any policy at all; it's a state of mind or it isn't honesty.

—Eugene L'Hote

Follow your honest convictions and be strong.

—William Makepeace Thackeray

It isn't the polls or public opinion of the moment that counts. It's right and wrong and leadership. Men with fortitude, honesty, and a belief in the right make epochs in the history of the world.

—Harry S. Truman

A commentary on the times is that the word *honesty* is now preceded by "old-fashioned."

—Larry Wolters

There is no admission charge to the straight and narrow path.

—Anonymous

HONEYMOON

A honeymoon is a short period between dating and debting.

—Ray C. Bandy

The honeymoon is over when he phones that he'll be late for supper—and she has already left a note that it's in the refrigerator.

—Bill Lawrence

A honeymoon is the time between *I do* and *You'd better.*

—Anonymous

HONOR

A man who permits his honor to be taken permits his life to be taken.
—Pietro Aretino

Honor is like a steep island without a shore: one cannot return once one is outside.
—Nicolas Boileau

No amount of ability is of the slightest avail without honor.
—Andrew Carnegie

No person was ever honored for what he received. Honor has been the reward for what he gave.
—Calvin Coolidge

It is more honorable to repair a wrong than to persist in it.
—Thomas Jefferson

He has honor if he holds himself to an ideal of conduct though it is inconvenient, unprofitable, or dangerous to do so.
—Walter Lippman

HOPE

The word *hope* I take for faith; and indeed hope is nothing else but the constancy of faith.
—John Calvin

Hope is the thing with feathers
That perches in the soul.
—Emily Dickinson

The men who build the future are those who know that greater things are yet to come. . . . Their minds are illumined by the blazing sun of hope.
—Melvin J. Evans

Hope is not the conviction that something will turn out well but the certainty that something makes sense, regardless of how it turns out.
—Vaclav Havel

Hope is the best possession. None are completely wretched but those who are without hope.
—William Hazlitt

Everything that is done in the world is done by hope. No husbandman would sow a grain of corn if he hoped not it would grow up and become seed. . . . Or tradesman would set himself to work if he did not hope to reap benefit thereby.
—Martin Luther

There is no medicine like hope, no incentive so great, and no tonic so powerful as expectation of something better tomorrow.
—Orison Swett Marden

Hope does not depend on having a blueprint for the future.
—Rebecca Manley Pippert

Hope is like the sun, which, as we journey toward it, casts the shadow of our burden behind us.
—Samuel Smiles

Our ground of hope is that God does not weary of mankind.
—Ralph W. Sockman

Behind the cloud the starlight lurks,
Through showers the sunbeams fall;
For God, who loveth all His works,
Has left His hope for all.

—John Greenleaf Whittier

HOPELESSNESS

There are no hopeless situations; there
are only people who have grown
hopeless about them.

—William Barclay

HOSPITALITY
(See also Guests)

Let not the emphasis of hospitality lie in
bed and board; but let truth and love and
honor and courtesy flow in all your deeds.

—Ralph Waldo Emerson

There is an emanation from the heart in
genuine hospitality that cannot be
described but is immediately felt, and
puts the stranger at once at his ease.

—Washington Irving

Hospitality should have no other nature
than love.

—Henrietta C. Mears

Hospitality is commended to be
exercised, even toward an enemy, when
he cometh to thine house. The tree does
not withdraw its shadow, even for the
woodcutter.

—Chinese Proverb

It is a sin against hospitality to open
your doors and shut up your
countenance.

—English Proverb

Hospitality is one form of worship.

—Jewish Proverb

Hospitality is the art of making people
want to stay without interfering with
their departure.

—Anonymous

HOSPITALS

A hospital bed is a parked taxi with the
meter running.

—Groucho Marx

A hospital should also have a recovery
room adjoining the cashier's office.

—Francis O'Walsh

HUMILITY

It is no great thing to be humble when
you are brought low; but to be humble
when you are praised is a great and rare
attainment.

—Saint Bernard of Clairvaux

Humility is not an ideal, it is the
unconscious result of the life being
rightly related to God.

—Oswald Chambers

Jesus Christ presented humility as a
description of what we shall be uncon-
sciously when we have become rightly
related to God and are rightly centered
in Jesus Christ.

—Oswald Chambers

He who receives a good turn should
never forget it; he who does a good turn
should never remember it.

—Pierre Charron

Humility is the root, mother, nurse, foundation, and bond of all virtue.
—Saint John Chrysostom

There is small chance of truth at the goal where there is not a child-like humility at the starting post.
—Samuel Taylor Coleridge

Humility is the hallmark of wisdom.
—Jeremy Collier

Humility is the solid foundation of all the virtues.
—Confucius

Nothing sets a person so much out of the Devil's reach as humility.
—Jonathan Edwards

True humility is not an abject, groveling, self-despising spirit; it is but a right estimate of ourselves as God sees us.
—Tryon Edwards

Humility must always be the portion of any man who receives acclaim earned in the blood of his followers and the sacrifices of his friends.
—Dwight D. Eisenhower

Without humility, we keep all our defects; and they are only crusted over by pride, which conceals them from others, and often from ourselves.
—François de La Rochefoucauld

Humility is the altar upon which God wishes that we should offer Him our sacrifices.
—François de La Rochefoucauld

Humility leads to strength and not to weakness. It is the highest form of self-respect to admit mistakes and to make amends for them.
—John J. McCloy

Humility, that low, sweet root
From which all heavenly virtues shoot.
—Thomas Moore

Do you want to enter what people call "the higher life"? Then go a step lower down.
—Andrew Murray

Humility is like underwear—essential, but indecent if it shows.
—Helen Nielsen

Being humble involves the willingness to be reckoned a failure in everyone's sight but God's.
—Roy M. Pearson

Sense shines with a double luster when it is set in humility. An able yet humble man is a jewel worth a kingdom.
—William Penn

The smaller we are, the more room God has for us.
—Croft M. Pentz

I believe that the first test of a truly great man is his humility. Really great men have a curious feeling that the greatness is not in them but through them. And they see something divine in every other man and are endlessly, incredibly merciful.
—John Ruskin

Humility is strong, not bold; quiet, not speechless; sure, not arrogant.

—Estelle Smith

The higher a man is in grace, the lower he will be in his own esteem.

—Charles H. Spurgeon

Do not consider yourself to have made any spiritual progress, unless you account yourself the least of all men.

—Thomas à Kempis

Humility, like darkness, reveals the heavenly lights.

—Henry David Thoreau

Humility means two things. One, a capacity for self-criticism.... The second feature is allowing others to shine, affirming others, empowering and enabling others. Those who lack humility are dogmatic and egotistical. That masks a deep sense of insecurity. They feel the success of others is at the expense of their own fame and glory.

—Cornel West

The flower of sweetest smell is shy and lowly.

—William Wordsworth

It is the laden bough that hangs low, and the most fruitful Christian who is the most humble.

—Anonymous

Humility is the acceptance of the place appointed by God, whether it be in the front or in the rear.

—Anonymous

The smaller we are the more room God has.

—Anonymous

HUMOR
(See also Laughter, Wit)

Good humor makes all things tolerable.

—Henry Ward Beecher

A person without a sense of humor is like a wagon without springs—jolted by every pebble in the road.

—Henry Ward Beecher

When humor goes, there goes civilization.

—Erma Bombeck

The great humorist forgets himself in his delighted contemplation of other people.

—Douglas Bush

True humor springs not more from the head than from the heart; it is not contempt, its essence is love; it issues not in laughter, but in still smiles, which lie far deeper.

—Thomas Carlyle

Our heavenly Father has an amazing sense of humor; He will bring across your path the kind of people who manifest to you what you have been to Him.

—Oswald Chambers

For health and the constant enjoyment of life, give me a keen and ever present sense of humor; it is the next best thing to an abiding faith in providence.

—G. B. Cheever

Men will confess to treason, murder, arson, false teeth, or a wig. How many of them will own up to a lack of humor?

—Frank M. Colby

Humor is not a postscript or an incidental afterthought; it is a serious and weighty part of the world's economy. One feels increasingly the height of the faculty in which it arises, the nobility of the things associated with it, and the greatness of the service it renders.

—Oscar W. Firkins

Humor is an affirmation of dignity, a declaration of man's superiority to all that befalls him.

—Romain Gary

A sense of humor is a sense of proportion.

—Kahlil Gibran

Humor involves sentiment and character. Humor is of a genial quality, dwells in the same character with pathos, and is always mingled with sensibility.

—Henry Giles

Humor is the salt of personality. Its presence is an evidence of good nature, of an appreciation of the real values of life, and of the lack of tenseness that characterizes some people. It is the most effective means of easing a difficult situation. Here it is important to differentiate between wit and humor; wit is of the mind, humor is of the heart.

—Charles Gow

There is of course something wrong with a man who is only partly humorous, or is only humorous at times, for humor ought to be a yeast, working through the whole of a man and his bearing.

—Theodor Haecker

Humor is laughing at what you haven't got when you ought to have it.

—Langston Hughes

I have never understood why it should be considered derogatory to the Creator to suppose that He has a sense of humor.

—William Ralph Inge

Good humor is a tonic for mind and body. It is the best antidote for anxiety and depression. It is a business asset. It attracts and keeps friends. It lightens human burdens. It is the direct route to serenity and contentment.

—Grenville Kleiser

Humor simultaneously wounds and heals, indicts and pardons, diminishes and enlarges; it constitutes inner growth at the expense of outer gain, and those who possess and honestly practice it make themselves more, through a willingness to make themselves less.

—Louis Kronenberger

The best definition of humor I know: Humor may be defined as the kindly contemplation of the incongruities of life, and the artistic expression thereof. I think this is the best I know because I wrote it myself.

—Stephen Leacock

A pun is the lowest form of humor—
when you don't think of it first.

—Oscar Levant

One must keep ever present a sense of
humor. It depends entirely on yourself
how much you see or hear or understand. But the sense of humor I have
found of use in every single occasion of
my life.

—Katherine Mansfield

Whence comes this idea that if what we
are doing is fun, it can't be God's will?
The God who made giraffes, a baby's
fingernails, a puppy's tail, a
crooknecked squash, the bobwhite's call,
and a young girl's giggle, has a sense of
humor. Make no mistake about that.

—Catherine Marshall

Think of what would happen to us . . . if
there were no humorists; life would be
one long Congressional Record.

—Thomas L. Masson

The humorist has a good eye for the
humbug; he does not always recognize
the saint.

—W. Somerset Maugham

Good humor is goodness and wisdom
combined.

—Owen Meredith

Humor is perhaps a sense of intellectual
perspective, an awareness that some
things are really important, others not;
and that the two kinds are most oddly
jumbled in everyday affairs.

—Christopher Morley

Humor is an expression, in terms of the
grotesque, of the appalling disparity
between human aspiration and human
performance.

—Malcolm Muggeridge

Humor distorts nothing, and only false
gods are laughed off their earthly pedestals.

—Agnes Repplier

There's no trick to being a humorist
when you have the whole government
working for you.

—Will Rogers

The only thing worth having in an
earthly existence is a sense of humor.

—Lincoln Steffens

God likes a little humor, as evidenced by
the fact that He made the monkey, the
parrot—and some of you people.

—Billy Sunday

Good humor is one of the best articles
of dress one can wear in society.

—William Makepeace Thackeray

Humor is the sense of the absurd, which
is despair refusing to take itself
seriously.

—Arland Ussher

A well-developed sense of humor is the
pole that adds balance to your step as
you walk the tightrope of life.

—William Arthur Ward

Humor, warm and all-embracing as the
sunshine, bathes its objects in a genial
and abiding light.

—Henry B. Whipple

The world likes humor, but it treats it patronizingly. It decorates its serious artists with laurel, and its wags with Brussels sprouts.

—E. B. White

Joy shatters pomposity and pride; it bubbles, is never heavy-handed, and is another name for the best kind of humor.

—Kenneth L. Wilson

HUNGER

They that die by famine die by inches.

—Matthew Henry

It is a lot easier emotionally to handle the fact that millions of people are starving if we don't see them as individuals.

—W. Stanley Mooneyham

I am full-fed and yet I hunger. What means this deeper hunger in my heart?

—Alfred Noyes

Hungry bellies have no ears.

—François Rabelais

No one can worship God or love his neighbor on an empty stomach.

—Woodrow Wilson

HURRY

Christ was never in a hurry. . . . Each day's duties were done as every day brought them, and the rest was left with God.

—Mary Slessor

Though I am always in haste, I am never in a hurry.

—John Wesley

HUSBANDS AND WIVES
(See also Marriage, Men and Women)

My wife and I have a perfect understanding. I don't try to run her life, and I don't try to run mine either.

—Milton Berle

Husbands are awkward things to deal with; even keeping them in hot water will not make them tender.

—Mary Buckley

A smart husband is one who saves all the barbershop gossip until after dinner—so his wife will help him with the dishes.

—Edna May Bush

If you want to be sure you never forget your wife's birthday, just try forgetting it once.

—Aldo Cammarota

An archaeologist is the best husband a woman can have; the older she gets, the more interested he is in her.

—Agatha Christie

Nothing has done so much to bring husbands and wives together as the button-up-the-back dress.

—Harold Coffin

The views expressed by husbands in their homes are not necessarily those of the management.

—John T. Dennis

Husbands and Wives

There's an after-shave lotion for husbands over sixty-five—Old Spouse.
—Shelby Friedman

Husbands are like fires. They go out when unattended.
—Zsa Zsa Gabor

I believe my wife is going to live forever. She has nothing but dresses she wouldn't be caught dead in.
—Bob Goddard

All that a husband or wife really wants is to be pitied a little, praised a little, appreciated a little.
—Oliver Goldsmith

Any housewife will tell you the most difficult meal for her to get is breakfast in bed.
—Howard Haynes

It's a wise wife who knows when to overlook and when to oversee.
—Anna Herbert

The "last word" is the most dangerous of infernal machines, and husband and wife should no more fight to get it than they would struggle for the possession of a lighted bombshell.
—Douglas Jerrold

An extravagance is anything you buy that is of no earthly use to your wife.
—Franklin P. Jones

For many wives, the season to be jolly is between the end of football and the beginning of baseball.
—A. L. Sheppard Jr.

Nothing makes a man and wife feel closer, these days, than a joint tax return.
—Gil Stern

Try praising your wife, even if it frightens her at first.
—Billy Sunday

When I think of how much you have meant to me all these years, it is almost more than I can do sometimes to keep from telling you so.
—Vermont Husband's Compliment

There are two kinds of people at parties—those who want to go home early and those who want to be the last ones in the place. The trouble is that they're usually married to each other.
—Anonymous

Probably a man's most profitable words are those spent praising his wife.
—Anonymous

A perfect wife is one who doesn't expect a perfect husband.
—Anonymous

A woman happy with her husband is better for their children than a hundred books on child welfare.
—Anonymous

A bride should make sacrifices for her husband, but not in the form of burnt offerings.
—Anonymous

Woman to marriage counselor: "The only thing my husband and I have in

common is that we were married on the
same day."

—Anonymous

HYPOCRISY

Lukewarmness toward God is hypocrisy
at its worst. If I truly believe He's
supreme, I must treat Him as such—I
must!

—Roc Bottomly

If we are not heedful of the way the
Spirit of God works in us, we will
become spiritual hypocrites. We see
where other folks are failing, and we
turn our discernment into the gibe of
criticism instead of intercession on
their behalf.

—Oswald Chambers

Hypocrites in the church? Yes, and in the
lodge and at the home. Don't hunt
through the church for a hypocrite. Go
home and look in the mirror. Hypocrites? Yes. See that you make the
number one less.

—Billy Sunday

The person who doesn't go to church
because so many hypocrites attend does
not hesitate to go to other places where
there are just as many hypocrites.

—Anonymous

1

IDEALS

Heads are wisest when they are cool,
and hearts are strongest when they beat
in response to noble ideals.
—Ralph J. Bunche

An idealist is one who, on noticing that a
rose smells better than a cabbage, concludes that it will also make better soup.
—H. L. Mencken

Blessed is he who carries within himself
a God, an ideal, and who obeys it.
—Louis Pasteur

There is a need to create ideals even
when you can't see any route by which
to achieve them, because if there are no
ideals then there can be no hope, and
then one would be completely in the
dark, in a hopeless blind alley.
—Andrei Sakharov

Ideals are like stars: You will not succeed
in touching them with your hands, but
like the seafaring man on the desert of
waters, you choose them as your guides,
and following them, you reach your
destiny.
—Carl Schurz

Nobody grows old by merely living a
number of years; people grow old only
by deserting their ideals.
—Samuel Ullman

IDEAS

A new idea is delicate. It can be killed by
a sneer or a yawn; it can be stabbed to
death by a quip and worried to death by
a frown on the right man's brow.
—Charles Brower

Ideas are the mightiest influence on
earth. One great thought breathed into a
man may regenerate him.
—William Ellery Channing

No idea is so antiquated that it was not
once modern. No idea is so modern that
it will not someday be antiquated.
—Ellen Glasgow

Man's mind stretched by a new idea
never returns to its original dimensions.
—Oliver Wendell Holmes

Many ideas grow better when trans-
planted into another mind than the one
where they sprang up.
—Oliver Wendell Holmes

An idea that is not dangerous is
unworthy of being called an idea at all.
—Elbert Hubbard

Greater than the tread of mighty armies
is an idea whose time has come.
—Victor Hugo

Ideas shape the course of history.
—John Maynard Keynes

An idea isn't responsible for the people who believe in it.

—Don Marquis

Ideas are not limited to territorial borders; they are the common inheritance of all free people.

—Franklin Delano Roosevelt

Getting an idea should be like sitting down on a pin; it should make you jump up and do something.

—E. L. Simpson

Ideas are like rabbits. You get a couple and learn how to handle them, and pretty soon you have a dozen.

—John Steinbeck

Ideas won't keep; something must be done about them.

—Alfred North Whitehead

Many great ideas have been lost because the people who had them could not stand being laughed at.

—Anonymous

Always keep a window open in your mind for new ideas.

—Anonymous

IDLENESS

If you are idle, you are on the way to ruin, and there are few stopping places upon it. It is rather a precipice than a road.

—Henry Ward Beecher

One of the tragedies of life is to have finished a tent and have nothing to do except play in it, with no new tent to begin.

—J. P. Cornette

Do not allow idleness to deceive you; for while you give him today he steals tomorrow from you.

—Alfred Crowquill

Idleness is the key of beggary and the root of all evil.

—Charles H. Spurgeon

IDOLATRY

You don't have to go to heathen lands today to find false gods. America is full of them. Whatever you love more than God is your idol.

—Dwight L. Moody

IGNORANCE

The reason there's so much ignorance is that those who have it are so eager to share it.

—Frank A. Clark

The recipe for perpetual ignorance: Be satisfied with your opinions and content with your knowledge.

—Elbert Hubbard

It is impossible to defeat an ignorant man in argument.

—William G. McAdoo

Everybody is ignorant, only on different subjects.

—Will Rogers

He who is not aware of his ignorance
will be only misled by his knowledge.

—Richard Whatley

Ignorance is not bliss—it is oblivion.

—Philip Wylie

ILLUSIONS

The illusion that times that were are
better than those that are has probably
pervaded all ages.

—Horace Greeley

Don't part with your illusions. When
they are gone you may still exist, but
you have ceased to live.

—Mark Twain

IMAGINATION
(See also Creativity)

Imagination is the highest kite that one
can fly.

—Lauren Bacall

I do not like the phrase "Never cross a
bridge until you come to it." The world
is *owned* by men who cross bridges in
their imaginations miles and miles in
advance of the procession.

—Bruce Barton

Your imagination has much to do with
your life. It pictures beauty, success,
desired results. On the other hand, it
brings into focus ugliness, distress, and
failure. It is for you to decide how you
want your imagination to serve you.

—Philip Conley

Imagination, not invention, is the
supreme master of art, as of life.

—Joseph Conrad

The source of genius is imagination
alone, or what amounts to the same
thing—senses that see what others do
not see, or see it differently.

—Eugene Delacroix

Imagination is greater than knowledge.

—Albert Einstein

Imagination is not a talent of some men
but is the health of every man.

—Ralph Waldo Emerson

One has to have the imagination to
think of something that has never been
seen before, never been heard of before.

—Richard Feynman

To know is nothing at all; to imagine is
everything.

—Anatole France

It is the imagination that makes the
world seem new to us every day. . . . It is
the imagination that wakens the dry
bones of any subject to sing about the
mystery of creation.

—Christopher Fry

He who has learning without imagination has feet but no wings.

—Stanley Goldstein

No man ever made a great discovery
without the exercise of the imagination.

—George Henry Lewes

Man consists of body, mind, and imagination. His body is faulty, his mind untrustworthy, but his imagination has made him remarkable. In some centuries, his imagination has made life on this planet an intense practice of all the lovelier energies.

—John Masefield

If you turn the imagination loose like a hunting dog, it will return with the bird in its mouth.

—William Maxwell

Imagination lit every lamp in this country, produced every article we use, built every church, made every discovery, performed every act of kindness and progress, created more and better things for more people. It is the priceless ingredient for a better day.

—Henry J. Taylor

You cannot depend on your eyes when your imagination is out of focus.

—Mark Twain

If you can imagine it, you can achieve it. If you can dream it, you can become it.

—William Arthur Ward

The seed, or germ, of all successful effort is in a trained imagination. If you can't picture your goal, you won't have the courage to start. Your imagination is working with you or against you every minute of every hour of every week of every year of your life.

—A. B. ZuTavern

IMITATION

Trust yourself. Think for yourself. Act for yourself. Speak for yourself. Be yourself. Imitation is suicide.

—Marva Collins

IMMORTALITY

Immortality is the glorious discovery of Christianity.

—William Ellery Channing

Our Creator would never have made such lovely days, and have given us the deep hearts to enjoy them, unless we were meant to be immortal.

—Nathaniel Hawthorne

I believe in the immortality of the soul because I have within me immortal longings.

—Helen Keller

Immortality is not darkness, for God is light. It is not lonely, for Christ is with you. It is not an unknown country, for Christ is there.

—Charles Kingsley

Surely God would not have created such a being as man . . . to exist only for a day! No, no, man was made for immortality.

—Abraham Lincoln

What we have done for ourselves alone dies with us. What we have done for others and the world remains and is immortal.

—Robert Pine

Immortality is the genius to move
others long after you yourself have
stopped moving.

—Frank Rooney

IMPOSSIBILITY

Impossibility is a word only to be found
in the dictionary of fools.

—Napoleon Bonaparte

The only way of discovering the limits
of the possible is to venture a little way
past them into the impossible.

—Arthur C. Clarke

It is kind of fun to do the impossible.

—Walt Disney

Only he who can see the invisible can do
the impossible.

—Frank L. Gaines

One of the main weaknesses of mankind is the average man's familiarity
with the word *impossible*.

—Napoleon Hill

The Wright brothers flew right through
the smoke screen of impossibility.

—Charles F. Kettering

It is often merely for an excuse that we
say things are impossible.

—François de La Rochefoucauld

No man has ever tested the resources of
God until he tries what is humanly
impossible.

—F. B. Meyer

I have learned to use the word impossible with the greatest of caution.

—Wernher Von Braun

IMPROVEMENT

People never improve unless they look
to some standard or example higher
and better than themselves.

—Tryon Edwards

Don't bother just to be better than your
contemporaries or predecessors. Try to
be better than yourself.

—William Faulkner

There's always room for improvement, you
know—it's the biggest room in the house.

—Louise Heath Leber

INCOME

If you live within your income, you'll be
without many things, the most important of which is worry.

—William Ward Ayer

Our incomes should be like our shoes: if
too small, they will gall and pinch, but if
too large, they will cause us to stumble.

—Charles Caleb Colton

If your income exceeds your outgo, then
your upkeep will be your downfall.

—Anonymous

INDECISION

There is no more miserable human
being than one in whom nothing is
habitual but indecision.

—William James

Indecision is fatal. It is better to make a wrong decision than build up a habit of indecision. If you're wallowing in indecision, you certainly can't act—and action is the basis of success.

—Marie Beynon Ray

Even when you're on the right track, you'll get run over if you just sit there.

—Will Rogers

An indecisive person is like a blind man looking in a dark room for a black cat that isn't there.

—Anonymous

INDEPENDENCE

It is not the greatness of a man's means that makes him independent, so much as the smallness of his wants.

—William Cobbett

Christianity promises to make men free; it never promises to make them independent.

—William Ralph Inge

It's easy to be independent when you've got money. But to be independent when you haven't got a thing—that's the Lord's test.

—Mahalia Jackson

INDIFFERENCE

The worst sin towards our fellow creatures is not to hate them, but to be indifferent to them. That's the essence of inhumanity.

—George Bernard Shaw

INDIVIDUALITY

No task is so humble that it does not offer an outlet for individuality.

—William Feather

Every individual has a place to fill in the world, and is important in some respect, whether he chooses to be so or not.

—Nathaniel Hawthorne

Be thankful not only that you are an individual but also that others are different. The world needs all kinds, but it also needs to use and respect that individuality.

—Donald A. Laird

Remember always that you have not only the right to be an individual, you have an obligation to be one.

—Eleanor Roosevelt

It is said that if Noah's ark had had to be built by a company, they would not have laid the keel yet; and it may be so. What is many men's business is nobody's business. The greatest things are accomplished by individual men.

—Charles H. Spurgeon

INERTIA

All that is necessary to break the spell of inertia and frustration is this: act as if it were impossible to fail.

—Dorothea Brande

Life leaps like a geyser for those who drill through the rock of inertia.

—Alexis Carrel

INFERIORITY

No man who says, "I am as good as you," believes it. He would not say it if he did. . . . The claim to equality is made only by those who feel themselves to be in some way inferior.

—C. S. Lewis

No one can make you feel inferior without your consent.

—Eleanor Roosevelt

INFLUENCE
(See also Example)

Every life is a profession of faith, and exercises an inevitable and silent influence.

—Henri Frédéric Amiel

The humblest individual exerts some influence, either for good or evil, upon others.

—Henry Ward Beecher

Blessed is the influence of one true, loving human soul on another.

—George Eliot

A man's influence works two ways: Positively or negatively—never neutrally! The man who doesn't take a stand for Christ . . . is taking a stand against Him.

—Richard C. Halverson

You cannot antagonize and influence at the same time.

—John Knox

The serene silent beauty of a holy life is the most powerful influence in the world, next to the might of God.

—Blaise Pascal

Influence is like a savings account. The less you use it, the more you've got.

—Andrew Young

INGENUITY

Never tell people how to do things. Tell them what you want them to achieve, and they will surprise you with their ingenuity.

—George S. Patton Jr.

INHERITANCE
(See also Ancestors, Heredity)

We pay for the mistakes of our ancestors, and it seems only fair that they should leave us the money to pay with.

—Don Marquis

Sometimes the poorest man leaves his children the richest inheritance.

—Ruth E. Renkel

INITIATIVE

Initiative is to success what a lighted match is to a candle.

—O. A. Battista

Take the initiative, take it yourself, take the step with your will now, make it impossible to go back. Burn your bridges behind you. . . . Make the thing inevitable.

—Oswald Chambers

How wonderful it is that nobody need wait a single moment before starting to improve the world.

—Anne Frank

INNOVATION

There is a common tendency to cling to old ways and methods. Every innovation has to fight for its life, and every good thing has been condemned in its day and generation.

—Elbert Hubbard

New and stirring things are belittled because, if they are not belittled, the humiliating question arises: Why, then, are you not taking part in them?

—H. G. Wells

INSOMNIA

I used to count sheep, but they made such a racket with their baaing that it kept me awake. Now I count oranges on an imaginary orange tree.

—Gracie Allen

The best cure for insomnia is a Monday morning.

—Sandy Cooley

INSPIRATION

Inspirations never go in for long engagements; they demand immediate marriage to action.

—Brendan Francis

My greatest inspiration is a challenge to attempt the impossible.

—Albert A. Michelson

INSTINCT

Good instincts usually tell you what to do long before your head has figured it out.

—Michael Burke

The operation of instinct is more sure and simple than that of reason.

—Edward Gibbon

INSULTS

Do not desire crosses, unless you have borne well those laid on you; it is an abuse to long after martyrdom while unable to bear an insult patiently.

—Saint Francis de Sales

The man who offers an insult writes it in sand, but for the man who receives it, it's chiseled in bronze.

—Giovanni Guareschi

Insults are the arguments employed by those who are in the wrong.

—Jean Jacques Rousseau

INTEGRITY
(See also Ethics)

To give real service you must add something that cannot be bought or measured with money, and that is sincerity and integrity.

—Donald A. Adams

Let unswerving integrity ever be your watchword.

—Bernard M. Baruch

Integrity has no need of rules.

—Albert Camus

Integrity

Nothing so completely baffles one who is full of trick and duplicity himself, than straightforward and simple integrity in another.

—Charles Caleb Colton

I am for integrity, if only because life is very short and truth is hard to come by.

—Kermit Eby

A great integrity makes us immortal.

—Ralph Waldo Emerson

Integrity is the basis of all true-blue success.

—B. C. Forbes

To let oneself be bound by a duty from the moment you see it approaching is a part of the integrity that alone justifies responsibility.

—Dag Hammarskjöld

Integrity without knowledge is weak and useless, and knowledge without integrity is dangerous and dreadful.

—Samuel Johnson

The integrity of men is to be measured by their conduct, not by their professions.

—Junius

You are already of consequence in the world if you are known as a man of strict integrity. If you can be absolutely relied upon; if when you say a thing is so, it is so; if when you say you will do a thing, you do it; then you carry with you a passport to universal esteem.

—Grenville Kleiser

Integrity is not a conditional word. It doesn't blow in the wind or change with the weather. It is your inner image of yourself, and if you look in there and see a man who won't cheat, then you know he never will.

—John D. MacDonald

Some persons are likable in spite of their unswerving integrity.

—Don Marquis

I would rather be the man who bought the Brooklyn Bridge than the man who sold it.

—Will Rogers

Men should be what they seem.

—William Shakespeare

Better keep yourself clean and bright; you are the window through which you must see the world.

—George Bernard Shaw

Integrity is the first step to true greatness. Men love to praise, but are slow to practice it.

—Charles Simmons

Give us the man of integrity, on whom we know we can thoroughly depend; who will stand firm when others fail; the friend, faithful and true; the adviser, honest and fearless; the adversary, just and chivalrous, such an one is a fragment of the Rock of Ages.

—A. P. Stanley

Integrity gains strength by use.

—John Tillotson

You cannot drive straight on a twisting lane.

—Russian Proverb

If men speak ill of you, live so that no one will believe them.

—Anonymous

Integrity: the virtue of being good without being watched.

—Anonymous

There is no admission charge to the straight and narrow path.

—Anonymous

INTELLIGENCE

I do not feel obliged to believe that the same God who has endowed us with sense, reason, and intellect has intended us to forgo their use.

—Galileo Galilei

One has to distinguish between two forms of intelligence, that of the brain and that of the heart, and I have come to regard the second as being far more important.

—George Gissing

The true test of intelligence is not how much we know how to do, but how we behave when we don't know what to do.

—John Holt

The intelligent man who is proud of his intelligence is like the condemned man who is proud of his large cell.

—Simone Weil

INTOLERANCE
(See also Bigotry, Prejudice)

Intolerance has been the curse of every age and state.

—Samuel Davies

Whoever kindles the flames of intolerance in America is lighting a fire underneath his own home.

—Harold E. Stassen

INVENTION

The march of invention has clothed mankind with powers that a century ago the boldest imagination could not have dreamt.

—Henry George

The wheel was man's greatest invention until he got behind it.

—Ford Jarrell

IRELAND

Solutions to problems in Ireland are never simple. . . . Anyone who isn't confused doesn't really understand the situation.

—Walter Bryan

For the great Gaels of Ireland
Are the men that God made mad,
For all their wars are merry,
And all their songs are sad.

—Gilbert Keith Chesterton

Ireland is a country in which the probable never happens and the impossible always does.

—J. P. Mahaffey

J

JEALOUSY

Jealousy sees things always with magnifying glasses that make little things large.

—Cervantes

Moral indignation is jealousy with a halo.

—H. G. Wells

Jealousy is a horse that the Devil likes to ride.

—Anonymous

JOBS

Whatever your job, it is important if it is what God wants you to do.

—Henry Jacobsen

JOURNALISM

(See also Freedom of the Press, News, Newspapers)

Serious, careful, honest journalism is essential, not because it is a guiding light but because it is a form of honorable behavior, involving the reporter and the reader.

—Martha Gellhorn

Journalism can never be silent: that is its greatest virtue and its greatest fault. It must speak, and speak immediately, while the echoes of wonder, the claims of triumph, and the signs of horror are still in the air.

—Henry Anatole Grunwald

Journalism, like history, is certainly not an exact science.

—John Gunther

Being a journalist is simply wonderful. It is a lifelong license to follow that most basic human trait—curiosity. It is permission to probe and delve into whatever interests you, as thoroughly or as superficially as you like, and then move on. You have a license to ask virtually any human being almost anything. You have an excuse to be a sidewalk superintendent, watching human beings work.

—Robert MacNeil

Journalists do not live by words alone, although sometimes they have to eat them.

—Adlai Stevenson

Journalism's ultimate purpose [is] to inform the reader, to bring him each day a letter from home and never to permit the serving of special interests.

—Arthur Ochs Sulzberger

JOY

Joy is the most infallible sign of the presence of God.

—Leon Bloy

When we speak of joy, we do not speak of something we are after, but of something that will come to us when we are after God and duty.

—Horace Bushnell

A man never knows joy until he gets
rightly related to God.
—Oswald Chambers

Joy is different from happiness, because
happiness depends on what happens.
There are elements in our circumstances we cannot help, joy is independent of them all.
—Oswald Chambers

A man is only joyful when he fulfills the
design of God's creation of him, and
that is a joy that can never be quenched.
—Oswald Chambers

Joy is the great note all through the
Bible. We have the notion of joy that
arises from good spirits or good health,
but the miracle of the joy of God has
nothing to do with a man's life or his
circumstances or the condition he is in.
Jesus does not come to a man and say
"Cheer up." He plants within a man the
miracle of the joy of God's own nature.
—Oswald Chambers

Joy is the sweet voice, joy the luminous
cloud.
—Samuel Taylor Coleridge

There are souls in this world who have
the gift of finding joy everywhere and
of leaving it behind them wherever
they go.
—Frederick W. Faber

Joy is an inward singing that cannot be
silenced by outward negative circumstances. Yes, even when life seemingly is
falling apart.
—Robert D. Foster

Joy shared is joy doubled.
—Johann von Goethe

Joyfulness is the mother of all virtues.
—Johann von Goethe

Real joy comes not from ease or riches
or from the praise of men, but from
doing something worthwhile.
—Wilfred T. Grenfell

Joy untouched by thankfulness is always
suspect.
—Theodor Haecker

Joy is a partnership,
Grief weeps alone;
Many guests had Cana,
Gethsemane had one.
—Frederic Lawrence Knowles

For happiness one needs security, but
joy can spring like a flower even from
the cliffs of despair.
—Anne Morrow Lindbergh

There's joy a-plenty in this world to fill
life's silver cup
If you'll only keep the corners of your
mouth turned up.
—Lulu Linton

Great joys, like griefs, are silent.
—Shackerley Marmion

This is the land of sin and death and
tears . . . but up yonder is unceasing joy.
—Dwight L. Moody

Joy descends gently upon us like the evening dew, and does not patter down like a hailstorm.

—Jean Paul Richter

If life seems full of struggle, it is also full of joy. Trouble is temporary; happiness is eternal.

—Charles M. Sheldon

Joy is the standard that flies on the battlements of the heart when the King is in residence.

—R. Leonard Small

Any man can again have the joy of his first meeting with God if he will go back over the same road.

—Roy L. Smith

Joy seems to me a step beyond happiness—happiness is a sort of atmosphere you can live in sometimes when you're lucky. Joy is a light that fills you with hope and faith and love.

—Adela Rogers St. John

There is sweet joy in feeling that God knows all and notwithstanding loves us still.

—J. Hudson Taylor

Profound joy of the heart is like a magnet that indicates the path of life. One has to follow it, even though one enters into a way full of difficulties.

—Mother Teresa

There is more joy in Jesus in twenty-four hours than there is in the world in 365 days. I have tried them both.

—R. A. Torrey

Grief can take care of itself, but to get the full value of joy, we must have somebody to divide it with.

—Mark Twain

He who takes pains to foster joy accomplishes a work as profitable for humanity as he who builds bridges, pierces tunnels, or cultivates the ground.

—Charles Wagner

Joy is not gush; joy is not jolliness. Joy is just perfect acquiescence in God's will because the soul delights itself in God Himself.

—Hammer William Webb-Peploe

Joy wholly from without is false, precarious, and short. Joy from within is like smelling the rose on the tree; it is more sweet, and fair, and lasting.

—Edward Young

One joy dispels a hundred cares.

—Oriental Proverb

Open the door, let in the air;
The winds are sweet and the flowers are
  fair.
Joy is abroad in the world today;
If our door is wide, it may come this
  way.

—Anonymous

JUDGMENT

You may juggle human laws, you may fool with human courts, but there is a judgment to come, and from it there is no appeal.

—Orin Philip Gifford

There is no fear of judgment for the man who judges himself according to the Word of God.

—Howard G. Hendricks

If you judge people, you have no time to love them.

—Mother Teresa

JUSTICE
(See also God's Justice)

Justice is that virtue that assigns to every man his due.

—Saint Augustine

Ethics and equity and the principles of justice do not change with the calendar.

—David Lawrence

Justice without strength is powerless, strength without justice is tyrannical. . . . Therefore, unable to make what is just strong, we have made what is strong just.

—Blaise Pascal

Justice will be achieved only when those who are not injured feel as indignant as those who are.

—Plato

Only love can transform calculating justice into creative justice. Love makes justice just. Justice without love is always injustice.

—Paul Tillich

We cannot be just if we are not kind-hearted.

—Marquis de Vauvenargues

KINDNESS

Kindness, a language that the dumb can speak and the deaf can understand.

—Christian Bovée

Without kindness there can be no true joy.

—Thomas Carlyle

Kindness makes a fellow feel good whether it's being done to him or by him.

—Frank A. Clark

A little kindness from person to person is better than a vast love for all human-kind.

—Richard Dehmel

I wonder why it is that we are not all kinder to each other than we are. How much the world needs it! How easily it is done!

—Henry Drummond

How beautiful a day can be when kindness touches it.

—George Elliston

You can never do a kindness too soon for you never know how soon it will be too late.

—Ralph Waldo Emerson

One of the most difficult things to give away is kindness—it is usually returned.

—Cort R. Flint

Kindness is the golden chain by which society is bound together.

—Johann von Goethe

Let me be a little kinder,
Let me be a little blinder
To the faults of those about me,
Let me praise a little more.

—John Grey

A kind heart is a fountain of gladness, making everything in its vicinity freshen into smiles.

—Washington Irving

A part of kindness consists in loving people more than they deserve.

—Joseph Joubert

Neither genius, fame, nor love show the greatness of the soul. Only kindness can do that.

—Jean Baptiste Henri Lacordaire

Kindness in us is the honey that blunts the sting of unkindness in another.

—Walter Savage Landor

He who has conferred a kindness should be silent; he who has received one should speak of it.

—Seneca

Kindness is never wasted. If it has no effect on the recipient, at least it benefits the bestower.

—S. H. Simmons

Kindness is more than deeds. It is an attitude, an expression, a look, a touch. It is anything that lifts another person.
—C. Neil Strait

Kind words can be short and easy to speak, but their echoes are truly endless.
—Mother Teresa

Kindness is a language that the deaf can hear and the blind can read.
—Mark Twain

Write kindness in marble, and write injuries in the dust.
—Persian Proverb

Don't expect to enjoy life if you keep your milk of human kindness all bottled up.
—Anonymous

Kindness has converted more sinners than zeal, eloquence, and learning.
—Anonymous

KISSING

A kiss is a course of procedure, cunningly devised, for the mutual stoppage of speech at a moment when words are superfluous.
—Oliver Herford

People who throw kisses are hopelessly lazy.
—Bob Hope

Kissing don't last: cookery do!
—George Meredith

High heels were invented by a woman who had been kissed on the forehead.
—Christopher Morley

Kissing is the glory of the human species.
—Tom Robbins

Bussing was a lot more popular when it meant kissing instead of hauling the kids around.
—Bill Vaughan

Kissing is a means of getting two people so close together that they can't see anything wrong with each other.
—Gene Yasenak

KNOWLEDGE

Any kind of knowledge gives a certain amount of power. A knowledge of details has served in many a crisis. A knowledge of details has often caught an error before it becomes a catastrophe.
—Aimee Buchanan

We owe almost all our knowledge not to those who have agreed, but to those who have differed.
—Charles Caleb Colton

Acquire new knowledge whilst thinking over the old, and you may become a teacher of others.
—Confucius

Knowledge is the eye of desire and can become the pilot of the soul.
—Will Durant

Knowledge

If you have knowledge, let others light their candles at it.

—Margaret Fuller

One half of knowing what you want is knowing what you must give up before you get it.

—Sidney Howard

Knowledge is the distilled essence of our intuitions, corroborated by experience.

—Elbert Hubbard

All knowledge is of itself of some value. There is nothing so minute or inconsiderable that I would not rather know it than not.

—Samuel Johnson

The love of anything is the fruit of our knowledge of it, and grows as our knowledge deepens.

—Leonardo da Vinci

The only people who achieve much are those who want knowledge so badly that they seek it while the conditions are still unfavorable. Favorable conditions never come.

—C. S. Lewis

It is much better to know something about everything than to know everything about one thing.

—Blaise Pascal

Knowledge comes by eyes always open and working hands.

—Jeremy Taylor

Knowledge, in truth, is the great sun in the firmament. Life and power are scattered with all its beams.

—Daniel Webster

LABOR

(See also Work)

Labor is life; from the inmost heart of the worker rises his God-given force, the sacred celestial life-essence breathed into him by almighty God.

—Thomas Carlyle

The fruit derived from labor is the sweetest of all pleasures.

—Luc de Clapiers

Labor disgraces no man; unfortunately, you occasionally find men who disgrace labor.

—Ulysses S. Grant

Genius begins great works; labor alone finishes them.

—Joseph Joubert

LANGUAGE

(See also Conversation, Speech)

Language is the apparel in which your thoughts parade before the public. Never clothe them in vulgar or shoddy attire.

—George Crane

Slang is a language that rolls up its sleeves, spits on its hands, and goes to work.

—Carl Sandburg

LAUGHTER

(See also Humor, Wit)

Laughter is a universal bond that draws all men closer.

—Nathan Ausubel

Laugh at yourself and the rest of the world will laugh with you instead of at you.

—O. A. Battista

Laughter is the sensation of feeling good all over and showing it principally in one place.

—Max Beerbohm

Strange, when you come to think of it, that of all the countless folk who have lived … on this planet, no one is known in history or in legend as having died of laughter.

—Max Beerbohm

Laughter has no accent.

—Jim Boren

How much lies in laughter: the cipher-key, wherewith we decipher the whole man.

—Thomas Carlyle

Laughter is regional: a smile extends over the whole face.

—Malcolm de Chazal

Laughter

Please feel free to laugh. Fred Allen said it was bad to suppress laughter. It goes back down and spreads your hips.

—Lloyd Cory

No man ever distinguished himself who could not bear to be laughed at.

—Maria Edgeworth

Laughter is a tranquilizer with no side effects.

—Arnold H. Glasow

Nothing is more significant of men's character than what they laugh at.

—Johann von Goethe

Laughter is the mind's intonation. There are ways of laughing that have the sound of counterfeit coins.

—Edmond de Goncourt

God cannot be solemn, or he would not have blessed man with the incalculable gift of laughter.

—Sydney J. Harris

It better befits a man to laugh at life than to lament over it. Laughter is wholesome. God is not so dull as some people make out. Did He not make the kitten to chase its tail?

—Heinrich Heine

Seriousness shows itself more majestic when laughter leads the way.

—Heinrich Heine

A man isn't poor if he can still laugh.

—Raymond Hitchcock

If you don't learn to laugh at trouble, you won't have anything to laugh at when you grow old.

—Edgar Watson Howe

Laughter is the sun that drives winter from the human face.

—Victor Hugo

Laughter is the jam on the toast of life. It adds flavor, keeps it from being too dry, and makes it easier to swallow.

—Diane Johnson

Joy and laughter are the products of faith. Men can laugh only when they believe.

—Gerald Kennedy

Shared laughter creates a bond of friendship. When people laugh together, they cease to be young and old, master and pupils, worker and driver. They have become a single group of human beings, enjoying their existence.

—W. Grant Lee

With the fearful strain that is on me night and day, if I did not laugh I should die.

—Abraham Lincoln

Everyone likes a man who can enjoy a laugh at his own expense.

—John Lubbock

Laughter brightens the eye, increases the perspiration, expands the chest, forces the poisoned air from the least-used cells, and tends to restore that exquisite poise or balance that we call health.

—Orison Swett Marden

A good laugh is a mighty good thing,
and rather too scarce a good thing: the
more's the pity.

—Herman Melville

Laughter is the best medicine for a long
and happy life. He who laughs—lasts!

—Wilfred A. Peterson

Laughter is God's hand upon a troubled
world.

—Zazu Pitts

It has been wisely said that we cannot
really love anybody at whom we never
laugh.

—Agnes Repplier

No one is more profoundly sad than he
who laughs too much.

—Jean Paul Richter

We are all here for a spell; get all the
good laughs you can.

—Will Rogers

The young man who has not wept is a
savage, and the old man who will not
laugh is a fool.

—George Santayana

It better befits a man to laugh at life
than to lament over it.

—Seneca

I am persuaded that every time a man
smiles, but much more when he laughs;
it adds something to this fragment of
life.

—Laurence Sterne

A woman without a laugh in her is the
greatest bore in existence.

—William Makepeace Thackeray

The human race has only one really
effective weapon and that is laughter.

—Mark Twain

Laugh and the world laughs with you,
Weep and you weep alone;
For the sad old earth must borrow its
     mirth,
But has trouble enough of its own.

—Ella Wheeler Wilcox

Laughter is not at all a bad beginning
for a friendship, and it is far the best
ending for one.

—Oscar Wilde

He who laughs last usually has a tooth
missing.

—Pat Williams and Ken Hussar

Whether laughter is healthful or not
depends on the size of the fellow you're
laughing at.

—Anonymous

The most completely lost of all days is
the one on which we have not laughed.

—Anonymous

When a person can no longer laugh at
himself, it is time for others to laugh at
him.

—Anonymous

Lord, teach us to laugh again but never let us forget we cried.

—Anonymous

LAW

If we could make a great bonfire of the thousands of laws we have in this country, and start all over again with only the Golden Rule and the Ten Commandments, I am sure we would get along much better.

—Coleman Cox

Laws should be like clothes. They should be made to fit the people they are meant to serve.

—Clarence Darrow

We have never stopped sin by passing laws; and in the same way, we are not going to take a great moral ideal and achieve it merely by law.

—Dwight D. Eisenhower

The law . . . dictated by God Himself is, of course, superior in obligation to any other. It is binding over all the globe, in all countries, and at all times. No human laws are of any validity if contrary to this.

—Alexander Hamilton

Law cannot restrain evil; for the freedom of man is such that he can make the keeping of the law the instrument of evil.

—Reinhold Niebuhr

You cannot legislate the human race into heaven.

—Charles Henry Parkhurst

We must reject the idea that every time a law is broken, society is guilty, rather than the lawbreaker. It is time to restore the American precept that each individual is responsible for his actions.

—Ronald Reagan

LAZINESS

Laziness grows on people; it begins in cobwebs and ends in iron chains.

—Thomas Buxton

Laziness travels so slowly that poverty soon overtakes him.

—Benjamin Franklin

Laziness is a secret ingredient that goes into failure. But it's only kept a secret from the person who fails.

—Robert Half

LEADERSHIP
(See also Management)

Leadership should be born out of the understanding of the needs of those who would be affected by it.

—Marian Anderson

The caliber of its leaders is the measure of a movement, for the caliber of men is indicated by the size of the things that challenge them, by the type and size of things that discourage and defeat them, by the caliber of the helpers they choose, by the size and the type of things that either irritate or please them, and by the reach of their shadow—their unconscious influence.

—J. B. Chapman

Leaders are leaders because they are the greater servants. The way up is down. The way to honor our Lord and Savior is to serve. There is always room for one more servant.

—Francis M. Cosgrove Jr.

The first responsibility of a leader is to define reality, the last is to say, "Thank you." In between the two, the leader must become a servant.

—Max De Pree

If leaders are to do what is required of them and to withstand the inherent pressures in their positions, then their character must be anchored in faith.

—Max De Pree

Leadership is much more an art, a belief, a condition of the heart, than a set of things to do. The visible signs of artful leadership are expressed, ultimately, in its practice.

—Max De Pree

I must follow the people. Am I not their leader?

—Benjamin Disraeli

You do not lead by hitting people over the head—that's assault, not leadership.

—Dwight D. Eisenhower

Leadership is the art of getting someone else to do something you want done, because he wants to do it.

—Dwight D. Eisenhower

Though leadership may be hard to define, the one characteristic common to all leaders is the ability to make things happen.

—Ted W. Engstrom

A leader's success as a motivator is directly related to his sincerity in showing concern for his subordinates.

—Ted W. Engstrom

Few men are born leaders. Leadership is achieved by ability, alertness, experience, and keeping posted; by willingness to accept responsibility; a knack for getting along with people; an open mind and a head that stays clear under stress.

—E. F. Girard

The leaders of today both in thought and action are real leaders in that they do not drive the men under them; they encourage them to greater effort.

—Charles Gow

For the visionary leader to require loyalty is prudent. To insist on blind loyalty is cult-like and dangerous.

—Olan Hendrix

If we could spend all our time preaching, teaching, and counseling, we would be happy. These tasks are the chocolate cake of the ministry diet. Unfortunately, a healthy leadership diet also includes lima beans and Brussels sprouts.

—Olan Hendrix

Leadership

The very essence of leadership is that you have to have a vision. It's got to be a vision you articulate clearly and forcefully on every occasion. You can't blow an uncertain trumpet.

—Theodore M. Hesburgh

Leadership is stirring people so they are moved from inside themselves. It is stating goals that excite them and lift their sights. It is setting the personal example, putting enthusiasm into the operation, communicating both ways (listening as well as talking).

—Frederick R. Kappel

The final test of a leader is that he leaves behind in other men the conviction and the will to carry on.

—Walter Lippmann

The art of leading, in operations large or small, is the art of dealing with humanity, of working diligently on behalf of men, of being sympathetic with them, but equally, of insisting that they make a square facing toward their own problems.

—S. L. A. Marshall

If you are in a position of power, and want to lead well, remember—allow those you lead . . . to . . . lead when they feel the need. All will benefit.

—Gordon MacKenzie

Leaders who develop people add. Leaders who develop leaders multiply.

—John C. Maxwell

Leadership is action, not position.

—Donald H. McGannon

I will pay more for the ability of a man to lead others than for any other asset.

—J. P. Morgan

Be willing to make decisions. That's the most important quality of a good leader. Don't fall victim to what I call the ready-aim-aim-aim syndrome. You must be willing to fire.

—T. Boone Pickens

A gifted leader is one who is capable of touching your heart.

—Jacob Samuel Potofsky

Leadership cannot be bought. It cannot be conferred. It cannot be inherited. It knows no divine right, it cannot be passed on by any process of succession. . . . It is acquired only by the personal mastery of each individual aspirant.

—Sterling Sill

Reason and judgment are the qualities of a leader.

—Tacitus

The rewards of godly leadership are so great and the responsibilities of the leader so heavy that no one can afford to take the matter lightly.

—A. W. Tozer

In periods where there is no leadership, society stands still. Progress occurs when courageous, skillful leaders seize the opportunity to change things for the better.

—Harry S. Truman

No training, uninspired by leadership, can produce more than technical competence.

—Lyndall Urwick

If you wish to be a leader you will be frustrated, for very few people wish to be led. If you aim to be a servant you will never be frustrated.

—Frank F. Warren

A follower of Jesus Christ who seeks to lead like Jesus must be willing to be treated like Jesus. Some will follow; others will throw stones.

—C. Gene Wilkes

There was never a world in greater need of men and women who know the way, and can keep ahead and draw others to follow.

—Samuel M. Zwemer

LEARNING
(See also Education, School, Teachers, Teaching, University)

Learning is not attained by chance. It must be sought for with ardor and attended to with diligence.

—Abigail Adams

You can teach a student a lesson for a day; but if you can teach him to learn by creating curiosity, he will continue the learning process as long as he lives.

—Clay P. Bedford

I think there is hope of one's finding a better way if only he can learn not to do things the way people do them who do not succeed.

—J. B. Chapman

I am always ready to learn, although I do not always like being taught.

—Winston Churchill

It is the studying that you do after your school days that really counts. Otherwise you know only that which everyone else knows.

—Henry L. Doherty

Always try to associate yourself closely with those who know more than you, who do better than you, who see more clearly than you. Don't be afraid to reach upward . . . such associations will make you a better person.

—Dwight D. Eisenhower

In my walks, every man I meet is my superior in some way, and in that I learn from him.

—Ralph Waldo Emerson

Tell me, and I forget,
Teach me, and I may remember,
Involve me, and I learn.

—Benjamin Franklin

Essentially, learning means a change in your thinking, a change in your feeling, a change in your behavior. Learning means that change takes place in the mind, in the emotions, and in the will.

—Howard G. Hendricks

The future belongs to the learners—not the knowers.

—Eric Hoffer

We never stop growing until we stop learning, and people who are learning this simple truth will grow old but never get old.

—Charlie "T" Jones

He who has imagination without learning has wings but no feet.

—Joseph Joubert

The important thing is not so much that every child should be taught, as that every child should be given the wish to learn.

—John Lubbock

Learn all your life—from your successes, from your failures. When you hit a spell of trouble, ask, "What is it trying to teach me?"

—Earl Nightingale

The hardest thing in life to learn is which bridge to cross and which to burn.

—David Russell

The illiterate of the future will not be the person who cannot read. It will be the person who does not know how to learn.

—Alvin Toffler

It's what you learn after you know it all that counts.

—John Wooden

LEGACY

We should so live and work in our lifetimes so that what came to us as seed might go to the next generation as blossom, and what came to us as blossom might go to the next generation as fruit.

—Henry Ward Beecher

LEISURE
(See also Relaxation, Rest)

Leisure is time for doing something useful.

—Benjamin Franklin

The advantage of leisure is mainly that we have the power of choosing our work, not certainly that it confers any privilege of idleness.

—John Lubbock

To be able to fill leisure intelligently is the last product of civilization, and at present very few people have reached that level.

—Bertrand Russell

Life lived amidst tension and busyness needs leisure—leisure that re-creates and renews. Leisure should be a time to think now thoughts, not ponder old ills.

—C. Neil Strait

LIBERTY
(See also Freedom)

Liberty will not long survive the total extinction of morals.

—Samuel Adams

If you love wealth better than liberty, the tranquillity of servitude better than the animating contest of freedom, go home from us in peace.

—Samuel Adams

The liberties of our country, the freedom of our civil constitution are worth defending at all hazards; and it is our duty to defend them against all attacks. We have received them as a fair inheritance.

—Samuel Adams

When the spirit of liberty, which now animates our hearts and gives success to our arms, is extinct, our numbers will accelerate our ruin and render us easier victims to tyranny.

—Samuel Adams

Our contest is not only whether we ourselves shall be free, but whether there shall be left to mankind an asylum on earth for civil and religious liberty.

—Samuel Adams

A day, an hour of virtuous liberty, is worth a whole eternity in bondage.

—Joseph Addison

Celebrating Independence Day, I'll reflect on God's gracious gift of liberty in this most favored land. . . . In our gatherings this Independence Day, let's all remember that "Where the Spirit of the Lord is, there is liberty."

—Gary L. Bauer

There is no man who does not love liberty; but the just demands it for all, the unjust only for himself.

—Ludwig Boerne

The framers knew that liberty is a fragile thing, and so should we.

—William Brennan

But what is liberty without wisdom, and without virtue? It is the greatest of all possible evils; for it is folly, vice, and madness, without tuition or restraint.

—Edmund Burke

Liberty is one of the most precious gifts that heaven has bestowed on man.

—Miguel de Cervantes

It is easy to take liberty for granted when you have never had it taken away from you.

—Dick Cheney

Liberty will not descend to a people; a people must raise themselves to liberty; it is a blessing that must be earned before it can be enjoyed.

—Charles Caleb Colton

The condition upon which God has given liberty to man is eternal vigilance.

—John Philpot Curran

Liberty is always dangerous, but it is the safest thing we have.

—Harry Emerson Fosdick

It is a common observation here that our cause is the cause of all mankind, and that we are fighting for their liberty in defending our own.

—Benjamin Franklin

They that give up essential liberty to obtain a little temporary safety deserve neither liberty nor safety.

—Benjamin Franklin

Natural liberty is a gift of the beneficent Creator, to the whole human race, and . . . civil liberty is founded in that, and cannot be wrested from any people without the most manifest violation of justice.

—Alexander Hamilton

Guard with jealous attention the public liberty. Suspect everyone who approaches that jewel. Unfortunately, nothing will preserve it but downright force. Whenever you give up that force, you are ruined.

—Patrick Henry

Eternal vigilance is the price of liberty.

—Thomas Jefferson

The God who gave us life gave us liberty at the same time.

—Thomas Jefferson

Timid men prefer the calm of despotism to the boisterous sea of liberty.

—Thomas Jefferson

The tree of liberty must be watered periodically with the blood of tyrants and patriots alike.

—Thomas Jefferson

Can the liberties of a nation be thought secure when we have removed their only firm basis, a conviction in the minds of the people that these liberties are the gift of God?

—Thomas Jefferson

We on this continent should never forget that men first crossed the Atlantic not to find soil for their plows but to secure liberty for their souls.

—Robert J. McCracken

He who would make his own liberty secure must guard even his enemy from oppression.

—Thomas Paine

A country cannot subsist well without liberty, nor liberty without virtue.

—Jean Jacques Rousseau

I tell you true, liberty is the best of all things; never live beneath the noose of a servile halter.

—William Wallace

God grants liberty only to those who love it and are always ready to guard and defend it. Let our object be our country. And, by the blessing of God, may that country itself become a vast and splendid monument, not of oppression and terror, but of wisdom, of peace and liberty, upon which the world may gaze with admiration forever.

—Daniel Webster

Liberty exists in proportion to wholesome restraint.

—Daniel Webster

The history of liberty is a history of resistance. The history of liberty is a history of limitations of governmental power, not the increase of it.

—Woodrow Wilson

Liberty is from God, liberties from the Devil.

—German Proverb

There is no liberty in wrongdoing. It chains and fetters its victims as surely as effect and cause.

—Anonymous

LIBRARY
(See also Books)

A library is a collection of friends.

—Lyman Abbott

A little library, growing larger every year, is an honorable part of a man's possessions. A library is not a luxury. It is one of the necessities of a full life.

—Henry Ward Beecher

Consider what you have in the smallest chosen library. A company of the wisest and wittiest men that could be picked out of all civil countries, in a thousand years, have set in best order the results of their learning and wisdom.

—Ralph Waldo Emerson

No possession can surpass or even equal a good library.

—J. A. Lankford

Many years ago, when I was just about as complete a failure as one can become, I began to spend a good deal of time in libraries, looking for some answers.... I found all the answers I needed in that golden vein of ore that every library has.

—Og Mandino

LIES

Whenever a child lies, you will always find a severe parent. A lie would have no sense unless the truth were felt to be dangerous.

—Alfred Adler

Nothing is rarer than a solitary lie, for lies breed like toads; you cannot tell one but out it comes with a hundred young ones on its back.

—Washington Allston

Sin has many tools, but a lie is the handle that fits them all.

—Oliver Wendell Holmes

He who permits himself to tell a lie once, finds it much easier to do it a second and third time, till at length it becomes habitual; he tells lies without attending to it, and truth without the world's believing him. This falsehood of the tongue leads to that of the heart, and in time depraves all its good disposition.

—Thomas Jefferson

A lie will easily get you out of a scrape, and yet, strangely and beautifully, rapture possesses you when you have taken the scrape and left out the lie.

—C. E. Montague

He who tells a lie is not sensible to how great a task he undertakes; for he must be forced to invent twenty more to maintain one.

—Alexander Pope

One of the most striking differences between a cat and a lie is that a cat has only nine lives.

—Mark Twain

LIFE

Life is my college. May I graduate well, and earn some honors!

—Louisa May Alcott

Life is short and we never have enough time for gladdening the hearts of those who travel the way with us. Oh, be swift to love! Make haste to be kind.

—Henri Frédéric Amiel

Life is at its noblest and its best when our effort cooperates with God's grace to produce the necessary loveliness.

—William Barclay

The life of every man is a diary in which he means to write one story, and writes another, and his humblest hour is when he compares the volume as it is with what he vowed to make it.

—James M. Barrie

The art of living lies less in eliminating our troubles than in growing with them.

—Bernard M. Baruch

God asks no man whether he will accept life. That is not a choice. You must take it. The only choice is how.

—Henry Ward Beecher

We sleep, but the loom of life never stops; and the pattern that was weaving when the sun went down is weaving when it comes up tomorrow.

—Henry Ward Beecher

Life is not lost by dying; life is lost minute by minute, day by dragging day, in all the thousand small uncaring ways.

—Stephen Vincent Benét

Life is not promised to you. Nor is it promised that it will go the way you want it to, and when you want it to.

—Rosalind Cash

Any idiot can face a crisis—it's the day-to-day living that wears you out.

—Anton Chekhov

Life often presents us with a choice of evils rather than of goods.

—Charles Caleb Colton

To live is so startling, it leaves little time for anything else.

—Emily Dickinson

There are two ways to live your life. One is as though nothing is a miracle. The other is as though everything is a miracle.

—Albert Einstein

Life is uncertain and no amount of control or manipulation or contriving will change it.

—John Eldredge

It is good to appreciate that life is now. Whatever it offers, little or much, life is now—this day—this hour.

—Charles Macomb Flandrau

I want to look at life . . . as if we had just turned a corner and run into it for the first time.

—Christopher Fry

The course of life is unpredictable . . . no one can write his autobiography in advance.

—Abraham Joshua Heschel

The greatest use of life is to spend it for something that will outlast it.

—William James

The trouble with life in the fast lane is that you get to the other end in an awful hurry.

—John Jensen

It isn't necessary to fly over the South Pole, climb the Matterhorn, nor swim the English Channel, to find adventure. Life itself is an adventure. . . . Doing things that lift or steer humanity to higher levels is not only an adventure but also a service to mankind and to God.

—Charlie "T" Jones

Life is either a glorious adventure or it's nothing at all.

—Helen Keller

Life must be understood backward. But . . . it must be lived forward.

—Sören Kierkegaard

Life is a short walk. There is so little time and so much living to achieve.

—John Oliver Killens

It's only when we truly know and understand that we have a limited time on earth—and that we have no way of knowing when our time is up that we begin to live each day to the fullest, as if it was the only one we had.

—Elizabeth Kubler-Ross

I think of life as a good book. The further you get into it, the more it begins to make sense.

—Harold S. Kushner

We must alter our lives in order to alter our hearts, for it is impossible to live one way and pray another.

—William Law

Life is a one-way street. No matter how many detours you take, none of them leads back.

—Isabel Moore

Life is a foreign language. All men mispronounce it.

—Christopher Morley

Fear not that your life shall come to an end, but rather that it shall never have a beginning.

—John Henry Newman

Life is easier than you'd think; all that is necessary is to accept the impossible, do without the indispensable, and bear the intolerable.

—Kathleen Norris

It's not as important to make a living as it is to make a life.

—Hugh Ross

Life is like an onion; you peel it off one layer at a time, and sometimes you weep.

—Carl Sandburg

Life is not the way it's supposed to be. It's the way it is. The way you cope with it is what makes the difference.

—Virginia Satir

I rejoice in life for its own sake. Life is no brief candle for me. It's a sort of splendid torch, which I've got hold of for the moment, and I want to make it burn as brightly as possible before handing it on to future generations.

—George Bernard Shaw

Only one life, 'twill soon be past; only what's done for Christ will last.

—C. T. Studd

May you live all the days of your life.

—Jonathan Swift

The measure of a life, after all, is not its duration, but its donation.

—Corrie ten Boom

The whole secret of life is to be interested in one thing profoundly, and a thousand things well.

—Horace Walpole

Life is all memory except for the one present moment that goes by so quick you can hardly catch it going.

—Tennessee Williams

Life is the greatest bargain; we get it for nothing.

—Yiddish Proverb

Life is full of ups and downs. The trick is to enjoy the ups and have courage during the downs.

—Anonymous

LIGHT

The hero is the one who kindles a great light in the world, who sets up blazing torches in the dark streets of life for men to see by. The saint is the man who walks through the dark paths of the world, himself a light.

—Felix Adler

You don't have to blow out the other fellow's light to let your own shine.

—Bernard M. Baruch

The way at times seems dark, but light will arise, if thou trust in the Lord, and wait patiently for Him.

—Elizabeth T. King

You are the light of the world, but the switch must be turned on.

—Austin Alexander Lewis

We are told to let our light shine, and if it does, we won't need to tell anybody it does. Lighthouses don't fire cannons to call attention to their shining—they just shine.

—Dwight L. Moody

Christ declared that He was the Light of the World. Religion must scatter that Light or fail in the accomplishment of its supreme mission.

—J. C. Penney

There are two kinds of light—the glow that illumines, and the glare that obscures.

—James Thurber

To walk in the light while darkness invades, envelops, and surrounds is to wait on the Lord.

—Howard Thurman

May the father of all mercies scatter light, and not darkness, upon our paths, and make us in all our several vocations useful here, and in His own due time and way everlastingly happy.

—George Washington

There are two ways of spreading light: to be the candle, or the mirror that reflects it.

—Edith Wharton

And I said to the man who stood at the gate of the year, "Give me a light that I may tread safely into the unknown!" And he replied, "Go out into the darkness and put thine hand into the hand of God. That shall be to thee better than light and safer than a known way."

—Anonymous

All the darkness of the world cannot put out the light of one small candle.

—Anonymous

LIMITATIONS

Anyone can walk right through the boundaries we ordinarily believe are our limitations.

—Henry Ford

LISTENING

Most of the successful people I've known are the ones who do more listening than talking.

—Bernard M. Baruch

If you have trouble finding listeners, try talking about somebody besides yourself.

—O. A. Battista

Listening to others is the first part of genuine Christian service.

—Dietrich Bonhoeffer

He who can no longer listen to his brother will soon be no longer listening to God.

—Dietrich Bonhoeffer

A man never listened himself out of a job.

—Calvin Coolidge

The effects of really good listening can be dramatic. These effects include the satisfied customer who will come back, the contented employee who will stay with the company, the manager who has the trust of his staff, and the salesman who tops his quota.

—John L. DiGaetani

The more faithfully you listen to the voice within you, the better you will hear what is sounding outside. And only he who listens can speak.

—Dag Hammarskjöld

I like to listen. I have learned a great deal from listening carefully. Most people never listen.

—Ernest Hemingway

No man would listen to you talk if he didn't know it was his turn next.

—Edgar Watson Howe

A good listener is a silent flatterer.

—Charlie "T" Jones

Then I want to sit and listen and have someone talk, tell me things . . . not to say anything—to listen and listen and be taught.

—Anne Morrow Lindbergh

Listening is an active pursuit that requires skill and practice.

—Stacey Lucas

Formula for handling people: 1) Listen to the other person's story; 2) Listen to the other person's full story; 3) Listen to the other person's full story first.

—George C. Marshall

Sainthood emerges when you can listen to someone's tale of woe and not respond with a description of your own.

—Andrew V. Mason

One friend, one person who is truly understanding, who takes the trouble to listen to us as we consider our problem, can change our whole outlook on the world.

—Elton Mayo

A good listener is not only popular everywhere, but after a while he knows something.

—Wilson Mizner

Nobody ever got into any trouble listening. That's about the safest thing that one can do in life. If you listen to people and you pay attention to them, then you're bound to learn.

—James O'Toole

Almost all employees, if they see that they will be listened to, and they have adequate information, will be able to find ways to improve their own performance and the performance of their small work group.

—James O'Toole

Know how to listen, and you will profit even from those who talk badly.

—Plutarch

The road to the heart is the ear.

—Voltaire

The one who listens is the one who understands.

—African Proverb

Listen, or thy tongue will keep thee deaf.
—Native American Proverb

There's no one as deaf as he who will not listen.
—Yiddish Proverb

LONELINESS

It is loneliness that makes the loudest noise. This is as true of men as of dogs.
—Eric Hoffer

We are born helpless. As soon as we are fully conscious we discover loneliness. We need others physically, emotionally, intellectually; we need them if we are to know anything, even ourselves.
—C. S. Lewis

People are lonely because they build walls instead of bridges.
—Joseph Fort Newton

LORD
(See also Christ)

If Christ is not Lord of all, he is not Lord at all.
—Anonymous

LOVE
(See also God's Love)

Love never asks how much must I do, but how much can I do.
—Frederick A. Agar

What does love look like? It has the hands to help others. It has the feet to hasten to the poor and needy. It has eyes to see misery and want. It has the ears to hear the sighs and sorrows of men. That is what love looks like.
—Saint Augustine

Real love stories never have endings.
—Richard Bach

What the world really needs is more love and less paperwork.
—Pearl Bailey

Young love is a flame; very pretty, often very hot and fierce, but still only light and flickering. The love of the older and disciplined heart is as coals, deep-burning, unquenchable.
—Henry Ward Beecher

True love is night jasmine, a diamond in darkness, the heartbeat no cardiologist has ever heard. It is the most common of miracles, fashioned of fleecy clouds—a handful of stars tossed into the night sky.
—Jim Bishop

True love never nags; it trusts. Love does not have to be tethered, either in time or in eternity.
—Anna Robertson Brown

Love does not die easily. It is a living thing. It thrives in the face of all life's hazards, save one—neglect.
—James D. Bryden

Love cannot be forced, love cannot be coaxed and teased. It comes out of heaven, unasked and unsought.
—Pearl Buck

It is astonishing how little one feels poverty when one loves.

—John Bulwer

Love sacrifices all things to bless the thing it loves.

—Edward G. Bulwer-Lytton

We ought to love our Maker for His own sake, without either hope of good or fear of pain.

—Miguel de Cervantes

In our life there is a single color, as on an artist's palette, which provides the meaning of life and art. It is the color of love.

—Marc Chagall

There are more people who wish to be loved than there are willing to love.

—Sebastien R. N. Chamfort

Loving means to love that which is unlovable—or it is no virtue at all.

—Gilbert Keith Chesterton

You can't put a price tag on love, but you can on all its accessories.

—Melanie Clark

Love has a thousand varied notes to move the human heart.

—George Crabbe

Love is a fire. But whether it's going to warm your hearth or burn down your house, you can never tell.

—Joan Crawford

Passion may be blind; but to say that love is, is a libel and a lie. Nothing is more sharp-sighted or sensitive than true love, in discerning, as by an instinct, the feelings of another.

—William Henry Davis

Real love is the universal language—understood by all. You may have real accomplishment or give your body to be burned; but, if love is lacking, all this will profit you and the cause of Christ nothing.

—Henry Drummond

We don't believe in rheumatism and true love until the first attack.

—Marie von Ebner-Eschenbach

To love somebody is not just a strong feeling—it is a decision, it is a judgment, it is a promise. If love were only a feeling, there would be no basis for the promise to love each other forever.

—Erich Fromm

This is the true measure of love: when we believe that we alone can love, that no one could ever have loved so before us, and that no one will ever love in the same way after us.

—Johann von Goethe

Love is not blind—it sees more, not less. But because it sees more, it is willing to see less.

—Julius Gordon

When one loves somebody, everything is clear—where to go, what to do—it all takes care of itself and one doesn't have to ask anybody about anything.

—Maxim Gorky

The story of a love is not important—
what is important is that one is capable
of love. It is perhaps the only glimpse we
are permitted of eternity.

—Helen Hayes

We too often love things and use people
when we should be using things and
loving people.

—Revel Howe

Love dies when it is monopolized—it
grows by giving.

—Elbert Hubbard

Love is never lost. If not reciprocated it
will flow back and soften and purify the
heart.

—Washington Irving

Love and time—those are the only two
things in all the world and in all of life
that cannot be bought, only spent.

—Gary Jennings

Love doesn't make the world go 'round.
Love is what makes the ride worthwhile.

—Franklin P. Jones

If we spend our lives in loving, we have
no leisure to complain, or to feel
unhappiness.

—Joseph Joubert

Engrave this upon thy heart: There isn't
anyone you couldn't love once you've
heard their story.

—Mary Lou Kownacki

Love doesn't just sit there, like a stone; it
has to be made, like bread, remade all
the time, made new.

—Ursula K. LeGuin

Love at first sight is easy to understand.
It's when two people have been looking
at each other for years that it becomes a
miracle.

—Sam Levenson

Love endures only when the lovers love
many things together and not merely
each other.

—Walter Lippmann

It is difficult to know at what moment
love begins; it is less difficult to know it
has begun.

—Henry Wadsworth Longfellow

Love gives itself, and is not bought.

—Henry Wadsworth Longfellow

They who love are but one step from
heaven.

—James Russell Lowell

Love is an image of God, and not a
lifeless image, but the living essence of
the divine nature, which beams full of
all goodness.

—Martin Luther

Blessed is the season that engages the
whole world in a conspiracy of love.

—Hamilton Wright Mabie

Love is proud of itself. It leaks out of us
even with the tightest security.

—Merrit Malloy

The most of us want very much to be loved. Perhaps we are not concerned enough about loving.

—Erwin McDonald

In loving, you lean on someone to hold them up.

—Rod McKuen

God is the source of love; Christ is the proof of love; service is the expression of love; boldness is the outcome of love.

—Henrietta C. Mears

Love talked about can be easily turned aside, but love demonstrated is irresistible.

—W. Stanley Mooneyham

Love is not measured by how many times you touch each other but by how many times you reach each other.

—Cathy Morancy

Absence in love is like water upon fire; a little quickens, but much extinguishes it.

—Hannah More

Love never reasons, but profusely gives—gives, like a thoughtless prodigal, its all, and trembles then lest it has done too little.

—Hannah More

Age doesn't protect you from love. But love, to some extent, protects you from age.

—Jeanne Moreau

There is no surprise more magical than the surprise of being loved. It is God's finger on man's shoulder.

—Charles Morgan

Love's reign is eternal,
The heart is his throne,
And he has all seasons
Of life for his own.

—George P. Morris

Anybody can be a heart specialist. The only requirement is loving somebody.

—Angie Papadakis

Love is like quicksilver in the hand. Leave the fingers open, and it stays. Clutch it, and it darts away.

—Dorothy Parker

Love is the fountain from which all goodness flows.

—Croft M. Pentz

We love those who know the worst of us and don't turn their faces away.

—Walker Percy

Love is the soy sauce on the chop suey of life.

—Wally Phillips

Love, recognizing germs of loveliness in the hateful, gradually warms it into life, and makes it lovely.

—Charles S. Pierce

Those who love deeply never grow old; they may die of old age, but they die young.

—Arthur Wing Pinero

Love does not consist in gazing at each other but in looking outward together in the same direction.

—Antoine de Saint-Exupéry

Love is a spendthrift, leaves its arithmetic at home, is always in the red.

—Paul E. Scherer

May you have the two greatest gifts of all . . . someone to love and someone who loves you.

—John Sinor

Nothing in love can be premeditated; it is as a power divine, but thinks and feels within us, unswathed by our control.

—Mme. Anne Louise de Staël

Knowledge is gained by learning; trust by doubt; skill by practice; and love by love.

—Thomas Szasz

Love is a fruit in season at all times, and within the reach of every hand.

—Mother Teresa

I have found the paradox that if I love until it hurts, then there is no hurt, but only more love.

—Mother Teresa

Love is what you've been through with somebody.

—James Thurber

I think that love is the only spiritual power that can overcome the self-centeredness that is inherent in being

alive. Love is the thing that makes life possible or, indeed, tolerable.

—Arnold Toynbee

The life that goes out in love to all is the life that is full, and rich, and continually expanding in beauty and in power.

—R. W. Trine

I am not one of those who do not believe in love at first sight, but I believe in taking a second look.

—Henry Vincent

To love and be loved is to feel the sun from both sides.

—David Viscott

Riches take wing, comforts vanish, hope withers away, but love stays with us. Love is God.

—Lew Wallace

The sun can break through the darkest cloud; love can brighten the gloomiest day.

—William Arthur Ward

People who are sensible about love are incapable of it.

—Douglas Yates

Love quickens all senses but the common.

—Anonymous

Love is the answer, no matter what the question.

—Anonymous

LOYALTY

I'm loyal to a fault. I've got a great many faults and I'm loyal to every one of them.

—Steve Allen

Christian service is not our work; loyalty to Jesus is our work.

—Oswald Chambers

The idea is not that we do work for God, but that we are so loyal to Him that He can do His work through us.

—Oswald Chambers

We are all in the same boat in a stormy sea, and we owe each other a terrible loyalty.

—Gilbert Keith Chesterton

Loyalty means nothing, unless it has at its heart the absolute principle of sacrifice.

—Woodrow Wilson

Loyalty is faithfulness, and effort, and enthusiasm. It is common decency plus common sense.

—Anonymous

LUCK

I believe in luck. How else can you explain the success of those you dislike?

—Jean Cocteau

The man who attracts luck carries with him the magnet of preparation.

—Clifton Fadiman

Luck is an accident that happens to the competent.

—Albert M. Greenfield

Luck is a word people use when they have no other plan.

—Joyce Hifler

Luck is the residue of design.

—Branch Rickey

Depend on the rabbit's foot if you will, but remember, it didn't work for the rabbit.

—R. E. Shay

Luck generally comes to those who look after it; and my notion is that it taps, once in a lifetime, at everybody's door, but if industry does not open it luck goes away.

—Charles H. Spurgeon

I had phenomenal luck with my garden this year—not a thing came up.

—Bill Yates

LUXURIES

Luxuries are what other people buy.

—David White

M

MAGNIFY

God does not prolong the lives of His people that they may pamper themselves with meat and drink, sleep as much as they please, and enjoy every temporal blessing, but to magnify Him.
—John Calvin

MAN

Whatever else is or is not true, this one thing is certain—man is not what he was meant to be.
—Gilbert Keith Chesterton

I believe that man will not merely endure; he will prevail. He is immortal, not because he alone among creatures has an inexhaustible voice, but because he has a soul, a spirit capable of compassion and sacrifice and endurance.
—William Faulkner

Man is the only animal that laughs and weeps; for he is the only animal that is struck by the difference between what things are and what they ought to be.
—William Hazlitt

To say that man is made up of certain chemical elements is a satisfactory description only for those who intend to use him as a fertilizer.
—Herbert J. Muller

God tells man who he is. God tells us that He created man in His image. So man is something wonderful.
—Francis Schaeffer

Man is the only animal that blushes— or needs to.
—Mark Twain

MANAGEMENT

I was so busy doing things I should have delegated, I didn't have time to manage.
—Charles Percy

Good management consists in showing average people how to do the work of superior people.
—John D. Rockefeller

MARRIAGE
(See also Husbands and Wives, Men and Women)

In every marriage more than a week old, there are grounds for divorce. The trick is to find, and continue to find, grounds for marriage.
—Robert Anderson

Marrying for love may be a bit risky, but it is so honest that God can't help but smile on it.
—Josh Billings

The great thing about marriage is that it enables one to be alone without feeling loneliness.

—Gerald Brenan

The particular charm of marriage is the duologue, the permanent conversation between two people who talk over everything and everyone.

—Cyril Connolly

The whole thing about matrimony is this: We fall in love with a personality, but we must live with a character.

—Peter De Vries

The goal in marriage is not to think alike, but to think together.

—Robert C. Dodds

When a marriage works, nothing on earth can take its place.

—Helen Gahagan Douglas

A sound marriage is not based on complete frankness; it is based on a sensible reticence.

—Morris L. Ernst

Getting married is easy. Staying married is more difficult. Staying happily married for a lifetime should rank among the fine arts.

—Roberta Flack

In marriage, being the right person is as important as finding the right person.

—Wilbert Donald Gough

Even if marriages are made in heaven, man has to be responsible for the maintenance.

—John Graham

Almost no one is foolish enough to imagine that he automatically deserves great success in any field of activity; yet almost everyone believes that he automatically deserves success in marriage.

—Sydney J. Harris

The marriages we regard as the happiest are those in which each of the partners believes that he or she got the best of it.

—Sydney J. Harris

The critical period in matrimony is breakfast-time.

—Alan Patrick Herbert

Whoever thinks marriage is a fifty-fifty proposition doesn't know the half of it.

—Franklin P. Jones

Marrying a man is like buying something you've been admiring for a long time in a shop window. You may love it when you get it home, but it doesn't always go with everything in the house.

—Jean Kerr

More marriages might survive if the partners realized that sometimes the better comes after the worse.

—Doug Larson

Marrying in the hope of avoiding conflict and loneliness is like jumping into a lake to avoid getting wet.

—Michael Levine

Marriage should, I think, always be a little bit hard and new and strange. It should be breaking your shell and going into another world, and a bigger one.
—Anne Morrow Lindbergh

There is no more lovely, friendly, and charming relationship, communion, or company than a good marriage.
—Martin Luther

Married life teaches one invaluable lesson: to think of things far enough ahead not to say them.
—Jefferson Machamer

In married conversation, as in surgery, the knife must be used with care.
—André Maurois

In a successful marriage, there is no such thing as one's way. There is only the way of both, only the bumpy, dusty, difficult, but always mutual path.
—Phyllis McGinley

A successful marriage requires falling in love many times, always with the same person.
—Mignon McLaughlin

Marriage is like vitamins: we supplement each other's daily requirements.
—Kathy Mohnke

Marriage should be a duet—when one sings, the other claps.
—Joe Murray

You don't marry one person; you marry three—the person you think they are, the person they are, and the person they are going to become as the result of being married to you.
—Richard Needham

The great secret of successful marriage is to treat all disasters as incidents and none of the incidents as disasters.
—Harold Nicolson

Marriage is an empty box. There is nothing in it. . . . Marriage was never intended to do anything for anybody. People are expected to do something for marriage. . . . Love, romance, consideration, generosity aren't in marriage, they are in people, and people put them into the marriage box.
—J. Allan Peterson

Marriage is like twirling a baton, turning handsprings, or eating with chopsticks. It looks easy until you try it.
—Helen Rowland

A good marriage is like an incredible retirement fund. You put everything you have into it during your productive life, and over the years it turns from silver to gold to platinum.
—Willard Scott

Chains do not hold a marriage together. It is threads, hundreds of tiny threads, that sew people together through the years.
—Simone Signoret

The most difficult years of marriage are those following the wedding.
—Gary Smalley

Marriage . . . resembles a pair of shears, so joined that they cannot be separated, often moving in opposite directions, yet always punishing anyone who comes between them.

—Sydney Smith

Story writers say that love is concerned only with young people, and the excitement and glamour of romance end at the altar. How blind they are. The best romance is inside marriage; the finest love stories come after the wedding, not before.

—Irving Stone

Why does a woman work ten years to change a man, and then complain that he's not the man she married?

—Barbra Streisand

One advantage of marriage is that, when you fall out of love with him or he falls out of love with you, it keeps you together until you fall in again.

—Judith Viorst

One great thing about marriage is the fun of living two at a time. You get not only your own life's journey but an extra ticket through another life as well. Also, you get two points of view for your money.

—Frances Lester Warner

Happiness is being married to your best friend.

—Barbara Weeks

The difference between courtship and marriage is the difference between the pictures in the seed catalog and what comes up.

—James Wharton

Marriage has teeth, and him bite very hot.

—Jamaican Proverb

A marriage seldom goes on the rocks when a couple finds something in common to laugh about. For instance, there's the old wedding pictures.

—Anonymous

Don't over-analyze your marriage; it's like yanking up a fragile indoor plant every twenty minutes to see how its roots are growing.

—Anonymous

A wedding is an event, but marriage is an achievement.

—Anonymous

Marital advice: 1) Keep your eyes wide open before marriage and half shut afterwards; 2) Never speak loudly to each other unless the house is on fire.

—Anonymous

Marriage is a refining process God uses to make us into the kind of person He wants us to be.

—Anonymous

MATERIALISM

Theirs is an endless road, a hopeless maze, who seek for goods before they seek for God.

—Saint Bernard of Clairvaux

Some day people will learn that material things do not bring happiness, that they are of little use in making men and women creative and forceful.

—Charles P. Steinmetz

MEDIA

(See also Freedom of the Press, Journalism, News, Newspapers)

Treat the media as you would any other watchdog. Stay calm. Be friendly. Let them sniff your hand—and never turn your back.

—Zack Burnett

Wooing the press . . . is an exercise roughly akin to picnicking with a tiger. You might enjoy the meal, but the tiger always eats last.

—Maureen Dowd

The press is like the peculiar uncle you keep in the attic—just one of those unfortunate things.

—G. Gordon Liddy

The media are far more powerful than the president in creating public awareness and shaping public opinion, for the simple reason that the media always have the last word.

—Richard M. Nixon

When a reporter sits down at the typewriter, he's nobody's friend.

—Theodore H. White

MEDIOCRITY

I have never met a Christian who sat down and planned to live a mediocre life. But if you keep going in the direction in which you are moving, you may land there.

—Howard G. Hendricks

Only a mediocre person is always at his best.

—W. Somerset Maugham

It isn't evil that's ruining the earth, but mediocrity. The crime is not that Nero played while Rome burned, but that he played badly.

—Ned Rorem

Mediocrity tends to draw downward what is up, but not upward what is down.

—Anonymous

MEDITATION

Prayer is the wing wherewith the soul flies to heaven; and meditation the eye with which we see God.

—Saint Ambrose

Elijah's servant went once, and saw nothing; therefore he was commanded to look seven times. So many of you look lightly on the Scripture and see nothing; meditate often upon it, and there you shall see a light like the light of the sun.

—Joseph Caryl

Take time. Give God time to reveal Himself to you. Give yourself time to be silent and quiet before Him, waiting to receive, through the Spirit, the assurance of His presence with you, His power working in you.

—Andrew Murray

Meditation is the activity of holy thought, consciously performed in the presence of God, under the eye of God, by the help of God, as a means of communion with God.

—J. I. Packer

MEEKNESS

Meekness is not . . . a mere contemplative virtue; it is maintaining peace and patience in the midst of pelting provocations.

—Henry Ward Beecher

Meek endurance and meek obedience, the acceptance of His dealings, of whatever complexion they are and however they may tear and desolate our hearts, without murmuring, without sulking, without rebellion or resistance, is the deepest conception of the meekness that Christ pronounced blessed.

—Alexander Maclaren

Spread abroad the name of Jesus in humility and with a meek heart; show him your feebleness, and he will become your strength.

—Thomas Merton

Meekness is power under control.

—Croft M. Pentz

Some glances of real beauty may be seen in the faces of those who dwell in true meekness.

—Henry David Thoreau

Meekness is the cherish'd bent
Of all the truly great and all the
   innocent.

—William Wordsworth

Meekness is the bridle of anger.

—Proverb

Meekness is not weakness, but strength harnessed for service.

—Anonymous

MEETINGS
(See also Committees, Conferences)

A meeting consists of people talking for hours to produce a result called minutes.

—Milton Berle

Meetings are indispensable when you don't want to do anything.

—John Kenneth Galbraith

It is said that the world is run by those willing to sit until the end of meetings.

—Hugh Park

MEMORIES

God gave us our memories so we might have roses in December.

—James M. Barrie

Everybody needs his memories. They keep the wolf of insignificance from the door.

—Saul Bellow

Recall it as often as you wish, a happy memory never wears out.

—Libbie Fudim

The best things you can give children, next to good habits, are good memories.
—Sydney J. Harris

The good memories are all of stopping and staying awhile. I realize I've always driven too fast through life, carrying in my baggage too much impatience and apprehension, missing too many chances, passing too many good people in the dust.
—Charles Kuralt

Memory is what tells a man that his wife's birthday was yesterday.
—Mario Rocco

Nothing is waste that makes a memory.
—Ned Rorem

Like a bird singing in the rain, let grateful memories survive in time of sorrow.
—Robert Louis Stevenson

Memory is a capricious and arbitrary character. You can never tell what pebble she will pick up from the shore of life to keep among her treasures.
—Henry Van Dyke

MEN AND WOMEN
(See also Husbands and Wives, Marriage, Women)

The ability to have our own way, and at the same time convince others that they are having their own way, is rare among men. Among women it is as common as eyebrows.
—Thomas Bailey Aldrich

A man who really loves a woman doesn't bother trying to understand her.
—O. A. Battista

Men and women chasing each other is what makes the human race.
—Mark Beltaire

A woman's best accessory is a well-dressed man.
—Albert Capraro

Being a woman is a terribly difficult task, since it consists primarily in dealing with men.
—Joseph Conrad

A woman is as old as she looks to a man who likes to look at her.
—Finley Peter Dunne

Charm is a woman's strength, just as strength is a man's charm.
—Havelock Ellis

Man once subscribed to the theory of male superiority—then woman cancelled his subscription.
—Shannon Fife

Women have more imagination than men. They need it to tell us how wonderful we are.
—Arnold H. Glasow

Sometimes I wonder if men and women really suit each other. Perhaps they should live next door and just visit now and then.
—Katharine Hepburn

A woman would no doubt need a great deal of imagination to love a man for his virtue.

—John Oliver Hobbes

After God created the world, he made man and woman. Then, to keep the whole thing from collapsing, he invented humor.

—Guillermo Mordillo

The happiest couples are those who spell *us* with a capital "you."

—Klare Provine

When a woman says, "Ah, I could love you if . . ."—fear not. She already loves you.

—Walter Pulitzer

Those people who have no trouble separating the men from the boys are called women.

—Howard Tamplin

Women still want men who are brawny enough to move a sofa, brave enough to attack a spider, and brilliant enough to put together a do-it-yourself bookcase from the instructions.

—Lois Wyse

MERCY

Moral indignation never led anyone to Christ, but mercy has.

—William Dever

Mercy shown in love and with great expectation can be life transforming. It is the essence of the Father's forgiveness through the person of Jesus. What is our response to this gift of mercy? Is there someone in your life who needs the love of Jesus shown through you by an act of mercy?

—Bob Snyder

Mercy is like the rainbow, which God hath set in the clouds; it never shines after it is night. If we refuse mercy here, we shall have justice in eternity.

—Jeremy Taylor

MIDDLE AGE

Middle age is when the only thing that can lead you down the garden path is a seed catalog.

—Ivern Boyett

If people fought sin as hard as they do middle age, earth would be a moral paradise.

—Hal Boyle

Middle age is when a woman takes her high school annual out of the bookcase and hides it where the children can't find it.

—Jacob M. Braude

Middle age is when your classmates are so gray and wrinkled and bald they don't recognize you.

—Bennett Cerf

The really frightening thing about middle age is the knowledge that you'll grow out of it.

—Doris Day

Middle age is when you still believe
you'll feel better in the morning.

—Bob Hope

I wouldn't mind being called middle-
aged if only I knew a few more one-
hundred-year-old people.

—Dean Martin

I am middle-aged and not ashamed of
it. It is not something you catch, like a
disease. It is not the flu. If a woman has
been filled with life, with joy and love
and tears, then waking up suddenly at
middle-age can be a wonderful
experience.

—Simone Signoret

The year is always portrayed as an old
man or a baby. Like most people, it
never gets any attention when it's
middle-aged.

—Bill Vaughan

In a man's middle years there is scarcely
a part of the body he would hesitate to
turn over to the proper authorities.

—E. E. White

MILLIONAIRES

Millionaires seldom smile.

—Andrew Carnegie

I'm opposed to millionaires, but it
would be dangerous to offer me the
position.

—Mark Twain

MIND
(See also Brains, Thought)

The mind is a wonderful thing. It starts
working the minute you are born and
never stops until you get up to speak in
public.

—John Mason Brown

The more accurately we search into the
human mind, the stronger traces we
everywhere find of the wisdom of Him
who made it.

—Edmund Burke

The empires of the future are the
empires of the mind.

—Winston Churchill

It is not enough to have a good mind.
The main thing is to use it well.

—René Descartes

Minds are like parachutes. They only
function when open.

—Thomas R. Dewar

Whatever the mind can conceive and
believe, the mind can achieve.

—Napoleon Hill

Little minds are interested in the
extraordinary; great minds in the
commonplace.

—Elbert Hubbard

Great minds have purposes; others have
wishes. Little minds are tamed and
subdued by misfortunes, but great
minds rise above them.

—Washington Irving

Where there is an open mind, there will always be a frontier.

—Charles F. Kettering

The mind is always the dupe of the heart.

—François de La Rochefoucauld

A mind, like a home, is furnished by its owner, so if one's life is cold and bare he can blame no one but himself.

—Louis L'Amour

Iron rusts from disuse; stagnant water loses its purity and in cold weather becomes frozen; even so does inaction sap the vigor of the mind.

—Leonardo da Vinci

The mind is its own place, and in itself can make a heaven of hell, a hell of heaven.

—John Milton

The mind is not a vessel to be filled, but a fire to be ignited.

—Plutarch

Our minds are not meant to rust in us unused.

—Fulton J. Sheen

The mind is like a clock that is constantly running down; it has to be wound up daily with good thoughts.

—Fulton J. Sheen

The only man who can't change his mind is a man who hasn't got one.

—Edward Noyes Wescott

MINISTERS

The minister is to be a live man, a real man, a simple man, great in his love, great in his life, great in his work, great in his simplicity, great in his gentleness.

—John Hall

The minister lives behind a "stained glass curtain." The layman has opportunities for evangelism that a minister will never have.

—James I. McCord

Some ministers would make good martyrs; they are so dry they would burn well.

—Charles H. Spurgeon

MIRACLES

In order to be a realist, you must believe in miracles.

—David Ben-Gurion

Miracles happen to those who believe in them.

—Bernard Berenson

There's nothing harder to stop than somebody who wants to believe a miracle.

—Leslie Ford

Difficulty is the very atmosphere of miracle; it is miracle in its first stage. If it is to be a great miracle, the condition is not difficulty, but impossibility.

—S. D. Gordon

When we do the best we can, we never know what miracle is wrought in our lives or in the life of another.

—Helen Keller

A coincidence is a small miracle where God chose to remain anonymous.

—Heidi Quade

You're not a realist unless you believe in miracles.

—Anwar Sadat

To me every hour of the light and dark is a miracle. Every cubic inch of space is a miracle.

—Walt Whitman

MISERY

If you want to be miserable think about yourself, about what you want, what you like, what respect people ought to pay you, and what people think of you.

—Charles Kingsley

If misery loves company, misery has company enough.

—Henry David Thoreau

MISFORTUNE

Misfortune makes of certain souls a vast desert through which rings the voice of God.

—Honoré de Balzac

If all our misfortunes were laid in one common heap whence everyone must take an equal portion, most people would be contented to take their own and depart.

—Socrates

MISSIONS/MISSIONARIES

Many of us cannot reach the mission fields on our feet, but we can reach them on our knees. Solid lasting missionary work is accomplished by prayer, whether offered in China, India, or the United States.

—J. O. Fraser

Christianity works, and if you want to see it most clearly, you must go to mission lands where the contrast between lives touched by Christianity and lives sunk in the depths of heathenism is most evident.

—Floyd E. Hamilton

Every heart with Christ is a missionary, and every heart without Christ is a mission field.

—Dick Hillis

God had only one Son—and He was a missionary.

—David Livingstone

The Spirit of Christ is the spirit of missions, and the nearer we get to Him the more intensely missionary we must become.

—Henry Martyn

If called to be a missionary, don't stoop to be a king.

—Charles H. Spurgeon

Some wish to live within the sound
Of Church or Chapel bell;
I want to run a Rescue Shop,
Within a yard of hell.

—C. T. Studd

MISTAKES

There is nothing final about a mistake except its being taken as final.

—Phyllis Bottome

No man ever became great except through many and great mistakes.

—William E. Gladstone

I've made mistakes all my life. And if there's one thing that's helped me, it's the fact that when I make a mistake, I never stop to talk about it—I just go ahead and make some more.

—Donald A. Laird

Mistakes are part of the dues one pays for a full life.

—Sophia Loren

No matter what mistakes you have made—no matter how you've messed things up—you can still make a new beginning. The person who fully realizes this suffers less from the shock and pain of failure and sooner gets off to a new beginning.

—Norman Vincent Peale

A life spent making mistakes is not only more honorable but more useful than a life spent doing nothing.

—George Bernard Shaw

He who never made a mistake never made a discovery.

—Samuel Smiles

I love to make a mistake. It is my only assurance that I cannot reasonably be expected to assume the responsibility of omniscience.

—Rex Stout

Only those who do nothing make no mistakes.

—Harry S. Truman

Learn from the mistakes of others. You can't live long enough to make them all yourself.

—Martin Vanbee

When you make a mistake, make amends immediately. It's easier to eat crow while it's still warm.

—Anonymous

MODERATION

Moderation is the inseparable companion of wisdom.

—Charles Caleb Colton

Moderation is the silken string running through the pearl chain of all virtues.

—Thomas Fuller

MODESTY

Modesty: the gentle art of enhancing your charm by pretending not to be aware of it.

—Oliver Herford

The Holy Spirit finds modesty so rare that He takes care to record it. Say much of what the Lord has done for you, but say little of what you have done for the Lord. Do not utter a self-glorifying sentence!

—Charles H. Spurgeon

Modesty is that certain feeling that others will discover how wonderful you are.

—Anonymous

MONEY

Money is a guarantee that we may have what we want in the future. Though we need nothing at the moment, it ensures the possibility of satisfying a necessary desire when it arises.

—Aristotle

If money be not thy servant, it will be thy master.

—Francis Bacon

Men no longer attempt to rule by the sword, but they find in money a weapon as sharp and more effective; and having lost none of the old lust for power, they seek to establish over their fellows the despotism of dollars.

—James Gordon Bennett

Money will not purchase character or good government.

—Calvin Coolidge

Make money your God, and it will plague you like the Devil.

—Henry Fielding

If you would know the value of money, go and try to borrow some.

—Benjamin Franklin

Money is a singular thing. It ranks with love as man's greatest source of joy— and with death as his greatest source of anxiety.

—John Kenneth Galbraith

Men make counterfeit money; in many more cases, money makes counterfeit men.

—Sydney J. Harris

Money may be the husk of many things, but not the kernel. It brings you food, but not appetite; medicine, but not health; acquaintances, but not friends; servants, but not faithfulness; days of joy, but not peace or happiness.

—Henrik Ibsen

Get to know two things about a man— how he earns his money and how he spends it—and you have the clue to his character, for you have a searchlight that shows up the inmost recesses of his soul. You know all you need to know about his standards, his motives, his driving desires, and his real religion.

—Robert J. McCracken

That most delicious of all privileges— spending other people's money.

—John Randolph

I have learned that money is not the measure of a man, but it is often the means of finding out how small he is.

—Oswald J. Smith

Money is not required to buy one necessity of the soul.

—Henry David Thoreau

One who thinks that money can do everything is likely to do anything for money.

—Anonymous

I don't lend money because it causes amnesia.

—Anonymous

Money will buy—
A bed but not sleep
Books but not brains
Food but not appetite
Finery but not beauty
A house but not a home
Medicine but not health
Amusements but not happiness
Religion but not salvation.

—Anonymous

Money is an article that may be used as a universal passport to everywhere except heaven, and as a universal provider of everything except happiness.

—Anonymous

MONOTONY

There is no monotony in living to him who walks ... with open and perceptive eyes. The monotony of life, if life is monotonous to you, is in you, not in the world.

—Phillips Brooks

MONUMENTS

A monument only says, "At least I got this far," while a footprint says, "This is where I was when I moved on."

—William Faulkner

Those only deserve a monument who do not need one; that is, who have raised themselves a monument in the minds and memories of men.

—William Hazlitt

MOODS
(See also Attitude)

We have absolutely no right to annoy others by our various moods. Let the prevailing mood be cheerful and serene; keep your other moods to yourself, or better still, get rid of them.

—Anne Gould

MORALITY

Opinions alter, manner changes, creeds rise and fall, but the moral law is written on the tables of eternity.

—Lord Acton

The bloom of human life is morality; whatever else we may possess, health and wealth, power, grace, knowledge, have a value only as they lead up to this, have a meaning only as they make this possible.

—Frederick Adler

Let us be true: this is the highest maxim of art and of life, the secret of eloquence and of virtue, and of all moral authority.

—Henri Frédéric Amiel

The moral life of any people rises or falls with the vitality or decay of its religious life.

—John S. Bonnell

Foundations of morality are like all other foundations; if you dig too much about them the superstructure will come tumbling down.

—Samuel Butler

Morals is not preaching, it is beauty of a rare kind.

—Ernest Dimnet

Morality regulates the acts of man as a private individual; honor, his acts as a public man.

—Esteban Echeverria

The most important human endeavor is striving for morality in our actions. Our inner balance and even our very existence depends on it. Only morality in our actions can give beauty and dignity to our lives.

—Albert Einstein

Nothing that is morally wrong can be politically right.

—William E. Gladstone

One of the greatest single needs in our world today is men and women who manifest a strong moral fiber day to day—whose lives are clean and sharp, with a cutting edge—who are strong with the health of righteousness.

—Richard C. Halverson

Our morality seems to me only a check on the ultimate domination of force, just as our politeness is a check on the impulse of every pig to put his feet in the trough.

—Oliver Wendell Holmes

My ideal man never would think about morality. He naturally would do the

kind, generous, splendid thing. While in all other departments we prefer native gifts to industry (which is also a gift of a less specialized sort), we have a queer notion that in morality industry is better than genius.

—Oliver Wendell Holmes Jr.

If only people would realize that moral principles are like measles [Eustace said]. They have to be caught. And only the people who've got them can pass on the contagion. . . . One doesn't have to catch the infection of goodness, if one doesn't want to. The will is always free.

—Aldous Huxley

The foundation of morality is to have done, once and for all, with lying.

—Thomas H. Huxley

Two things fill the mind with ever new and increasing wonder and awe—the starry heavens above me and the moral law within me.

—Immanuel Kant

Morality is not properly the doctrine of how we may make ourselves happy, but how we may make ourselves worthy of happiness.

—Immanuel Kant

In reality, moral rules are directions for running the human machine. Every moral rule is there to prevent a breakdown, or a strain, or a friction, in running that machine. That is why these rules at first seem to be constantly interfering with our natural inclinations.

—C. S. Lewis

Morality

To give a man full knowledge of true morality, I would send him to no other book than the New Testament.

—John Locke

To restore morality we must first recognize the source from which all morality springs. From our earliest history in 1776, when we were declared to be the United States of America, our forefathers recognized the sovereignty of God.

—Roy Moore

Of all the lessons history teaches this one is plainest: the person who tries to achieve ends through force is always unscrupulous and is always cruel. We should remember this in an age where morality seems to be disappearing and is being replaced by politics.

—Eustace Percy

Though economic science and moral discipline are guided each by its own principles in its own sphere, it is false that the two orders are so distinct and alien that the former in no way depends upon the latter.

—Pope Pius XI

Without civic morality communities perish; without personal morality their survival has no value.

—Bertrand Russell

Morality is not respectability.

—George Bernard Shaw

Morality is moral only when it is voluntary.

—Lincoln Steffens

We must never delude ourselves into thinking that physical power is a substitute for moral power, which is the true sign of national greatness.

—Adlai Stevenson

If your morals make you dreary, depend upon it, they are wrong.

—Robert Louis Stevenson

The readiness to do justly and to love mercy springs from moral attitudes implanted early in life. But the attitudes aren't enough. We need some clues as to what constitutes justice and mercy in a confusing world. Those clues do not issue full-blown from the moral strivings of youth. They ripen slowly and not without cultivation.

—D. Sutten

Aim above morality. Be not simply good; be good for something.

—Henry David Thoreau

Moral education is impossible without the habitual vision of greatness.

—Alfred North Whitehead

I've looked for answers in many ways—religious, political, humanistic, in different places. I have come to believe there is only one response, the moral response. Whatever we do must be measured in moral terms.

—Elie Wiesel

MORNING

(See also Dawn, Sunrise)

The moment when first you wake up in the morning is the most wonderful of the twenty-four hours. No matter how weary or dreary you may feel, you possess the certainty that, during the day that lies before you, absolutely anything can happen.

—Monica Baldwin

The first hour of the morning is the rudder of the day. It is a blessed baptism that gives the first waking thoughts into the bosom of God.

—Henry Ward Beecher

Those who run from God in the morning will scarcely find Him the rest of the day.

—John Bunyan

I have never known an early riser to be compelled to hurry.

—J. B. Chapman

To be seeing the world being made new every morning, as if it were the morning of the first day, and then to make the most of it for the individual soul, as if it were the last day—is the daily curriculum of the mind's desire.

—John H. Finley

The morning is the gate of the day, and should be well-guarded with prayer. The morning is one end of the thread on which the day's actions are strung, and should be well-knotted with devotion. If we felt more the majesty of life, we should be more careful of its mornings.

—Robert D. Foster

I don't ask for the meaning of the song of a bird or the rising of the sun on a misty morning. They are there, and they are beautiful.

—Pete Hamill

Life begins each morning! . . . Each night of life is a wall between today and the past. Each morning is the open door to a new world—new vistas, new aims, new tryings.

—Leigh Mitchell Hodges

Morning is in my heart. . . . The rich spoils of memory are mine. Mine, too, are the precious things of today— books, flowers, pictures, nature, and sport. The best of life is always further on.

—William Mulock

A tender, gentle pink steals silently over the horizon, giving life to the world before it. The clouds are touched with a lacy gold, and the heavens are of speechless beauty.

—Irene Potocki

I have always been delighted at the prospect of a new day, a fresh try, one more start, with perhaps a bit of magic waiting somewhere behind the morning.

—J. B. Priestly

The rose is sweetest washed with morning dew.

—Walter Scott

I know the morning—I am acquainted with it and I love it. I love it fresh and sweet as it is—a daily new creation, breaking forth and calling all that have life and breath and being to a new adoration, new enjoyments, and new gratitude.

—Daniel Webster

Outside the open window
The morning air is all awash with
    angels.

—Richard Purdy Wilbur

MOTHERS

Any mother could perform the jobs of several air-traffic controllers with ease.

—Lisa Alther

Instant availability without continuous presence is probably the best role a mother can play.

—Lotte Bailyn

The God to whom little boys say their prayers has a face very much like their mother's.

—James M. Barrie

The mother's heart is the child's schoolroom.

—Henry Ward Beecher

Anyone who thinks mother love is as soft and golden-eyed as a purring cat should see a cat defending her kittens.

—Pam Brown

A suburban mother's role is to deliver children obstetrically once, and by car forever after.

—Peter De Vries

A mother is not a person to lean on, but a person to make leaning unnecessary.

—Dorothy Canfield Fisher

Men want to improve only the world, but mothers want to improve their whole family. That is a much harder task.

—Harriet Freezer

Only mothers can think of the future, because they give birth to it in their children.

—Maxim Gorky

If I cannot give my children a perfect mother I can at least give them more of the one they've got—and make that one more loving. I will be available. I will take time to listen, time to play, time to be home when they arrive from school, time to counsel and encourage.

—Ruth Bell Graham

Maternal love is a miraculous substance that God multiplies as He divides it.

—Victor Hugo

The memory of my mother and her teachings were ... the only capital I had to start life with, and on that capital I have made my way.

—Andrew Jackson

You never get over being a child, as long as you have a mother to go to.

—Sarah Orne Jewett

Now, as always, the most automated appliance in a household is the mother.

—Beverly Jones

The mother is the most precious possession of the nation, so precious that society advances its highest well-being when it protects the functions of the mother.

—Ellen Key

I remember my mother's prayers and they have always followed me. They have clung to me all my life.

—Abraham Lincoln

No man is poor who has had a godly mother.

—Abraham Lincoln

All that I am or hope to be, I owe to my angel mother.

—Abraham Lincoln

There is no such thing as a *non*-working mother.

—Hester Mundis

Every mother is like Moses. She does not enter the promised land. She prepares a world she will not see.

—Pope Paul VI

No man is really old until his mother stops worrying about him.

—William Ryan

I don't think there are enough devils in hell to take a young person from the arms of a godly mother.

—Billy Sunday

Mother is the name for God on the lips and hearts of little children.

—William Makepeace Thackeray

All that I am I owe to my mother. I attribute all my success in life to the moral, intellectual, and physical education I received from her.

—George Washington

God could not be everywhere, and so He made mothers.

—Jewish Proverb

Automation is a technological process that does all the work while you just sit there. When you were younger, this was called "Mother."

—Anonymous

MOTIVATION

I'm not in the business of making steel. I'm in the business of building men. They make steel.

—Andrew Carnegie

The job of a football coach is to make men do what they don't want to do, in order to achieve what they've always wanted to be.

—Tom Landry

If you want to build a ship, don't drum up the men to gather wood, divide the work, and give orders. Instead, teach them to yearn for the vast and endless sea.

—Antoine de Saint-Exupéry

MOUNTAINS

You never conquer a mountain. You stand on the summit a few moments; then the wind blows your footprints away.

—Arlene Blum

The mountains are fountains of men as well as of rivers, of glaciers, of fertile soil. The great poets, philosophers, prophets, able men whose thoughts and deeds have moved the world, have come down from the mountains—mountain-dwellers who have grown strong there with the forest trees in nature's work-shops.

—John Muir

Climb the mountains and get their good tidings. The winds will blow their own freshness into you, and the storms their energy, while cares drop away from you like the leaves of autumn.

—John Muir

MUSIC

All music is folk music. I ain't never heard no horse sing a song.

—Louis Armstrong

Music washes away from the soul the dust of everyday life.

—Berthold Auerbach

I consider music as a very innocent diversion, and perfectly compatible with the profession of a clergyman.

—Jane Austen

Music is well said to be the speech of angels.

—Thomas Carlyle

Music is the only language in which you cannot say a mean or sarcastic thing.

—John Erskine

After silence, that which comes nearest to expressing the inexpressible is music.

—Aldous Huxley

My heart, which is full to overflowing, has often been solaced and refreshed by music when sick and weary.

—Martin Luther

Music is often called the language of the emotions.

—Charles O'Connell

NATURE

Nature is the armory of genius.... The eye craves the spectacle of the horizon, of mountains, ... the clouds and stars, actual contact with the elements, sympathy with the seasons as they rise and roll.

—Amos Bronson Alcott

In all things of nature, there is something of the marvelous.

—Aristotle

I love to think of nature as an unlimited broadcasting system through which God speaks to us every hour, if we will only tune in.

—George Washington Carver

Nature is too thin a screen; the glory of the omnipresent God bursts through everywhere.

—Ralph Waldo Emerson

How thoughtful of Mother Nature! By the time we reach the sitting around state of life, she endows us with a bigger cushion.

—Francis Gay

Assuredly all nature informs us that man is born for happiness.

—André Gide

Nature is the living, visible garment of God.

—Johann von Goethe

The "amen" of nature is always a flower.

—Oliver Wendell Holmes

Let us permit nature to have her way; she understands her business better than we do.

—Michel de Montaigne

Nature is man's religious book, with lessons for every day.

—Theodore Parker

Nature holds out her hands brimming with gifts, and we buzz about in the shadow of them, heads down, wondering why it is so dark.

—C. M. Skinner

Nature never quite goes along with us. She is somber at weddings, sunny at funerals, and she frowns on ninety-nine out of a hundred picnics.

—Alexander Smith

Go into the woodland if you seek for
    peace of mind,
At this time when nature's mood is
    gentle, quiet and kind ...
When soft winds fan the trembling
    leaves about the cloistered glade,
And paths go winding deep into the
    green and breathless shade.

—Patience Strong

Come forth into the light of things, let nature be your teacher.

—William Wordsworth

NEEDS

The more needs there are, the more God does, for God operates on the basis of need. If God is to do more, there must be more need. Need is the springboard of His doing! He only operates amid need.

—Jack R. Taylor

NEGLECT

The untended garden will soon be overrun with weeds; the heart that fails to cultivate truth and root out error will shortly be a theological wilderness.

—A. W. Tozer

Our faith and our friendships are not shattered by one big act, but by many small neglects.

—J. Gustav White

NEIGHBORS

All the blessings we enjoy are divine deposits, committed to our trust on this condition, that they should be dispensed for the benefit of our neighbors.

—John Calvin

Every man takes care that his neighbor shall not cheat him. But a day comes when he begins to care that he do not cheat his neighbor. Then all goes well.

—Ralph Waldo Emerson

The question is not "Who is my neighbor?" but "Am I a neighbor?" In other words, the burden of proof does not lie with another as to whether or not he is a neighbor in order to qualify for my love. The question is, "Am I a neighbor to any and all, especially to those who are needy?"

—Richard C. Halverson

The spirit of liberty is more than jealousy for your own rights.... The love of liberty cannot be separated from loving your neighbor as yourself.

—Christian Herter

It is easier to love humanity as a whole than to love one's neighbor.

—Eric Hoffer

Borrow trouble for yourself, if that's your nature, but don't lend it to your neighbors.

—Rudyard Kipling

We all have strength to bear the misfortunes of our neighbors.

—François de La Rochefoucauld

It is impossible to be truly converted to God without being thereby converted to our neighbor.

—John R. W. Stott

Love of God is the root, love of our neighbor the fruit of the Tree of Life. Neither can exist without the other, but the one is cause and the other effect.

—William Temple

The love of our neighbor in all its fullness simply means being able to say to him, "What are you going through?"

—Simone Weil

The most amiable man on earth can live at peace with his neighbor only as long as the neighbor chooses.

—Anonymous

NEW YEAR
(See also Resolutions)

The old year dies and we face the new year as though it were an entity, new as a newborn babe.... Yet all our yesterdays are summarized in our now, and all the tomorrows are ours to shape,... and year's end is neither an end nor a beginning but a going on, with all the wisdom that experience can instill in us.

—Hal Borland

Some people have a regular practice of making New Year's resolutions— generally shattering them before January has hidden its cold head out of sight.

—Will Carleton

New Year is not only the oldest and the most universal of festivals; it is also, in a sense, the parent of them all. More than a mere accident of the calendar, it is a triumphant reassertion, from year to year, that life is in the end victorious and that death is swallowed up forever.

—Theodor Gaster

As a new year dawns, we stand before an open door. Looking through its arch, we see all things new. Behind us the door is closing, closing forever,... sealed to everything but our memories.

—E. Paul Hovey

At each New Year it is common to make new resolutions, but in the life of the individual, each day is the beginning of a new year, if he will only make it so. A mere date on the calendar is no more a divider of time than a particular grain of sand divides the desert.

—William G. Jordan

The beauty of human life consists in the fact that, as we review our last New Year's resolutions, we find we have fulfilled one-third of them, left unfilled another third, and can't remember what the other third was.

—Lin Yü-t'ang

Time has no divisions to mark its passage; there is never a thunderstorm to announce the beginning of a new year. It is only we mortals who ring bells and fire off pistols.

—Thomas Mann

What the New Year brings to you will depend a great deal on what you bring to the New Year.

—Vern McLellan

NEWS
(See also Freedom of the Press, Journalism, Media, Newspapers)

News is the first rough draft of history.

—Benjamin Bradlee

News, like substances, ought to be divided into solids, fluids, and gases— and appropriately labeled as such for publication.

—Sydney J. Harris

The news on an ordinary day [is] a strange assembly that swoops down on one's life like cousins from Oslo one has never seen before, will never see again, and who, between planes, thought they would call to say hello.

—Roger Rosenblatt

NEWSPAPERS

(See also Freedom of the Press, Journalism, Media, News)

The morning paper is just as necessary for an American as dew is to the grass.

—Josh Billings

A newspaper is lumber made malleable. It is ink made into words and pictures. It is conceived, born, grows up, and dies of old age in a day.

—Jim Bishop

A newspaper should be the maximum of information, and the minimum of comment.

—Richard Cobden

Were it left to me to decide whether we should have a government without newspapers, or newspapers without a government, I should not hesitate a moment to prefer the latter.

—Thomas Jefferson

Newspapers have two great advantages over television. They can be used by men as barriers against their wives. It is still the only effective screen against the morning features of the loved one and, as such, performs a unique human service. The second advantage is that you can't line a garbage pail with a television set—it's usually the other way around.

—Marya Mannes

NOBILITY

The noblest question in the world is, What good may I do in it?

—Benjamin Franklin

To be good is noble, but to teach others how to be good is nobler—and less trouble.

—Mark Twain

There is nothing noble about being superior to some other man. The true nobility is in being superior to your previous self.

—Hindu Proverb

NOISE

Perhaps it would be a good idea, fantastic as it sounds, to muffle every telephone, stop every motor, and halt all activity for one hour some day just to give people a chance to ponder for a few minutes on what it is all about, why they are living, and what they really want.

—James Truslow Adams

Traditionally, noise is used to ridicule, embarrass, denigrate, and curse, while silence is used for worship, respect, anticipation, and love. Do we hate each other as much as our noise level suggests?

—John Hillaby

He who sleeps in continual noise is wakened by silence.

—William Dean Howells

All noise is waste. So cultivate quietness in your speech, in your thoughts, in your emotions. Speak habitually low. Wait attention and then your low words will be charged with dynamite.

—Elbert Hubbard

The more noise a man or motor makes, the less power there is available.

—W. R. McGeary

He who establishes his argument by noise and command—shows that his reason is weak.

—Michel de Montaigne

We are usually surrounded by so much outer noise that it is hard to truly hear our God when he is speaking to us. We have often become deaf, unable to know when God calls us and unable to understand in which direction he calls us. Thus, our lives have become absurd. . . . When, however, we learn to listen, our lives become obedient.

—Henri H. M. Nouwen

Everybody else is noisier than God.

—Eugene Peterson

The amount of noise that anyone can bear undisturbed stands in inverse proportion to his mental capacity.

—Arthur Schopenhauer

They that govern most make the least noise.

—John Selden

Noise produces nothing. Often a hen who has merely laid an egg cackles as though she has laid an asteroid.

—Mark Twain

Strongest minds
Are often those of whom the noisy world
Hears least.

—William Wordsworth

What grows makes no noise.

—German Proverb

What a terrific din there would be if we made as much noise when things go right as we do when they go wrong.

—Anonymous

Honk if you love peace and quiet.

—Anonymous

NOSTALGIA

A trip to nostalgia now and then is good for the spirit, as long as you don't set up housekeeping.

—Dan Bartolovic

It's hard to be nostalgic when you can't remember anything.

—Anonymous

O

OBEDIENCE

Obedience is the means whereby we show the earnestness of our desire to do God's will.

—Oswald Chambers

The greatest cure for infidelity is obedience to the Spirit of God.

—Oswald Chambers

When we do our duty, not for duty's sake, but because we believe that God is engineering our circumstances in that way, then at the very point of our obedience the whole superb grace of God is ours.

—Oswald Chambers

Throughout the Bible ... when God asked a man to do something, methods, means, materials, and specific directions were always provided. The man had one thing to do: obey.

—Elisabeth Elliot

It is a great deal easier to do that which God gives us to do, no matter how hard it is, than to face the responsibilities of not doing it.

—James R. Miller

See in the meantime that your faith bringeth forth obedience, and God in due time will cause it to bring forth peace.

—John Owen

Obedience is the fruit of faith, patience the bloom on the fruit.

—Christina Rossetti

Where the need is greatest let us be found gladly obeying the Master's command.

—J. Hudson Taylor

OBJECTIONS

Nothing will ever be attempted if all possible objections must be first overcome.

—Samuel Johnson

OBSTACLES

The block of granite that was an obstacle in the pathway of the weak becomes a stepping-stone in the pathway of the strong.

—Thomas Carlyle

If you find a path with no obstacles, it probably doesn't lead anywhere.

—Frank A. Clark

Ride on! Rough-shod if need be, smooth-shod if that will do, but ride on! Ride on over all obstacles, and win the race.

—Charles Dickens

Obstacles are the muscles of achievement.

—Ella E. Dodson

The greater the obstacle, the more glory in overcoming it.

—Jean Baptiste Molière

The majority see the obstacles; the few see the objectives; history rewards the successes of the latter, while oblivion is the reward of the former.

—Alfred A. Montapert

Obstacles are those frightful things you see when you take your eyes off the goal.

—Hannah More

Looking back, my life seems like one long obstacle race, with me as the chief obstacle.

—Jack Paar

What on earth would a man do with himself if something did not stand in his way?

—H. G. Wells

OLD AGE

I'm going to be eighty soon, and I guess the one thing that puzzles me most is how quick it got here.

—Roy Acuff

A man is not old till regrets take the place of dreams.

—John Barrymore

I'm celebrating my seventy-fifth birthday, which is sort of embarrassing because I'm eighty-five.

—Victor Borge

A comfortable old age is the reward of a well-spent youth. Instead of its bringing sad and melancholy prospects of decay, it should give us hopes of eternal youth in a better world.

—Jacob M. Braude

You know you're old when you've lost all your marvels.

—Merry Browne

I stay away from natural foods. At my age I need all the preservatives I can get.

—George Burns

I should have been a country-western singer. After all, I'm older than most western countries.

—George Burns

A man who is always living in the midst of his studies and labors does not perceive when old age creeps upon him.

—Marcus Porcius Cato

Old age, especially an honored old age, has so great authority, that this is of more value than all the pleasures of youth.

—Cicero

To enter the country of old age is a new experience, different from what you supposed it to be. Nobody, man or woman, knows the country until he has lived in it and has taken out his citizenship papers.

—Malcolm Cowley

Some lives, like evening primroses, blossom most beautifully in the evening of life.

—Charles E. Cowman

Old Age

I'm saving the rocker for the day when I feel as old as I really am.
> —Dwight D. Eisenhower

We do not count a man's years, until he has nothing else to count.
> —Ralph Waldo Emerson

It is really something of a feat to have lived seventy-five years, in spite of illnesses, germs, accidents, disasters, and wars. And now every fresh day finds me more filled with wonder and better qualified to draw the last drop of delight from it.
> —Maurice Goudeket

When people tell you how young you look, they are also telling you how old you are.
> —Cary Grant

Old age, believe me, is a good and pleasant time. It is true that you are quietly shouldered off the stage, but then you are given such a comfortable front seat as spectator, and if you have really played your part you are more content to sit down and watch.
> —Jane Ellen Harrison

When you're my age, it's as if you're a car. First a tire blows, and you get that fixed. Then a headlight goes and you get that fixed. And then one day you drive into a garage and the man says, "Sorry, miss, they don't make that kind of car anymore."
> —Katharine Hepburn

Old age is not a disease—it is strength and survivorship, triumph over all kinds of vicissitudes and disappointments, trials and illnesses.
> —Maggie Kuhn

Age is not all decay; it is the ripening, the swelling of the fresh life within, that withers and bursts the husk.
> —George MacDonald

Old age is like a plane flying through a storm. Once you are aboard there is nothing you can do.
> —Golda Meir

Memory, wit, fancy, acuteness, cannot grow young again in old age, but the heart can.
> —Jean Paul Richter

As winter strips the leaves from around us, so that we may see the distant regions they formerly concealed, so old age takes away our enjoyments only to enlarge the prospects of the coming eternity.
> —Jean Paul Richter

As for old age, embrace and love it. It abounds with pleasure if you know how to use it. The gradually declining years are among the sweetest in a man's life, and I maintain that, even when they have reached the extreme limit, they have their pleasure still.
> —Seneca

When a noble life has prepared for old age, it is not decline that it reveals, but the first days of immortality.
> —Mme. Anne Louise de Staël

Cherish all your happy moments; they make a fine cushion for old age.

—Booth Tarkington

Old age is the most unexpected of all the things that happen to a man.

—Leon Trotsky

Old age is when you get out of the shower, and you're glad the mirror is all fogged up.

—Anonymous

Old age is a blessed time. It gives us leisure to put off our earthly garments one by one, and dress ourselves for heaven. Blessed are they that are homesick, for they shall get home.

—Anonymous

OPINIONS

The man who never alters his opinion is like standing water, and breeds reptiles of the mind.

—William Blake

A biased opinion is one you don't agree with.

—David Brinkley

If in the last few years you hadn't discarded a major opinion or acquired a new one, check your pulse. You may be dead.

—Gelett Burgess

He that never changes his opinions never corrects his mistakes, and will never be wiser on the morrow than he is today.

—Tryon Edwards

The foolish and the dead alone never change their opinions.

—James Russell Lowell

The fact that an opinion has been widely held is no evidence whatever that it is not utterly absurd.

—Bertrand Russell

The notion that one opinion is as good as another will not work in any other area of human experience. Why should it work in the area of faith?

—David E. Trueblood

OPPORTUNITY

A wise man will make more opportunities than he finds.

—Francis Bacon

Opportunity is closest at hand when everybody is against taking advantage of it.

—O. A. Battista

When one door closes, another opens; but we often look so long and so regretfully upon the closed door that we do not see the one that has opened for us.

—Alexander Graham Bell

If opportunity doesn't knock, build a door.

—Milton Berle

Today's opportunities erase yesterday's failures.

—Gene Brown

Opportunity

The lure of the distant and the difficult is deceptive. The great opportunity is where you are.

—John Burroughs

The man who grasps an opportunity as it is paraded before him, nine times out of ten makes a success; but the man who makes his own opportunities is, barring an accident, a sure-fire success.

—Dale Carnegie

How often do we sigh for opportunities for doing good, whilst we neglect the openings of providence in little things, which would frequently lead to the accomplishment of most important usefulness!

—George Crabbe

Small opportunities are often the beginning of great enterprises.

—Demosthenes

For the highest task of intelligence is to grasp and recognize genuine opportunity, possibility.

—John Dewey

The secret of success in life is for a man to be ready for his opportunity when it comes.

—Benjamin Disraeli

Great opportunities come to all, but many do not know they have met them. The only preparation to take advantage of them is simple fidelity to what each day brings.

—A. E. Dunning

We are all continually faced with a series of great opportunities, brilliantly disguised as insoluble problems.

—John W. Gardner

For every man the world is as it was at the first day, and as full of untold novelties for him who has the eyes to see them.

—Thomas H. Huxley

He who refuses to embrace a unique opportunity loses the prize as surely as if he had failed.

—William James

To improve the golden moment of opportunity, and catch the good that is within our reach, is the great art of life.

—Samuel Johnson

Men do with opportunities as children do at the seashore; they fill their little hands with sand, and then let the grains fall through, one by one, till all are gone.

—T. Jones

Problems are only opportunities in work clothes.

—Henry J. Kaiser

One can present people with opportunities. One cannot make them equal to them.

—Rosamond Lehmann

I will study and get ready and the opportunity will come.

—Abraham Lincoln

There is no security on this earth— only opportunity.

—Douglas MacArthur

If opportunity came disguised as temptation, one knock would be enough.

—Lane Olinghouse

Opportunities should never be lost, because they can hardly be regained.

—William Penn

Vigilance in watching opportunity; tact and daring in seizing upon opportunity; force and persistence in crowding opportunity to its utmost of possible achievement—these are the martial virtues that must command success.

—Austin Phelps

We are surrounded by insurmountable opportunities.

—Pogo (Walt Kelly)

Life is not a collection bureau for power and wealth, but an opportunity for service.

—John W. Raley

God's best gift to us is not things, but opportunities.

—Alice W. Rollins

Do what you're afraid to do. When you run away because you are afraid to do something big, you pass opportunity by.

—W. Clement Stone

An opportunity grasped and used produces at least one other opportunity.

—Chester A. Swor

When we stop to think, we often miss our opportunity.

—Publilius Syrus

Only the day dawns to which we are awake.

—Henry David Thoreau

An opportunity well taken is the only weapon of advantage.

—John Udale

Opportunities are swarming around us all the time, thicker than gnats at sundown. We walk through a cloud of them.

—Henry Van Dyke

The greatest achievement of the human spirit is to live up to one's opportunities and make the most of one's resources.

—Marquis de Vauvenargues

The opportunity for doing mischief is found a hundred times a day, and of doing good once in a year.

—Voltaire

Opportunity is often difficult to recognize; we usually expect it to beckon us with beepers and billboards.

—William Arthur Ward

I believe in America because … we have great dreams and because we have the opportunity to make these dreams come true.

—Wendell Willkie

Opportunity is frequently overlooked because it disguises itself as work.

—Anonymous

The commonest form, one of the most often neglected, and the safest opportunity for the average man to seize, is hard work.

—Anonymous

OPPOSITION

A certain amount of opposition is a great help to a man. Kites rise against, not with the wind.

—John Neal

OPTIMISM
(See also Pessimism)

An optimist is the human personification of spring.

—Susan J. Bissonette

Being an optimist after you've got everything you want doesn't count.

—Frank McKinney Hubbard

Optimism is the faith that leads to achievement. Nothing can be done without hope and confidence.

—Helen Keller

A pessimist is one who makes difficulties of his opportunities; an optimist is one who makes opportunities of his difficulties.

—Robert Mansell

An optimist is someone who tells you to cheer up when things are going his way.

—Edward R. Murrow

An optimist is a fellow who believes a housefly is looking for a way to get out.

—George Jean Nathan

An optimist may see a light where there is none, but why must the pessimist always run to blow it out?

—Michel de Saint-Pierre

Both optimists and pessimists contribute to our society. The optimist invents the airplane and the pessimist the parachute.

—Gil Stern

If it wasn't for the optimist, the pessimist would never know how happy he wasn't.

—Anonymous

ORIGINALITY
(See also Imitation)

Originality is simply a pair of fresh eyes.

—Thomas W. Higginson

The principal mark of genius is not perfection but originality, the opening of new frontiers.

—Arthur Koestler

All good things that exist are the fruits of originality.

—John Stuart Mill

OTHERS
(See also People, Relationships)

Those who bring sunshine into the lives of others cannot keep it from themselves.

—James M. Barrie

The most attractive people in the world are the ones who are interested in others—turned outward in cheerfulness, kindness, appreciation, instead of turned inward to be constantly centered in themselves.

—Pat Boone

Blessed is he that does good to others and desires not that others should do him good.

—Brother Giles

The pleasure we derive from doing favors is partly in the feeling it gives us that we are not altogether worthless.

—Eric Hoffer

It is well to remember . . . that the entire population of the universe, with one trifling exception, is composed of others.

—John Andrew Holmes

Doing nothing for others is the undoing of ourselves.

—Horace Mann

You have not lived a perfect day, even though you have earned your money, unless you have done something for someone who will never be able to repay you.

—Ruth Smeltzer

Put the golden sunshine in each day;
Others need the cheer that comes
    through you—
Need it most when outer sky's dull gray
Leaves the sunshine-making yours
    to do.

—Juniata Stafford

Let God love you through others and let God love others through you.

—D. M. Street

We cannot hold a torch to light another's path without brightening our own.

—Ben Sweetland

Unless life is lived for others, it is not worthwhile.

—Mother Teresa

Success has nothing to do with what you gain in life or accomplish for yourself. It's what you do for others.

—Danny Thomas

PAIN
(See also Empathy)

If I had to choose between pain and nothing, I would choose pain.
—William Faulkner

Pain insists on being attended to. God whispers to us in our pleasures, speaks in our conscience, but shouts in our pains; it is His megaphone to rouse a deaf world.
—C. S. Lewis

PARANOIA

This is a do-it-yourself test for paranoia: you know you've got it when you can't think of anything that's your fault.
—Robert M. Hutchins

Just because you're paranoid doesn't mean they're not out to get you.
—Anonymous

PARENTS
(See also Heredity)

When should a parent turn authority over to a child? When the child stops reaching for authority and reaches for responsibility, and not before.
—Donald Barr

The best inheritance a parent can give to his children is a few minutes of his time each day.
—O. A. Battista

We never know the love of the parent until we become parents ourselves.
—Henry Ward Beecher

By the time parents are ready to enjoy the comforts of life, their children are using them.
—Bob Brown

Every parent is at some time the father of the unreturned prodigal, with nothing to do but keep his house open to hope.
—John Ciardi

In their eagerness for their children to acquire skills and to succeed, parents may forget that youngsters need time to think, and privacy in which to do it.
—James Cox

If I were asked what single qualification was necessary for one who has the care of children, I should say patience— patience with their tempers, with their understandings, with their progress.
—François de la Fenelon

Parents never really appreciate teachers until it rains all weekend.
—Bob Goddard

Most of us don't expect to be admired by our children, but we wouldn't mind just a slight closing of the generation gap.
—Troy Gordon

Only as genuine Christian holiness and Christlike love are expressed in the life of a parent, can the child have the opportunity to inherit the flame and not the ashes.

—Stephen G. Green

A measure of good parenthood could be when our children exceed our own achievements.

—Tom Haggai

The best combination of parents consists of a father who is gentle beneath his firmness, and a mother who is firm beneath her gentleness.

—Sydney J. Harris

The beauty of "spacing" children many years apart lies in the fact that parents have time to learn the mistakes that were made with the older ones—which permits them to make exactly the opposite mistakes with the younger ones.

—Sydney J. Harris

Life is but one continual course of instruction. The hand of the parent writes on the heart of the child the first faint characters that time deepens into strength so that nothing can efface them.

—Richard Hill

True parenthood is self-destructive. The wise parent is one who effectively does himself out of his job as parent. The silver cord must be broken. It must not be broken too abruptly, but it must be broken.... The wise parent delivers his child over to society.

—Robert Holmes

Perhaps one way of coping with the population explosion would be to give every potential parent some experience in driving a school bus.

—Franklin P. Jones

Note on church bulletin board: "Parents, be the soul support of your children."

—Vern McLellan

Perhaps parents would enjoy their children more if they stopped to realize that the film of childhood can never be run through for a second showing.

—Evelyn Nown

Parents need to fill a child's bucket of self-esteem so high that the rest of the world can't poke enough holes in it to drain it dry.

—Alvin Price

The frightening thing about heredity and environment is that parents provide both.

—Walt Schriebman

Parenthood remains the greatest single preserve of the amateur.

—Alvin Toffler

Parents are the bones on which children cut their teeth.

—Peter Ustinov

Before I got married I had six theories about bringing up children; now I have six children and no theories.

—John Wilmot

Parents often talk about the younger generation as if they didn't have anything to do with it.

—Anonymous

The parent's life is the child's copybook.

—Anonymous

The toughest thing about raising kids is convincing them you have seniority.

—Anonymous

Don't be discouraged if your children reject your advice. Years later they will offer it to their own offspring.

—Anonymous

PASSION
(See also Fire)

We live in the present, we dream of the future, but we learn eternal truths from the past.

—Madame Chiang Kai-shek

One person with passion is better than forty who are merely interested.

—Tom Connellan

God, light these idle sticks of my life and let me burn out for Thee.

—Jim Elliot

The early Christians were aflame. And, just as moths are attracted to the flame, so will others be drawn to us if we burn brightly and intensely for God. But proximity alone will not ignite them; we must touch them with the spark that will burst them into flames—to pass along to them the spark of Jesus Christ.

—Archie B. Parrish

Let a man in a garret but burn with enough intensity, and he will set fire to the world.

—Antoine de Saint-Exupéry

If I had three hundred men who feared nothing but God, hated nothing but sin, and were determined to know nothing among men but Jesus Christ, and Him crucified, I would set the world on fire.

—John Wesley

PAST

The past should be a springboard, not a hammock.

—Edmund Burke

The past is the only dead thing that smells sweet.

—Cyril Connolly

The past always looks better than it was; it's only pleasant because it isn't here.

—Finley Peter Dunne

The past is a foreign country; they do things differently there.

—L. P. Hartley

We must, like Paul, forget everything that is behind us, refusing to allow the dead hand of the past to be laid upon our present or future, and turn a deaf ear to the satanic suggestion that the past, with its failures . . . is only the prophecy of the future.

—J. Gregory Mantle

Shut out all your past except that which will help you weather your tomorrows.

—William Osler

The past is a bucket of ashes, so live not in your yesterdays, nor just for tomorrow, but in the here and now. Keep moving and forget the post-mortems.

—Carl Sandburg

Those who cannot remember the past are condemned to repeat it.

—George Santayana

PATIENCE

Life on the farm is a school of patience; you can't hurry the crops or make an ox in two days.

—Henri Fournier Alain

There is no patience equal to the patience of God.

—Oswald Chambers

Patience is a necessary ingredient of genius.

—Benjamin Disraeli

Patience is the greatest of all shock absorbers. The only thing you can get in a hurry is trouble.

—Thomas R. Dewar

Adopt the pace of nature; her secret is patience.

—Ralph Waldo Emerson

Patience defined: God took a forty-year-old conceited *somebody*, spent forty years showing him he was a *nobody*, and forty more years to demonstrate what He can do with *anybody*.

—Robert D. Foster

The key to everything is patience. You get the chicken by hatching the egg, not by smashing it open.

—Arnold H. Glasow

Exasperation is the mind's way of spinning its wheels until patience restores traction.

—George L. Griggs

Patience is the ballast of the soul, that will keep it from rolling and tumbling in the greatest storms.

—Charles Hopkins

Patience often gets the credit that belongs to fatigue.

—Franklin P. Jones

Never cut what you can untie.

—Joseph Joubert

Patience is something you admire in the driver behind you, but not in the one ahead.

—Bill McGlashen

This would be a fine world if all men showed as much patience all the time as they do while they're waiting for the fish to bite.

—Vaughn Monroe

Be patient enough to live one day at a time as Jesus taught us, letting yesterday go and leaving tomorrow till it arrives.

—John F. Newton

With patience, a well can be dug with a needle.

—Croft M. Pentz

Only those who have the patience to do simple things perfectly will acquire the skill to do difficult things easily.

—Johann Friedrich von Schiller

Patience! The windmill never strays in search of the wind.

—Andy J. Sklivis

How can a society that exists on instant mashed potatoes, packaged cake mixes, frozen dinners, and instant cameras teach patience to its young?

—Paul Sweeney

Patience is willingness to become what we can, not readiness to accept what we are.

—Robert K. Thomas

Patience wears out stones.

—Gaelic Proverb

Be patient! God always uses the yielded life—but in His own way.

—Anonymous

The real secret of patience is to find something else to do in the meantime.

—Anonymous

PATRIOTISM

A patriot without religion in my estimation is as great a paradox as an honest man without the fear of God.

—Abigail Adams

To love is ... the real duty of patriotism, whereas, in the mouths of many of its noisiest professors, the point would rather seem to be hate.

—John Ayscough

Patriotism must be founded on great principles and supported by great virtue.

—Henry St. John Bolingbroke

I realize that patriotism is not enough. I must have no hatred or bitterness toward anyone.

—Edith Louise Cavell

A man's country is not a certain area of land, of mountains, rivers, and woods, but it is a principle; and patriotism is loyal to that principle.

—George William Curtis

True patriotism hates injustice in its own land more than anywhere else.

—Clarence Darrow

The really patriotic citizen is the one who loves.

—Patrick J. Hayes

It is now the moment when by common consent we pause ... to recall what our country has done for each of us, and to ask ourselves what we can do for our country in return.

—Oliver Wendell Holmes Jr.

I fought in three wars and three more would not be too many to defend my country. I love America and as she has weaknesses or ills I'll hold her hand.

—Daniel "Chappie" James

The first object of my heart is my own country. In that is embarked my family, my fortune, and my own existence.

—Thomas Jefferson

Patriotism means to stand by the country. It does not mean to stand by the president.

—Theodore Roosevelt

Patriotism is as much a virtue as justice, and is as necessary for the support of societies as natural affection is for the support of families.

—Benjamin Rush

True patriotism is of no party.

—Tobias Smollett

I venture to suggest that patriotism is not short, frenzied outbursts of emotion, but the tranquil and steady dedication of a lifetime.

—Adlai Stevenson

PEACE
(See also God's Peace, Peace of Mind, War)

All things that speak of heaven speak of peace.

—Philip J. Bailey

True peace could come instantly to the world if we all treated each other as though today was the last day of our lives—which it could very well be!

—O. A. Battista

We lose the peace of years when we hunt after the rapture of moments.

—Edward G. Bulwer-Lytton

Peace is the fairest form of happiness.

—William Ellery Channing

There is no joy that lies so deep as peace,
No peace so deep as that by struggle won.

—Helen Gray Cone

What is peace? Is it war? No. Is it strife? No. Is it lovely, and gentle, and beautiful, and pleasant, and serene, and joyful? Oh yes! Therefore, my friends, I wish for peace, upon you and upon yours.

—Charles Dickens

Peace comes only from loving, from mutual self-sacrifice and self-forgetfulness.

—Horace W. B. Donegan

Without peace, our property and possessions, much or little, are of no value, and without the Prince of Peace there can be no peace.

—R. E. Dudley

You have to take chances for peace, just as you take chances in war. The ability to get to the verge without getting into the war is the necessary art. If you try to run away from it, if you are scared to go to the brink, you are lost.

—John Foster Dulles

Peace, sweet peace is ever found
In her eternal home on holy ground.

—Emma C. Embury

The peace of the man who has forsworn the use of the bullet seems to me not quite peace, but a canting impotence.

—Ralph Waldo Emerson

Peace is such a precious jewel that I would give anything for it but truth.

—Matthew Henry

Yes, we love peace, but we are not willing to take wounds for it, as we are for war.

—John Andrew Holmes

The only condition of peace in this world is to have no ideas, or, at least, not to express them.

—Oliver Wendell Holmes

Peace is not made at the council table, or by treaties, but in the hearts of men.

—Herbert Hoover

Universal peace sounds ridiculous to the head of an average family.

—Frank McKinney Hubbard

We love peace, but not peace at any price. There is a peace more destructive of the manhood of living man than war is destructive of his body. Chains are worse than bayonets.

—Douglas Jerrold

Peace is more important than all justice; and peace was not made for the sake of justice, but justice for the sake of peace.

—Martin Luther

If man does find the solution for world peace it will be the most revolutionary reversal of his record we have ever known.

—George C. Marshall

God will keep no nation in supreme peace that will not do supreme duty.

—William McKinley

There will be no peace so long as God remains unseated at the conference tables.

—William M. Peck

True, lasting peace cannot be secured through the strength of arms alone. Among free peoples, the open exchange of ideas ultimately is our greatest security.

—Ronald Reagan

Peace, like charity, begins at home.

—Franklin Delano Roosevelt

Peace, like war, can succeed only where there is a will to enforce it, and where there is available power to enforce it.

—Franklin Delano Roosevelt

I want our great democracy to be wise enough to realize that aloofness from war is not promoted by unawareness of war. In a world of mutual suspicions, peace must be affirmatively reached for. It cannot just be wished for. It cannot just be waited for.

—Franklin Delano Roosevelt

We wish peace; but we wish the peace of justice, the peace of righteousness. We wish it because we think it is right, and not because we are afraid.

—Theodore Roosevelt

Peace won by compromise is usually a short-lived achievement.

—Winfield Scott

Peace has to be created, in order to be maintained. It is the product of faith, strength, energy, will, sympathy, justice, imagination, and the triumph of principle. It will never be achieved by passivity and quietism. Passivity and quietism are invitations to war.

—Dorothy Thompson

They have not wanted peace at all; they have wanted to be spared war—as though the absence of war was the same as peace.

—Dorothy Thompson

Nations have no existence apart from their people. If every person in the world loved peace, every nation would love peace.

—J. Sherman Wallace

To be prepared for war is one of the most effectual means of preserving peace.

—George Washington

There is a price that is too great to pay for peace, and that price can be put in one word. One cannot pay the price of self-respect.

—Woodrow Wilson

Peace comes not by establishing a calm outward setting so much as by inwardly surrendering to whatever the setting.

—Hubert van Zeller

Peace is not so much a goal to be achieved as a way to be walked.

—Anonymous

Peace begins when expectation ends.

—Anonymous

Peace comes not from the absence of conflict in life but from the ability to cope with it.

—Anonymous

Peace is not a season; it is a way of life.

—Anonymous

PEACE OF MIND
(See also God's Peace, Peace)

Acquire inner peace and a multitude will find their salvation near you.

—Catherine de Hueck Doherty

For peace of mind, resign as general manager of the universe.

—Larry Eisenberg

Peace does not mean the end of all our
    striving;
Joy does not mean the drying of our
    tears;
Peace is the power that comes to souls
    arriving
Up to the light where God Himself
    appears.

—G. A. Studdart Kennedy

If we have not peace within ourselves, it is vain to seek it from outward sources.

—François de La Rochefoucauld

No God, no peace; know God, know peace.

—Croft M. Pentz

I never have found
Peace of mind
By giving folks a
Piece of mine.

—Laurence C. Smith

One of the great hindrances to internal peace that the Christian encounters is the common habit of dividing our lives into two areas—the sacred and the secular.

—A. W. Tozer

Peace rules the day when Christ rules the mind.

—Anonymous

Peace is the deliberate adjustment of my life to the will of God.

—Anonymous

PEOPLE
(See Others, Relationships)

Expect people to be better than they are; it helps them to become better. But don't be disappointed when they are not; it helps them to keep trying.

—Merry Browne

We either love people or we control them. There's little room for anything else. And it's far easier to control them than to love them.

—John Eldredge

It's not the difference between people that's the difficulty. It's the indifference.

—Lillian G. Geden

People change, and forget to tell each other.

—Lillian Hellman

People are like stained glass windows: they sparkle and shine when the sun's out, but when the darkness sets in, their true beauty is revealed only if there is light within.

—Elizabeth Kubler-Ross

A different world cannot be built by indifferent people.

—Peter Marshall

You understand people better if you look at them—no matter how old or impressive or important they may be— as if they were children. For most men never mature; they simply grow taller.

—Leo Rosten

Some people come into our lives and quickly go. Some stay for a while and leave footprints on our hearts, and we are never ever the same.

—Flavia Weedn

The world needs people . . .
who do not have a price at which they
   can be bought;
who do not borrow from integrity to
   pay for expediency;
whose handshake is an ironclad
   contract;
who are not afraid of risk;
who have opinions instead of prejudices;
who are as honest in large matters as in
   small ones;
whose ambitions are big enough to
   include others;
who know how to win with grace and
   lose with dignity;
who still have friends they made twenty
   years ago;
who are occasionally wrong and always
   willing to admit it.

—Anonymous

People are like tea bags; you don't know how strong they are until they get into hot water.

—Anonymous

People will forget what you said; people will forget what you did; but people will never forget how you made them feel.

—Anonymous

PERCEPTION

Sometimes you think the whole world is falling, and it's only yourself that's leaning.

—Pearl Bailey

We don't see things as they are; we see them as we are.

—Anaïs Nin

PERFECTION

The nearest to perfection most people ever come is when filling out an employment application.

—Ken Kraft

A perfectionist is one who takes infinite pains, and often gives them to other people.

—Kenneth L. Krichbaum

Trifles make perfection, but perfection is no trifle.

—Michelangelo

PERSECUTION

Whenever you see persecution, there is more than a probability the truth is on the persecuted side.

—Hugh Latimer

Whoever is right, the persecutor must be wrong.

—William Penn

PERSEVERANCE
(See also Determination, Persistence)

Genius, that power that dazzles mortal eyes, is oft but perseverance in disguise.

—Henry W. Austin

To break our own record, to outstrip yesterdays by todays, to bear our trials more beautifully than we ever dreamed we could, to whip the tempter inside and out as we never whipped him before, to give as we never have given, to do our work with more force and a finer finish than ever—this is the true idea—to get ahead of ourselves.

—Maltbie D. Babcock

Great effects come of industry and perseverance; for audacity doth almost bind and mate the weaker sort of minds.

—Francis Bacon

Victory belongs to the most persevering.

—Napoleon Bonaparte

Most of the important things in the world have been accomplished by people who have kept on trying when there seemed to be no hope at all.

—Dale Carnegie

Be like a postage stamp—stick to one thing until you get there.

—Margaret Carty

Press on: nothing in the world can take the place of perseverance.

—Calvin Coolidge

Perseverance is not a long race; it is many short races one after another.

—Walter Elliott

To persevere, trusting in what hopes he has, is courage in a man. The coward despairs.

—Euripides

Perseverance lies within the affordings of everyone; its power increases with its progress, and it but rarely misses its aim.

—Johann von Goethe

Perseverance gives power to weakness, and opens to poverty the world's wealth. It spreads fertility over the barren landscape, and bids the choicest fruits and flowers spring up and flourish in the desert abode of thorns and briers.

—S. G. Goodrich

Perseverance is the ingredient of life that sometimes makes up for lack of genius.

—W. Ballentine Henley

Effort only fully releases its reward after a person refuses to quit.

—Napoleon Hill

Great works are performed not by strength but by perseverance.

—Samuel Johnson

Keep on going, and the chances are you will stumble on something, perhaps when you are least expecting it. I have never heard of anyone stumbling on something sitting down.

—Charles F. Kettering

Perseverance can lend the appearance of dignity and grandeur to many actions, just as silence in company affords wisdom and apparent intelligence to a stupid person.

—G. C. Lichtenberg

Perseverance is a great element of success. If you only knock long enough and loud enough at the gate, you are sure to wake somebody.

—Henry Wadsworth Longfellow

Big shots are only little shots who keep on shooting.

—Christopher Morley

It takes time and perseverance to do big things.

—Jawaharlal Nehru

Perseverance is more prevailing than violence; and many things that cannot be overcome when they are together, yield themselves up when taken little by little.

—Plutarch

You just can't beat the person who never gives up.

—Babe Ruth

The will to persevere is often the difference between failure and success.

—David Sarnoff

The repetition of small efforts will accomplish more than the occasional use of great talents.

—Charles H. Spurgeon

'Tis known by the name of perseverance in a good cause, and of obstinacy in a bad one.

—Laurence Sterne

The man with average mentality, but with control, a definite goal and a clear conception of how it can be gained and, above all, with the power of application and labor, wins in the end.

—William Howard Taft

One may walk over the highest mountain one step at a time.

—John Wanamaker

One cold [winter] day a snail started climbing an apple tree. As he inched slowly upward, a worm stuck its head from a crevice in the bark to offer some advice. "You're wasting your energy. There isn't a single apple up there." The snail kept up his slow climb. "There will be when I get there," he said.

—Anonymous

All the performances of human art, at which we look with praise or wonder, are instances of the resistless force of perseverance: it is by this that the quarry becomes a pyramid, and that distant countries are united with canals.

—Anonymous

Often genius is just another way of spelling perseverance.

—Anonymous

Perseverance has been defined as sticking to something you're not stuck on.

—Anonymous

Perseverance is the result of a strong will. Obstinacy is the result of a strong won't.

—Anonymous

The basic rules for success may be defined as follows: Know what you want. Find out what it takes to get it. Act on it and persevere.

—Anonymous

PERSISTENCE
(See also Determination, Perseverance)

Nothing in the world can take the place of persistence. Talent will not; nothing is more common than unsuccessful men with talent. Genius will not; unrewarded genius is almost a proverb. Education will not; the world is full of educated failures. Persistence and determination alone are omnipotent.

—Calvin Coolidge

It is never too late to be what you might have been.

—George Eliot

So long as there is breath in me, that long will I persist. For now I know one of the greatest principles of success: if I persist long enough I will win.

—Og Mandino

PERSONALITY

An appealing personality is not something grafted on from without.... It is expressed through the body, the mind, the heart, and the spirit.

—Edith Johnson

Men have yet to learn the value of human personality. The fact that a person is white, or black, or yellow, of one race or another, of this religion or that—these things are not all-important. It is the human personality that should come first.

—John R. Van Sickle

PERSPECTIVE

One never notices what has been done; one can only see what remains to be done.

—Marie Curie

As followers of Jesus, we should be seeking God's perspective.... Are you, like me, overwhelmed and losing perspective? We need to stop and climb the mast of the ship of faith, to see life from God's perspective. It will change completely what we see.

—Bob Snyder

It's a recession when your neighbor loses his job, it's a depression when you lose yours.

—Harry S. Truman

We mutter and splutter, we fume and we spurt,
We mumble and grumble, our feelings get hurt,

We can't understand things, our vision gets dim,
When all that we need is a moment with HIM.

—Anonymous

PERSUASION

I would rather try to persuade a man to go along, because once I have persuaded him, he will stick. If I scare him, he will just stay as long as he is scared, and then he is gone.

—Dwight D. Eisenhower

PESSIMISM
(See also Optimism)

More than one pessimist got that way by financing an optimist.

—Fred W. Bender

There isn't a pessimistic note in the New Testament after the Resurrection.

—Andrew W. Blackwood Jr.

Believe. No pessimist ever discovered the secrets of the stars, or sailed to an uncharted land, or opened a new heaven to the human spirit.

—Helen Keller

PILGRIMS

Measured by the standards of men of their time, [the Pilgrims] were the humble of the earth. Measured by later accomplishments, they were the mighty. In appearance weak and persecuted they came—rejected, despised—an insignificant band, in reality strong and independent, a mighty host of whom the world was not worthy, destined to free mankind.

—Calvin Coolidge

The Pilgrims came to America not to accumulate riches but to worship God, and the greatest wealth they left unborn generations was their heroic example of sacrifice that their souls might be free.

—Harry Moyle Tippett

PLANNING

We can't cross a bridge until we come to it, but I always like to lay down a pontoon ahead of time.

—Bernard M. Baruch

Make no little plans; they have no magic to stir the blood.

—Daniel Burnham

Just because something doesn't do what you planned it to do doesn't mean it's useless.

—Thomas Edison

You and I must not complain if our plans break down, if we have done our part. That probably means that the plans of One who knows more than we do have succeeded.

—Edward Everett Hale

Our plans miscarry because they have no aim. When you don't know what harbor you're aiming for, no wind is the right wind.

—Seneca

Dig a well before you are thirsty.

—Chinese Proverb

PLEASURE

Your greatest pleasure is that which rebounds from hearts that you have made glad.

—Henry Ward Beecher

We thoroughly enjoy only the pleasure that we give.

—Alexandre Dumas

Do not bite at the bait of pleasure till you know there is no hook beneath it.

—Thomas Jefferson

Pleasure is very seldom found where it is sought. Our brightest blazes are commonly kindled by unexpected sparks.

—Samuel Johnson

A life merely of pleasure, or chiefly of pleasure, is always a poor and worthless life.

—Theodore W. Parker

We tire of those pleasures we take, but never of those we give.

—J. Petit-Senn

POET/POETRY

A poet is, before anything else, a person who is passionately in love with language.

—W. H. Auden

Poetry is the renewal of words, setting them free, and that's what a poet is doing: loosening the words.

—Robert Frost

You will find poetry nowhere unless you bring some of it with you.

—Joseph Joubert

POLITENESS

One of the great victories you can gain over a man is to beat him at politeness.

—Josh Billings

Politeness is an inexpensive way of making friends.

—William Feather

Politeness has been well defined as benevolence in small things.

—Thomas B. Macaulay

Politeness is real kindness kindly expressed.

—John Witherspoon

POLITICIANS

(See also Politics)

A politician thinks of the next election; a statesman, of the next generation.

—James Freeman Clarke

Since a politician never believes what he says, he is always astonished when others do.

—Charles de Gaulle

One of the shallowest disdains is the sneer against the professional politician.

—Felix Frankfurter

America was built not by politicians running for something, but by statesmen standing for something.

—Vance Havner

A statesman is a politician who is held up by equal pressure from all directions.

—Eric A. Johnston

We all work for the government but the politician is wise. He gets paid for it.

—Charlie "T" Jones

A successful politician is one who can get in the public eye without irritating it.

—Vesta M. Kelly

Public interest is a term used by every politician to support his ideas.

—W. M. Kiplinger

America is the only country in the world where you can go on the air and kid politicians—and where politicians can go on the air and kid the people.

—Groucho Marx

Politics is becoming a precarious game. One week a politician may appear on the cover of *Time*, and the next week he may be serving it.

—Vern McLellan

Politicians are wonderful people as long as they stay away from things they don't understand, such as working for a living.

—P. J. O'Rourke

Professional politicians like to talk about the value of experience in government. Nuts! The only experience you gain in politics is how to be political.

—Ronald Reagan

A man to be a sound politician and in any degree useful to his country must be governed by higher and steadier considerations than those of personal sympathy and private greed.

—Martin Van Buren

I knew how to say no, but seldom could bring myself to say it. A woman and a politician must say that word often, and mean it—or else.

—James J. Walker

POLITICS
(See also Politicians)

Politics is the gentle art of getting votes from the poor and campaign funds from the rich, by promising to protect each from the other.

—Oscar Ameringer

Politics is not a good location or a vocation for anyone lazy, thin-skinned, or lacking a sense of humor.

—John Bailey

In politics, an absurdity is not an impediment.

—Napoleon Bonaparte

Our national politics has become a competition for images or between images, rather than between ideals.

—Daniel J. Boorstin

Political ability is the ability to foretell what is going to happen tomorrow, next week, next month, and next year. And to have the ability afterward to explain why it didn't happen.

—Winston Churchill

Politics should be the part-time profession of every citizen.

—Dwight D. Eisenhower

Politics is not the art of the possible. It consists in choosing between the disastrous and the unpalatable.

—John Kenneth Galbraith

In politics as on the sickbed people toss from one side to the other, thinking they will be more comfortable.

—Johann von Goethe

Politics makes strange postmasters.

—Frank McKinney Hubbard

Politics defined: Poly is a Greek word meaning "many" and tics are little bloodsuckers.

—Charlie "T" Jones

Politics is war without bloodshed, and war is politics with blood.

—Mao Tse-tung

Those who would treat politics and morality apart will never understand the one or the other.

—John Morley

Politics is not a bad profession. If you succeed, there are many rewards; if you disgrace yourself, you can always write a book.

—Ronald Reagan

I have learned that one of the most important rules in politics is poise—which means looking like an owl after you have behaved like a jackass.

—Ronald Reagan

Some of you may remember that in my early days I was a sort of a bleeding heart liberal. Then I became a man and put away childish ways.

—Ronald Reagan

All politics are based on the indifference of the majority.

—James Reston

Times have proven only one good thing and that is you can't ruin this country even with politics.

—Will Rogers

I tell you folks, all politics is applesauce.

—Will Rogers

Politics is perhaps the only profession for which no preparation is thought necessary.

—Robert Louis Stevenson

In politics, if you want anything said, ask a man. If you want anything done, ask a woman.

—Margaret Thatcher

The basis of our political system is the right of the people to make and to alter their constitutions of government.

—George Washington

POSSESSIONS

Let us soar above our worldly possessions. The bee does not less need its wings when it has gathered an abundant store; for if it sinks in the honey it dies.

—Saint Augustine

There is one advantage in having nothing—it never needs repair.

—Frank A. Clark

If I have any possessions I refuse to part with, I don't own them; they own me.

—Keith Jesperson

Our most valuable possessions are those that can be shared without lessening, those which, when shared, multiply.

—Hugh Prather

I have held many things in my hands, and I have lost them all; but whatever I have placed in God's hands, that I still possess.

—Corrie ten Boom

What you possess in the world will be found at the day of your death to belong to someone else, but what you are will be yours forever.

—Henry Van Dyke

POSSIBILITIES

Rebellion against your handicaps gets you nowhere. Self-pity gets you nowhere. One must have the adventurous daring to accept oneself as a bundle of possibilities and undertake the most interesting game in the world—making the most of one's best.

—Harry Emerson Fosdick

It is very dangerous to go into eternity with possibilities that one has himself prevented from becoming realities. A possibility is a hint from God. One must follow it; . . . if God does not wish it then let him prevent it, but one must not hinder oneself.

—Sören Kierkegaard

There comes a moment when you begin to realize that virtually anything is possible—that nothing is too good to be true.

—Kobi Yamada

POTENTIAL

There is a great deal of unmapped country within us.

—George Eliot

You now have within you all the elements that are necessary to make you all the Father dreamed that you would be in Christ.

—E. W. Kenyon

The best picture has not yet been painted; the greatest poem is still unsung; the mightiest novel remains to be written; the divinest music has not been conceived even by Bach.

—Lincoln Steffens

POVERTY
(See also Debt)

Poverty often deprives a man of all spirit and virtue; it is hard for an empty bag to stand upright.

—Benjamin Franklin

Poverty is a virtue greatly overrated by those who no longer practice it.

—Barnaby C. Keeney

The great thing about serving the poor is that there is no competition.

—Eugene Rivers

Poverty is no disgrace to a man, but it is confoundedly inconvenient.

—Sydney Smith

A poor man is not the one who has too little; he is the one who constantly craves more.

—Anonymous

POWER

Power always thinks it has a great soul and vast views beyond the comprehension of the weak, and that it is doing God's service when it is violating all His laws.

—John Adams

The qualities that get a man into power are not those that lead him, once established, to use power wisely.

—Lyman Bryson

Power will intoxicate the best hearts, as wine the strongest heads. No man is wise enough, nor good enough, to be trusted with unlimited power.

—Charles Caleb Colton

Power doesn't corrupt people. People corrupt power.

—William Gaddis

Power depends on good connections—the train with the locomotive, machinery with the engine, the electrical mechanism with the powerhouse. And in the Christian life the follower of Jesus with the Spirit of Jesus.

—S. D. Gordon

Human nature will never part with power. Look for an example of a voluntary relinquishment of power from one end of the globe to another—you will find none.

—Patrick Henry

You all have powers you never dreamed of. You can do things you never thought you could do.... Don't think you cannot. Think you can!

—Alfred Kingston

Unlimited power is apt to corrupt the minds of those who possess it.

—William Pitt

Power has an incredible ability to corrupt. Yet must power always corrupt? Jesus demonstrated that power could be wielded in new, creative, and constructive ways—ways that evidenced servant leadership to empower, equip, and educate others.

—Bob Snyder

When you have robbed a man of everything, he is no longer in your power. He is free again.

—Alexander Solzhenitsyn

He is truly great in power who has power over himself.

—Charles H. Spurgeon

Lust of power is the most flagrant of all the passions.

—Tacitus

Being powerful is like being a lady. If you have to tell people you are, you aren't.

—Margaret Thatcher

Human beings will generally exercise power when they can get it, and they will exercise it most undoubtedly in popular governments under pretense of public safety.

—Daniel Webster

PRAISE
(See also Prayer—Praise, Prayer—Thanksgiving)

Praise others in public—and watch how your own reputation grows behind your back.

—O. A. Battista

Praise is something that will make you sick if you feed on it.

—O. A. Battista

The meanest, most contemptible kind of praise is that which first speaks well of a man and then qualifies it with a but.

—Henry Ward Beecher

I never yet knew a man so blasé that his face did not change when he heard that some action or creation of his had been praised; yes, even when that praise came from men most insignificant.

—Hilaire Belloc

The advantage of doing one's praising to one's self is that one can lay it on so thick and exactly in the right places.
—Samuel Butler

I praise loudly; I blame softly.
—Catherine II of Russia

Modesty is the only sure bait when you angle for praise.
—Gilbert Keith Chesterton

A hammer sometimes misses its mark—a bouquet never.
—Monta Crane

One thing scientists have discovered is that often praised children become more intelligent than blamed ones. There's a creative element in praise.
—Thomas Dreier

Most people like praise. . . . Many people have an unreasonable fear of administering it. . . . When it is really deserved, most people expand under it into richer and better selves.
—Joseph Farrell

The attention span of a typical human is ten praises, six promises, or one preachment.
—Jocco Grand

If our aim is to praise, we should forget to criticize; if our aim is to criticize, we should remember to praise.
—Charlie "T" Jones and Bob Phillips

Consider carefully before you say a hard word to a man, but never let a chance to say a good one go by. Praise, judiciously bestowed, is money invested.
—G. H. Lorimer

Once in a century a man may be ruined or made insufferable by praise. But surely once in a minute something generous dies for want of it.
—John Masefield

Remember that praise is more valuable than blame.
—George S. Patton Jr.

The trouble with most of us is that we would rather be ruined by praise than saved by criticism.
—Norman Vincent Peale

The greatest efforts of the race have always been traceable to the love of praise, as the greatest catastrophes to the love of pleasure.
—John Ruskin

I have never committed the least matter to God, that I have not had reason for infinite praise.
—Anna Shipton

Even in the best, most friendly and simple relations in life, praise and commendation are as indispensable as the oil that greases the wheels of a machine to keep them running smoothly.
—Leo Tolstoy

He who merits praise he never receives is better off than he who receives praise he never merits.
—Anonymous

PRAYER

Prayer is not a way of making use of God; prayer is a way of offering ourselves to God in order that he should be able to make use of us. It may be that one of our great faults in prayer is that we talk too much and listen too little. When prayer is at its highest, we wait in silence for God's voice to us.

—William Barclay

When life knocks you to your knees, and it will, get up! If it knocks you to your knees again, as it will, isn't that the best position in which to pray?

—Ethel Barrymore

Prayer is a wine that makes glad the heart of man.

—Saint Bernard of Clairvaux

Prayer is the language of a man burdened with a sense of need. It is the voice of the beggar, conscious of his poverty, asking of Another the things he needs.

—E. M. Bounds

Praying is the best school in which to learn to pray, prayer the best dictionary to define the art and the nature of praying.

—E. M. Bounds

Prayer is a shield to the soul, a sacrifice to God, and a scourge to Satan.

—John Bunyan

In prayer it is better to have a heart without words than words without a heart.

—John Bunyan

The meaning of prayer is that we get hold of God, not of the answer.

—Oswald Chambers

If you have ever prayed in the dawn you will ask yourself why you were so foolish as not to do it always: it is difficult to get into communion with God in the midst of the hurly-burly of the day.

—Oswald Chambers

Let our prayers, like the ancient sacrifices, ascend morning and evening. Let our days begin and end with God.

—William Ellery Channing

Really to pray is to stand to attention in the presence of the King and to be prepared to take orders from Him.

—Donald Coggan

Most of us have much trouble praying when we are in little trouble, but we have little trouble praying when we are in much trouble.

—Richard P. Cook

Prayer is the key of the morning and the bolt of the evening.

—Mohandas K. Gandhi

Prayer is the frame of the bridge from weeping to doing, built across the canyon of despair.

—James Gilliom

Prayer is putting the lens of your soul on time exposure. Prayer is putting on earphones that shut out all noises but the voice of you and your God.

—James Gilliom

Morning prayer: Good morning, God, I love You! What are you up to today? I want to be part of it.

—Norman Grubb

Prayer is the slender nerve that moves the muscle of Omnipotence.

—Edwin Hartsill

We carry checks on the bank of heaven and never cash them at the window of prayer. . . . We lie to God in prayer if we do not rely on God after prayer.

—Vance Havner

Prayer is a summit meeting in the very throne room of the universe. There is no higher level.

—Ralph Herring

Our prayers will see answers when we believe in what we ask for.

—John Iverson

I know there's a God. With the hand of prayer, I knocked at His door, and He opened it.

—Bob Jones Sr.

Prayer is exhaling the spirit of man and inhaling the spirit of God.

—Edwin Keith

He who has learned to pray has learned the greatest secret of a holy and happy life.

—William Law

Prayer is the most important thing in my life. If I should neglect prayer for a single day, I should lose a great deal of the fire of faith.

—Martin Luther

How often we look upon God as our last resource! We go to him because we have nowhere else to go. And then we learn that the storms of life have driven us, not upon the rocks, but into the desired haven.

—George MacDonald

Behind every work of God you will always find some kneeling form.

—Dwight L. Moody

I'd rather be able to pray than be a great preacher; Jesus Christ never taught his disciples how to preach, but only how to pray.

—Dwight L. Moody

He who prays as he ought will endeavor to live as he prays.

—John Owen

The law of prayer is the law of harvest: sow sparingly in prayer, reap sparingly; sow bountifully in prayer, reap bountifully. The trouble is that we are trying to get from our efforts what we never put into them.

—Leonard Ravenhill

The Bible doesn't say we should preach all the time, but it does say we should pray all the time.

—John R. Rice

Pray not for lighter burdens but for stronger backs.

—Theodore Roosevelt

Don't pray to escape trouble. Don't pray to be comfortable in your emotions. Pray to do the will of God in every situation. Nothing else is worth praying for.

—Samuel M. Shoemaker

Prayers are heard in heaven very much in proportion to our faith. Little faith will get very great mercies, but great faith still greater.

—Charles H. Spurgeon

Do not have your concert first, then tune your instrument afterwards. Begin the day with the Word of God and prayer, and get first of all in harmony with Him.

—J. Hudson Taylor

Don't bother to give God instructions; just report for duty.

—Corrie ten Boom

Prayer enlarges the heart until it is capable of containing God's gift of himself.

—Mother Teresa

It is time we put a stop to the coercive and compulsory bans on religious expression in our public schools. Those who oppose such expression constantly point to their desire to protect constitutional rights and intents. However, they seem oblivious to the fact that those who wrote and adopted the U.S. Constitution also made frequent references to the importance of prayer in the public area and the need for moral instruction based on biblical values in our schools.

—Forrest Turpen

Prayer is the gymnasium of the soul.

—Samuel M. Zwemer

PRAYER—ANSWERED

The whole canon of Bible teaching is to illustrate the great truth that God hears and answers prayer.

—E. M. Bounds

God's way of answering the Christian's prayer for more patience, experience, hope, and love often is to put him into the furnace of affliction.

—Richard Cecil

I believe we get an answer to our prayers when we are willing to obey what is implicit in the answer. I believe that we get a vision of God when we are willing to accept what that vision does to us.

—Elsie Chamberlain

Keep praying, but be thankful that God's answers are wiser than your prayers.

—William Culbertson

The privilege of prayer, to me, is one of the most cherished possessions, because faith and experience alike convince me that God Himself sees and answers, and His answers I will never venture to criticize. It is only my part to ask.

—Wilfred T. Grenfell

Listen, my friend! Your helplessness is your best prayer. It calls from your heart to the heart of God with greater effect than all your uttered pleas. He hears it from the very moment that you are seized with helplessness, and He becomes actively engaged at once in hearing and answering the prayer of your helplessness.

—O. Hallesby

I have lived to thank God that all my prayers have not been answered.

—Jean Ingelow

There are four ways God answers prayer: (1) No, not yet; (2) No, I love you too much; (3) Yes, I thought you'd never ask; (4) Yes, and here's more.

—Anne Lewis

Prayer is as vast as God because He is behind it. Prayer is as mighty as God because He has committed Himself to answer it.

—Leonard Ravenhill

I don't know of a single foreign product that enters this country untaxed except the answer to prayer.

—Mark Twain

PRAYER—CONFESSION

For a successful season of prayer, the best beginning is confession.

—Charles H. Spurgeon

PRAYER—INTERCESSION

Honest interceding is one of the means by which we come to a better under-
standing of God's will. Interceding causes us to look beyond our own needs to what God desires for mankind.

—Bobb Biehl and James W. Hagelganz

Talking to men for God is a great thing, but talking to God for men is greater still.

—E. M. Bounds

Intercessory prayer might be defined as loving our neighbor on our knees.

—Charles H. Brent

Jesus Christ carries on intercession for us in heaven; the Holy Ghost carries on intercession in us on earth; and we the saints have to carry on intercession for all men.

—Oswald Chambers

By intercessory prayer we can hold off Satan from other lives and give the Holy Ghost a chance with them. No wonder Jesus put such tremendous emphasis on prayer!

—Oswald Chambers

The prayer of intercession is the . . . level of prayer in which we share the burden of Christ for a person, circumstance, or need anywhere in the world.

—Paul Y. Cho

The prayers of Jesus verbally reported in the Gospels are not many in number and are few in words; but the indications of his habit of intercession are abundant and convincing.

—Harry Emerson Fosdick

Intercession . . . is love on its knees.

—Harry Emerson Fosdick

Can the humble request of believing lips restrain, accelerate, change the settled order of events? Can prayer make things that are not to be as though they were? Yes, a thousand times yes! Intercession is the mother tongue of the whole family of Christ.

—Dora Greenwell

Intercession is simply love at prayer.

—Henrietta C. Mears

Don't put people down—unless it's on your prayer list.

—Stan Michalski

PRAYER—PETITION

All who call on God in true faith, earnestly from the heart, will certainly be heard, and will receive what they have asked and desired, although not in the hour or in the measure, or the very thing which they ask; yet they will obtain something greater and more glorious than they had dared to ask.

—Martin Luther

Spread out your petition before God, and then say, "Thy will, not mine, be done." The sweetest lesson I have learned in God's school is to let the Lord choose for me.

—Dwight L. Moody

In our Lord's teaching about petitionary prayer there are three main principles. The first is confidence, the second is perseverance, and the third, for lack of a better word, I will call correspondence with Christ.

—William Temple

PRAYER—POWER

Men may spurn our appeals, reject our message, oppose our arguments, despise our persons, but they are helpless against our prayers.

—J. Sidlow Baxter

It would be well to remember the more we pray, the more power we have in prayer. Faith is not like gasoline, in danger of running out if we go too far. It is more like a muscle that strengthens from practice.

—Rex Humbard

Distance is no bar, space no barrier, to reaching the remotest place on earth. Nor is the power of prayer diminished by the distance between the person who prays and the person who is prayed for.

—Harold Lindsell

When we pray for rain we should get our umbrellas ready! When we pray for God's power, we should get ready to act.

—William McBirnie

God does not hear us because of the length of our prayer, but because of the sincerity of it. Prayer is not to be measured by the yard nor weighed by the pound. It is the might and force of it—the truth and reality of it—the energy and the intensity of it.

—Charles H. Spurgeon

PRAYER—PRAISE

Praise is almost the only thing we do on earth that we shall not cease to do in heaven.

—Samuel L. Brengle

You don't have to be afraid of praising God too much; unlike humans He never gets a big head.

—Paul Dibble

Praise is like a plow set to go deep into the soil of believers' hearts. It lets the glory of God into the details of daily living.

—C. M. Hanson

I have never committed the least matter to God that I have not had reason for infinite praise.

—Anna Shipton

PRAYER—THANKSGIVING

Thou who hast given so much to me, Give one thing more—a grateful heart.

—George Herbert

Lord, we're not just thankful for what You give us. We're thankful most of all for the privilege of learning to be thankful.

—Charlie "T" Jones

For three things I thank God every day of my life: thanks that He has vouch-safed me knowledge of His Works; deep thanks that He has set in my darkness the lamp of faith; deep, deepest thanks that I have another life to look forward to—a life joyous with light and flowers and heavenly song.

—Helen Keller

Our Father in heaven . . . if we do not have the grace to thank Thee for all that we have and enjoy, how can we have the effrontery to seek Thy further blessings? God, give us grateful hearts. For Jesus' sake. Amen

—Peter Marshall

O Lord, that lends me life, lend me a heart replete with thankfulness.

—William Shakespeare

PREACHERS/PREACHING
(See also Sermons)

The preacher's life must be a life of large accumulation. He must not be always trying to make sermons, but always seeking truth, and out of the truth that he has won, the sermons will make themselves.

—Phillips Brooks

No matter in what age or in what land he lives, the soul-winning preacher is, and must be, a pioneer in spirit. . . . He must set his soul to seek other souls, and must not permit any interference with his purpose.

—J. B. Chapman

In a live church the preacher does not do all the talking. Dependable witnesses are as indispensable in the church as in the courtroom. Lawyers and preachers are helpless if there are no witnesses.

—J. B. Chapman

If a man does not like sweat and toil and suffering and hardship and blood, he will not like the preacher-calling.

—J. B. Chapman

There has been too much preaching. Let's just take an outline and go into the pulpit and tell the story of Jesus and how He died for our sins and how He took them away, and sets us free. That's what we need to hear.

—J. Wilbur Chapman

I would have every minister of the gospel address his audience with the zeal of a friend, the generous energy of a father, and the exuberant affection of a mother.

—François de la Fenelon

The test of a preacher is that his congregation goes away saying, not what a lovely sermon, but, "I will do something!"

—Saint Francis de Sales

When I hear a man preach, I like to see him act as if he were fighting bees.

—Abraham Lincoln

Even the angels cannot preach the gospel. This is reserved for the church of Jesus Christ alone.

—Harold Lindsell

My grand point in preaching is to break the hard heart, and to heal the broken one.

—John F. Newton

Most preachers handle sin as they would handle snakes, at arm's length and with no greater intimacy and for no longer time than is absolutely necessary.

—Samuel M. Shoemaker

Give me one hundred preachers who fear nothing but sin and desire nothing but God, and I care not a straw whether they be clergymen or laymen; such alone will shake the gates of hell and set up the kingdom of God upon earth.

—John Wesley

PREJUDICE
(See also Bigotry, Intolerance)

Prejudices, it is well known, are most difficult to eradicate from the heart whose soil has never been loosened or fertilized by education; they grow there, firm as weeds among stones.

—Charlotte Bronté

Prejudices are rarely overcome by argument; not being founded in reason, they cannot be destroyed by logic.

—Tryon Edwards

I am free of all prejudices. I hate everyone equally.

—W. C. Fields

Every bigot was once a child free of prejudice.

—Sister Mary de Lourdes

Too many of our prejudices are like pyramids upside down. They rest on tiny, trivial incidents, but they spread upward and outward until they fill our minds.

—William McChesney Martin Jr.

Reasoning against a prejudice is like fighting against a shadow; it exhausts the reasoner without visibly affecting the prejudice.

—Charles Mildmay

A great many people think they are thinking when they are really rearranging their prejudices.

—Edward R. Murrow

An individual is as strong as his or her prejudice. Two things reduce prejudice—education and laughter.

—Laurence J. Peter

It is not possible for Christians to take part in anti-Semitism. We are Semites spiritually.

—Pope Pius XI

Never try to reason the prejudice out of a man. It was not reasoned into him and cannot be reasoned out.

—Sidney Smith

Prejudice is a disease caused by hardening of the categories.

—William Arthur Ward

PREPARATION

It ought to be the business of every day to prepare for the last day.

—Matthew Henry

God is preparing His heroes; and when the opportunity comes, He can fit them into their places in a moment.

—A. B. Simpson

PRESENT, THE
(See also Today)

One of the illusions of life is that the present hour is not the critical, decisive hour. Write it on your hearts that every day is the best day of the year.

—Ralph Waldo Emerson

It is wise to think about the past and learn from it. But it is unwise for us to be in the past.... It is also wise for us to think about the future and plan for it. But it is unwise for us to be in the future.... The present moment is the only reality we will ever experience.

—Spencer Johnson

In rivers, the water that you touch is the last of what has passed and the first of that which comes: so it is with the present time.

—Leonardo da Vinci

I can feel guilty about the past, apprehensive about the future, but only in the present can I act. The ability to be in the present is a major component of mental wellness.

—Abraham Maslow

We are not living in eternity. We have only this moment, sparkling like a star in our hand—and melting like a snowflake. Let us use it before it is too late.

—Marie Beynon Ray

Now is the watchword of the wise.

—Charles H. Spurgeon

He who governed the world before I was born shall take care of it likewise when I am dead. My part is to improve the present moment.

—John Wesley

PRESIDENCY

In America, anyone can become president. That's one of the risks you take.

—Adlai Stevenson

Within the first few months I discovered that being a president is like riding a tiger. A man has to keep riding or be swallowed.

—Harry S. Truman

From forty to sixty percent of the presidential office is not in administration but in morals, politics, and spiritual leadership.... As President of the United States and servant of God, he has much more to do than to run a desk as the head of the greatest corporation in the world. He has to guide a people in the greatest adventure ever undertaken on this planet.

—William Allen White

PRICE

What you get free costs too much.

—Jean Anouilh

There is hardly anything in the world that some man cannot make a little worse and sell a little cheaper, and the people who consider price only are this man's lawful prey.

—John Ruskin

The cost of a thing ... is the amount of life it requires to be exchanged for it, immediately or in the long run.

—Henry David Thoreau

I judge all things only by the price they shall gain in eternity.

—John Wesley

PRIDE

Pride slays thanksgiving, but a humble mind is the soil out of which thanks naturally grow. A proud man is seldom a grateful man, for he never thinks he gets as much as he deserves.

—Henry Ward Beecher

When a little child becomes conscious of being a little child, the child-likeness is gone; and when a saint becomes conscious of being a saint, something has gone wrong.

—Oswald Chambers

To be proud of virtue is to poison yourself with the antidote.

—Benjamin Franklin

It is the eyes of other people that ruin us. If all but myself were blind, I should want neither a fine house nor fine furniture.

—Benjamin Franklin

Pride is to the character what the attic is to the house—the highest part, and generally the most empty.

—Henrietta C. Mears

Let me give you the history of pride in three small chapters. The beginning of pride was in heaven. The continuance of pride is on earth. The end of pride is in hell. This history shows how inconvenient it is.

—R. Newton

He that is proud eats up himself. Pride is his own glass, his own trumpet, his own chronicle, and whatever praises itself but in the deed, devours the deed in the praise.

—William Shakespeare

Swallow your pride occasionally. It's non-fattening.

—Frank Tyger

If you feel that you are indispensable, put your finger in a glass of water, withdraw it, and note the hole you have left.

—Anonymous

PRINCIPLES

He or she who floats with the current, who does not guide himself, according to higher principles, who has no ideal, no real standards . . . such a person is a mere article of the world's furniture—a thing moved, instead of a living and moving being—an echo not a voice.

—Henri Frédéric Amiel

Expedients are for the hour, but principles are for the ages.

—Henry Ward Beecher

Most men, in politics as in everything, attribute the results of their imprudence to the firmness of their principles.

—Benjamin Constant

Temporary deviations from fundamental principles are always more or less dangerous. When the first pretext fails, those who become interested in prolonging the evil will rarely be at a loss for other pretexts.

—James Madison

No free government, or the blessings of liberty, can be preserved to any people, but by a firm adherence to justice, moderation, temperance, frugality, and virtue, and by frequent recurrence to fundamental principles.

—George Mason

It is often easier to fight for principles than to live up to them.

—Adlai Stevenson

PRIORITIES

Why are you doing what others can do, when you are leaving undone what only you can do?

—Bruce Bugbee

Prioritize! It's one of the most important words in the English language.

—Ted W. Engstrom

It is not so important to be serious as it is to be serious about the important things. The monkey wears an expression that would do credit to any college student, but the monkey is serious because it itches.

—Robert M. Hutchins

I thank God I live in a country where dreams can come true, where failure is the first step to success, and where success is only another form of failure if we forget what our priorities should be.

—Harry Lloyd

It is good not to have too many trades. "Many trades, few blessings."

—Jewish Proverb

PROBLEMS

A man with fifty problems is twice as alive as a man with twenty-five. If you haven't got problems, you should get down on your knees and ask, Lord, don't You trust me anymore?

—John Bainbridge

One of the surest ways to bolster your ego is suddenly to find a simple solution to what you always felt was a most difficult problem.

—O. A. Battista

One man who never hesitates to tackle a problem is worth a dozen who prefer to talk about a solution to it.

—O. A. Battista

The troubles of the world will continue to increase as long as we train people how to spot problems instead of how to solve them.

—O. A. Battista

I think the next best thing to solving a problem is finding some humor in it.

—Frank A. Clark

Having problems may not be so bad. We have a special place for folks who have none—it's called a cemetery.

—Frank A. Clark

The best way to forget your own problems is to help someone else solve his.

—Lloyd Cory

The message from the moon . . . is that no problem need any longer be considered insoluble.

—Norman Cousins

Progress implies both new and continuing problems and, unlike presidential administrations, problems rarely have terminal dates.

—Dwight D. Eisenhower

Most people spend more time and energy going around problems than in trying to solve them.

—Henry Ford

You must live with people to know their problems, and live with God in order to solve them.

—Peter T. Forsyth

Total absence of problems would be the beginning of death for a society or an individual. We aren't constructed to live in that kind of world. We are problem-solvers by nature, problem-seekers, problem-requirers.

—John W. Gardner

All problems become smaller if you don't dodge them but confront them. Touch a thistle timidly and it pricks you; grasp it boldly and its spine crumbles.

—William F. Halsey

It is wise not to solve any problems that you do not have to solve. Save your time, your nerves, and your brains until you are certain that a problem exists and that you are the person who has to do the solving. Many problems, like storms, never arrive in spite of threatening skies.

—Edward Hodnett

Problems breed problems; but problems also are the main breeding ground for success. Seldom does real success, real progress, come in any other manner.

—Gerald Jaggers

Why can't problems hit us when we're seventeen and know everything?

—A. C. Jolly

The easiest way to solve a problem is to pick an easy one.

—Franklin P. Jones

Problems are only opportunities in work clothes.

—Henry J. Kaiser

If you keep your head when all about you are losing theirs, you don't understand the problem.

—Gerald F. Lieberman

I'm afraid we have become a nation of plodders, who feel that all problems can be found in books and that the answers are on a certain page.

—Clarence Linder

The world now has so many problems that if Moses had come down from Mount Sinai today the two tablets would have been aspirin.

—Robert Orben

When it comes to defining real problems, the main pitfall to look out for is this: we are inclined to take the

first possible solution that happens to pop into our minds, and make the mistake of thinking that's our problem. The result is that we sometimes overlook the real problem and do not give ourselves a chance to consider all possible solutions.

—William J. Reilly

The basic problem most people have is that they're doing nothing to solve their basic problem.

—Bob Richardson

So you've got a problem? That's good! Why? Because repeated victories over your problems are the rungs on your ladder to success. With each victory you grow in wisdom, stature, and experience. You become a bigger, better, more successful person each time you meet a problem and tackle and conquer it with a positive mental attitude.

—W. Clement Stone

Let God's promises shine on your problems.

—Corrie ten Boom

To welcome a problem without resentment is to cut its size in half.... Problems are challenges we can complain about, dwell on, give in to—or think through.... We can spend our time aimlessly licking our wounds or aggressively licking our problems.... Our Goliaths can be feared or fought, succumbed to or slain.

—William Arthur Ward

PROCRASTINATION

God has promised forgiveness to your repentance, but He has not promised tomorrow to your procrastination.

—Saint Augustine

When there is a hill to climb, don't think that waiting will make it any smaller.

—H. Jackson Brown

Stop procrastinating! I have only to see those words and I'm jerked into starting immediately, because I know only too well from personal experience how easy it is to put off getting down to solid work.

—John Creasy

My advice is, never do tomorrow what you can do today. Procrastination is the thief of time. Collar him!

—Charles Dickens

Conditions are never just right. People who delay action until all factors are favorable do nothing.

—William Feather

One of the greatest labor-saving devices of today is tomorrow.

—Vincent T. Foss

Procrastination is opportunity's natural assassin.

—Victor Kiam

No unwelcome tasks become any the less unwelcome by putting them off till tomorrow. Undone, they stand threatening and disturbing our tranquility, and hindering our communion with God.

—Alexander Maclaren

Look to today. Procrastination is the art of keeping up with yesterday.

—Don Marquis

Only put off until tomorrow what you are willing to die having left undone.

—Pablo Picasso

By the streets of "by and by," one arrives at the house of "never."

—Spanish Proverb

The sooner you fall behind, the more time you have to catch up.

—Anonymous

PROFIT

It is a socialist idea that making profits is a vice; I consider the real vice is making losses.

—Winston Churchill

Profit is the ignition system of our economic engine.

—Charles Sawyer

PROGRESS

We should so live and labor in our time that what came to us as seed may go to the next generation as blossom, and that which came to us as blossom may go to them as fruit. That is what we mean by progress.

—Henry Ward Beecher

Restlessness and discontent are the first necessities of progress.

—Thomas Edison

Progress is made by correcting the mistakes resulting from the making of progress.

—Claude Gibb

Progress is our ability to complicate simplicity.

—Thor Heyerdahl

You can't sit on the lid of progress. If you do, you will be blown to pieces.

—Henry J. Kaiser

The test of our progress is not whether we add more to the abundance of those who have much; it is whether we provide enough for those who have too little.

—Franklin Delano Roosevelt

All progress has resulted from people who took unpopular positions.

—Adlai Stevenson

Progress is not created by contented people.

—Frank Tyger

PROMISES
(See also God's Promises)
He who is most slow in making a promise is usually the most faithful in the performance of it.

—Jean Jacques Rousseau

PROSPERITY
Watch lest prosperity destroy generosity.

—Henry Ward Beecher

Prosperity is only an instrument to be used, not a deity to be worshipped.

—Calvin Coolidge

Few of us can stand prosperity. Another man's, I mean.

—Mark Twain

It is poor prosperity that is blind to the need of God's favor.

—John Wanamaker

PSYCHIATRY
A psychiatrist is a fellow who asks you a lot of expensive questions your wife asks for nothing.

—Joey Adams

Anybody who goes to see a psychiatrist ought to have his head examined.

—Samuel Goldwyn

Freud's discarding of moral values has contributed toward making the analyst just as blind as the patient.

—Karen Horney

PUNCTUALITY
I am a believer in punctuality, though it makes me very lonely.

—E. V. Lucas

I owe my success in life to having always been a quarter of an hour beforehand.

—Horatio Nelson

The trouble with being punctual is that nine times out of ten there is nobody there to appreciate it.

—Anonymous

PURITY

It is safe to tell the pure in heart that they shall see God, for only the pure in heart want to.

—C. S. Lewis

PURPOSE

Have a purpose in life, and having it, throw into your work such strength of mind and muscle as God has given you.

—Thomas Carlyle

We're not primarily put on this earth to see through one another, but to see one another through.

—Peter De Vries

It is better to die for something than it is to live for nothing.

—Bob Jones Sr.

Every life should have a purpose to which it can give the energies of its mind and the enthusiasms of its heart. That life without a purpose will be prey to the perverted ways waiting for the uncommitted life.

—C. Neil Strait

QUALITY

Quality is not an act. It is a habit.

—Aristotle

The best things and best people rise out of their separateness. I'm against a homogenized society because I want the cream to rise.

—Robert Frost

Quality is never an accident; it is always the result of intelligent effort.

—John Ruskin

QUESTIONS
(See also Answers)

The first key to wisdom is assiduous and frequent questioning. . . . For by doubting we come to inquiry, and by inquiry we arrive at truth.

—Peter Abelard

The important thing is not to stop questioning.

—Albert Einstein

Language was invented to ask questions. Answers may be grunts and gestures, but questions must be spoken. Humanness came of age when man asked the first question. Social stagnation results not from lack of answers but from absence of the impulse to ask questions.

—Eric Hoffer

In all affairs, business and personal, it's a healthy thing now and then to hang a big question mark on the things you've long taken for granted.

—Bertrand Russell

No man really becomes a fool until he stops asking questions.

—Charles P. Steinmetz

QUIET
(See also Solitude)

If we have not quiet in our minds, outward comfort will do no more for us than a golden slipper on a gouty foot.

—John Bunyan

The happiest heart that ever beat
Was in some quiet breast
That found the common daylight sweet,
And left to Heaven the rest.

—John Vance Cheney

Be still; only a silent mind can absorb.

—Diogenes

Only in quiet waters things mirror themselves undistorted. Only in a quiet mind is adequate perception of the world.

—Hans Margolius

I delight to steal away for days and weeks together, and bathe my spirit in the freedom of the old woods, and to grow young again, . . . counting the white clouds that sail along the sky, softly and tranquilly. . . . I like to steep my soul in a sea of quiet, with nothing floating past me . . . but the perfume of flowers, and soaring birds, and shadows of clouds.

—Donald G. Mitchell

All the misfortunes of men spring from their not knowing how to live quietly at home in their own rooms.

—Blaise Pascal

QUIET TIME
(See also Devotions)

Time alone with God is absolutely imperative for the man who desires to be *his best!* It tempers—seasons— settles the man, builds strength into the very fiber of his life!

—Richard C. Halverson

Be still, and in the quiet moments, listen to the voice of your heavenly Father. His words can renew your spirit. No one knows you and your needs like He does.

—Janet Weaver

QUOTATIONS

To quote copiously and well requires taste, judgment, and erudition, a feeling for the beautiful, an appreciation of the noble, and a sense of the profound.

—Christian Bovée

It is a good thing for an educated man to read books of quotations.

—Winston Churchill

The wisdom of the wise and the experience of ages may be preserved by quotation.

—Benjamin Disraeli

When a thing has been said and said well, have no scruple. Take it and copy it.

—Anatole France

A book that furnishes no quotations is no book—it is a plaything.

—Thomas Love Peacock

A fine quotation is a diamond on the finger of a man of wit, and a pebble in the hand of a fool.

—Joseph Roux

I often quote myself. It adds spice to my conversation.

—George Bernard Shaw

RAINBOWS

A rainbow is the ribbon nature puts on after washing her hair.

—Ramon Gomez

Rainbows apologize for angry skies.

—Sylvia A. Voirol

Rainbows are a beautiful reminder that God always keeps His promises.

—Anonymous

READING

(See also Books)

My early and invincible love of reading I would not exchange for the treasures of India.

—Edward Gibbon

Every man who knows how to read has it in his power to magnify, to multiply the ways in which he exists, to make his life full, significant, and interesting.

—Aldous Huxley

What is reading but silent conversation?

—Walter Savage Landor

To acquire the habit of reading is to construct for yourself a refuge from almost all the miseries of life.

—W. Somerset Maugham

Reading is to the mind what exercise is to the body.

—Richard Steele

REALITY

I have lived long enough to be battered by the realities of life, and not too long to be downed by them.

—John Mason Brown

Reality is that which, when you stop believing in it, doesn't go away.

—Philip K. Dick

REASON

He who will not reason is a bigot; he who cannot is a fool; and he who dares not is a slave.

—William Drummond

If you do not hear reason she will rap you on the knuckles.

—Benjamin Franklin

People who are driven by their appetites perish by ignoring their reason; and people who are governed by their reason too often perish by ignoring their appetites; and . . . only a few wise ones are able to sustain a creative tension between those opposites.

—Sydney J. Harris

In quiet places, reason abounds.

—Adlai Stevenson

It is useless to attempt to reason a man out of a thing he was never reasoned into.

—Jonathan Swift

REASONS

A man always has two reasons for what he does—a good one, and the real one.

—J. P. Morgan

Some men have thousands of reasons why they cannot do what they want to do, when all they need is one reason why they can.

—Willis R. Whitney

RECONCILIATION

Why should the world believe in reconciliation when it doesn't see the church reconciled? And the church is not going to be reconciled even if it gets all the issues solved. It will be reconciled only through Jesus Christ. He is the Reconciler.

—Richard C. Halverson

REDEMPTION

(See also Salvation)

Redemption is a word implying helplessness. The "picture of redemption" is of one held captive by forces that cannot be overcome. Only a third party can intervene to rescue. Redemption never comes by our own efforts.... Spiritually, redemption cannot happen without a Redeemer. This word is precious because it reminds followers of Jesus that relationship with Him has been purchased at great cost.

—Bob Snyder

REFLECTION

If we would only give, just once, the same amount of reflection to what we want out of life that we give to the question of what to do with a two weeks' vacation, we would be startled at our false standards and the aimless procession of our busy days.

—Dorothy Canfield

To doubt everything or to believe everything are two equally convenient solutions; both dispense with the necessity of reflection.

—Jules Henri Poincaré

The man who acts is always devoid of conscience. No man has any conscience except the man who pauses to reflect.

—Johann von Goethe

REGENERATION

(See also Born Again, Salvation)

The old nature must be cast aside as a complete wreck, and good for nothing, and the man made a new creation in Christ Jesus. But willing as we may be to admit this truth, few lessons are harder to learn.

—J. Gregory Mantle

Self can never cast out self, even in the regenerate man. Praise God! The death of Jesus, once and forever, is the death to self. And the gift of the Holy Spirit makes our very own the power of the death-life.

—Andrew Murray

REGRET

Regret for time wasted can become a power for good in the time that remains, if we will only stop the waste, and the idle, useless regretting.

—Arthur Brisbane

Regret is an appalling waste of energy. You can't build on it; it's only good for wallowing in.

—Katherine Mansfield

The feet of regret step into the shoes of opportunity neglected.

—Anonymous

RELATIONSHIPS
(See also Others, People)

Your greatest pleasure is that which rebounds from hearts that you have made glad.

—Henry Ward Beecher

Blessed are the happiness-makers. Blessed are they who know how to shine on one's gloom with their cheer.

—Henry Ward Beecher

When dealing with people, let us remember we are not dealing with creatures of logic. We are dealing with creatures of emotion, creatures bustling with prejudices and motivated by pride and vanity.

—Dale Carnegie

People who matter are most aware that everyone else does too.

—Malcolm S. Forbes

In a world that is focused on improved techniques and newer and newer technologies, there has never been discovered a shortcut to building relationships—not with people, and especially not with God.

—Joe Hesh

Whenever two people meet there are really six people present. There is each man as he sees himself, each as the other person sees him, and each man as he really is.

—William James

Be charitable and indulgent to every one but thyself.

—Joseph Joubert

I always prefer to believe the best of everybody—it saves so much time.

—Rudyard Kipling

One of the reasons our society has become such a mess is that we're isolated from each other.

—Maggie Kuhn

It is the nature of man to feel as much bound by the favors they do as by those they receive.

—Niccolo Machiavelli

RELAXATION
(See also Leisure, Rest)

The time to relax is when you don't have time for it.

—Sydney J. Harris

RELIABILITY

Flash powder makes a more brilliant light than the arc lamp, but you cannot use it to light your street corner because it doesn't last long enough. Stability is more essential to success than brilliancy.

—Anonymous

God has never been able to use any man in a large way who could not be trusted in an emergency.

—Anonymous

Stick to the fight when you're hardest hit—
It's when things seem worst that you must not quit.

—Anonymous

RELIGION

The strength of a country is the strength of its religious convictions.

—Calvin Coolidge

I've noticed that, among religious people, many are cold and a few are frozen.

—Charlie "T" Jones

I didn't find God—He found me. Religions teach man's search for God, and the gospel teaches God's search for man.

—E. Stanley Jones

Religion is the best armor in the world, but the worst cloak.

—John F. Newton

Should a man happen to err in supposing the Christian religion to be true, he could not be a loser by the mistake. But how irreparable is his loss, and how inexpressible his danger, who should err in supposing it to be false.

—Blaise Pascal

One of the very worst sins of religious people is that they go about the world looking as if God were dead.

—A. Maude Royden

Most men, indeed, play at religion as they play at games, religion itself being of all games the one most universally played.

—A. W. Tozer

Our religion must not alone be the concern of the emotions, but must be woven into the warp and woof of our everyday lives.

—Booker T. Washington

Reason and experience both forbid us to expect that national morality can prevail in exclusion of religious principle.

—George Washington

Educate people without religion and you make them but clever devils.

—Arthur Wellesley

Christianity is not about religion—it's about relationship.

—Anonymous

REPENTANCE

There is one case of death-bed repentance recorded—the penitent thief—that no one should despair; and only one, that no one should presume.

—Saint Augustine

Of all acts of man, repentance is the most divine. The greatest of all faults is to be conscious of none.

—Thomas Carlyle

You cannot repent too soon, because you do not know how soon it may become too late.

—Thomas Fuller

Repentance was perhaps best defined by a small girl: "It's to be sorry enough to quit."

—C. H. Kilmer

Man is born with his back toward God. When he truly repents, he turns right around and faces God. Repentance is a change of mind.

—Dwight L. Moody

There is no repentance in the grave.

—Isaac Watts

REPUTATION
(See also Character)

You can't build a reputation on what you are *going* to do.

—Henry Ford

A reputation once broken may possibly be repaired, but the world will always keep their eyes on the spot where the crack was.

—Joseph Hall

Many a man's reputation would not know his character if they met on the street.

—Elbert Hubbard

A man's reputation is the opinion people have of him; his character is what he really is.

—Jack Miner

If I take care of my character, my reputation will take care of itself.

—Dwight L. Moody

The way to gain a good reputation is to endeavor to be what you desire to appear.

—Socrates

Life is for one generation; a good name is forever.

—Japanese Proverb

RESEARCH

The feeling of "aha, that's it," which accompanies the clothing of a situation with meaning, is emotionally very satisfying, and is the major charm of scientific research, or artistic creation, and of the solution of crossword puzzles. It is why the intellectual life is fun.

—Hudson Hoagland

Research is an organized method for keeping you reasonably dissatisfied with what you have.

—Charles F. Kettering

A research laboratory is not simply a building that contains apparatus for conducting experiments. I contend that it is a state of mind. . . . The research man ought to be thought of as the fellow you keep up in the crows-nest to see beyond your horizon, to tell you where there is another prize ship to be taken or a man-o'-war to be avoided.

—Charles F. Kettering

Research is exemplified in the problem-solving mind as contrasted with the let-well-enough-alone mind. It is the composer mind instead of the fiddler mind. It is the *tomorrow* mind instead of the *yesterday* mind.

—Charles F. Kettering

If politics is the art of the possible, research is surely the art of the soluble.

—Peter Medawar

If you copy from one author, it's plagiarism. If you copy from two, it's research.

—Wilson Mizner

Research is to see what everybody has seen, and to think what nobody else has thought.

—Albert Szent-Györgyi

Research means going into the unknown with the hope of finding something new to bring home. If you know what you're going to do, or even to find there, then it is not research at all, then it is only a kind of honorable occupation.

—Albert Szent-Györgyi

True research requires an objective, even if the results turn out to be different from expectation.

—Anonymous

RESOLUTIONS

Nothing relieves and ventilates the mind like a resolution.

—John Burroughs

Resolved, to live with all my might while I do live. Resolved, never to lose one moment of time, to improve it in the most profitable way I possibly can. Resolved, never to do anything that I should despise or think meanly of in another. Resolved, never to do anything out of revenge. Resolved, never to do anything that I should be afraid to do if it were the last hour of my life.

—Jonathan Edwards

Just as soon as we make a good resolution we get into a situation that makes its observance unbearable.

—William Feather

You may be whatever you resolve to be. Determine to be something in the world, and you will be something. "I cannot" never accomplished anything; "I will try" has wrought wonders.

—J. Hawes

Empty pieties and good resolutions are part of the natural equipment of every proper man. They were never meant to be performed or fulfilled, but in the scheme of things, they serve their purpose.

—Holbrook Jackson

Make your resolutions so clear and firm that nothing can lure you from your chosen path. Substitute doing for dreaming and achievement for apathy.
—Grenville Kleiser

Always bear in mind that your own resolution to succeed is more important than any other one thing.
—Abraham Lincoln

Good resolutions are a pleasant crop to sow.
—Lucas Malet

Resolve that whatever you do, you will bring the whole man to it; that you will fling the whole weight of your being into it.
—Orison Swett Marden

What you are to be, or become, depends upon the character of your resolutions.
—Walter Matthews

I believe that the resolutions less likely to be kept are those most likely to be made—the high that proved too high, the heroic for earth too hard.
—Rose McCaulay

You are not going to have the laugh on me by luring me into resolutions. I know my weaknesses.... I shall continue to be pleasant to insurance agents, from sheer lack of manhood, and to keep library books out over the date and so incur a fine. My only hope, you see, is resolutely to determine to persist in these failings. Then by sheer perversity, I may grow out of them.
—Christopher Morley

We always, it seems, do better with resolutions if we tell others, for we fear their mockery more than the prickings of our conscience.
—Gorham Munson

Good resolutions are often checks drawn on an account with insufficient funds.
—Jules Renard

Every mind is a great slumbering power until awakened by keen desire and by definite resolution to do.
—Edgar Roberts

When you rise in the morning, form a resolution to make the day a happy one to a fellow creature.
—Sydney Smith

RESPECT

Respect is love in plain clothes.
—Frankie Byrne

The respect of those you respect is worth more than the applause of the multitude.
—Arnold H. Glasow

RESPONSIBILITY

No snowflake in an avalanche ever feels responsible.
—Stanislaw Lec

You can't escape the responsibility of tomorrow by evading it today.
—Abraham Lincoln

We are not put here on earth to play around. There is work to be done. There are responsibilities to be met. Humanity needs the abilities of every man and woman.

—Alden Palmer

It is the mark of weak men that they break down under unusual responsibilities, of strong men that they are developed by them.

—C. I. Scofield

People need responsibility. They resist assuming it, but they cannot get along without it.

—John Steinbeck

With every right there is a responsibility. Just once, I wish someone would demand his responsibility.

—Paul Sweeney

REST
(See also Leisure, Relaxation)

We do not rest because our work is done; we rest because God commanded it and created us to have a need for it.

—Gordon MacDonald

Rest is the sweet sauce of labor.

—Plutarch

Rest has cured more people than all the medicine in the world.

—Harold J. Reilly

RESULTS

The world expects results. Don't tell others about the labor pains. Show them the baby.

—Arnold H. Glasow

RESURRECTION
(See also Easter)

I believe in the miracle of the Resurrection, everywhere apparent, for it assures me that life is triumphant and that death is but another phase of life.

—Waldemar W. Argow

Our Lord has written the promise of the Resurrection, not in books alone, but in every leaf in springtime.

—Martin Luther

Every time a man finds that his heart is troubled, that he is not rejoicing in God, a resurrection must follow; a resurrection out of the night of troubled thought into the gladness of the truth.

—George MacDonald

The stone was rolled away from the door, not to permit Christ to come out, but to enable the disciples to go in.

—Peter Marshall

The bodily resurrection of Jesus Christ from the dead is the crowning proof of Christianity.

—Henry Morris

The Gospels do not explain the Resurrection; the Resurrection explains the Gospels.

—John S. Whale

Belief in the Resurrection is not an appendage to the Christian faith; it *is* the Christian faith.

—John S. Whale

RETIREMENT

Some people are born about sixty-five years old and are always ready to retire. Some stay twenty-one until they are ninety.

—Sir William Beveridge

Retirement at sixty-five is ridiculous. When I was sixty-five, I still had pimples.

—George Burns

To retire is to begin to die.

—Pablo Casals

A foundation of good sense, and a cultivation of learning, are required to give a seasoning to retirement and make us taste of its blessings.

—John Dryden

Retirement should be based on the tread, not the mileage.

—Allen Ludden

The best time to start thinking about your retirement is before your boss does.

—Anonymous

REVENGE
(See also Forgiveness)

A man who studies revenge keeps his own wounds green.

—Francis Bacon

Revenge is the poor delight of little minds.

—Juvenal

There is no passion of the human heart that promises so much and pays so little as that of revenge.

—H. B. Shaw

REVERENCE

The soul of the Christian religion is reverence.

—Johann von Goethe

Reverence is the very first element of religion; it cannot but be felt by every one who has right views of the divine greatness and holiness, and of his own character in the sight of God.

—Charles Simmons

REVIVAL

The best way to revive a church is to build a fire in the pulpit.

—Dwight L. Moody

The call to revival is given not to the unbelieving but to the family of God.

—Robert Boyd Munger

Revival is absolutely essential to restrain the righteous anger of God, to restore the conscious awareness of God, and to reveal the gracious activity of God.

—Stephen Olford

REVOLT

Revolt is revolt whether it is militant, blatant rebellion, or quiet, respectable indifference.

—Richard C. Halverson

REVOLUTION

If the average church would suddenly take seriously the notion that every lay member—man or woman—is really a minister of Christ, we could have something like a revolution in a very short time.

—Elton Trueblood

REWARD

The highest reward for a person's toil is not what they get for it, but what they become by it.

—John Ruskin

RICHES
(See also Wealth)

You don't make the poor richer by making the rich poorer.

—Winston Churchill

The riches we impart are the only wealth we shall always retain.

—Matthew Henry

The richest I have ever been was when I was a boy and found a five-dollar bill. It is the only time in my life I ever had enough money to buy more than I wanted. I guess you can't get richer than that.

—Walling Keith

A man is rich in proportion to the number of things that he can afford to let alone.

—Henry David Thoreau

The truly rich are satisfied with what they have, no matter how little; the truly poor are dissatisfied with what they have, no matter how much.

—Anonymous

RIGHT AND WRONG
(See also Honesty)

It may make a difference to all eternity whether we do right or wrong today.

—James Freeman Clarke

If mankind had wished for what is right, they might have had it long ago.

—William Hazlitt

Rise above principle and do what's right.

—Walter Heller

The eternal difference between right and wrong does not fluctuate. It is immutable. And if the moral order does not change, then it imposes on us obligations toward God and man. Duty, then, requires the willingness to accept responsibility and to sacrifice one's desires to a higher law.

—Patrick Henry

Let us have faith that right makes might, and in that faith let us to the end dare to do our duty as we understand it.

—Abraham Lincoln

Lord, when we are wrong, make us willing to change; and when we are right, make us easy to live with.
— Peter Marshall

Before you can help make the world right, you must be made right within.
— John Miller

Right is right even if everyone is against it. Wrong is wrong even if everyone is for it.
— William Penn

Whatever people may think of you, do that which you believe to be right. Be alike indifferent to censure or praise.
— Pythagoras

RIGHTEOUSNESS

The fear of doing right is the grand treason in times of danger.
— Henry Ward Beecher

You can always tell when you are on the road of righteousness—it's uphill.
— Ernest Blevins

He who walks straight seldom falls.
— Leonardo Da Vinci

Nothing is settled until it is settled right.
— Abraham Lincoln

Always do right. This will surprise some people and astonish the rest.
— Mark Twain

God never alters the robe of righteousness to fit man, but the man to fit the robe.
— Anonymous

RIGHTS

I am the inferior of any man whose rights I trample underfoot.
— Horace Greeley

The sacred rights of mankind are not to be rummaged for among old parchments, or musty records. They are written, as with a sunbeam, in the whole volume of human nature by the hand of the divinity itself; and can never be erased or obscured by mortal power.
— Alexander Hamilton

RISK

Any life truly lived is a risky business, and if one puts up too many fences against the risks, one ends up shutting out life itself.
— Kenneth S. Davis

If the Creator had a purpose in equipping us with a neck, he surely meant us to stick it out.
— Arthur Koestler

Don't be afraid to take a big step if one is indicated. You can't cross a chasm in two small jumps.
— David Lloyd George

Take calculated risks. That is quite different from being rash.
— George S. Patton

It's this simple: if I never try anything, I never learn anything. If I never take a risk, I stay where I am.

—Hugh Prather

Take risks. You can't fall off the bottom.

—Barbara Proctor

Far better it is to dare mighty things, to win glorious triumphs, even though checkered by failure, than to take rank with those poor spirits who neither enjoy much nor suffer much, because they live in the gray twilight that knows neither victory nor defeat.

—Theodore Roosevelt

Why not go out on a limb? Isn't that where the fruit is?

—Frank Scully

ROMANCE

In a great romance, each person basically plays a part that the other really likes.

—Elizabeth Ashley

I'm convinced romance is here to stay. So is hot soup. With me, the soup comes first.

—George Burns

Romance is the irresistible desire to be irresistibly desired.

—Robert Frost

Romance is like a game of chess: one false move and you're mated.

—Anonymous

ROYALTY

Christ brought to the world a new conception of royalty. He rules by love and not by force. That, as he expressly said, is the difference between His kingdom and the kingdoms of the world.

—William Temple

RULES

Don't ask too much of any set of rules. Think of how long it is taking to put over the ones Moses presented.

—David Bentham

People have rules for when they can't trust their instincts.

—Kenneth A. Fisher

The young man knows the rules, but the old man knows the exceptions.

—Oliver Wendell Holmes

Rules are for when brains run out.

—George Papashvily

S

SABBATH
(See also Sunday)

Through the week we go down into the valleys of care and shadow. Our Sabbaths should be hills of light and joy in God's presence; and so as time rolls by we shall go from mountain top to mountain top, till at last we catch the glory of the gate, and enter in to go no more out forever.

—Henry Ward Beecher

A world without a Sabbath would be like a man without a smile, like a summer without flowers, and like a homestead without a garden. It is the joyous day of the whole week.

—Henry Ward Beecher

The Sabbath is God's present to the working man, and one of its chief objects is to prolong his life. . . . The savings bank of human existence is the weekly Sabbath.

—William G. Blaikie

I feel as if God had, by giving the Sabbath, given fifty-two springs in every year.

—Samuel Taylor Coleridge

You show me a nation that has given up the Sabbath, and I will show you a nation that has got the seed of decay.

—Dwight L. Moody

The longer I live the more highly do I estimate the Christian Sabbath, and the more grateful do I feel to those who impress its importance on the community.

—Daniel Webster

SACRIFICE

The altar of sacrifice is the touchstone of character.

—O. P. Clifford

I never made a sacrifice. We ought not to talk of "sacrifice" when we remember the great sacrifice that He made, who left His Father's throne on high to give Himself for us.

—David Livingstone

It is the habit of making sacrifices in small things that enables us for making them in great, when it is asked of us.

—Anthony W. Thorold

SADNESS
(See also Sorrow)

Sadness needs its own time to be.

—Karen Berry

Sad soul, take comfort nor forget
The sunrise never failed us yet.

—Celia Laighton Thaxter

SAINTS

Some of us always want to be illuminated saints with golden haloes and the flush of inspiration.... A gilt-edged saint is no good; he is abnormal, unfit for daily life.... We must never make our moments of inspiration our standard.

—Oswald Chambers

The saints are God's jewels, highly esteemed and dear to Him; they are a royal diadem in His hand.

—Matthew Henry

A man can be as truly a saint in a factory as in a monastery, and there is as much need of him in the one as in the other.

—Robert J. McCracken

The mark of a saint is not perfection, but consecration. A saint is not a man without faults, but a man who has given himself without reserve to God.

—W. T. Richardson

Saints are persons who make it easier for others to believe in God.

—Nathan Söderblom

The saints are the sinners who keep on trying.

—Robert Louis Stevenson

SALT

As long as salt retains its identity, it is useless. It must penetrate to benefit, and when it does, it disappears! Salt is doing its work only when it is invisible.

—Richard C. Halverson

They say that you can lead a horse to water, but you can't make him drink. Maybe not, but I can put lots of salt in his oats.

—Charlie "T" Jones

SALVATION
(See also Born Again, Conversion, Redemption, Regeneration)

He who created us without our help will not save us without our consent.

—Saint Augustine

Salvation is a gift and you can't boast about a gift. You can only be thankful.

—D. James Kennedy

The Son of God became a man to enable men to become the sons of God.

—C. S. Lewis

The recognition of sin is the beginning of salvation.

—Martin Luther

If salvation could be attained only by working hard, then surely horses and donkeys would be in heaven.

—Martin Luther

Salvation may come quietly, but we cannot remain quiet about it.

—Anonymous

Why should men pay such a high price for damnation, when salvation is free?

—Anonymous

SANCTIFICATION

Sanctification is the work of Christ in me, the sign that I am no longer independent, but completely dependent on Him.

—Oswald Chambers

Many of God's children long for a better life, but do not realize the need of giving God time day by day in their inner chamber by the Spirit to renew and sanctify their lives.

—Andrew Murray

SATISFACTION

(See also Contentment)

The stomach is the only part of a man that can be fully satisfied. The yearning of man's brain for new knowledge and experience and for more pleasant and comfortable surroundings can never be completely met. It is an appetite that cannot be appeased.

—Thomas Edison

Show me a thoroughly satisfied man and I will show you a failure.

—Thomas Edison

A man who is always satisfied with himself is seldom satisfied with others.

—François de La Rochefoucauld

Most of us learn too late that it is just as easy, under most conditions, to be satisfied as it is to be dissatisfied. And it's much more healthful.

—Anonymous

SCHOOL

(See also Education, Learning, Teachers, Teaching, University)

Life is a school, and we teach others better when we ourselves are learning.

—J. B. Chapman

We are shut up in schools and college recitation rooms for ten or fifteen years, and come out at last with a bellyful of words and do not know a thing.

—Ralph Waldo Emerson

Everything you've learned in school as "obvious" becomes less obvious as you begin to study the universe.

—Buckminster Fuller

A school should not be a preparation for life. A school should be life.

—Elbert Hubbard

School is a building that has four walls—with tomorrow inside.

—Lon Watters

SCIENCE

Science is but a mere heap of facts, not a gold chain of truths, if we refuse to link it to the throne of God.

—Frances P. Cobbe

Science has not found a substitute for God.

—Henry Drummond

Science is not a sacred cow. Science is a horse. Don't worship it. Feed it.

—Aubrey Eben

Science can give us only the tools in a box, mechanical miracles that it has already given us. But of what use to us are miraculous tools until we have mastered the humane, cultural use of them? We do not want to live in a world where the machine has mastered the man; we want to live in a world where man has mastered the machine.

—Frank Lloyd Wright

SECULARISM

Secularism is to live as though God does not exist. We believe in Him, but that's as far as it goes! Our home life, business life, social life are conducted along lines that leave God out.... But the ultimate course of secularism leads to spiritual bankruptcy—expediency rather than principle.

—Richard C. Halverson

SECURITY

If virtue and knowledge are diffused among the people, they will never be enslaved. This will be their great security.

—Samuel Adams

Security is the priceless product of freedom. Only the strong can be secure.

—B. E. Hutchinson

Life is either a daring adventure or nothing at all. Security is mostly a superstition. It does not exist in nature.

—Helen Keller

You cannot establish security on borrowed money.

—Abraham Lincoln

In these days of increasing pressure for a welfare state, it behooves us to remember that Patrick Henry did not say, "Give me *security* or give me death."

—John Davis Lodge

SELF
(See also Ego)

It is always easier to confess the sins of others than to acknowledge our own faults, and to point out the delinquencies of others than to mend our own nets. Men, like water, are prone to take the easy way from the mountains to the sea.

—J. B. Chapman

Self is the opaque veil that hides the face of God from us.

—Richard J. Foster

When we make ourselves more than nothing, we make God less than everything.

—Robert D. Foster

There is only one corner of the universe you can be certain of improving, and that's your own self.

—Aldous Huxley

I have had more trouble with myself than with any other man I have ever met.

—Dwight L. Moody

As long as we are something, God cannot be all.

—Andrew Murray

The greatest burden we have to carry in life is self; the most difficult thing we have to manage is self.

—Hannah Whitall Smith

Beware of no man more than of yourself; we carry our worst enemies within us.

—Charles H. Spurgeon

Self is the only prison that can bind the soul.

—Henry Van Dyke

SELF-CENTEREDNESS

The investment of a self-centered life yields no dividends that are satisfying or eternal.

—Robert D. Foster

A self-centered life is totally empty, while an emptied life leaves room for God.

—Tom Haggai

SELF-CONFIDENCE

Nothing splendid has ever been achieved except by those who dared believe that something inside them was superior to circumstance.

—Bruce Barton

SELF-CONTROL

I count him braver who overcomes his desires than him who conquers his enemies; for the hardest victory is the victory over self.

—Aristotle

What it lies in our power to do, it lies in our power not to do.

—Aristotle

To break our own record, to outstrip yesterdays by todays, to bear our trials more beautifully than we ever dreamed we could, to whip the tempter inside and out as we never whipped him before, to give as we never have given, to do our work with more force and a finer finish than ever—this is the true idea, to get ahead of ourselves.

—Maltbie D. Babcock

Hold yourself responsible for a higher standard than anybody else expects of you. Never excuse yourself. Never pity yourself. Be a hard master to yourself—and be lenient to everybody else.

—Henry Ward Beecher

Man without self-restraint is like a barrel without hoops, and tumbles to pieces.

—Henry Ward Beecher

No man is such a conqueror as the man who has defeated himself.

—Henry Ward Beecher

The only conquests that are permanent, and leave no regrets, are our conquests over ourselves.

—Napoleon Bonaparte

No one is free who is not master of himself.

—Claudius

Self-control is more often called for
than self-expression.
—William M. Comfort

Few are those who err on the side of
self-restraint.
—Confucius

He that requires much from himself and
little from others will keep himself from
being the object of resentment.
—Confucius

Self-command is the main elegance.
—Ralph Waldo Emerson

No man is free who is not master of
himself.
—Epictetus

It's not the mountain we conquer, but
ourselves.
—Edmund Hillary

There's only one corner of the universe
you can be certain of improving and
that's your own self.
—Aldous Huxley

You will get much more done if you will
only crack the whip at yourself.
—Donald A. Laird

He who conquers others is strong.
He who conquers himself is mighty.
—Lao-Tze

He who would govern others, first
should be the master of himself.
—Philip Massinger

He who reigns within himself and rules
his passions, desires, and fears, is more
than a king.
—John Milton

The first and best victory is to conquer
self; to be conquered by self is, of all
things, most shameful and vile.
—Plato

They have great powers, and they waste
them pitifully, for they have not the
greater power—the power to rule the
use of their powers.
—Frederick W. Robertson

There never did and never will exist
anything permanently noble and
excellent in a character that was a
stranger to the exercise of resolute self-
denial.
—Walter Scott

Man who man would be,
Must rule the empire of himself.
—Percy Bysshe Shelley

The poorest education that teaches self-
control is better than the best that
neglects it.
—George Sterling

No conflict is so severe as his who
labors to subdue himself.
—Thomas à Kempis

Self-denial is an excellent guard of
virtue.
—Thomas Townson

Master selfishness or it will master you.
—Anonymous

SELF-DECEPTION

It is a delusion to seek a sort of ready-made perfection that can be assumed like a garment; it is a delusion, too, to aim at a holiness that costs no trouble, although such holiness would no doubt be exceedingly agreeable to nature. We think that if we could discover the secret of sanctity we should become saints quickly and easily.

—J. Gregory Mantle

We possess a marvelous capacity for self-deception. This capacity the enemy finds to be one of his most effective weapons for destroying the souls of men.

—J. Gregory Mantle

Man's capacity for self-deception is unlimited.

—George H. Tausch

SELF-DISCIPLINE

(See also Discipline, Self-control)

We go wrong because we refuse to discipline ourselves, physically, morally, or mentally.

—Oswald Chambers

God will not discipline us, we must discipline ourselves. God will not bring every thought and imagination into captivity; we have to do it.

—Oswald Chambers

Self-discipline is the free man's yoke.

—John W. Gardner

Self-discipline is when your conscience tells you to do something and you don't talk back.

—W. K. Hope

The most valuable of all education is the ability to make yourself do the thing you have to do when it has to be done, whether you like it or not.

—Aldous Huxley

The best discipline, maybe the only discipline that really works, is self-discipline.

—Walter Kiechel III

What we do upon some great occasion will probably depend on what we already are, and what we are will be the result of previous years of self-discipline.

—H. P. Liddon

The difference between winning and losing is self-discipline.

—Anonymous

SELF-ESTEEM

It is difficult to make a man miserable while he feels worthy of himself and claims kindred to the great God who made him.

—Abraham Lincoln

The picture you have of yourself, your self-esteem, will have a profound effect on the way you see the world and the way your world sees you.

—Earl Nightingale

SELF-IMPROVEMENT

We shall be better tomorrow if we shake off complacency and press hard after that better standard of excellence in life and service that ever beckons us onward.

—J. B. Chapman

SELFISHNESS

All the trouble in the world is due to selfishness. It always has been and always will be.

—Joseph F. Flannelly

No indulgence of passion destroys the spiritual nature so much as respectable selfishness.

—George MacDonald

SELF-LOVE

Self-love is a cup without any bottom; you might pour all the great lakes into it, and never fill it up.

—Oliver Wendell Holmes

Every man is prompted by the love of himself to imagine that he possesses some qualities superior, either in kind or degree, to those that he sees allotted to the rest of the world.

—Samuel Johnson

The greatest of all flatterers is self-love.

—François de La Rochefoucauld

SELF-PITY

Self-pity in its early stages is as snug as a feather mattress. Only when it hardens does it become uncomfortable.

—Maya Angelou

If you indulge in self-pity, the only sympathy you can expect is from the same source.

—Bill Copeland

SELF-RESPECT

Self-respect is the fruit of discipline; the sense of dignity grows with the ability to say no to one's self.

—Abraham Joshua Heschel

SENTIMENTALITY

Sentimentality is no indication of a warm heart. Nothing weeps more copiously than a chunk of ice.

—Anonymous

SERENITY

Boredom is the feeling that everything is a waste of time; serenity, that nothing is.

—Thomas Szasz

Great people are not affected by each puff of wind that blows ill. Like great ships, they sail serenely on, in a calm sea or a great tempest.

—George Washington

Serenity isn't gray resignation. It's a golden, smiling quality. . . . I pray daily, not to be resigned to old age, not to yield supinely to its limitations, but to accept with a cheerful serenity what remains to me of accomplishment and experience.

—I. A. R. Wylie

SERMONS
(See also Preachers/Preaching)

The most powerful part of a sermon is the man behind it.

—Phillips Brooks

Do I listen to the pastor because my life needs a sermon, or do I listen to the pastor to learn how my life can be a sermon?

—Hugh Ross

If I had but one sermon to preach, it would be on the homesickness of the soul for God.

—Samuel M. Shoemaker

Few sinners are saved after the first twenty minutes of a sermon.

—Mark Twain

Once in seven years I burn all my sermons; for it is a shame if I cannot write better sermons now than I did seven years ago.

—John Wesley

A good sermon leaves you wondering how the preacher knew all about you.

—Anonymous

One minister says that he does not mind a man looking at his watch during a sermon, but he does resent his shaking it to find out if it is still going.

—Anonymous

SERVICE

If you are dissatisfied with your lot in life, build a service station on it.

—Samuel L. Brengle

Service to a just cause rewards us with more real happiness and satisfaction than any other venture of life.

—Carrie Lane Chapman Catt

My love for serving the Lord with my whole time and strength makes it a privilege to sacrifice other enjoyments.

—J. B. Chapman

If you want to become the greatest in your field, no matter what it may be, equip yourself to render greater service than anyone else.

—Clinton Davidson

God forces no one, for love cannot compel, and God's service, therefore, is a thing of perfect freedom.

—Hans Denk

It is not fitting, when one is in God's service, to have a gloomy face or a chilling look.

—Saint Francis of Assisi

Serving God is doing good to man. But praying is thought an easier service and is therefore more generally chosen.

—Benjamin Franklin

The service we render for others is really the rent we pay for our room on this earth.

—Wilfred T. Grenfell

You've got to be a servant to *somebody*—or *something*.

—Charles F. Kettering

Find out where you can render a service, and then render it. The rest is up to the Lord.

—S. S. Kresge

A Christian man is the most free lord of all, and subject to none; a Christian man is the most dutiful servant to all, and subject to everyone.

—Martin Luther

The world cannot always understand a person's profession of faith, but it can understand service.

—Ian Maclaren

I don't know what your destiny will be, but one thing I know: the only ones among you who will be really happy are those who have sought and found how to serve.

—Albert Schweitzer

Do something for someone every day, for which you do not get paid.

—Albert Schweitzer

Life is a place of service, and in that service to suffer a great deal that is hard to bear, but more often to experience a great deal of joy. But that joy can be real only if people look upon their lives as a service, and have a definite object in life outside themselves and their personal happiness.

—Leo Tolstoy

Christ will have no servants except by consent. His people are a willing people. He will be all in all, or He will be nothing.

—John Wesley

Nothing liberates our greatness like the desire to help, the desire to serve.

—Marianne Williamson

SHADOWS
Never fear shadows. They simply mean there's a light shining somewhere.

—Ruth E. Renkel

SHINE
We are stars, bold, blazing, light-giving stars! No need to shout, scream, or make a scene. Just shine.

—Charles Swindoll

There is no shining without burning.

—Anonymous

SILENCE
(See also Noise)
There are times when silence has the loudest voice.

—Leroy Brownlow

Silence is a friend who will never betray.

—Confucius

I've never been hurt by anything I didn't say.

—Calvin Coolidge

To be alone with silence is to be alone with God.

—Samuel Miller Hageman

Silence is a great peacemaker.

—Henry Wadsworth Longfellow

True silence is the rest of the mind; it is to the spirit what sleep is to the body—nourishment and refreshment.

—William Penn

No one has a finer command of language than the person who keeps his mouth shut.

—Sam Rayburn

God is the friend of silence. Trees, flowers, grass grow in silence. See the stars, moon, and sun, how they move in silence.

—Mother Teresa

SIMPLICITY

The obvious is that which is never seen until someone expresses it simply.

—Kahlil Gibran

Simplicity is truth's most becoming garb.

—Bob Jones Sr.

Life grows wondrously beautiful when we look at is as simple, when we can brush aside trivial cares, sorrows, worries, and failures. . . . Simplicity is a mental soil where selfishness, deceit, treachery, and low ambition cannot grow.

—William G. Jordan

In character, in manners, in style, in all things, the supreme excellence is simplicity.

—Henry Wadsworth Longfellow

Simplicity, of all things, is the hardest to be copied.

—Richard Steele

Simplify your life. Don't waste the years struggling for things that are unimportant. Don't destroy your peace of mind by looking back, worrying about the past. Live in the present, enjoy the present. Simplify!

—Henry David Thoreau

SIN

Our first problem is that our attitude toward sin is more self-centered than God-centered. We are more concerned about our own "victory" over sin than we are about the fact that our sins grieve the heart of God.

—Jerry Bridges

Two thousand years of failure have not taught some reformers that you can't stop sin by declaring it illegal.

—Joy Davidman

What a paradox: The sinner forever free from the slightest traces of sin—the sinless Son bearing forever in His body the marks of sin's sacrifice.

—Richard C. Halverson

There are . . . few stronger indications of ignorance of the power and evil of sin than the confident assertion of our ability to resist and subdue it.

—Charles Hedge

Contradiction is obliteration of the line of demarcation between good and evil, it means calling humanism what is actually "sin."

—Pope John Paul II

Frightful this is in a sense, but it is true, and every one who has merely some little knowledge of the human heart can verify it: there is nothing to which a man holds so desperately as to his sin.

—Sören Kierkegaard

The wages of sin is death—thank God I quit before payday.

—Reamer Loomis

Sin arises out of mistrust. Man is afraid to trust the divine destiny and to accept his limits. The rebellion that follows is a decisive act of repudiation, a trusting of self over against God.

—James I. McCord

You seldom meet a bankrupt sinner. Most of them think they can pay about seventy-five cents on the dollar; some ninety-nine percent—they just come up a little bit short and think the Almighty will make it up somehow.

—Dwight L. Moody

Perhaps no sin so easily besets us as a sense of self-satisfied superiority to others.

—William Osler

Sin and the child of God are incompatible. They may occasionally meet; they cannot live together in harmony.

—John R. W. Stott

One reason that sin flourishes is that it is treated like a cream puff instead of a rattlesnake.

—Billy Sunday

No sin is small. It is against an infinite God, and may have consequences immeasurable. No grain of sand is small in the mechanism of a watch.

—Jeremy Taylor

SINCERITY

Sincerity is no test of truth, no evidence of correctness of conduct. You may take poison, sincerely believing it the necessary medicine, but will it save your life?

—Tryon Edwards

Sincerity is an open heart. Few people show it; usually what we see is an imitation put on to snare the confidence of others.

—François de La Rochefoucauld

Sincerity is to speak as we think, to do as we profess, to perform what we promise, and really to be what we would seem and appear to be.

—John Tillotson

SIZE

Big doesn't necessarily mean better. Sunflowers aren't better than violets.

—Edna Ferber

SLANDER
(See also Gossip)

To murder character is as truly a crime as to murder the body: the tongue of the slanderer is brother to the dagger of the assassin.

—Tryon Edwards

Slander is the revenge of a coward.

—Samuel Johnson

The worthiest people are the most injured by slander, as is the best fruit that the birds have been pecking at.

—Jonathan Swift

SLAVERY

Peace is liberty in tranquility; servitude the last of all evils, one to be repelled, not only by war but even by death.

—Cicero

Whenever I hear anyone arguing for slavery, I feel a strong impulse to see it tried on him personally.

—Abraham Lincoln

Humanism is man's rebellion against and alienation from God. This is man's slavery. How can that which produced man's slavery set him free from it? All man's efforts to possess a self-contained freedom, to find the meaning of life by his own wisdom, to build a worthy human society without God, are self-defeating, for they are a denial of man's essential nature.

—Donald G. Miller

It isn't always others who enslave us. Sometimes we let circumstances enslave us; sometimes we let routines enslave us; sometimes we let things enslave us; sometimes, with weak wills, we enslave ourselves.

—Anonymous

SLEEP

The best bridge between despair and hope is a good night's sleep.

—Harry Ruby

It is a common experience that a problem difficult at night is resolved in the morning after the committee of sleep has worked on it.

—John Steinbeck

SMILES

What sunshine is to flowers, smiles are to humanity. They are but trifles, to be sure, but scattered along life's pathway, the good they do is inconceivable.

—Joseph Addison

A smile is the shortest distance between two people.

—Victor Borge

While enormous strides have been made in communications in recent years, there's still a lot to be said for a smile.

—Franklin P. Jones

If you can't do anything else to help along, just smile.

—Eleanor Kirk

There are no language barriers when you are smiling.

—Allen Klein

Any road you travel in life is made infinitely better if you remember to pack a smile in your luggage and take it out frequently on your trip.

—Anthony Vespugio

A smile is the welcome mat at the doorway of kindness.

—William Arthur Ward

SMOKING

As kids, we started smoking because it was smart. Why don't we stop for the same reason?

—Harold Emery

Everyone eventually stops smoking. Mother Nature—the most permissive of parents—sees to that. Those who smoke heaviest stop earliest.

—Pat McGrady

I'm glad I don't have to explain to a man from Mars why each day I set fire to dozens of little pieces of paper, and then put them in my mouth.

—Mignon McLaughlin

Most people quit smoking in two stages: first, they give up *their* cigarettes, then they give up *yours*.

—Mickey Porter

SOLITUDE

Be able to be alone. Don't lose the advantage of solitude.

—Thomas Browne

What a lovely surprise to discover how un-lonely being alone can be.

—Ellen Burstyn

Only alone can I draw close enough to God to discover His secrets.

—George Washington Carver

It is easy in the world to live after the world's opinion; it is easy in solitude to live after our own; but the great man is he who in the midst of the crowd keeps with perfect sweetness the independence of solitude.

—Ralph Waldo Emerson

Get apart in solitude so you can hear His voice, watch His movements, and wait for His bidding.

—Robert D. Foster

Solitude is as needful to the imagination as society is wholesome for the character.

—James Russell Lowell

It is in solitude that we discover that being is more important than having and that we are worth more than the results of our efforts. In solitude we discover that our life is not a possession to be defended, but a gift to be shared.

—Henri H. M. Nouwen

I have never found the companion that was so companionable as solitude.

—Henry David Thoreau

SONS
(See also Boys)

You don't raise heroes, you raise sons. And if you treat them like sons, they'll turn out to be heroes, even if it's just in your own eyes.

—Walter Schirra Sr.

Nearly every man is a firm believer in heredity until his son makes a fool of himself.

—Anonymous

SORROW
(See also Compassion, Grief, Sadness, Tears)

He who has most of heart knows most of sorrow.

—Philip J. Bailey

Sorrows are often like clouds, which though black when they are passing over us, when they are past become as if they were the garments of God thrown off in purple and gold along the sky.

—Henry Ward Beecher

We have no right to ask when sorrow comes, "Why did this happen to me?" unless we ask the same question for every joy that comes our way.

—Philip S. Bernstein

Disappointment, in life, is inevitable. Pain is the common lot. Sorrow is not given to us alone that we may mourn. It is given us that, having felt, suffered, wept, we may be able to understand, love, bless.

—Anna Robertson Brown

In times of deep sorrow it is not the people who tell you why you are suffering who are of any use; the people who help you are those who give expression to your state of mind; often they do not speak at all.

—Oswald Chambers

I walked a mile with Sorrow
And ne'er a word said she;
But, oh, the things I learned from her
When Sorrow walked with me.

—Robert Browning Hamilton

Sorrow is a fruit; God does not make it grow on limbs too weak to bear it.

—Victor Hugo

Often the clouds of sorrow reveal the sunshine of His face.

—Hilys Jasper

When the clouds of sorrow gather over us we see nothing beyond them, nor can imagine how they will be dispelled; yet a new day succeeds the night, and sorrow is never long without a dawn of ease.

—Samuel Johnson

In this sad world of ours, sorrow comes to all, and it often comes with bitter agony. Perfect relief is not possible, except with time. You cannot now believe that you will ever feel better. But this is not true. You are sure to be happy again. Knowing this, truly believing it, will make you less miserable now.

—Abraham Lincoln

Only the soul that knows the mighty grief can know the mighty rapture. Sorrows come to stretch out spaces in the heart for joy.

—Edwin Markham

Our sorrows are like thunderclouds, which seem black in the distance, but grow lighter as they approach.

—Jean Paul Richter

When sorrows come, they come not single spies, but in battalions.

—William Shakespeare

There is a sweet joy that comes to us through sorrow.

—Charles H. Spurgeon

You cannot stop the bird of sorrow from flying over your head, but you can prevent it from nesting in your hair.

—Chinese Proverb

SOUL

Our bodies are where we stay; our souls are what we are.

—Cecil Baxter

The body—that is but dust; the soul is a bud of eternity.

—Nathaniel Culverwell

I believe that man will not merely endure, he will prevail. He is immortal not because he alone among creatures has an inexhaustible voice, but because he has a soul.

—William Faulkner

Since the soul is large enough to contain the infinite God, nothing less than Himself can satisfy or fill it.

—Edward B. Pusey

A sad soul can kill you quicker, far quicker, than a germ.

—John Steinbeck

SOUL WINNING

(See also Evangelism, Witnessing)

Christians are to *be* good news before they *share* the good news. The *music* of the gospel must precede the *words* of the gospel and prepare the context in which there will be a hunger for those words. What is the music of the gospel? It is the beauty of the indwelling Christ in the everyday relationships of life.

—Joe Aldrich

Men are won, not so much by being blamed, as by being encompassed by love.

—William Ellery Channing

Every one comes between men's souls and God, either as a brick wall or as a bridge. Either you are leading men to God or you are driving them away.

—Lindsay Dewar

Lord, make me a crisis man. Bring those I contact to decision. Let me not be a milepost on a single road. Make me a fork, that men must turn one way or another on facing Christ in me.

—Jim Elliot

There is no greater honor than to be the instrument in God's hands of leading one person out of the kingdom of Satan into the glorious light of heaven.

—Dwight L. Moody

Surely there can be no greater joy than that of saving souls.

—Lottie Moon

There is a net of love by which you can catch souls.

—Mother Teresa

Soul winners are not soul winners because of what they know, but because of Who they know, and how well they know Him, and how much they long for others to know Him.

—Dawson Trotman

SPEECH
(See also Conversation, Eloquence, Talk, Tongue, Words)

Watch your speech . . . command of the language is most important. Next to kissing, it's the most exciting form of communication mankind has evolved.

—Oren Arnold

When I want to speak let me think first. Is it true? Is it kind? Is it necessary? If not let it be unsaid.

—Maltbie D. Babcock

The shortest distance between two jokes makes a perfect speech.

—O. A. Battista

Speak not at all, in any wise, till you have somewhat to speak; care not for the reward of your speaking, but simply and with undivided mind for the truth of your speaking.

—Thomas Carlyle

The manner of speaking is full as important as the matter, as more people have ears to be tickled, than understandings to judge.

—Lord Chesterfield

Say what you have to say, and the first time you come to a sentence with a grammatical ending—sit down.

—Winston Churchill

It is difficult to tell how much men's minds are conciliated by a kind manner and gentle speech.

—Cicero

Think all you speak, but speak not all you think. Thoughts are all your own; your words are so no more.

—Patrick Delany

Don't say giddy-up to your mouth before your head is hitched up.

—Buddy Ebsen

Have something to say; say it, and stop when you're done.

—Tryon Edwards

Blessed is the man who, having nothing to say, abstains from giving wordy evidence of the fact.

—George Eliot

The sweetest music is not in the oratorio, but in the human voice when it speaks from its instant life tones of tenderness, truth, or courage.

—Ralph Waldo Emerson

First, learn the meaning of what you say, and then speak.

—Epictetus

The commencement speaker represents the continuation of a barbaric custom that has no basis in logic. If the state of oratory that inundates our educational institutions during the month of June could be transformed into rain for southern California, we should all be happily awash or waterlogged.

—Samuel Gould

Speak clearly, if you speak at all;
Carve every word before you let it fall.

—Oliver Wendell Holmes

Why doesn't the fellow who says, "I'm
no speechmaker," let it go at that instead
of giving a demonstration?

—Frank McKinney Hubbard

There is as much eloquence in the tone
of voice, in the eyes, and in the air of a
speaker as in his choice of words.

—François de La Rochefoucauld

In general those who have nothing to
say
Contrive to spend the longest time in
doing it;
They turn and vary it in every way,
Hashing it, stewing it, mincing it,
 ragout-ing it.

—James Russell Lowell

If you're offered an honorarium for a
speech, you can be sure the money is of
no consequencium.

—Merle Miller

Oratory is the art of making deep noises
from the chest sound like important
messages from the brain.

—H. I. Phillips

We are much more affected by the
words that we hear, for though what you
read in books may be more pointed, yet
there is something in the voice, the look,
the carriage, and even the gesture of the
speaker, that makes a deeper impression upon the mind.

—Pliny the Younger

For a message to be immortal, it doesn't
have to be everlasting.

—Lorne Sanny

If silence is golden, then speech is
platinum. It spreads wisdom, dispels
ignorance, ventilates grievances,
stimulates curiosity, lightens the spirits
and lessens the fundamental loneliness
of the soul.

—Jan Struther

It usually takes more than three weeks
to prepare a good impromptu speech.

—Mark Twain

If all my possessions were taken away
from me with one exception, I would
choose the power of speech. For by it, I
would regain all the rest of my
possessions.

—Daniel Webster

SPIRITUAL GIFTS

God has said that every Christian has at
least one spiritual gift for the benefit of
the whole body of Christ. No one has all
the gifts, all have at least one gift, and
some have two or more. We are dependent on each other.

—Francis M. Cosgrove Jr.

Spiritual gifts are given, not for competition, but for cooperation.

—Gerald W. Cox

SPIRITUALITY

We never become truly spiritual by
sitting down and wishing to become so.

You must undertake something so great that you cannot accomplish it unaided.

—Phillips Brooks

We are not human beings having a spiritual experience. We are spiritual beings having a human experience.

—Teilhard de Chardin

The basic need of the world is spirituality.

—Douglas MacArthur

SPORTS

Sports do not build character. They reveal it.

—Heywood Broun

Sports: the toy department of human life.

—Jimmy Cannon

Sports serve society by providing vivid examples of excellence.

—George F. Will

Skiing is best when you have lots of white snow and plenty of Blue Cross.

—Earl Wilson

SPRING

The nicest thing about the promise of spring is that sooner or later she'll have to keep it.

—Mark Beltaire

Spring is the time when youth dreams and old age remembers.

—Margaret L. Creager

All the veneration of Spring connects itself with love.

—Ralph Waldo Emerson

Spring unlocks the flowers to paint the laughing soil.

—Reginald Heber

Spring is wonderful. It makes you feel young enough to do all the things you're old enough to know you can't.

—Franklin P. Jones

Soon will come eternal Spring,
And eternal songs to sing;
Loud our "hallelujahs" ring,
To our Savior, Lord and King.

—B. K.

If Spring came but once in a century, instead of once a year, or burst forth with the sound of an earthquake and not in silence, what wonder and expectation there would be in all hearts to behold the miraculous change.

—Henry Wadsworth Longfellow

There is no time like spring,
When life's alive in every thing.

—Christina Rossetti

Sweet lovers love the Spring.

—William Shakespeare

Blossom by blossom the spring begins.

—Algernon G. Swinburne

In the spring a young man's fancy lightly turns to thoughts of love.

—Alfred Lord Tennyson

It is always springtime in the heart that loves God.

—Jean-Marie Vianney

STARS

If the stars should appear but one night in a thousand years, how would men believe and adore and preserve for many generations the remembrance of the city of God that had been shown!

—Ralph Waldo Emerson

There is more gold in one star than in all the dust of the earth. Look up!

—Joaquin Miller

STATISTICS

I can prove anything by statistics— except the truth.

—George Canning

Statistics are no substitute for judgment.

—Henry Clay

Somewhere on this globe, every ten seconds, there is a woman giving birth to a child. She must be found and stopped.

—Sam Levenson

You cannot feed the hungry on statistics.

—David Lloyd George

Children are very adept at comprehending modern statistics. When they say, "Everyone else is allowed to," it is usually based on a survey of one.

—Paul Sweeney

Just try explaining the value of statistical summaries to the widow of the man who drowned crossing a stream with an average depth of four feet.

—Anonymous

A recent survey indicates that three out of four people make up 75 percent of the world's population.

—Anonymous

STEWARDSHIP
(See also Generosity, Gifts/Giving)

Stewardship is what a man does after he says, "I believe."

—W. H. Greever

Stewardship is not leaving a tip on God's tablecloth; it is the confession of an unpayable debt at God's Calvary.

—Paul S. Rees

Stewardship is not a classroom exercise in fractions. It is a homework assignment in total living.

—Kenneth L. Wilson

STRENGTH

I've never been one who thought the good Lord should make life easy; I've just asked Him to make me strong.

—Eva Bowring

Do not pray for easy lives. Pray to be stronger men! Do not pray for tasks equal to your powers. Pray for powers equal to your tasks. Then the doing of your work shall be no miracle, but you shall be a miracle.

—Phillips Brooks

If you're strong enough, there
are no precedents.

—F. Scott Fitzgerald

Some people think it's holding on that
makes one strong. Sometimes it's
letting go.

—Sylvia Robinson

It is the mark of weak men that they
break down under unusual responsibilities, of strong men that they are
developed by them.

—C. I. Scofield

Inside each of us is a well of strength
that you could call upon if you're only
willing to reach inside and get it.

—Beck Weathers

STUBBORNNESS

Stubbornness does have its helpful
features. You always know what you are
going to be thinking tomorrow.

—Glen Beaman

SUBMISSION

Let God put you on His wheel and whirl
you as He likes, and as sure as God is
God and you are you, you will turn out
exactly in accordance with the vision He
gave you. Don't lose heart in the process.

—Oswald Chambers

Submission! That word has received
such a bad reputation that we rarely use
it. It is the willful act of yielding to the
power, control, or authority of another.
Submission is a voluntary act. It is a
critical part of the learning process.

Submission is a key concept in the Bible.
. . . To be true followers of Jesus, we must
learn to be submissive.

—Bob Snyder

SUCCESS
(See also Failure)

All that is necessary to break the spell of
inertia and frustration is this: Act as if it
were impossible to fail. That is the
talisman, the formula, the command of
right-about-face that turns us from
failure to success.

—Dorothea Brande

I believe the true road to preeminent
success in any line is to make yourself
master of that line.

—Andrew Carnegie

The difference between a successful
person and a failure often lies in the fact
that the successful man will profit by his
mistakes and try again in a different
way.

—Dale Carnegie

Success is knowing the difference
between cornering people and getting
them in your corner.

—Bill Copeland

You've removed most of the roadblocks
to success when you've learned the
difference between motion and
direction.

—Bill Copeland

The secret of success is constancy to
purpose.

—Benjamin Disraeli

The measure of success is not whether you have a tough problem to deal with, but whether it's the same problem you had last year.

—John Foster Dulles

A successful man keeps looking for work after he has found a job.

—Raymond Duncan

Success in your work, the finding a better method, the better understanding that insures the better performing, is hat and coat, is food and wine, is fire and horse and health and holiday. At least, I find that any success in my work has the effect on my spirits of all these.

—Ralph Waldo Emerson

Success has a simple formula: do your best, and people may like it.

—Sam Ewing

Whether it's marriage or business, patience is the first rule of success.

—William Feather

Success seems to be largely a matter of hanging on after others have let go.

—William Feather

Don't aim for success if you want it; just do what you love and believe in, and it will come naturally.

—David Frost

Success doesn't always go to the head. Sometimes it goes to the mouth.

—Arnold H. Glasow

Success isn't a result of spontaneous combustion. You must set yourself on fire.

—Arnold H. Glasow

Success is enjoying the journey through life, not reaching a destination.

—Raymond E. Hill

The door to the room of success swings on the hinge of opposition.

—Bob Jones Sr.

The most successful men have used seeming failures as stepping stones to better things.

—Grenville Kleiser

The conditions of success in life are the possession of judgment, experience, initiative, and character.

—Gustave LeBon

Just remember—God does not judge success the way the world does; His measurement is for eternity. So don't let the world's evaluation discourage you. Just keep working. If you can remember this, you will have a happy, satisfying, rewarding, and successful life in God's service.

—Richard LeTourneau

The frustrating thing is that the key to success doesn't always fit your ignition.

—Roger C. Meyer

Success without honor is an unseasoned dish; it will satisfy your hunger, but it won't taste good.

—Joe Paterno

We must never be afraid to go too far, for success lies just beyond.
—Marcel Proust

If you want to succeed, you should strike out on new paths rather than travel the worn paths of accepted success.
—John D. Rockefeller

Success and failure. We think of them as opposites, but they are really not. They're *companions*—the hero and the sidekick.
—Laurence Shames

Success is a little like wrestling a gorilla. You don't quit when you're tired—you quit when the gorilla is tired.
—Robert Strauss

Success does for living what sunshine does for stained glass.
—Bob Talbert

Why should we be in such a desperate haste to succeed, and in such desperate enterprises? If a man does not keep pace with his companions, perhaps it is because he hears a different drummer.
—Henry David Thoreau

God may allow His servant to succeed when He has disciplined him to a point where he does not need to succeed to be happy. The man who is elated by success and is cast down by failure is still a carnal man. At best his fruit will have a worm in it.
—A. W. Tozer

The most successful businessman is the man who holds onto the old just as long as it is good, and grabs the new just as soon as it is better.
—Robert P. Vanderpoel

Nothing recedes like success.
—Walter Winchell

Success is more attitude than aptitude.
—Anonymous

The door of success is guarded, and no one is permitted to enter who has not worked and waited and overcome.
—Anonymous

The road to success is always under construction.
—Anonymous

If at first you don't succeed, try reading the instructions.
—Anonymous

God gave us two ends, one to sit on and the other to think with. Success depends upon which end we use most. Heads, we win. Tails, we lose.
—Anonymous

SUFFERING
(See also Adversity, Affliction, Trials, Troubles)

Present suffering is not enjoyable, but life would be worth little without it. The difference between iron and steel is fire, but steel is worth all it costs.
—Maltbie D. Babcock

God can mend a broken heart if we give Him all the pieces.

—J. Sidlow Baxter

Out of suffering have emerged the strongest souls; the most massive characters are seared with scars.

—Edwin H. Chapin

Although the world is full of suffering, it is also full of the overcoming of it.

—Helen Keller

Suffering: the fertile soil into which God transplants every growing Christian.

—Anonymous

SUMMER

Summer afternoon—summer afternoon; to me they have always been the two most beautiful words in the English language.

—Henry James

If I could ... pull back each summer's
   curtain from off this changing sod!
Upon earth's mighty easel God paints
   His pictures rare
And grants His humble creatures
   sanctuary there.

—Janet Miller

SUN

The commonplace sun in the commonplace sky
Makes up the commonplace day;
The moon and the stars are commonplace things,
And the flower that blooms, and the
   bird that sings;

But dark is the world and sad our lot,
If the flowers failed, and the sun shone
   not.

—Susan Coolidge

The sun, with all those planets revolving around it and dependent on it, can still ripen a bunch of grapes as if it had nothing else in the universe to do.

—Galileo Galilei

The sun shines not on us, but in us.

—John Muir

SUNDAY
(See also Sabbath)

Too many persons try to make Sunday a sponge with which to wipe out sins of the week.

—Henry Ward Beecher

Sunday is the golden clasp that binds together the volume of the weeks.

—Henry Wadsworth Longfellow

O what a blessing is Sunday, interposed between the waves of worldly business like the divine path of the Israelites through the sea.

—Samuel Wilberforce

SUNDAY SCHOOL

In Sunday School we invest our lives in the lives of others; they in turn invest their lives in still other lives.

—Henrietta C. Mears

SUNRISE

Each golden sunrise ushers in new
opportunities for those who retain faith
in themselves, and keep their chins up.
No one has ever seen a cock crow with
its head down.... Meet the sunrise with
confidence.

—Alonzo Newton Benn

I don't ask for the meaning of the song
of a bird or the rising of the sun on a
misty morning. There they are, and they
are beautiful.

—Pete Hamill

The grand show is eternal. It is always
sunrise somewhere.... Eternal sunrise,
eternal sunset, eternal dawn and
gleaming, on sea and continents and
islands, each in its turn, as the round
earth rolls.

—John Muir

Climb up on some hill at sunrise.
Everybody needs perspective once in a
while, and you'll find it there.

—Robb Sagendorph

And lo! in a flash of crimson splendor,
with blazing scarlet clouds running
before his chariot, and heralding his
majestic approach, God's sun rises upon
the world.

—William Makepeace Thackeray

SUNSET

Sunsets are so beautiful that they
almost seem as if we were looking
through the gates of heaven.

—John Lubbock

SUNSHINE

Keep your face to the sunshine and you
cannot see the shadow.

—Helen Keller

Put the golden sunshine in each day;
Others need the cheer that comes
        through you—
Need it most when outer sky's dull gray
Leaves the sunshine-making yours to do.

—Juniata Stafford

SUPERNATURAL

Take away the supernatural, and what
remains is the unnatural.

—Gilbert Keith Chesterton

The supernatural is the native air of
Christianity

—Dora Greenwell

SUPERSTITION

Superstition is the religion of feeble
minds.

—Edmund Burke

Superstition is the poison of the mind.

—Joseph Lewis

SURPRISE

Be ready for the sudden surprise visits
of God. A ready person never needs to
get ready.

—Oswald Chambers

It must be very dull not to be a searching Christian and never know the
surprise of Christ.

—Lois Cheney

SURRENDER

God does not always choose great people to accomplish what He wishes, but He chooses a person who is wholly yielded to Him.

—Henrietta C. Mears

I can understand why so many Christians do not have the joy they might have, or do not have overflowing praise in their hearts. There must be a full surrender of life to the Savior to have the fullness of the Holy Spirit.

—Robert E. Nicholas

If we will only surrender ourselves utterly to the Lord, and will trust Him perfectly, we shall find our souls "mounting up with wings as eagles," where earthly annoyances have no power to disturb us.

—Hannah Whitall Smith

SUSPICIONS

Most of our suspicions of others are aroused by what we know about ourselves.

—Henry S. Haskins

SYMPATHY

(See also Compassion, Empathy)

We are living at a time when creeds and ideologies vary and clash. But the gospel of human sympathy is universal and eternal.

—Samuel Hopkins Adams

Next to love, sympathy is the divinest passion of the human heart.

—Edmund Burke

The more sympathy you give, the less you need.

—Malcolm S. Forbes

Sympathy is never wasted except when you give it to yourself.

—John W. Raper

Sympathy is two hearts tugging at one load.

—Anonymous

TACT

Tact is the rare ability to keep silent
while two friends are arguing, and you
know both of them are wrong.
                              —Hugh Allen

Tact: the ability to describe others as
they see themselves.
                              —Abraham Lincoln

Tact is the knack of making a point
without making an enemy.
                              —Howard W. Newton

Tact is the ability to tell a man he has an
open mind when he has a hole in his head.
                              —Anonymous

TALENT

Genius is the gold in the mine; talent is
the miner who works and brings it out.
                              —Marguerite Blessington

Everyone has talent. What is rare is the
courage to follow the talent to the dark
place where it leads.
                              —Erica Jong

One of the greatest talents of all is the
talent to recognize and to develop talent
in others.
                              —Frank Tyger

Use what talents you possess: the woods
would be very silent if no bird sang
there except those that sang best.
                              —Henry Van Dyke

TALK
*(See also Communication, Conversation,
Speech)*

Most men talk too much. Much of my
success has been due to keeping my
mouth shut.
                              —J. Ogden Armour

Talking is like playing on the harp; there
is as much in laying the hands on the
strings to stop their vibrations as in
twanging them to bring out their music.
                              —Oliver Wendell Holmes

Most men talk *at* one another rather
than *with* one another. Each person
thinks he is making meaningful points,
but rarely do they add up to genuine
communication.
                              —Eugene Rand

Talk is by far the most accessible of
pleasures. It costs nothing in money, it is
all profit, it completes our education,
founds and fosters our friendships, and
can be enjoyed at any age and in almost
any state of health.
                              —Robert Louis Stevenson

TAXES

Why does a light tax increase cost you
two hundred dollars and a substantial
tax cut save you thirty cents?
                              —Peg Bracken

When more of the people's sustenance is exacted through the form of taxation than is necessary to meet the just obligations of government and expenses of its economical administration, such exaction becomes ruthless extortion and a violation of the fundamental principles of free government.

—Grover Cleveland

The art of taxation consists in so plucking the goose as to obtain the largest amount of feathers with the least possible amount of hissing.

—J. B. Colbert

Some taxpayers close their eyes, some stop their ears, some shut their mouths, but all pay through the nose.

—Evan Esar

Don't get excited about a tax cut. It's like a mugger giving you back carfare.

—Arnold H. Glasow

We're taxed right and left. Report our taxes right and have nothing left.

—Arnold H. Glasow

I'm proud to be paying taxes in the United States. The only thing is—I could be just as proud for half the money.

—Arthur Godfrey

Sending money to Washington to have it administered and sent back is like getting a blood transfusion from your right arm to your left arm with a leaky valve.

—Ernest Hollings

The tax collector must love poor people—he's created so many of them.

—Charlie "T" Jones

It's awfully hard to believe that only about two hundred years ago we went to war to avoid taxation.

—Charlie "T" Jones

The power to tax involves the power to destroy.

—John Marshall

Where there is an income tax, the just man will pay more and the unjust less on the same amount of income.

—Plato

Next to being shot at and missed, nothing is really quite as satisfying as an income tax refund.

—F. J. Raymond

The taxpayer—that's someone who works for the federal government but doesn't have to take a civil service examination.

—Ronald Reagan

Taxation under every form presents but a choice of evils.

—David Ricardo

The income tax has made more liars out of the American people than golf has.

—Will Rogers

One difference between death and taxes is that death doesn't get worse every time Congress meets.

—Roy L. Schaeffer

The thing generally raised on city land is taxes.

—Charles Dudley Warner

The IRS has a special toll-free number for persons having problems figuring their tax forms. It's designed especially for those who like to listen to busy signals.

—Pat Williams and Ken Hussar

The income tax evader soon finds it would have been better to give than to deceive.

—Anonymous

TEACHERS
(See also Education, Learning, School, Teaching, University)

A teacher affects eternity; he can never tell where his influence stops.

—Henry Brooks Adams

The true teacher defends his pupils against his own personal influence.

—Amos Bronson Alcott

Those who educate children well are more to be honored than parents, for these only gave life, those the art of living well.

—Aristotle

A great teacher is not simply one who imparts knowledge to his students, but one who awakens their interest in it and makes them eager to pursue it for themselves. He is a spark plug, not a fuel pipe.

—M. J. Berrill

[Teacher,] I beg of you to stop apologizing for being a member of the most important . . . profession in the world.

—William G. Carr

A teacher should know more than he teaches, and if he knows more than he teaches, he will teach more than he knows.

—Eleanor L. Doan

No mechanical device can replace the teacher. Thus far no substitute has been found for the impact of mind upon mind, personality upon personality. Teachers may overcome limitations in environment, but they themselves are absolutely essential.

—Eleanor L. Doan

The great teacher is not the man who supplies the most facts, but the one in whose presence we become different people.

—Ralph Waldo Emerson

The great teacher . . . performs certain actions, says certain things that create another teacher. This other teacher is the one hidden inside the student. When the master teacher is finished, the newborn professor inside the youngster takes over, and with any luck the process of education continues until death.

—Clifton Fadiman

The educator becomes God's mind at work to help grow the best possible plants in God's garden. He exists to prepare the soil, to sow the good seed, to weed, to water, and to harvest.

—Nels F. S. Ferre

I have always felt that the true text book for the pupil is his teacher.

—Mohandas K. Gandhi

The job of a teacher is to excite in the young a boundless sense of curiosity about life, so that the growing child shall come to apprehend it with an excitement tempered by awe and wonder.

—John Garrett

A good teacher feels his way, looking for response.

—Paul Goodman

If I had a child who wanted to be a teacher, I would bid him Godspeed as if he were going to a war. For indeed the war against prejudice, greed, and ignorance is eternal, and those who dedicate themselves to it give their lives no less because they may live to see some fraction of the battle won.

—James Hilton

Successful teachers . . . share certain traits that have contributed greatly to their success. For one thing, they prize creativity. For another thing, they know how and when to maintain discipline. They can also judge and evaluate people accurately. They have a sense of humor. And they have open minds—they are alert to new ideas and new developments in teaching.

—Patricia Hockstad

The question mark is the teacher's badge.

—Herman H. Horne

A professor who had taught for many years was counseling a young teacher. "You will discover," he said, "that in nearly every class there will be a youngster eager to argue. Your first impulse will be to silence him, but I advise you to think carefully before doing so. He probably is the only one listening."

—Jim Kelly

The teacher who is attempting to teach without inspiring the pupil with a desire to learn is hammering on cold iron.

—Horace Mann

Every child is born with a great capacity for knowledge. . . . The purpose of the teacher is to "draw out," not to "cram in." We must create interest in the heart and mind of the child that will make him reach out and take hold upon the things he is taught.

—Henrietta C. Mears

Old teachers never die, they just grade away.

—Bob Phillips

The true aim of everyone who aspires to be a teacher should be, not to impart his own opinions, but to kindle minds.

—Frederick W. Robertson

A great teacher has always been measured by the number of his students who have surpassed him.

—Don Robinson

When our children will run to school and walk from school, I will know that our teachers are fulfilling their sacred mission well.

—J. A. Rosenkranz

Teachers can be found after school— taking aspirin, picking up spitballs, washing blackboards, rehearsing plays, sewing angel costumes for Christmas pageants—and just sitting at a desk waiting for strength to go home.

—Dan Valentine

In addition to knowing all there is to know about reading, writing, and arithmetic, not to mention science, biology, history, and music, a teacher has to be an authority on—baseball . . . grasshoppers . . . little girls . . . snakes . . . young love . . . little boys . . . and how to live three months of the year without a paycheck.

—Dan Valentine

The mediocre teacher tells. The good teacher explains. The superior teacher demonstrates. The great teacher inspires.

—William Arthur Ward

The teacher is like the candle, which lights others in consuming itself.

—Italian Proverb

Most of all, a teacher is somebody who likes somebody else's children—and has strength left to go to the PTA meeting.

—Anonymous

Good teachers are the ones who are able to challenge young minds without losing their own.

—Anonymous

When asked the subjects she taught, she answered that she did not teach subjects—she taught children!

—Anonymous

Filling out a series of reports at the end of the school year, one tired teacher came upon this line: "List three reasons for entering the teaching profession." Without hesitation she filled in "(1) June, (2) July, (3) August."

—Anonymous

TEACHING
(See also Education, Learning, School, Teachers, University)

In teaching you cannot see the fruit of a day's work. It is invisible and remains so, maybe for twenty years.

—Jacques Barzun

You can teach a student a lesson for a day; but if you can teach him to learn by creating curiosity, he will continue the learning process as long as he lives.

—Clay P. Bedford

It is not what is poured into a student, but what is planted, that counts.

—Eugene P. Berten

What nobler employment . . . than that of instructing the younger generation?

—Cicero

I do not teach children, I give them joy.

— Isadora Duncan

Let us teach our children to study man as well as mathematics and to build cathedrals as well as power stations.

— David Eccles

Let our teaching be full of ideas. Hitherto it has been stuffed only with facts.

— Anatole France

The whole art of teaching is only the art of awakening the natural curiosity of young minds for the purpose of satisfying it afterwards.

— Anatole France

To teach is to learn twice.

— Joseph Joubert

There are three things to remember when teaching school: know your stuff; know whom you are stuffing; and then stuff them elegantly.

— Lola May

I touch the future: I teach.

— Christa McAuliffe

Your pupils are not bowls to be filled, but torches to be lighted.

— Henrietta C. Mears

You teach a little by what you say. You teach most by what you are.

— Henrietta C. Mears

If you want to fill a dozen milk bottles, you must not stand back and spray at them with a hose. You may get them wet, but you won't fill them. You must take them one by one.

— Henrietta C. Mears

Children can take in but a little each day; they are like vases with a narrow neck; you may pour little or pour much, but much will not enter at a time.

— Jules Michelet

Teaching kids to count is fine, but teaching them what counts is best.

— Bob Talbert

The art of teaching is the art of assisting discovery.

— Mark Van Doren

The secret of teaching is to appear to have known all your life what you learned this afternoon.

— Anonymous

TEAMWORK

It marks a big step in a man's development when he comes to realize that other men can be called in to help him do a better job than he can do alone.

— Andrew Carnegie

Bees accomplish nothing save as they work together, and neither do men.

— Elbert Hubbard

No one can whistle a symphony. It takes an orchestra to play it.

— Halford E. Luccock

Two men working as a team will produce more than three men working as individuals.

—Charles P. McCormick

People acting together as a group can accomplish things that no individual acting alone could ever hope to bring about.

—Franklin Delano Roosevelt

TEARS

(See also Grief, Sorrow)

Tears of joy, like summer rain-drops, are pierced by sunbeams.

—Hosea Ballou

God washes the eyes by tears until they can behold the invisible land where tears shall come no more.

—Henry Ward Beecher

Tears are often the telescope through which men see far into heaven.

—Henry Ward Beecher

Tears are nature's lotion for the eyes. The eyes see better for being washed with them.

—Christian Bovée

The soul would have no rainbow had the eye no tears.

—John Vance Cheney

Happiness is the fine and gentle rain that penetrates the soul, but that afterwards gushes forth in springs of tears.

—M. de Guerin

Tears shed for self are tears of weakness, but tears shed for others are a sign of strength.

—Billy Graham

Every tear of sorrow sown by the righteous springs up a pearl.

—Matthew Henry

Tears are the noble language of the eye.

—Robert Herrick

Remember that the tears of life belong to the interlude, not the finale, of your story.

—Alice Huff

There is a sacredness in tears. They are not the mark of weakness, but of power. They speak more eloquently than ten thousand tongues. They are the messengers of overwhelming grief, of deep contrition and of unspeakable love.

—Washington Irving

We have lived and loved together
Through many changing years;
We have shared each other's gladness,
And wept each other's tears.

—Charles Jefferys

I do believe there is many a tear in the heart that never reaches the eyes.

—Norman MacEwan

My God, I have never thanked Thee for my thorn. I have thanked Thee a thousand times for my roses, but not once for my thorn. I have been looking forward to a world where I shall get compensation for my cross; but I have never thought of my cross as itself a present glory. Teach me the glory of my cross; teach me the value of my thorn. Show me that I have climbed to Thee by the path of pain. Show me that my tears have made my rainbows.

—George Matheson

This is the land of sin and death and tears . . . but up yonder is unceasing joy.

—Dwight L. Moody

There is a certain joy in weeping, for by tears grief is sated and relieved.

—Ovid

Tears of joy are the dew in which the sun of righteousness is mirrored.

—Jean Paul Richter

Jesus wept once, possibly more than once. There are times when God asks nothing of His children except silence, patience, and tears.

—Charles S. Robinson

Tears are the softening showers that cause the seed of heaven to spring up in the human heart.

—Walter Scott

Tears are the safety valve of the heart when too much pressure is laid on.

—Albert Smith

The bitterest tears shed over graves are for words left unsaid and deeds left undone.

—Harriet Beecher Stowe

You may forget with whom you laughed, but you will never forget with whom you wept.

—Arab Proverb

What soap is for the body, tears are for the soul.

—Jewish Proverb

TEENAGERS
(See also Adolescence, Youth)

Most of the criticism adults make about teenagers stems from envy.

—O. A. Battista

Most teenagers think that their family circle is composed of squares.

—Dan Bennett

Remember that as a teenager you are in the last stage of your life when you will be happy that the phone is for you.

—Fran Lebowitz

A baby-sitter is a teenager who comes in to act like an adult while the adults go out and act like teenagers.

—Henry Mason

If you have teenagers in your house, you'll find it difficult to understand how farmers could possibly grow a surplus of food.

—Vern McLellan

If you think there are no new frontiers, watch a boy ring the front doorbell on his first date.

—Olin Miller

Teenagers are the vanguard of tomorrow. They are a fresh breeze in a stale world.

—Dan Valentine

I like teenagers. It would be a sorry, stagnant, boring, standstill world without them.

—Dan Valentine

In conversing with teenagers, parents envy the United Nations those earphones, which give instant, simultaneous translations.

—Bill Vaughan

To grown people a girl of fifteen and a half is a child still; to herself she is very old and very real—more real, perhaps, than ever before or after.

—Margaret Widdemer

Heredity is what makes the parents of teenagers wonder a little about each other.

—Anonymous

Since teenagers are too old to do the things kids do and not old enough to do the things adults do, they do things nobody else does.

—Anonymous

TELEVISION

Television is the first truly democratic culture—the first culture available to everybody and entirely governed by what the people want. The most terrifying thing is what the people want.

—Clive Barnes

You can never hope to become a skilled conversationalist until you learn how to put your foot tactfully through the television set.

—M. Dale Baughman

If it weren't for Philo T. Farnsworth, inventor of television, we'd still be eating frozen radio dinners.

—Johnny Carson

Television hasn't done much for speakers, but it has improved conversation. There is much less of it.

—Edward L. Friedman

Television is an invention that permits you to be entertained in your living room by people you wouldn't have in your home.

—David Frost

If television encouraged us to work as much as it encourages us to do everything else, we could better afford to buy more of everything it is advertising.

—Cullen Hightower

One trouble with television . . . is too much tell and not enough vision.

—Marjorie Johnson

You do have to admire one thing about TV-sitcom families—they never waste time watching television.

—Kris Lee

I must say I find television very educational. The minute somebody turns it on, I go to the library and read a good book.

—Groucho Marx

Television has changed the American child from an irresistible force into an immovable object.

—Laurence J. Peter

Television? The word is half Latin and half Greek. No good can come of it.

—Charles P. Scott

We keep our radio right on top of the TV set. With the radio playing there, it gives us something to think about while we're watching television.

—Herb Shriner

Television will never completely replace the newspaper—no one can swat a fly with it.

—Anonymous

TEMPER
(See also Anger)

Bad temper is its own scourge. Few things are more bitter than to feel bitter. A man's venom poisons himself more than his victim.

—Charles Buxton

Temperament is temper that is too old to spank.

—Charlotte Greenwood

My life is in the hands of any fool who makes me lose my temper.

—Joseph Hunter

The worst-tempered people I ever met were people who knew they were wrong.

—Wilson Mizner

Temper, if ungoverned, governs the whole man.

—Anthony Shaftesbury

Temper is a valuable possession—don't lose it.

—Anonymous

TEMPERANCE

Temperance is a bridle of gold.

—Burton

Temperance means the abstinence from all that is evil, and the moderate use of all that is good.

—Ned H. Holmgren

TEMPTATION

Temptation usually comes in through a door that has deliberately been left open.

—Arnold H. Glasow

What makes resisting temptation difficult, for many people, is that they don't want to discourage it completely.

—Franklin P. Jones

Temptation is an irresistible force at work on a movable body.

—H. L. Mencken

Some temptations come to the industrious, but all temptations attack the idle.

—Charles H. Spurgeon

Temptation rarely comes in working hours. It is in their leisure time that men are made or marred.

—William M. Taylor

Every temptation that we meet in the path of duty is another chance of filling our souls with the power of heaven.

—Frederick Temple

Most of us keep one eye on the temptation we pray not to be led into.

—Mary H. Waldrip

No degree of temptation justifies any degree of sin.

—Nathaniel Parker Willis

Temptations are like bums: treat one nice and he'll return—with his friends.

—Anonymous

If you have been tempted into evil, fly from it. It is not falling into the water, but lying in it, that drowns.

—Anonymous

When you flee temptation, don't leave a forwarding address.

—Anonymous

TEN COMMANDMENTS

The reason why the Ten Commandments are short and clear is that they were handed down direct, not through several committees.

—Dan Bennett

The Ten Commandments are like an "Operator's Manual" from the factory.

Its instructions are fundamental to proper operation and maintenance.

—Richard C. Halverson

We have staked the future of all our political institutions upon the capacity of mankind for self-government—upon the capacity of each and all of us to govern ourselves, to control ourselves, to sustain ourselves according to the Ten Commandments of God.

—James Madison

I sometimes think if someone appealed the Ten Commandments to some of our courts, they would rule, "Thou shalt not, unless you feel strongly to the contrary."

—Ronald Reagan

It is not said that after keeping God's commandments, but in keeping them, there is great reward. God has linked these two things together, and no man can separate them—obedience and peace.

—Frederick W. Robertson

The Lord gave us commandments—He didn't mention amendments.

—Anonymous

THANKFULNESS
(See also Gratitude, Prayer—Thanksgiving)

A thankful heart is not only the greatest virtue, but the parent of all other virtues.

—Cicero

It is always possible to be thankful for what is given rather than to complain about what is not given. One or the other becomes a habit of life.

—Elisabeth Elliot

Every breath you breathe will be filled with thankfulness when you realize Jesus Christ is your blesser, giver, and healer.

—Charlie "T" Jones

The greatest saint in the world is not he who prays most or fasts most; it is not he who gives alms, or is most eminent for temperance, chastity, or justice. It is he who is most thankful to God, and who has a heart always ready to praise Him.

—William Law

All that I see teaches me to thank the Creator for all I cannot see.

—Henrietta C. Mears

Thanksgiving is nothing if not a glad and reverent lifting of the heart to God in honor and praise for His goodness.

—James R. Miller

Gratitude does nothing but love God because of the greatness of His bounty and proclaims His goodness unceasingly.

—Ottokar Prohaszka

It will be a foretaste of heaven to us here below if we are able to thank God for all His infinite goodness with all our hearts.

—Ottokar Prohaszka

God gave you the gift of 86,400 seconds today. Have you used one to say, "thank you"?

—William Arthur Ward

God has two dwellings: one in heaven, and the other in a meek and thankful heart.

—Izaak Walton

THEOLOGY

The world doesn't hear Jesus Christ any more. The world hears about our pet theological distinctives.

—Richard C. Halverson

Your theology is what you are when the talking stops and the action starts.

—Colin Morris

The best theology is rather a divine life than a divine knowledge.

—Jeremy Taylor

The Devil is a better theologian than any of us and is a devil still.

—A. W. Tozer

THEORY

There is no sadder sight in the world than to see a beautiful theory killed by a brutal fact.

—Thomas H. Huxley

First a new theory is attacked as absurd; then it is admitted to be true, but obvious and insignificant; finally, it is seen to be so important that its adversaries claim that they themselves discovered it.

—William James

The moment a person forms a theory, his imagination sees, in every object, only the traits that prove that theory.

—Thomas Jefferson

THOUGHT
(See also Mind)

You are today where your thoughts have brought you; you will be tomorrow where your thoughts take you.

—James Lane Allen

The pleasantest things in the world are pleasant thoughts, and the great art in life is to have as many as possible.

—Christian Bovée

Thinking, for many, is life's most painful activity. For the fortunate others, there's not much in life that approaches it.

—Carth Cate

We are ruined not by what we really want, but by what we think we do.

—Charles Caleb Colton

It is nonsense to say there is not enough time to be fully informed.... Time given to thought is the greatest time-saver of all.

—Norman Cousins

The best thinking is done in solitude. The worst has been in turmoil.

—Thomas Edison

Thoughts lead on to purposes; purposes go forth in action; actions form habits; habits decide character; and character fixes our destiny.

—Tryon Edwards

If a man sits down to think, he is immediately asked if he has a headache.

—Ralph Waldo Emerson

Thinking is the hardest work there is, which is the probable reason why so few engage in it.

—Henry Ford

Many people have played themselves to death. Many people have eaten and drunk themselves to death. Nobody ever thought himself to death.

—Gilbert Highet

You have absolute control over but one thing, and that is your thoughts. This is the most significant and inspiring of all facts known to man! It reflects man's divine nature.

—Napoleon Hill

A man is not idle because he is absorbed in thought. There is a visible labor and there is an invisible labor.

—Victor Hugo

The reason some of us find it difficult to think is that we haven't had any previous experience.

—Charlie "T" Jones

Thoughts, like fleas, jump from man to man. But they don't bite everybody.

—Stanislaw Lec

Thought

Think wrongly, if you please, but in all cases think for yourself.

—Doris Lessing

To think is to meander from highway to byway, and from byway to alleyway, till we come to a dead end. Stopped dead in our alley, we think what a feat it would be to get out. That is when we look for the gate to the meadows beyond.

—Antonio Machado

The dissenter is every human being at those moments of his life when he resigns momentarily from the herd and thinks for himself.

—Archibald MacLeish

Every man has a train of thought on which he travels when he is alone. The dignity and nobility of his life, as well as his happiness, depend upon the direction in which that train is going, the baggage it carries, and the scenery through which it travels.

—Joseph Fort Newton

Make for yourselves nests of pleasant thoughts. None of us yet know, for none of us have been taught in early youth, what fairy palaces we may build of beautiful thoughts—proof against all adversity.

—John Ruskin

Few people think more than two or three times a year. I have made an international reputation for myself by thinking once or twice a week.

—George Bernard Shaw

Good thoughts are blessed guests, and should be heartily welcomed, well-fed, and much sought after. Like rose leaves, they give out a sweet smell, if laid up in the jar of memory.

—Charles H. Spurgeon

Negative thoughts breed doubts and despair. Such thinking enslaves life and keeps it from reaching out for the best. Such thinking makes life a stranger to possibility. . . . Negative thoughts poison the mind. What a mind poisoned with negative thoughts contributes, then, to life is not progress, but problems.

—C. Neil Strait

To him whose elastic and vigorous thought keeps pace with the sun, the day is a perpetual morning.

—Henry David Thoreau

Life does not consist mainly—or even largely—of facts and happenings. It consists mainly of the storm of thoughts that is forever blowing through one's head.

—Mark Twain

Thoughts should be tested before they are transmitted. If our thoughts taste unkind, critical, or unfair, we should refuse to release them into the dangerous world of words.

—William Arthur Ward

If we Americans do not start to think, if we let slip the old practice of self-exile in a silent place, we shall presently become a nation of superficial men and women, identical and interchangeable.

—Philip Wylie

THRIFT

Thrift used to be a basic American virtue. Our folklore is full of it. Now the American virtue is to spend money.
—David Brinkley

Thrift is a wonderful virtue—especially in ancestors.
—Anonymous

TIME

Lost time is never found again.
—John H. Aughey

I wish I could stand on a busy corner, hat in hand, and beg people to throw me all their wasted hours.
—Bernard Berenson

There's never enough time to do it right, but there's always time to do it over.
—Jack Bergman

Time is like money; the less we have of it to spare, the further we make it go.
—Josh Billings

Be wise in the use of time. The question of life is not, "How much time have we?" The question is, "What shall we do with it?"
—Anna Robertson Brown

Time does not become sacred to us until we have lived it, until it has passed over us and taken with it a part of ourselves.
—John Burroughs

Time is the reef upon which our frail mystic ships are wrecked.
—Noel Coward

Wasting time is just as serious as breaking any of the Ten Commandments. The Lord allotted us a certain amount of time on earth and wasting it is being ungrateful and selfish, not only to the God above, but to our fellow citizens.
—Bob Feller

Time is a circus, always packing up and moving away.
—Ben Hecht

Time is a versatile performer. It flies, marches on, heals all wounds, runs out, and will tell.
—Franklin P. Jones

The surest way to be late is to have plenty of time.
—Leo Kennedy

Time is childhood's leaden wings, it is age's rushing, soundless river.
—Walter de la Mare

What is time? The shadow on the dial, the striking of the clock, the running of the sand, day and night, summer and winter, months, years, centuries—these are but arbitrary and outward signs, the measure of time, not time itself. Time is the life of the soul.
—Henry Wadsworth Longfellow

Most time is wasted, not in hours, but in minutes. A bucket with a small hole in the bottom gets just as empty as a bucket that is deliberately kicked over.

—Paul J. Meyer

How you spend your time is more important than how you spend your money. Money mistakes can be corrected, but time is gone forever.

—David B. Norris

Time neither subtracts nor divides, but adds at such a pace it seems like multiplication.

—Bob Talbert

During a very busy life I have often been asked, "How did you manage to do it all?" The answer is simple: Because I did everything *promptly*.

—Richard Tangye

Time is but a stream I go a-fishing in. I drink at it. But while I drink, I see the sandy bottom and detect how shallow it is. Its thin current slips by, and eternity remains.

—Henry David Thoreau

Suspect each moment, for it is a thief, tiptoeing away with more than it brings.

—John Updike

God made time, but man made haste.

—Irish Proverb

TODODAY
TODAY
(See also The Present)

Do not look back on happiness—or dream of it in the future. You are only sure of today; do not let yourself be cheated out of it.

—Henry Ward Beecher

Every day is the best day of the year. He is rich who owns the day. And no one owns the day who allows it to be invaded by fret and anxiety. Finish every day and be done with it. You have done what you could. Tomorrow is a new day. Too dear, with its hopes and invitations, to waste a single thought on tomorrow.

—Ralph Waldo Emerson

Today is your day and mine, the only day we have, the day in which we play our part. What our part may signify in the great whole we may not understand; but we are here to play it, and now is the time.

—David Starr Jordan

That we are alive today is proof positive that God has something for us to do today.

—Anna R. B. Lindsay

I will forget the happenings of the day that is gone, where they were good or bad, and greet the new sun with confidence that this will be the best day of my life.

—Og Mandino

May every day be a new beginning, and every dawn bring us closer to that shining city upon a hill.

—Ronald Reagan

Each day comes bearing its gifts. Untie
the ribbons.

—Ann Schabacker

I believe in today. It is all that I possess.
The past is of value only as it can make
the life of today fuller and freer. There is
no assurance of tomorrow. I must make
good today!

—Charles Stelzle

Today is a day that we never had before,
that we shall never have again. It rose
from the great ocean of eternity, and
again sinks into its unfathomable
depths.

—T. DeWitt Talmadge

Wipe out the past, trust the future, and
live in a glorious now.

—Elizabeth Towne

Time and life are made up of one today
after another. Yesterday is a fallen leaf;
tomorrow is still a dream; but today is
here.

—Esther Baldwin York

The past is history; the future is a
mystery; today is a gift; that's why it's
called the "PRESENT."

—Anonymous

Life is lived in the present. Yesterday has
gone, tomorrow is yet to be. Today is the
miracle.

—Anonymous

TOMORROW

Every tomorrow has two handles; we
can take hold by the handle of anxiety
or by the handle of faith.

—Henry Ward Beecher

God's tomorrow will be better than any
yesterday you have ever known.

—Thomas A. Carruth

It is a great deed to leave nothing for
tomorrow.

—Baltasar Gracian

I do not fear tomorrow, for I remember
yesterday and I love today.

—William Allen White

Tomorrow is the day when idlers work,
and fools reform, and mortal men lay
hold of heaven.

—Anonymous

TONGUE

One of the first things a physician says
to his patient is, "Let me see your
tongue." A spiritual advisor might often
do the same.

—Nehemiah Adams

Mistakes of the tongue have destroyed
more people, ruined more marriages,
and cost more businessmen their jobs
and their futures than any other kind of
mistake.

—O. A. Battista

When we advance a little into life, we
find that the tongue of man creates
nearly all the mischief in the world.

—Edward Paxton Hood

A sharp tongue is the only edged tool that grows keener with constant use.

—Washington Irving

The second most deadly instrument is a loaded gun. The first is the human tongue. The gun merely kills bodies. The tongue kills reputations and oftentimes ruins character.

—William G. Jordan

It is the wise head that makes the still tongue.

—William James Lucas

There is danger when a man throws his tongue into high gear before he gets his brain a-going.

—C. C. Phelps

The tongue is but three inches long, yet it can kill a man six feet high.

—Japanese Proverb

TRAGEDY

The tragedy of life is what dies inside a man while he lives.

—Albert Einstein

The great tragedy of life is not that men perish, but that they cease to love.

—W. Somerset Maugham

TRANQUILITY

The time of business does not differ from the time of prayer; and in the noise and clutter of my kitchen, while several persons are at the same time calling for different things, I possess God in as great tranquillity as if I were on my knees.

—Brother Lawrence

I delight to steal away for days and weeks together, and bathe my spirit in the freedom of the old woods, and to grow young again, . . . counting the white clouds that sail along the sky, softly and tranquilly. . . . I like to steep my soul in a sea of quiet, with nothing floating past me . . . but the perfume of flowers, and soaring birds, and shadows of clouds.

—Donald G. Mitchell

TRAVEL

I have wandered all my life, and I have also traveled; the difference between the two being this, that we wander for distraction, but we travel for fulfillment.

—Hilaire Belloc

If you look anything like your passport photo, you're not well enough to travel.

—Jill Briscoe

TRIALS
(See also Adversity, Affliction, Burdens, Misfortune, Suffering, Troubles)
The beauty of the soul shines out when a man bears with composure one heavy mischance after another, not because he does not feel them, but because he is a man of high and heroic temper.

—Aristotle

We are always in the forge or on the anvil; by trials God is shaping us for higher things.

—Henry Ward Beecher

Wherever souls are being tried and ripened, in whatever commonplace and homely way, there God is hewing out the pillars for his temple.

—Phillips Brooks

Sufficient to each day are the duties to be done and the trials to be endured. God never built a Christian strong enough to carry today's duties and tomorrow's anxieties piled on top of them.

—Theodore Ledyard Cuyler

Blessed is any weight, however overwhelming, that God has been so good as to fasten with His own hand upon our shoulders.

—Frederick W. Faber

All sunshine and blue skies make for a Sahara Desert; there must be the fall and winter to make for a beautiful spring. Sweet wine comes from crushed grapes.

—Robert D. Foster

The chief pang of most trials is not so much the actual suffering itself as our own spirit of resistance to it.

—Jean Nicolas Grou

Into each life some rain must fall. Some days must be dark and dreary.

—Henry Wadsworth Longfellow

God is testing us, to see whether we can trust Him in the dark as well as in the light; and whether we can be as true to Him when all pleasurable emotions have faded off our hearts, as when we walked with Him in the light.

—F. B. Meyer

That which caused us trial shall yield us triumph; and that which made our heart ache shall fill us with gladness.... We must pass through the darkness to reach the light.

—Albert Pike

It would seem, indeed, to be God's usual method to prepare men for extensive usefulness by the personal discipline of trial.

—W. M. Punshon

As sure as God ever puts His children into the furnace, He will be in the furnace with them.

—Charles H. Spurgeon

Hard times have a way of teaching us lessons that we refuse to learn in good times. That is the one university we all get to attend—tuition free.

—Clarence Thomas

Botanists say that trees need the powerful March winds to flex their trunks and main branches, so that the sap is drawn up to nourish the budding leaves. Perhaps we need the gales of life in the same way, though we dislike enduring them. A blustery period in our fortunes is often the prelude to a new spring of life and health, success and happiness, when we keep steadfast in faith and look to the good in spite of appearances.

—Jane Truax

A smooth sea never made a skilled mariner.

—English Proverb

My friend, I don't know what you're going through, but look and see if God is trying to direct you, inspect you, correct you, protect you, or perfect you.

—Anonymous

TROUBLES
(See also Adversity, Affliction, Burdens, Misfortune, Suffering, Trials)

When we are flat on our backs, there is no way to look but up.

—Roger Babson

Troubles are often the tools by which God fashions us for better things.

—Henry Ward Beecher

Trouble is a sieve through which we sift our acquaintances. Those too big to pass through are our friends.

—Arlene Francis

Nothing lasts forever—not even your troubles.

—Arnold H. Glasow

If you would kick the person responsible for most of your troubles, you wouldn't be able to sit down for six months.

—Gordon Gray

Never attempt to bear more than one kind of trouble at once. Some people bear three kinds—all they have had, all they have now, and all they ever expect to have.

—Edward Everett Hale

Trouble makes us one with every human being in the world.

—Oliver Wendell Holmes

Trouble creates a capacity to handle it.

—Oliver Wendell Holmes Jr.

Troubles are like babies—they only grow by nursing.

—Douglas Jerrold

People who invite trouble always complain when it accepts.

—Lane Olinghouse

In the presence of trouble, some people grow wings; others buy crutches.

—Harold W. Ruoff

There are people who are always anticipating trouble, and in this way they manage to enjoy many sorrows that never really happen to them.

—Henry Wheeler Shaw

If you tell your troubles to God, you put them into the grave; they will never rise again when you have committed them to Him.

—Charles H. Spurgeon

I am an old man and have known a great many troubles, but most of them never happened.

—Mark Twain

All the water in the world cannot sink a ship—unless the water starts getting inside. . . . All the troubles in the world can't sink a human being—unless those troubles invade his inner life.

—Vera Werblo

TRUST/TRUSTWORTHINESS

Trust is the emotional glue that binds followers and leaders together.

—Warren G. Bennis

Trust God for great things; with your five loaves and two fishes, He will show you a way to feed thousands.

—Horace Bushnell

The man who trusts men will make fewer mistakes than he who distrusts them.

—Camillo di Cavour

You can trust the man who died for you.

—Lettie Cowman

What loneliness is more lonely than distrust?

—George Eliot

All I have seen teaches me to trust the Creator for all I have not seen.

—Ralph Waldo Emerson

Trust men, and they will be true to you; treat them greatly and they will show themselves great.

—Ralph Waldo Emerson

People whom we trust tend to become trustworthy.

—Solomon Freehof

I prefer to have too much confidence, and thereby be deceived, than to be always mistrustful. For, in the first case, I suffer for a moment at being deceived and, in the second, I suffer constantly.

—Paul Gauguin

When a man assumes a public trust, he should consider himself as public property.

—Thomas Jefferson

It is better to suffer wrong than to do it, and happier to be sometimes cheated than not to trust.

—Samuel Johnson

Trust him little who praises all, him less who censures all, and him least who is indifferent about all.

—Johann K. Lavater

To be trusted is a greater compliment than to be loved.

—George MacDonald

Trust in yourself and you are doomed to disappointment; trust in your friends and they will die and leave you; trust in money and you may have it taken from you; trust in reputation and some slanderous tongue may blast it; but trust in God, and you are never to be confounded in time or eternity.

—Dwight L. Moody

Better to trust the man who is frequently in error than the one who is never in doubt.

—Eric Sevareid

Trust in that man's promise who dares to refuse that which he fears he cannot perform.

—Charles H. Spurgeon

The only way to make a man trustworthy is to trust him.

—Henry L. Stimson

When a train goes through a tunnel and it gets dark, you don't throw away the ticket and jump off. You sit still and trust the engineer.

—Corrie ten Boom

I think that we may safely trust a good deal more than we do.

—Henry David Thoreau

Trust is a treasured item and relationship. Once it is tarnished, it is hard to restore it to its original glow.

—William Arthur Ward

He who mistrusts most should be trusted least.

—Greek Proverb

It is an equal failing to trust everybody, and to trust nobody.

—Proverb

The more you trust people the less are the chances that their friendships will rust.

—Anonymous

The person I trust the least is one who is suspicious of everybody else.

—Anonymous

A man's trust in God diminishes in direct proportion to the growth of his power over people.

—Anonymous

TRUTH
(See also Candor)

The language of truth is unadorned and always simple.

—Marcellinus Ammianus

To labor in season and out of season, under every discouragement, by the power of truth . . . that requires a heroism that is transcendent.

—Henry Ward Beecher

He that would make real progress in knowledge must dedicate his age as well as youth—the latter growth as well as the first fruits—at the altar of truth.

—George Berkeley

As scarce as truth is, the supply has always been in excess of the demand.

—Josh Billings

Truth is a gem that is found at great depth; whilst on the surface of the world all things are weighed by the false scale of custom.

—Lord Byron

Truth will rise above falsehood as oil above water.

—Miguel de Cervantes

Men occasionally stumble over the truth, but most pick themselves up and hurry off as if nothing had happened.

—Winston Churchill

The pursuit of truth shall set you free,
even if you never catch up with it.

—Clarence Darrow

I believe, absolutely, that truth is the
strongest and most powerful weapon a
man can use, whether he is fighting for
a reform or fighting for a sale.

—Arthur Dunn

The greatest homage we can pay to the
truth is to use it.

—Ralph Waldo Emerson

Craft must have clothes, but truth loves
to go naked.

—Thomas Fuller

I love agitation and investigation and
glory in defending unpopular truth
against popular error.

—James A. Garfield

The question is not whether a doctrine
is beautiful but whether it is true. When
we wish to go to a place, we do not ask
whether the road leads through a pretty
country, but whether it is the right road.

—A. W. and J. C. Hare

Truth is tough. It will not break like a
bubble, at a touch; nay, you may kick it
about all day, like a football, and it will
be round and full at evening.

—Oliver Wendell Holmes

There is no wisdom save in truth. Truth
is everlasting.

—Martin Luther

In the mountains of truth you never
climb in vain.

—Friedrich Nietzsche

Truth often suffers more by the heat of
its defenders than from the arguments
of its opposers.

—William Penn

Those who know the truth learn to
love it; those who love the truth learn
to live it.

—Bob Proctor

There is no power on earth more
formidable than truth.

—Margaret Lee Runbeck

Truth has no special time of its own. Its
hour is now—always.

—Albert Schweitzer

Truth is a glorious but hard mistress.
She never consults, bargains, or
compromises.

—A. W. Tozer

Truth is the most valuable thing we
have. Let us economize it.

—Mark Twain

Let's not drag God's standard of truth
down to our level of performance.

—Morris Vendon

If you do not tell the truth about
yourself you cannot tell it about other
people.

—Virginia Woolf

TYRANNY

The only tyrant I accept in this world is
the "still small voice" within me.

>   —Mohandas K. Gandhi

Resistance to tyrants is obedience to
God.

>   —Thomas Jefferson

These are the times that try men's souls.
The summer soldier and the sunshine
patriot will, in this crisis, shrink from
the service of their country; but he that
stands it now, deserves the love and
thanks of man and woman. Tyranny,
like hell, is not easily conquered; yet we
have this consolation with us, that the
harder the conflict, the more glorious
the triumph.

>   —Thomas Paine

When the administration of justice goes
awry, citizens are doomed to tyranny.

>   —Paul Craig Roberts

Beware the tyranny of the minority.

>   —Latin Proverb

The tyrant confuses those he can't
convince, corrupts those he can't
confuse, and crushes those he can't
corrupt.

>   —Anonymous

U

UNDERSTANDING

The great need today in every phase of our social, economical, and political life is understanding. It has always been so.
—Charles R. Hook

If you wish to please people, you must begin by understanding them.
—Charles Reade

There can be no happiness equal to the joy of finding a heart that understands.
—Victor Robinsoll

UNIQUENESS

I narrow-mindedly outlawed the word *unique.* Practically every press release contains it. Practically nothing ever is.
—Fred M. Hechinger

God made each of us unique, and there is a vast mystery and beauty surrounding the human soul.
—Alan Loy McGinnis

UNITY

All your strength is in union—all your danger is in discord.
—Henry Wadsworth Longfellow

Christian unity is not found in uniformity, organization, or a particular church, but rather in Jesus and our commitment to His teachings, and living them out in our lives. . . . It is only as we join together with others who

look different than we do but share a common love and commitment to the Truth that is Jesus, that we can know the completeness of the body of Christ.
—Bob Snyder

UNIVERSE

The universe is a stairway leading nowhere unless man is immortal.
—Edgar Young Mullins

The universe is full of magical things, patiently waiting for our wits to grow sharper.
—Eden Phillpotts

UNIVERSITY
(See also Education, Learning, School, Teachers, Teaching)

If you feel that you have both feet planted on level ground, then the university has failed you.
—Robert Goheen

The world is a great university. From the cradle to the grave we are always in God's great kindergarten, where everything is trying to teach us a lesson.
—Orison Swett Marden

There are few earthly things more beautiful than a university . . . a place where those who hate ignorance may strive to know, where those who perceive truth may strive to make others see.
—John Masefield

URGENCY

Don't let the urgent take the place of the important in your life. Oh, the urgent will really fight, claw, and scream for attention. It will plead for our time and even make us think we've done the right thing in calming its nerves. But the tragedy of it all is this: When you and I were putting out the fires of the urgent, the important was again left in a holding pattern.

—Charles E. Hummel

VALUES

The real values are those that stay by you, give you happiness, and enrich you. They are the human values.

—George Matthew Adams

Our American values are not luxuries but necessities—not the salt in our bread but the bread itself. Our common vision of a free and just society is our greatest source of cohesion at home and strength abroad—greater than the bounty of our material blessings.

—Jimmy Carter

In a world where so much seems to be hidden by the smoke of falsity and moral degeneration, we Americans must grasp firmly the ideals that have made this country great. We must reaffirm the basic human values that have guided our forefathers. A revival of old-fashioned patriotism and a grateful acknowledgment of what our country has done for us would be good for all our souls.

—Manton S. Eddy

Try not to become a man of success, but rather a man of value.

—Albert Einstein

There is too much stress today on material things. I try to teach my children not so much the value of cents as a sense of values.

—Morris Franklin

It is not our affluence, or our plumbing, or our clogged freeways that grip the imagination of others. Rather, it is the values upon which our system is built. These values imply our adherence not only to liberty and individual freedom, but also to international peace, law, and order, and constructive social purpose. When we depart from these values, we do so at our peril.

—J. William Fulbright

Values are not trendy items that are casually traded in.

—Ellen Goodman

Beauty, truth, friendship, love, creation—these are the great values of life. We can't prove them, or explain them, yet they are the most stable things in our lives.

—Jesse Herman Holmes

The aim of education is the knowledge not of facts but of values.

—William Ralph Inge

Get a right idea of values. Material possessions that you do not need and cannot use may be only an encumbrance. Let your guiding rule be not how much but how good.

—Grenville Kleiser

Civilization ceases when we no longer respect and no longer put into their correct places the fundamental values such as work, family, and country, such as the individual, honor, and religion.

—R. P. Lebret

We shall be rich or poor only as we seek or reject those values that make us so.

—Elmer G. Leterman

Today we are afraid of simple words like goodness and mercy and kindness. We don't believe in the good old words because we don't believe in the good old values anymore.

—Lin Yü-t'ang

The ultimate determinant in the struggle now going on for the world will not be bombs and rockets but a test of wills and ideas—a trial of spiritual resolve: the values we hold, the beliefs we cherish, and the ideals to which we are dedicated.

—Ronald Reagan

Conscience is the voice of values long and deeply infused into one's sinews and blood.

—Elliot L. Richardson

The hope of free man in a frightened world is the values that man puts ahead of inventions when his back is to the wall. These values are beauty, truth, goodness, and having a faith, all of which are bombproof.

—Ralph W. Sockman

A people that values its privileges above its principles soon loses both.

—Anonymous

VICE

The inherent vice of capitalism is the unequal sharing of blessings; the inherent virtue of socialism is the equal sharing of miseries.

—Winston Churchill

There is a capacity of virtue in us, and there is a capacity of vice to make your blood creep.

—Ralph Waldo Emerson

VICTORY

Victory at all costs, victory in spite of all terror, victory however long and hard the road may be; for without victory there is no survival.

—Winston Churchill

I glory in conflict that I may hereafter exult in victory.

—Frederick Douglass

We have all eternity to tell of victories won for Christ, but we have only a few hours before sunset in which to win them.

—Jonathan Goforth

Be ashamed to die until you have won some victory for humanity.

—Horace Mann

Those who know how to win are much more numerous than those who know how to make proper use of their victories.

—Polybius

VIOLENCE

Violence is the last refuge of the incompetent.

—Isaac Asimov

Nothing good ever comes from violence.

—Martin Luther

In violence we forget who we are.

—Mary McCarthy

VIRTUE

Virtue is like a rich stone, best plain set.

—Francis Bacon

The virtues that keep this world sweet and the faithfulness that keeps it steadfast are chiefly those of the average man.

—W. R. Bowie

Virtue, like a plant, will not grow unless its root be hidden, buried from the eye of the sun.

—Thomas Carlyle

Loving means to love that which is unlovable—or it is no virtue at all; forgiving means to pardon the unpardonable—or it is no virtue at all; and to hope means hoping when things are hopeless—or it is no virtue at all.

—Gilbert Keith Chesterton

Virtue shows quite as well in rags and patches as she does in purple and fine linen.

—Charles Dickens

The best way to teach a virtue is to live it.

—Paul R. Frothingham

Virtue, morality, and religion. This is the armor, my friend, and this alone that renders us invincible. These are the tactics we should study. If we lose these, we are conquered, fallen indeed.

—Patrick Henry

The virtuous soul is pure and unmixed light, springing from the body as a flash of lightning darts from the cloud.

—Heraclitus

Virtue is the health of the soul; it gives a flavor to the smallest leaves of life.

—Joseph Joubert

Virtue is the fount whence honor springs.

—Christopher Marlowe

Virtue and goodness tend to make men powerful in this world; but they who aim at the power have not the virtue.

—John Henry Newman

Whenever we are planning for posterity, we ought to remember that virtue is not hereditary.

—Thomas Paine

One advantage resulting from virtuous actions is that they elevate the mind and dispose it to attempt others more virtuous still.

—Jean Jacques Rousseau

Virtue is bold, and goodness never fearful.

—William Shakespeare

Virtue consists, not in abstaining from vice, but in not desiring it.

—George Bernard Shaw

Few men have virtue to withstand the highest bidder.

—George Washington

Virtue is stronger than a battering-ram.

—Proverb

VISION

We all live under the same sky, but we don't all have the same horizon.

—Konrad Adenauer

The vision that you glorify in your mind, the ideal that you enthrone in your heart—this you will build your life by, this you will become.

—James Lane Allen

Good vision consists in seeing as far ahead as you can and, on getting there, never looking back.

—O. A. Battista

The greatest danger inherent in pride is the effectiveness with which our own brilliance can blind our vision.

—O. A. Battista

Good vision consists of being able to see the trees and the forest.

—O. A. Battista

The degree of vision that dwells in a man is a correct measure of the man.

—Thomas Carlyle

The sorriest man in town is the one who has caught up with his vision.

—Paul Elliott

Poor eyes limit your sight; poor vision limits your deeds.

—Franklin Field

I'm looking for people who have the infinite capacity to not know what can't be done.

—Henry Ford

A blind man's world is bounded by the limits of his touch; an ignorant man's world by the limits of his knowledge; a great man's world by the limits of his vision.

—E. Paul Hovey

The most pathetic person in the world is someone who has sight but has no vision.

—Helen Keller

There are so many wonderful things in your everyday experience, lucrative opportunities, glorious occasions, that do not exist for you because you do not have the vision for discerning them.

—Edward Kramer

Two men look out through the same
   bars:
One sees the mud, and one the stars.
                —Frederick Langbridge

Now man cannot live without some
vision of himself. But still less can he
live without a vision that is true to his
inner experience and inner feeling.
                —D. H. Lawrence

A vision foretells what may be ours. It is
an invitation to do something. With a
great mental picture in mind we go
from one accomplishment to another,
using the materials about us only as
steppingstones to that which is higher
and better and more satisfying. We thus
become possessors of the unseen values
that are eternal.
                —Katherine Logan

Vision is of God. A vision comes in
advance of any task well done.
                —Katherine Logan

Vision is the world's most desperate
need. There are no hopeless situations,
only people who think hopelessly.
                —Winifred Newman

True vision is always twofold. It involves
emotional comprehension as well as
physical perception. Yet how rarely we
have either. We generally only glance at an
object long enough to tag it with a name.
                —Ross Parmenter

Visionary people are visionary partly
because of the very great many things
they don't see.
                —Berkeley Rice

The fellow who can only see a week
ahead is always the popular fellow, for
he is looking with the crowd. But the
one who can see years ahead, he has a
telescope but he can't make anybody
believe he has it.
                —Will Rogers

Hundreds of people can talk for one
who can think, but thousands can think
for one who can see. To see clearly is
poetry, prophecy, and religion—all in
one.
                —John Ruskin

A rock pile ceases to be a rock pile the
moment a single man contemplates it,
bearing within him the image of a
cathedral.
                —Antoine de Saint-Exupéry

Every man takes the limits of his own
field of vision for the limits of the
world.
                —Arthur Schopenhauer

There is no gain except by loss; there is
no life except by death; there is no
vision but by faith.
                —Walter Chalmers Smith

Vision is the art of seeing things
invisible.
                —Jonathan Swift

If your vision is for a year, plant wheat.
If your vision is for ten years, plant
trees. If your vision is for a lifetime,
plant people.
                —Chinese Proverb

Tomorrow belongs to those who have vision today.

—Anonymous

Vision is the Aladdin's Lamp of the soul. It is the divine spark that lights the lamp of progress. It is the hand that pushes aside the curtains of night to let the sunrise in.

—Anonymous

A vision without a task is a dream;
A task without a vision is drudgery;
A vision and a task equal the hope of the world.

—Anonymous

VOCATION

In the divine economy, each call or vocation is of equal importance with the others—each is the work of the church—each is done in submission and obedience to God.

—Richard C. Halverson

Everyone has a vocation by which he earns his living, but he also has a vocation in an older sense of the word—the vocation to use his powers and live his life well.

—Richard W. Livingstone

The test of a vocation is the love of the drudgery it involves.

—Logan Pearsall Smith

VOTING

Always vote for a principle, though you vote alone, and you may cherish the sweet reflection that your vote is never lost.

—John Quincy Adams

Vote for the man who promises least; he'll be the least disappointing.

—Bernard M. Baruch

A good citizen votes regularly and intelligently at election time. The greatest menace to freedom is an inert people.

—Louis D. Brandeis

Did you ever stop to think what the word *vote* means? To me it means "**V**oice **o**f **T**axpayers **E**verywhere."

—Martin Buxbaum

At the bottom of all the tributes paid to democracy is the little man, walking into the little booth, with a little pencil, making a little cross on a little bit of paper.

—Winston Churchill

Applause, mingled with boos and hisses, is about all that the average voter is able or willing to contribute to public life.

—Elmer Davis

The first step toward liberation for any group is to use the power in hand . . . and the power in hand is the vote.

—Helen Gahagan Douglas

I always voted at my party's call,
And I never thought of thinking for
    myself at all.
                        —Gilbert and Sullivan

Some experts say the women hold the
balance in voting. Which shows the
importance of making a good impression on the Eve of the election.
                        —Quin Ryan

Whenever a fellow tells me he's
bipartisan, I know he's going to vote
against me.
                        —Harry S. Truman

America is a land where a citizen will
cross the ocean to fight for democracy
and won't cross the street to vote.
                        —Bill Vaughan

It makes no difference who you vote
for—the two parties are really one
party representing four percent of the
people.
                        —Gore Vidal

What's real in politics is what the voters
decide is real.
                        —Ben J. Wattenberg

WAITING

Everything comes to him who hustles while he waits.

—Thomas Edison

We must wait for God, long, meekly, in the wind and wet, in the thunder and lightning, in the cold and dark. Wait, and He will come. He never comes to those who do not wait.

—Frederick W. Faber

Let God take the initiative. If you will wait, God will work! Cease from your trying; start to trust and praise Him for what He is going to do.

—Robert D. Foster

Simply wait upon Him. So doing, we shall be directed, supplied, protected, corrected, and rewarded.

—Vance Havner

Quiet waiting before God would save from many a mistake and from many a sorrow.

—J. Hudson Taylor

WAR

(See also Peace)

We make war that we may live in peace.

—Aristotle

A just fear of an imminent danger, though there be no blow given, is a lawful cause of war.

—Francis Bacon

Men acquainted with the battlefield will not be found among the numbers that glibly talk of another war.

—Dwight D. Eisenhower

No one is fool enough to choose war instead of peace. For in peace sons bury fathers, but in war fathers bury sons.

—Herodotus

It is fatal to enter any war without the will to win it.

—Douglas MacArthur

War is an ugly thing but not the ugliest of things; the decayed and degraded state of moral and patriotic feelings that thinks that nothing is worth war is much worse.

—John Stuart Mill

Wars may be fought with weapons, but they are won by men. It is the spirit of the men who follow and of the man who leads that gains the victory.

—George S. Patton

A just war is in the long run far better for a nation's soul than the most prosperous peace obtained by acquiescence in wrong or injustice.

—Theodore Roosevelt

WASHINGTON (D.C.)

The more I observed Washington, the more frequently I visited it, and the more people I interviewed there, the more I understood how prophetic L'Enfant was when he laid it out as a city that goes around in circles.

—John Mason Brown

People only leave [Washington] by way of the box—ballot or coffin.

—Claiborne Pell

It's hard when you're up to your armpits in alligators to remember you came here [to Washington] to drain the swamp.

—Ronald Reagan

WEAKNESS

Weakness of attitude becomes weakness of character.

—Albert Einstein

You cannot run away from weakness. You must somehow fight it or perish; and if that be so, why not now and where you are?

—Robert Louis Stevenson

WEALTH

Wealth unused might as well not exist.

—Aesop

Wealth, after all, is a relative thing, since he who has little, and wants less, is richer than he who has much, and wants more.

—Charles Caleb Colton

If rich men would remember that shrouds have no pockets, they would, while living, share their wealth with their children, and give for the good of

others, and so know the highest pleasure wealth can give.

—Tryon Edwards

Wealth consists not in having great possessions but in having few wants.

—Epicurus

The real measure of our wealth is how much we should be worth if we lost our money.

—J. H. Jowett

There is nothing that makes men rich and strong but that which they carry inside of them. Wealth is of the heart, not of the hand.

—John Milton

WEATHER

If we want to go somewhere intensely enough, we call the bad weather "bracing."

—Sydney J. Harris

Don't knock the weather; nine-tenths of the people couldn't start a conversation if it didn't change once in a while.

—Frank McKinney Hubbard

Sunshine is delicious, rain is refreshing, wind braces us up, snow is exhilarating; there is really no such thing as bad weather, only different kinds of good weather.

—John Ruskin

Each of us makes his own weather, determines the color of the skies in the emotional universe that he inhabits.

—Fulton J. Sheen

WELCOME

Come in the evening, or come in the
  morning,
Come when you're looked for, or come
  without warning.

—Thomas Osborne Davis

You are as welcome as the flowers in
May.

—Charles Macklin

A most moving and pulse-stirring
honor—the heartfelt grip of the hand,
and the welcome that does not descend
from the pale, gray matter of the brain
but rushes up with the red blood of the
heart.

—Mark Twain

WILDERNESS

Though in the wilderness, a man is
never alone.

—Thomas Brown

In God's wilderness lies the hope of the
world—the great fresh unblighted,
unredeemed wilderness.

—John Muir

In this silent, serene wilderness, the
weary can gain a heart-bath in perfect
peace.

—John Muir

WILL POWER

Lack of will power has caused more
failure than lack of intelligence or
ability.

—Flower A. Newhouse

Many men have too much will power.
It's won't power they lack.

—John A. Shedd

WINNERS

It is harder to be a good winner than a
good loser—one has less practice.

—T. E. B. Clarke

A winner knows how much he still has
to learn, even when he is considered an
expert by others. A loser wants to be
considered an expert by others, before
he has learned enough to know how
little he knows.

—Sydney J. Harris

Often the best way to win is to forget to
keep score.

—Marianne Espinosa Murphy

WINTER

Winter tames man, woman, and beast.

—William Shakespeare

What fire could ever equal the sunshine
of a winter's day?

—Henry David Thoreau

WISDOM

A prudent question is one-half of
wisdom.

—Francis Bacon

Learning sleeps and snores in libraries,
but wisdom is everywhere, wide awake,
on tiptoes.

—Josh Billings

A man doesn't begin to attain wisdom until he recognizes that he is no longer indispensable.

—Richard E. Byrd

A man begins getting his wisdom teeth the first time he bites off more than he can chew.

—Herb Caen

I do not believe in the collective wisdom of individual ignorance.

—Thomas Carlyle

It is always wise to look ahead, but difficult to look further than you can see.

—Winston Churchill

The function of wisdom is discriminating between good and evil.

—Cicero

Common sense in an uncommon degree is what the world calls wisdom.

—Samuel Taylor Coleridge

Knowledge is proud that he has learn'd
    so much;
Wisdom is humble that he knows no
    more.

—William Cowper

Intelligence and education can ascertain the facts. Wisdom can discover the truth.

—Max De Pree

A loving heart is the truest wisdom.

—Charles Dickens

It requires the eye of wisdom and bravery to see the radiance of a dark day, and impart its brightness to the world.

—Ella E. Dodson

The attempt to combine wisdom and power has only rarely been successful and then only for a short while.

—Albert Einstein

He is a wise man who does not grieve for the things that he has not, but rejoices for those that he has.

—Epictetus

It is a wise man who said that there is no greater inequality than the equal treatment of unequals.

—Felix Frankfurter

Wisdom too often never comes, and so one ought not to reject it merely because it comes late.

—Felix Frankfurter

He is a wise man who wastes no energy on pursuits for which he is not fitted, and is still wiser who, among the things he can do well, chooses and resolutely follows the best.

—William E. Gladstone

No man is really wise until he is kind and courteous.

—Charles Haas

The road to wisdom?
Well, it's plain, and simple to express:
Err and err and err again,
But less and less and less.

—Piet Hein

Wisdom

Wisdom denotes the pursuing of the best ends by the best means.
—Francis Hutcheson

It is astonishing with how little wisdom mankind can be governed, when that little wisdom is its own.
—William Ralph Inge

The art of being wise is the art of knowing what to overlook.
—William James

Make wisdom your provision for the journey from youth to old age, for it is a more certain support than all other possessions.
—Diogenes Laertius

Besides the art of getting things done, there is the noble art of leaving things undone. The wisdom of life consists in the elimination of non-essentials.
—Lin Yü-t'ang

It requires wisdom to understand wisdom; the music is nothing if the audience is deaf.
—Walter Lippmann

The older I get, the more I distrust the familiar doctrine that age brings wisdom.
—H. L. Mencken

The most manifest sign of wisdom is a continual cheerfulness.
—Michel de Montaigne

We can be knowledgeable with other men's knowledge, but we cannot be wise with other men's wisdom.
—Michel de Montaigne

The growth of wisdom may be gauged exactly by the diminution of ill-temper.
—Friedrich Nietzsche

We don't receive wisdom; we must discover it for ourselves after a journey no one can take for us or spare us.
—Marcel Proust

Nine-tenths of wisdom consists in being wise in time.
—Theodore Roosevelt

Wisdom comes by disillusionment.
—George Santayana

Wisdom is ever a blessing; education is sometimes a curse.
—John A. Shedd

The wise want love; and those who love want wisdom.
—Percy Bysshe Shelley

Wise men and women in every major culture have maintained that the secret of happiness is not in getting more but in wanting less.
—Philip Slater

Wisdom outweighs any wealth.
—Sophocles

O then that wisdom may we know,
Which yields a life of peace below!
—Charles Sprague

The doorstep to the temple of wisdom is a knowledge of our own ignorance.
—Charles H. Spurgeon

Knowledge comes, but wisdom lingers.
—Alfred Lord Tennyson

It is characteristic of wisdom not to do desperate things.
—Henry David Thoreau

Wisdom is not finally tested by the schools,
Wisdom cannot be pass'd from one having it to another not having it,
Wisdom is of the soul, is not susceptible of proof, is its own proof.
—Walt Whitman

The wiser man shapes into God's plan as water shapes into a vessel.
—Ella Wheeler Wilcox

Wisdom doesn't necessarily come with age. Sometimes age just shows up all by itself.
—Tom Wilson

Wisdom is ofttimes nearer when we stoop than when we soar.
—William Wordsworth

A wise man will change his mind. A fool never does.
—Anonymous

WISHING

It is always wise to stop wishing for things long enough to enjoy the fragrance of those now flowering.
—Patricia Clafford

A man will sometimes devote all his life to the development of one part of his body—the wishbone.
—Robert Frost

Many of us spend half our time wishing for things we could have if we didn't spend half our time wishing.
—Alexander Woollcott

WIT
(See also Humor, Laughter)

Wit ought to be a glorious treat, like caviar; never spread it about like marmalade.
—Noel Coward

Wit is the salt of conversation, not the food.
—William Hazlitt

Wit has truth in it; wisecracking is simply calisthenics with words.
—Dorothy Parker

Wit, by itself, is of little account. It becomes of moment only when grounded in wisdom.
—Mark Twain

WITNESSING
(See also Evangelism, Soul Winning)

We are here to represent Christ—to present Him again, to re-present Him.
—Maltbie D. Babcock

Jesus Christ didn't commit the gospel to an advertising agency; He commissioned disciples. And He didn't command them to put up signs and pass out tracts; He said that they would be His witnesses.

—Joe Bayly

My mind is not so timid that I deny the existence of mysteries. But I am wary of those who profess to live by them, who with their finger to their lips, proclaim themselves God's elect and keep the uninitiated in ignorance.

—Jacques de Borbbon Busset

We have the Bible bound in morocco, bound in all kinds of beautiful leather. What we need is the Bible bound in shoe leather.

—Oswald Chambers

We were not saved to go to heaven. If so, why didn't we go to heaven right then? Heaven is a by-product. We were saved to tell others and to let Jesus Christ live in us.

—Jimmy Draper

Life is like a river, with the unsaved rushing downstream heading for the waterfalls, as we Christians are standing on the shore, waving goodbye.

—Ted Limpic

It's always a privilege to sit down and explain how forgiveness, cleansing, and power can be individually ours in and through the Lord Jesus Christ.

—Paul Little

Live the gospel first! Tell about it afterward!

—Henrietta C. Mears

People will understand as much of the love of God as they see in our own lives. The first Bible many people will read will be your life.

—Rebecca Manley Pippert

The real problem of Christianity is not atheism or skepticism, but the non-witnessing Christian trying to smuggle his own soul into heaven.

—James S. Stewart

To hoard the message of salvation and refuse to share it with an expanding world population . . . is to fail in our solemn obligation to God.

—Paul Van Gorder

We are commanded to be God's witnesses, not soul winners. We are commanded to make disciples, not win souls. We are the witnesses, but the Holy Spirit is the real soul winner.

—Anonymous

WOMEN

The way to fight a woman is with your hat. Grab it and run.

—John Barrymore

The problem with life is, by the time you can read women like a book, your library card has expired.

—Milton Berle

Next to God we are indebted to women, first for life itself, and then for making it worth having.

—Christian Bovée

A good and true woman is said to resemble a Cremona fiddle—age but increases its worth and sweetens its tone.

—Oliver Wendell Holmes

There is in every true woman's heart a spark of heavenly fire, which lies dormant in the broad daylight of prosperity, but which kindles up and blazes in the dark hour of adversity.

—Washington Irving

If you don't think women are explosive, drop one.

—Gerald F. Lieberman

Nothing makes a woman more beautiful than the belief that she is beautiful.

—Sophia Loren

There are two theories to arguing with women. Neither one works.

—Anonymous

WONDER

The wonder of a single snowflake outweighs the wisdom of a million meteorologists.

—Francis Bacon

Wonder is the basis of worship.

—Thomas Carlyle

Wonder is the very essence of life. Beware always of losing the wonder.... The only evidence of salvation or sanctification is that the sense of wonder is developing, not at things as they are, but at the One who made them as they are.

—Oswald Chambers

The world will never starve for want of wonders, but only for want of wonder.

—Gilbert Keith Chesterton

He who can no longer pause to wonder and stand rapt in awe, is as good as dead; his eyes are closed.

—Albert Einstein

Wonder is the attitude of reverence for the infinite values and meaning of life, and of marveling over God's purpose and patience in it all.

—George W. Fiske

Everything has its wonders, even darkness and silence, and I learn, whatever state I may be in, therein to be content.

—Helen Keller

WORDS
(See also Writers, Writing)

We have too many high-sounding words, and too few actions that correspond with them.

—Abigail Adams

All words are pegs to hang ideas on.

—Henry Ward Beecher

Words

There's a great power in words, if you don't hitch too many of them together.
— Josh Billings

We rule the world by our words.
— Napoleon Bonaparte

To speak of "mere words" is much like speaking of "mere dynamite."
— C. J. Ducasse

Gentle words, quiet words, are, after all, the most powerful words. They are more convincing, more compelling, more prevailing.
— Washington Gladden

When you doubt between words, use the plainest, the commonest, the most idiomatic. Avoid big words as you would rouge, and love simple ones as you would native roses in your cheek.
— August W. Hare

Words—so innocent and powerless as they are, as standing in a dictionary, how potent for good and evil they become in the hands of one who knows how to combine them.
— Nathaniel Hawthorne

Words form the threads on which we string our experiences.
— Aldous Huxley

The most valuable talent is that of never using two words when one will do.
— Thomas Jefferson

Words are, of course, the most powerful drug used by mankind.
— Rudyard Kipling

Oh, words are action good enough, if they're the right words.
— D. H. Lawrence

Apt words have power to assuage the tumors of a troubled mind.
— John Milton

Cold words freeze people, and hot words scorch them, and bitter words make them bitter, and wrathful words make them wrathful. Kind words also produce their image on men's souls, and a beautiful image it is. They smooth, and quiet, and comfort the hearer.
— Blaise Pascal

Be brief; for it is with words as with sunbeams. The more they are condensed, the deeper they burn.
— Robert Southey

Words are vehicles that can transport us from the drab sands to the dazzling stars.
— M. Robert Syme

All our words will be useless unless they come from within—words that do not give the light of Christ increase the darkness.
— Mother Teresa

Words are seductive and dangerous material to be used with caution.
— Barbara Tuchman

The difference between the almost right word and the right word is really a large matter—'tis the difference between the lightning bug and the lightning.
— Mark Twain

As to the adjective—when in doubt, strike it out.

—Mark Twain

Words must be weighed, not counted.

—Polish Proverb

What's in a word? Consider the difference between "wise man" and "wise guy."

—Anonymous

WORK
(See also Labor)

Nothing is really work unless you would rather be doing something else.

—James M. Barrie

As a remedy against all ills—poverty, sickness, and melancholy—only one thing is absolutely necessary: a liking for work.

—Charles Baudelaire

Anyone can do any amount of work provided it isn't the work he is supposed to be doing at that moment.

—Robert Benchley

We are tired by the work we do not do, not by what we do.

—Florence C. Brillhart

Choose a job you love and you will never have to work a day in your life.

—Confucius

God gave man work, not to burden him, but to bless him, and useful work, willingly, cheerfully, effectively done, has always been the finest expression of the human spirit.

—Walter R. Courtenay

I never did anything worth doing by accident, nor did any of my inventions come by accident; they came by work.

—Thomas Edison

How do I work? I grope.

—Albert Einstein

Three rules of work: Out of clutter, find simplicity. From discord, find harmony. In the middle of difficulty lies opportunity.

—Albert Einstein

No other technique for the conduct of life attaches the individual so firmly to reality as laying emphasis on work; for his work at least gives him a secure place in a portion of reality, in the human community.

—Sigmund Freud

By working faithfully eight hours a day, you may eventually get to be a boss and work twelve hours a day.

—Robert Frost

The world is full of willing people; some willing to work, the rest willing to let them.

—Robert Frost

It is good to dream, but it is better to dream and work. Faith is mighty, but action with faith is mightier. Desiring is helpful, but work and desire are invincible.

—Thomas Robert Gain

Work

There are two kinds of people, those who do the work and those who take the credit. Try to be in the first group; there is less competition there.

—Indira Gandhi

I learned to work mornings, when I could skim the cream off the day and use the rest for cheese-making.

—Johann von Goethe

I've met a few people in my time who were enthusiastic about hard work. And it was just my luck that all of them happened to be men I was working for at the time.

—Bill Gold

When work is a pleasure, life is a joy! When work is a duty, life is slavery.

—Maxim Gorky

When you are making a success of something, it's not work. It's a way of life. You enjoy yourself because you are making your contribution to the world.

—Andy Granatelli

People who never do any more than they get paid for, never get paid for any more than they do.

—Elbert Hubbard

I'm a great believer in luck, and I find the harder I work the more I have of it.

—Thomas Jefferson

God didn't make things to work for us; He made us to make things work, in order for Him to make us.

—Charlie "T" Jones

When your work speaks for itself, don't interrupt.

—Henry J. Kaiser

Thank God every morning when you get up that you have something to do that day that must be done, whether you like it or not. Being forced to work and forced to do your best will breed in you temperance and self-control, diligence and strength of will, cheerfulness and contentment, and a hundred virtues that the idle will never know.

—Charles Kingsley

The harder you work, the harder it is to surrender.

—Vince Lombardi

A man's work is his dilemma: his job is his bondage, but it also gives him a fair share of his identity and keeps him from being a bystander in somebody else's world.

—Melvin Maddocks

When a man tells you he got rich through hard work, ask him whose?

—Don Marquis

Your life's work is your statue. You cannot get away from it. It is beautiful or hideous, lovely or ugly, or inspiring, as you make it.

—Alfred A. Montapert

When I pray, I pray like it all depends on God, but when I get through praying, I get up and work like it all depends on me.

—Dwight L. Moody

If you don't want to work you have to work to earn enough money so that you won't have to work.

—Ogden Nash

We must get rid of the extraordinary notion that manual work is degrading. There is nothing more ennobling than manual work and nothing better for physical and mental health.

—Jawaharlal Nehru

Live neither in the past nor in the future, but let each day's work absorb all your interest, energy, and enthusiasm. The best preparation for tomorrow is to do today's work superbly well.

—William Osler

Work is accomplished by those employ- ees who have not yet reached their level of incompetence.

—Laurence J. Peter

I am only an average man but, by George, I work harder at it than the average man.

—Theodore Roosevelt

Far and away the best prize that life offers is the chance to work hard at work worth doing.

—Theodore Roosevelt

Work is not man's punishment. It is his reward and his strength, his glory and his pleasure.

—George Sand

When I was a young man I observed that nine out of ten things I did were

failures. I didn't want to be a failure, so I did ten times more work.

—George Bernard Shaw

The great thing with work is to be on top of it, not constantly chasing after it.

—Dorothy Thompson

Work spares us from three evils: boredom, vice, and need.

—Voltaire

It is not sufficiently realized that work is a great, if not the greatest, factor in keeping us well.

—Paul Dudley White

Work is the refuge of people who have nothing better to do.

—Oscar Wilde

The better work men do is always done under stress and at great personal cost.

—William Carlos Williams

WORLD

We treat this world of ours as if we had a spare in the trunk.

—Al Bernstein

The world has achieved brilliance without wisdom, power without conscience. Ours is a world of nuclear giants and ethical infants. We know more about war than we know about peace, more about killing than we know about living.

—Omar N. Bradley

This world, after all our science and sciences, is still a miracle; wonderful, inscrutable, magical, and more, to whosoever will think of it.

—Thomas Carlyle

Of all the joys of life ... there is nothing more great, more refreshing, more beneficial in the widest sense of the word than a real love of the beauty of the world.

—Sir Edward Grey

The world is as fresh as it was at the first day, and as full of untold novelties for him who has the eyes to see them.

—Thomas H. Huxley

He does most in God's great world who does his best in his own little world.

—Thomas Jefferson

If you would win the world, melt it, do not hammer it.

—Alexander Maclaren

Come, come, my conservative friend, wipe the dew off your spectacles, and see that the world is moving.

—Elizabeth Cady Stanton

The world is a looking-glass, and gives back to every man the reflection of his own face. Frown at it, and it in turn will look sourly upon you; laugh at it and with it, and it is a jolly, kind companion.

—William Makepeace Thackeray

You don't have to do the grand gesture to heal the world. It can happen one person at a time.

—Susan Vreeland

If the world were like me, what kind of world would this be?

—Anonymous

WORLDLINESS

Worldliness is horizontal life. Worldliness has nothing of the vertical in it. It has ambition; it has no aspirations. Its motto is success, not holiness. It is always saying, "Onward," never "Upward." A worldly man or woman is a man or woman who never says, "I will lift up mine eyes unto the hills."

—J. H. Jowett

WORRY
(See also Anxiety, Fear)

Blessed is the person who is too busy to worry in the daytime and too sleepy to worry at night.

—Leo Aikman

Worry is the down payment on ninety percent of the trouble you won't have.

—John Benton

Worry is spiritual nearsightedness, a fumbling way of looking at little things, and of magnifying their value.

—Anna Robertson Brown

The bridges you cross before you come to them are over rivers that aren't there.

—Gene Brown

Every evening, I turn worries over to God. He's going to be up all night anyway.

—Mary C. Crowley

We experience moments absolutely free from worry. These brief respites are called panic.

—Cullen Hightower

There is little peace or comfort in life if we are always anxious as to future events. He that worries himself with the dread of possible contingencies will never be at rest.

—Samuel Johnson

Cross your bridges before you come to them and you have to pay the toll twice.

—Franklin P. Jones

Worry is the most popular form of suicide. It impairs appetite, spoils digestion, disturbs sleep, irritates disposition, weakens mind, warps character, saps bodily strength, and stimulates disease. Worry is the real cause of death in thousands of instances where some other disease is named on the death certificate.

—William G. Jordan

A man ninety years old was asked to what he attributed his longevity. "I reckon," he said, with a twinkle in his eye, "it's because most nights I went to bed and slept when I should have sat up and worried."

—Dorothea Kent

To be upset over what you don't have is to waste what you do have.

—Ken S. Keyes Jr.

Worry is the interest paid by those who borrow trouble.

—G. W. Lyon

Worriers spend a lot of time shoveling smoke.

—Claude McDonald

We probably wouldn't worry about what other people think of us if we could know how seldom they do.

—Olin Miller

If I spent as much time doing the things I worry about getting done as I do worrying about them, I wouldn't have anything to worry about.

—Beryl Pfizer

Worry is a thin stream of fear trickling through the mind. If encouraged, it cuts a channel into which all other thoughts are drained.

—Arthur Somers Roche

There is a great difference between worry and concern. A worried person sees a problem, and the concerned person solves a problem.

—Harold Stephens

Worry does not empty tomorrow of its sorrow; it empties today of its strength.

—Corrie ten Boom

Worry not about the Future,
The Present is all thou hast.
The Future will soon be Present,
And the Present will soon be Past.

—Lowell Thomas

Every moment of worry weakens the soul for its daily combat.

—Henry Wood

Schedule all your worrying for a specific half-hour about the middle of the day. Then take a nap during this period.

—Anonymous

Oh, I worry over this thing and I worry
  over that,
But I notice when the atmosphere has
  cleared,
That the bad luck I had looked for
Didn't come and knock me flat,
And I didn't have the trouble that I
  feared.
Oh, I like to start the morning with an
  apprehensive sigh,
For I find a bit of worry to my taste;
But I cannot help a'thinking,
As the years go speeding by,
That an awful lot of worry goes to waste.

—Anonymous

WORSHIP

God has no need for our worship. It is we who need to show our gratitude for what we have received.

—Saint Thomas Aquinas

I never knew how to worship until I knew how to love.

—Henry Ward Beecher

It is only when men begin to worship that they begin to grow.

—Calvin Coolidge

If worship does not change us, it has not been worship. To stand before the Holy One of eternity is to change. Worship begins in holy expectancy; it ends in holy obedience.

—Richard J. Foster

God does not need our worship! But we need to worship God! Our humanness depends on it. Not to worship God is to deny our essential humanity. It is of the very essence of authentic humanness to worship God. Made to worship, man becomes something less than human when he refuses to worship. It is not God who suffers when we do not worship—it is we who suffer!

—Richard C. Halverson

Worship is not simply something done on set occasions or on certain days. It is an entire way of life. It is the proclamation of God's character as revealed in Jesus Christ, acted out in the life of the worshipper before a world that has "lost its memory of God."

—Wes Harty

Worship changes people; we become like whatever it is we worship.

—Wes Harty

It is worship that is man's most distinctive activity, not work and not play.

—Arthur F. Holmes

Our worshipping God through Christ in front of the world may well be making the most important statement to culture that can possibly be made.

—Jay Kesler

The worship most acceptable to God comes from a thankful and cheerful heart.

—Plutarch

When Christian worship is dull and joyless, Jesus Christ has been left outside—that is the only possible explanation.

—James S. Stewart

The gem that has been lost to the evangelical church is worship.

—A. W. Tozer

WRINKLES

Wrinkles should only indicate where smiles have been.

—Ethel Barrymore

When grace is joined with wrinkles, it is adorable. There is an unspeakable dawn in happy old age.

—Victor Hugo

I enjoy my wrinkles and regard them as badges of distinction—I've worked hard for them.

—Maggie Kuhn

If God had to give a woman wrinkles, he might at least have put them on the soles of her feet.

—Ninon de Lenclos

Years may wrinkle the skin, but to give up interest wrinkles the soul.

—Douglas MacArthur

I'm at that age where if you flattened out all the wrinkles I'd be seven feet tall.

—Robert Orben

A wrinkled face is a firm face, a steady face, a safe face. Wrinkles are the dried-up riverbeds of a lifetime's tears, the nostalgic remnants of a million smiles. Wrinkles are the crannies and footholds on the smooth visage of life on which man can cling and gain some comfort and security.

—Anonymous

First person: "I have the body of a twenty-year-old."
Second person: "Well, you'd better give it back. You're getting it all wrinkled."

—Anonymous

WRITERS
(See also Words, Writing)

There is only one trait that marks the writer. He is always watching. It's a kind of trick of the mind and he is born with it.

—Morley Callaghan

The discipline of the writer is to learn to be still and listen to what his subject has to tell him.

—Rachel Carson

The most original thing a writer can do is write like himself. It is also his most difficult task.

—Robertson Davies

The way I see it, every one of us in the writing business starts off with precisely the same tools, the twenty-six letters of the alphabet. All we can do is try to arrange those twenty-six letters in a different way than anyone else has before.

—Bob Greene

Many people who want to be writers don't really want to be writers. They want to have been writers. They wish they had a book in print.

—James Michener

Every writer must acknowledge, and be able to handle the unalterable fact, that he has, in effect, given himself a life sentence in solitary confinement.

—Peter Straub

Every writer, by the way he uses the language, reveals something of his spirit, his habits, his capacities, his bias. . . . Avoid the elaborate, the pretentious, the coy, and the cute. Do not be tempted by a twenty-dollar word when there is a ten-center handy, ready and able.

—William Strunk Jr. and E. B. White

The whole duty of a writer is to please and satisfy himself, and the true writer always plays to an audience of one.

—William Strunk Jr. and E. B. White

I have yet to see a piece of writing, political or non-political, that doesn't have a slant. All writing slants the way a writer leans, and no man is born perpendicular, although many men are born upright.

—E. B. White

WRITING
(See also Words, Writers)

Writing is an apprenticeship that leads to soul, to self. It involves digging deeply into territory that we keep hidden, not only from others, but even more dangerously from ourselves.

—Catherine Bauer

Writing a book is an adventure. To begin with, it is a toy and an amusement. Then it becomes a mistress, then it becomes a master, then it becomes a tyrant. The last phase is that just as you are about to be reconciled to your servitude, you kill the monster, and fling him to the public.

—Winston Churchill

Writing is easy. All you do is stare at a blank sheet of paper until drops of blood form on your forehead.

—Gene Fowler

If you would not be forgotten as soon as you are gone, either write things worth reading or do things worth writing.

—Benjamin Franklin

Your manuscript is both good and original; but the parts that are good are not original, and the parts that are original are not good.

—Samuel Johnson

Write "tight," using short sentences and short paragraphs and eliminating unnecessary verbiage.

—Raymond J. Kelly

Writing is not hard. Just get paper and pencil, sit down, and write it as it occurs to you. The writing is easy—it's the occurring that's hard.

—Stephen Leacock

If you want to change the world, pick up your pen.

> —Martin Luther

WRONG

If things go wrong, don't go with them.

> —Roger Babson

If you think the world is all wrong, remember that it contains people like you.

> —Mohandas K. Gandhi

It is better to suffer wrong than to do it.

> —Samuel Johnson

If you have always done it that way, it's probably wrong.

> —Charles F. Kettering

It's often wrong to do the thing you have a right to do.

> —Frank Tyger

YOUTH
(See also Adolescence, Teenagers)

You never know how wonderful the youth of America really are until you turn off the television and talk to them.
—O. A. Battista

There is a place in God's sun for the youth "farthest down" who has the vision, the determination, and the courage to reach it.
—Mary McLeod Bethune

At nineteen, everything is possible and tomorrow is friendly.
—Jim Bishop

One good thing about being young is that you are not experienced enough to know you cannot possibly do the things you are doing.
—Gene Brown

The young do not know enough to be prudent, and therefore they attempt the impossible—and achieve it, generation after generation.
—Pearl Buck

The best thing about being young is, if you had it to do all over again, you would still have time.
—Sandra Clarke

Youth is when you blame all your troubles on your parents; maturity is when you learn that everything is the fault of the younger generation.
—Harold Coffin

That's what being young is all about. You have the courage and the daring to think that you can make a difference.
—Ruby Dee

If we keep well and cheerful we are always young, and at last die in youth, even when years would count us old.
—Tryon Edwards

Never tell a young person that anything cannot be done. God may have been waiting for centuries for somebody ignorant enough of the impossible to do that very thing.
—John Andrew Holmes

Every young man should learn to take criticism. He'll probably be a parent someday.
—Franklin P. Jones

One of the virtues of being very young is that you don't let the facts get in the way of your imagination.
—Sam Levenson

I do beseech you to direct your efforts more to preparing youth for the path and less to preparing the path for the youth.
—Ben Lindsey

Each youth is like a child born in the
night who sees the sun rise and thinks
that yesterday never existed.

        —W. Somerset Maugham

Youth do not think into the future far
enough. There are great tomorrows we
must encourage youth to dream of.

        —Henrietta C. Mears

Don't laugh at a youth for his affecta-
tions; he is only trying on one face after
another to find a face of his own.

        —Logan Pearsall Smith

What are our young people coming to?
Slowly, but surely, to the time when they
will ask the same question.

        —H. M. Stansifer

Youth is when you're allowed to stay up
late on New Year's Eve. Middle age is
when you're forced to.

        —Bill Vaughan

Life goes on and there comes a time
when you don't have to pay girls to
spend the evening with your son.

        —Gene Yasenak

The person who says youth is a state of
mind invariably has more state of mind
than youth.

        —Anonymous

Never give up learning and listening,
and keep in touch with the younger
generation, even if you can only tolerate
them in small doses.

        —Anonymous

Z

ZEAL

Zeal without knowledge is fire without light.

—Thomas Fuller

The self-righteous zealot relishes playing the role of a merciful, compassionate person. After crushing a sinner under the weight of his indignation, he enjoys condescendingly lifting him up again as a gesture of sham mercy.

—Dietrich von Hildebrand

Zeal without tolerance is fanaticism.

—John Kelman

Be zealous! Be active! Time is short!

—John Wesley

Subject Index

Subject Index

Source Index